0   20 miles

0   20 km

N

P A C I F I C   O C E A N

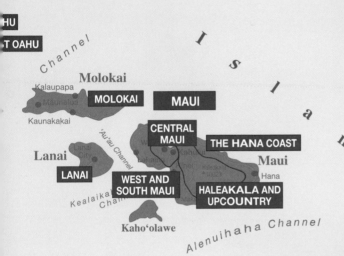

HU

T OAHU

Channel

i

a

n   *I s l a n d s*

Molokai

Kalaupapa

MOLOKAI   **MAUI**

Maunaloa

Kaunakakai

'Au'au Channel

CENTRAL MAUI

THE HANA COAST

Lanai

Lanai City

Maui

Hana

LANAI

WEST AND SOUTH MAUI

HALEAKALA AND UPCOUNTRY

Kealaika Chan

Kaho'olawe

Alenuihaha Channel

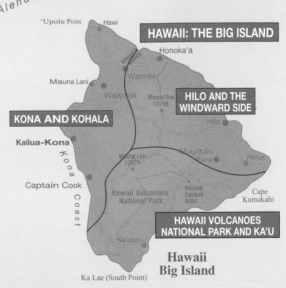

'Upolu Point   Hawi

HAWAII: THE BIG ISLAND

Honoka'a

Waimea

Mauna Lani

Waikoloa

Mauna Kea
13796

HILO AND THE WINDWARD SIDE

KONA AND KOHALA

Hilo

Kailua-Kona

Mauna Loa
13679

Mountain View

Pahoa

Kona Coast

Captain Cook

Hawaii Volcanoes National Park

Kilauea Caldera
4091

Cape Kumukahi

HAWAII VOLCANOES NATIONAL PARK AND KA'U

Na'alahu

Hawaii Big Island

Ka Lae (South Point)

Hawaiian Archipelago

0   100 miles

0   100 km

N

l a n d s

Kauai

Oahu

Molokai

Honolulu   Lanai   Maui

Kaho'olawe

see above

Hilo

Hawaii Big Island

Mauna Loa

INSIGHT ◉ GUIDES

HAWAII

PLAN & BOOK
YOUR TAILOR-MADE TRIP

BRAZIL CHILE ECUADOR

TAILOR-MADE TRIPS & UNIQUE EXPERIENCES CREATED BY LOCAL TRAVEL EXPERTS AT INSIGHTGUIDES.COM/HOLIDAYS

Insight Guides has been inspiring travellers with high-quality travel content for over 45 years. As well as our popular guidebooks, we now offer the opportunity to book tailor-made private trips completely personalised to your needs and interests. By connecting with one of our local experts, you will directly benefit from their expertise and local know-how, helping you create memories that will last a lifetime.

HOW INSIGHTGUIDES.COM/HOLIDAYS WORKS

STEP 1

Pick your dream destination and submit an enquiry, or modify an existing itinerary if you prefer.

STEP 2

Fill in a short form, sharing details of your travel plans and preferences with a local expert.

STEP 3

Your local expert will create your personalised itinerary, which you can amend until you are completely satisfied.

STEP 4

Book securely online. Pack your bags and enjoy your holiday! Your local expert will be available to answer questions during your trip.

BENEFITS OF PLANNING & BOOKING AT
INSIGHTGUIDES.COM/HOLIDAYS

PLANNED BY LOCAL EXPERTS

The Insight Guides local experts are hand-picked, based on their experience in the travel industry and their impeccable standards of customer service.

SAVE TIME & MONEY

When a local expert plans your trip, you save time and money when you book, even during high season. You won't be charged for using a credit card either.

TAILOR-MADE TRIPS

Book with Insight Guides, and you will be in complete control of the planning process, from the initial selections to amending your final itinerary.

BOOK & TRAVEL STRESS-FREE

Enjoy stress-free travel when you use the Insight Guides secure online booking platform. All bookings come with a money-back guarantee.

WHAT OTHER TRAVELLERS THINK ABOUT TRIPS BOOKED AT
INSIGHTGUIDES.COM/HOLIDAYS

Trip to Portugal

Every step of the planning process and the trip itself was effortless and exceptional. Our special interests, preferences and requests were accommodated resulting in a trip that exceeded our expectations.

Corinne, USA   ★★★★★

Trip to Vietnam

The organization was superb, the drivers professional, and accommodation quite comfortable. I was well taken care of! My thanks to your colleagues who helped make my trip to Vietnam such a great experience. My only regret is that I couldn't spend more time in the country.

Heather   ★★★★★

CONTENTS

Introduction

The best of Hawaii 6
Aloha 19
Volcanic Isles 21

History & Features

Decisive dates 30
Beginnings: Ancient Hawaii..................... 33
    🔍 Hawaiian Gods 39
Arrival of Captain Cook............................ 41
The Hawaiian Monarchy............................ 45
Modern Hawaii 53
Hawaii's People.. 63
    🔍 Traditional Beliefs........................ 66
📷 Ancient Ways and Places 72
Outdoor Activities.................................... 75
Music and Hula 81
📷 Lei 88
An Eclectic Cuisine 91
    🔍 The Lu'au 95
Hawaii on Screen 97

Places

Introduction.. 107
⬛ Oahu 111
Honolulu... 115
Waikiki.. 127
    🔍 Duke Kahanamoku......................... 132
Greater Honolulu 139
Southeast Oahu.. 148
Windward Oahu 153
North Shore 158
    🔍 Surfing.. 161
Central Oahu and the Wai'anae Coast........ 163
    🔍 The Leeward Islands...................... 169
⬛ Maui.. 173
Central Maui 177
West and South Maui 180
    🔍 Humpback Whales......................... 182
Haleakala and Upcountry 189
The Hana Coast 195
📷 Disappearing Flora and Fauna 202
Molokai... 207
Lanai... 218

■ Hawaii: The big island............................227
Kona and Kohala...229
Hilo and The Windward Side.......................241
Hawaii Volcanoes National Park and Ka'u . 251
◉ A State of Fire in the Pacific Ocean 258
■ Kauai 263
North and West Kauai.................................267
South and East Kauai.................................275
    🔍 Ni'ihau 278

Travel Tips

TRANSPORTATION

Getting there 284
    By air 284
    By sea 285
Getting around 285
    By air 285
    By bicycle 285
    On foot 285
    By bus...286
    By car 286
    By sea...287
    By taxi...287

A – Z

Accommodations 288
Admission charges 288
Animals 288
Budgeting for your trip 288
Children...288
Climate and weather 289
Crime and safety.......................................289
Customs regulations 289
Disabled travelers.....................................289
Eating out 290
Emergencies 290
Embassies and consulates 290
Electricity 290
Festivals 290
Health and medical care............................292
Internet 292
LGBTQ travelers..293
Maps..293
Media...293
Money..293

Opening hours..293
Postal services 294
Public holidays 294
Religion 294
Shopping 294
Tax 296
Telephones 296
Time zone 297
Tipping...297
Tourist information 297
Tour operators 297
Visas and passports...................................297
Weights and measures 297
What to bring 297
What to wear..297

LANGUAGE

Background...298
A language of the Pacific 298
Pronunciation guidelines...........................299

FURTHER READING

Non-fiction 300
Fiction 300

Maps

Hawaiian Islands...108
Oahu..112
Honolulu Center..116
Waikiki..130
Honolulu..136
Maui...174
Lahaina 183
Molokai..208
Lanai..218
Hawaii (Big Island)......................................226
Hilo..242
Kilauea Volcano...252
Kauai and Ni'ihau..264
Inside front cover Hawaii
Inside back cover Honolulu

LEGEND
🔍 Insight on
◉ Photo story

THE BEST OF HAWAII: TOP ATTRACTIONS

△ **Hawaii Volcanoes National Park.** There aren't many places on Earth where you can see new land being born. That – and the omnipresent evidence of lava flows from years past – is what makes this destination on Hawaii Island a must-see. See page 251.

▽ **Hana Highway.** It's about 45 miles from Paia to Hana along the world-famous Hana Highway on Maui, and every turn brings new sights to see. Be sure to stop and get out to experience some of the dozens of waterfalls along the way. See page 195.

△ **Na Pali Coast.** The lush coastline on the North Shore of Kauai is arguably one of the most picturesque spots in all of Hawaii. Take a boat trip from Hanalei to see the 4,000ft (1,220-meter) cliffs from the water, or hike the hamstring-straining 11-mile (18km) Kalalau Trail for a closer look. See page 269.

△ **Surfing.** Legends are born (and crushed) on the North Shore of Oahu, where winter brings some of the biggest waves in all of Hawaii. See page 161.

△ **Waikiki Beach.** Sun-drenched sand meets busy metropolis on Honolulu's iconic Waikiki Beach, where high-rise hotels tower over some of the most pristine oceanfront property in Hawaii. See page 127.

△ **Kalaupapa National Historic Park.** Few visitors to Hawaii make the trek to Molokai, but this national park, famous for its history as a colony for those suffering from Hansen's Disease, is worth the extra effort. See page 210.

△ **Whale-watching.** Ka'anapali Beach is Maui's most famous white-sand stretch, but also happens to be one of the best places on Earth to watch humpback whales from shore. See page 184.

▷ **USS Arizona Memorial.** As President Franklin Roosevelt predicted, December 7, 1941, the day the Japanese attacked the US military at Pearl Harbor, has "lived in infamy." Today, visitors to the Oahu site can pay respects to soldiers who lost lives in the attack at the floating memorial over one of the sunken carriers. See page 146.

△ **Bishop Museum.** This museum, on the outskirts of downtown Honolulu, contains the most comprehensive and mind-boggling collection of art and artifacts from pre-contact Hawaii. See page 139.

▽ **Pu'uhonua 'O Honaunau National Historical Park.** This religious site on the South Kona side of Hawaii Island once was a place for criminals to take refuge, receive absolution, and reform. Today, it is a living museum, where visitors can learn about ancient Hawaiian laws and rituals. See page 232.

THE BEST OF HAWAII: EDITOR'S CHOICE

Sliding Sands Trail, Haleakala National Park.

MAJOR HIGHLIGHTS

Na Pali Coast, Kauai. Familiar from many a Hollywood movie, the pleated, towering cliffs of Kauai's North Shore are mythic in scale. See page 269.

Diamond Head, Oahu. This dormant volcanic tuff named for the crystals in its soil sits just beyond the soft sands of Waikiki Beach; an invitation to exploration. See page 148.

Haleakala, Maui. The crumbling, multi-colored sands in the summit caldera of Maui's highest volcano serve as a haven for rare species. See page 192.

Kilauea, Hawaii Island. Watch new land burst into life, literally at your feet, as the world's most active volcano makes the Big Island even bigger, day by day. See page 251.

Na Pali coastline.

BEST SURFING SITES

Honolua Bay, Maui. Beautifully located bay at the top of verdant West Maui, blessed with dependably towering waves. See page 185.

Honoli'i Bay, Hawaii Island. A lovely spot on the windward side of the Big Island, where Hilo's best surfers battle with fierce surf. See page 244.

Hanalei Bay, Kauai. This huge curving bay, in view of the Na Pali cliffs, is the spiritual home to Kauai's surfing community. See page 268.

Sunset Beach, Oahu. The regular site for several major world championships, Oahu's North Shore attracts the world's premier surfers every winter. Novices beware. See page 158.

Waimea Bay, Oahu. Probably the world's most famous surfing venue, with the biggest rideable waves you will ever see anywhere in the world. Extremely dangerous in winter. See page 158.

Surfing in the waters off Maui.

Hiking in the Na Pali Coast State Wilderness Park.

BEST WALKS

Kalalau Trail, Kauai. This legendary hike along Kauai's Na Pali cliffs offers Hawaii's most breathtaking scenery. See page 270.
Sliding Sands Trail, Maui. An unforgettable hike through the extraordinary moonscape at the summit of Maui's mighty Haleakala volcano. See page 193.

Alaka'i Swamp Trail, Kauai. The only way to explore the eerie rainforest swamplands with stupendous ocean views along the way. See page 271.
Koko Head Trail, Oahu. Not for novices, the hike to the top of Koko Head includes more than 1,000 steps. See page 149.

Kailua Beach, Oahu.

BEST BEACHES

Kailua Beach, Oahu. Tempting turquoise waters lap Oahu's Windward Shore. Ideal for kayaking. See page 153.
Papohaku Beach, Moloka. The perfect spot for swimming and beachcombing. See page 214.

Ka'anapali Beach, Maui. Hawaii's best family beach is great for relaxing with the kids. See page 184.
Waikiki Beach, Oahu. Warm waters and gentle waves make this Hawaii's most famous beach. See page 127.

BEST MUSEUMS AND GALLERIES

Bishop Museum, Honolulu, Oahu. For anyone interested in Hawaii and its Polynesian heritage, the Bishop Museum is the best place to start. See page 139.
'Imiloa Astronomy Center, Hilo, Hawaii Island. A fascinating, hands-on museum that explores the links between modern astronomers and ancient Hawaiian beliefs. See page 243.
Honolulu Museum of Art, Honolulu, Oahu. This sophisticated gallery houses a globe-spanning collection of artistic treasures. See page 122.
Polynesian Cultural Center, La'ie, Oahu. One part history museum, one part live entertainment venue, the PCC boasts the best *lu'aus* in Hawaii. See page 156.
Whaling Village Museum, Ka'anapali, Maui. An enlightening introduction to the part Hawaii played in the whaling industry. See page 184.

Inside the 'Imiloa Astronomy Center.

Windsurfing at Ho'okipa.

BEST HISTORIC SITES

Pearl Harbor, Oahu. A sombre memorial to the "date which will live in infamy," Hawaii's finest harbor hauntingly evokes the surprise Japanese attack of 1941. See page 146.

Pu'uhonua O Honaunau, South Kona, Hawaii Island. A beautiful spot in its own right, this so-called "place of refuge" was once a royal precinct, and is still adorned with fearsome carved images. See page 232.

Kealakekua Bay, South Kona, Hawaii Island. A stark white obelisk marks the precise location where Captain Cook lost his life in 1779. See page 232.

Pi'lanihale Heiau, Hana, Maui. The largest ancient temple in all Polynesia, this fabulous multi-tiered oceanfront pyramid looms above Maui's ravishing Hana coast. See page 197.

Pu'ukohola Heiau, South Kohala, Hawaii Island. The "war temple," where Kamehameha the Great performed human sacrifices before he conquered all the islands, still dominates the Kohala shoreline. See page 235.

'Iolani Palace, Honolulu, Oahu. Built in 1882, this imposing palace in the heart of Honolulu served as a prison for Hawaii's last queen, after her kingdom was overthrown. See page 115.

BEST OCEAN ACTIVITIES

Windsurfing at Ho'okipa, Maui. Crowds of spectators gather on the hillsides to watch the amazing feats at the world's premier spot for windsurfers at the top of their game. See page 190.

Snorkeling at Hanauma Bay, Oahu. Shoals of iridescent fish congregate in this gorgeous nature preserve; a volcanic crater that's a short ride out from Waikiki. See page 150.

Diving at Molokini. The crystal-clear waters, a few miles off South Maui, attract boat-loads of divers daily. See page 187.

Whale-watching off Maui. Every winter, the shallow waters that separate Maui from Lanai and Molokai are teeming with migratory humpback whales. See page 182.

Kayaking in Kailua Bay, Oahu. There's no better place to paddle a rented kayak than in the beautiful shallow waters off Oahu's finest beach. See page 153.

'Iolani Palace, Honolulu.

BEST SMALL TOWNS

Hanapepe, Kauai. Loop off Kauai's circle-island highway to while away an hour or two in this delightful little village, with its fading antique stores and swinging rope-bridge. See page 280.

Hawi, Hawaii Island. Hidden at the quiet northernmost tip of the Big Island, Hawi makes a great half-way stopping point on a tour of the lovely North Kohala district. See page 238.

Lanai City, Lanai. Once the pineapple capital of the world, this former plantation town, with its pretty gardens and simple cafés, is unlike any city you've ever seen. See page 220.

Hale'iwa, Oahu. The only town on Oahu's North Shore is a laidback hangout for surfers and backpackers, with quirky stores, galleries, and wholefood restaurants on all sides. See page 160.

Makawao, Maui. This one-horse town still evokes the days when Maui's verdant Upcountry was home to the Hispanic cowboys known as *paniolos*. See page 190.

Kaunakakai, Molokai. Molokai's sleepy little capital is the perfect place to hang out for a lazy afternoon of simply "talking story". See page 208.

The beautiful 'Akaka Falls.

HAWAII'S NATURAL WONDERS

'Akaka Falls, Hawaii Island. This towering, majestic waterfall is reached by a short hike deep into the rainforest of the Big Island's Hamakua coast. See page 244.

Nu'uanu Pali Lookout, Oahu. Travelers crossing the Ko'olau Mountains are suddenly confronted by the vast sweeping cliffs that line the Windward Coast. See page 143.

'Iao Needle, Maui. An abrupt, velvet-coated pinnacle buried deep in Central Maui's lush mountains. See page 179.

Waimea Canyon, Kauai. This deep chasm is slowly splitting Kauai in two, and glows green, gold, and red as the sun crosses the sky. See page 271.

Garden of the Gods, Lanai. These eerie red badlands are more like something you'd find in the Wild West than in lush Hawaii. See page 221.

Halawa Valley, Molokai. This magnificent valley was home to some of Hawaii's earliest Polynesian settlers. See page 213.

Storefronts in Makawao, Maui.

MONEY-SAVING TIPS

Inter-island travel. Hawaii's airlines are constantly in fare-cutting competition to lure inter-island passengers. Check their websites for current rates, rather than booking your flights between the islands as part of your trans-Pacific itinerary.

Getting around. On Oahu's excellent public bus network, TheBus (www.thebus.org), fares are much cheaper, and the range of routes is much wider, than on the various overpriced "trolley" services that operate in Waikiki. You can even travel around the entire island for just $5.50 (one-day pass). Public transportation is less helpful on other islands, but rental car specials are available every season.

Cheap eating. Visitors can save on inflated prices by dining at farmers' markets, or in the food courts at shopping centers. "Local" restaurants operated by Hawaii's various immigrant groups offer more varied cuisine at bargain prices.

Adventuring on land and sea. Access to all beaches in Hawaii is always free. Bring your own surfing or snorkeling equipment, or rent it cheaply on the islands. Similarly, most of Hawaii's best hiking trails, such as on the volcanoes of Maui and Hawaii Island, are clearly marked routes in national and state parks.

'Ehukai Beach Park, home
of the Banzai Pipeline, Ōahu.

Hire a 4x4 and drive the Munro
Trail on Lanai.

The Milky Way from Mauna Kea Observatory on Big Island.

Kailua Beach, Oahu.

ALOHA

On the six major, freely visitable islands of Hawaii, spectacular scenery, colorful history, and modern comforts add up to paradise.

Waterfalls near the Hana Highway, Maui.

Smack in the middle of the Pacific Ocean, the eight major inhabited islands of the Hawaiian archipelago rise from the sea like oases out of a desert. In reality, they are giant volcanoes – one of which is still active. But for many, including the Polynesians who discovered them hundreds of years ago, the islands represent paradise. Secluded beaches, fragrant rainforests, mountains that soar above the mists, and waterfalls shimmering like silvery ribbons in valleys unmarred by human footsteps: Hawaii is one of the most alluring destinations on Earth.

But physical beauty is only the beginning, for Hawaii is rich in culture and history as well. In modern times, the islands have become home to an amazingly diverse gathering of peoples from all over the world. These cultures have grown together, creating a new, distinctly Hawaiian take on food, fashion, and art.

Today, Hawaii's economy is driven largely by tourism. Over 10.4 million people visited the islands in 2019, pumping $17.75 billion into the state. Covid-19 may have obliterated travel in 2020, but the industry started to pick up again in 2022 thanks to the vaccine rollout. While Oahu – the island with the state's largest city (Honolulu) – typically draws the crowds, other islands, such as Maui, Kauai, and Hawaii Island ("The Big Island"), have grown in popularity in recent years. Lanai and Molokai receive the fewest visitors, and Ni'ihau, the westernmost island, is open only to native Hawaiians. Kaho'olawe isn't open to visitors at all. Think of the eight islands like siblings from the same family; while each has a distinct personality, all are very much part of the same whole.

A wiliwili tree blooms by the windy road to Hana, Maui.

No matter how you experience Hawaii, you will be touched by *aloha* (*alo*, to face, and *ha*, the breath of life). It is the spiritual glue that binds the islanders, whatever the ethnic or cultural background. It is also the best way to describe how locals greet visitors: welcoming, inviting, and eager to share.

⊘ A NOTE TO READERS

At Insight Guides, we always strive to bring you the most up-to-date information. This book was produced during a period of continuing uncertainty caused by the Covid-19 pandemic, so please note that content is more subject to change than usual. We recommend checking the latest restrictions and official guidance.

Sunrise over Haleakala National Park, Maui.

VOLCANIC ISLES

Technically, the Hawaiian Islands are volcanoes rising out of the sea; what is visible is just the tops of these hulking landmasses that have emerged from the ocean floor.

It's difficult to think about things in geologic time; because most of us are only here for around three quarters of a century (if we're lucky), pondering the past in the context of so many years can boggle the mind. Nevertheless, this type of long-term perspective is critical for understanding how the islands of Hawaii came to be, because each and every one of the islands is – or once was – a volcano that rose from the depths of the sea and weathered over time.

Consider Kilauea, the active volcano on Hawaii Island. Kilauea has been continuously erupting in one form or another since 1983, most dramatically in the violent eruption of 2018. Every time lava oozed from the Earth and dropped into the sea, the island grew another few inches. Over hundreds of thousands of years, this is how the entire archipelago was born – a necklace of volcanoes in the middle of the Pacific Ocean.

Scientists believe it all began about 28 million years ago, when lava from the fiery interior of the Earth rumbled and surged, blasting through a jagged vent 15,000ft (4,600 meters) below the ocean's surface. A fraction of an inch at a time – 2 to 3ins (5 to 8cm) a year – the Pacific Plate of the Earth's crust crept northwest, rafting the volcano that had formed away from the hot spot and allowing a new sea mount to build under the water. A number of islands broke the ocean's surface, grew, and then eroded away into atolls, while at the same time newer islands formed. Eons later, a line of subterranean mountains, some rising to 15,000ft (4,600 meters) above sea level, stretched majestically in a row across 1,600 miles (2,500km) of the Pacific Ocean, from Hawaii Island to Kure Atoll, far to the northwest.

After these cataclysmic geologic events, biology took over. Over the centuries, floating seeds, fish,

Na Pali Coast State Wilderness Park, Kauai.

and marine larvae drifted to the islands on ocean currents. Winds carried fern spores, tiny seeds, and insects. Birds, sometimes full of fertile eggs or viable seeds, landed here, often propelled by storm winds. These isolated colonists adapted to suit their environment, making them unique, or endemic, to Hawaii. Over time, they have interacted with other non-native species (many brought by man) to populate an ecosystem that is now uniquely Hawaiian.

HAWAII'S SHIELD VOLCANOES

More than 10,000 years from now, we may write about Hawaii having nine major islands. Some 30 miles (50km) southeast of Hawaii Island's southernmost point, far beneath the surface of the ocean, a new island – Lo'ihi – is forming over a hot spot in the Earth's crust. Such eruptions, which begin on the ocean bottom, are the first stage in building Hawaii's broad shield volcanoes; the name derives from their supposed resemblance to the shields of ancient warriors, lying on

---

With its 132 islands, atolls, reefs, and shoals, Hawaii has the fourth-greatest length of coastline in the United States.

Mauna Loa, Hualalai (all have been active within the past 200 years), Mauna Kea, and Kohala, the oldest volcano on Hawaii Island. Basaltic lava from ancient and more recent eruptions is the most common rock in the Hawaiian chain. A drive around the Volcano area and Ka'u reveals two types of hardened lava: *paho'eho 'e* and *'a 'a*. Both have the same chemical composition. *Paho'eho 'e*, because it retains more gas, is hotter when it erupts, producing a fluid flow that hardens to smooth, ropy lava. *'A 'a*, on the other hand, hardens to rough, chunky, and sharp lava.

Sliding Sands Trail in Haleakala National Park, Maui.

the ground. Each volcano slowly grows as a thin layer of lava covers earlier layers. Underwater, lava hardens into pumice – light rocks full of gas bubbles – and pillow lava, or rock hummocks with rounded, smoother shapes.

Lo'ihi is predicted to jut from the ocean as a new sheer-sided, cliff-rimmed island some tens of thousands of years from now. Depending on the forces of nature – or on the whim of the volcano goddess Pele – it may eventually connect with Hawaii above sea level, making Hawaii Island even bigger.

When seamounts break the ocean's surface, the lava erupts in fiery fountains, flowing from craters and rifts in the mountain's sides. Five such seamount volcanoes formed Hawaii Island: Kilauea,

Eventually, the tops of the volcanoes collapse, creating wide depressions known as calderas. On Hawaii Island, Kilauea (which is currently erupting) and Mauna Loa both have calderas. When lava from these active volcanoes reaches the sea, you can witness the awesome process of island creation.

Hot lava pouring into the ocean turns shore waters into churning cauldrons, giving rise to towers of steam and cloud build-up. Sulfur dioxide released by active calderas combines with rain from these clouds, falling as dilute sulfuric acid. Chlorine gas freed from boiling sea water mixes with the sulfur, giving the area a chemical odor. It's a primordial scene not to be missed, but it can be dangerous.

THE LIFE CYCLE OF AN ISLAND

Once the volcano-building stops, other forces take over. Wind and sun eat away at the land, surf carves the coastlines, and rain cuts valleys and ridges into the new mountains. Volcanic rocks break down and gradually turn into soil. Plants arrive, then animals. Eventually, humans take over. What was once just a hot spot on the ocean floor is now fertile, life-supporting land.

Like the creatures that populate them, islands become middle-aged, grow old, and die. This aging process is visible in the Hawaiian Island

underwater, creating an atoll – a coral reef enclosing a lagoon. The coral reef rises above the ocean unevenly, forming numerous low islands in a circular shape. Kure, at the northwest end of the Hawaiian chain, is such an atoll. Molokini, a popular snorkeling spot between Maui and Kahoʻolawe, is another.

Forces of erosion have turned gentle slopes similar to those found on Mauna Loa into breathtaking ridges like those of Kauai's Na Pali coast. The towering North Shore cliffs of Molokai are the tallest ocean cliffs in the world, rising

Carlsmith Beach Park, Hilo, Big Island.

chain. After new islands form, coral reefs start growing at the edges, circling the island like underwater *lei* (garlands). As an island erodes and sinks toward the northwest with the shifting tectonic plate, the coral grows upward, searching for the sunshine so it can survive. Reefs growing on the outskirts of middle-aged islands like Maui, Molokai, Lanai, Oahu, and Kauai are called fringing reefs. The fringing reef associated with Hawaii Island is only now just beginning to be formed.

As the Pacific Plate continues to sink, lagoons tend to appear between the reef and its island. These barrier reefs can be seen in some of the older Hawaiian islands of the northwest chain. Eventually, the island in the center vanishes

nearly 2,000ft (600 meters) above the sea. Sandy beaches, rocky shores, and crater-shaped bays line other coastal areas throughout the state.

CLIMATE

Ecosystems in Hawaii are many and varied, depending not only on the location of the islands on the Earth's surface, but also on the topography of the land and the amount of wind, rain, and sunshine in each area.

Because Hawaii is in the sub-tropics, seasonal differences are slight. Temperatures are relatively stable, varying from an average of 80°F (25°C) around the coastal areas in winter months to 88°F (31°C) in the summer. At higher elevations, the difference increases. On the same latitude as Mexico

City, Hong Kong, and Cairo, Hawaii's longest day is 13 hours and 20 minutes compared to Seattle's 16 hours; the shortest day is 10 hours and 50 minutes, while Seattle's is 8 hours and 20 minutes.

Rainfall in the islands is most sparse in leeward areas – central mountains drain the northeasterly trade winds – and atop the highest mountains of Hawaii Island. The average annual rainfall ranges from less than 10ins (25cm) to more than 430ins (10 meters).

Weather develops as the trade winds carrying clouds across the ocean ascend the moun-

Papakolea Green Sand Beach,
Big Island.

tains and the air is cooled. Condensation causes rainfall on the windward side of the mountain ranges, leaving little moisture to fall as the depleted winds pass over the leeward side of each island. The climates of the islands mimic climates of much larger continents, with tropical rainforests, grasslands, deserts, and even areas of tundra represented on a smaller scale.

ECOSYSTEMS OF HAWAII

Narrow bands around each island where land and ocean meet are called coastal vegetation zones. Here, hundreds of plant and animal species live, each having adapted in its own way to this unique environment. There has been human

settlement in coastal zones for so long that it is difficult to find a place that hasn't been altered by human activity.

However, even with so much human influence, researchers recognize 150 different plant communities in Hawaii, which are named according to elevation, moisture, and vegetation. Within each of these, the plants and animals interact with one another and their environment to form ecosystems. In some areas, preserves – rainforests or shifting sand dunes that might hide traces of former lives, the bones of extinct birds, or ancient Hawaiian burial grounds – have been set aside. In these ecosystems, native species are protected.

A wetland is one kind of ecosystem. The term wetland refers to areas where water dominates the environment and its plants and animals. Wetlands can contain salty, brackish (salt and fresh), or fresh water, and can be up to 6ft (2 meters) deep. Anything deeper is a lake. Hawaii's bogs, estuaries, swamps, and streams contain and nurture unique scenery, plant life and bird life that's well worth checking out. Luckily, much of what remains undeveloped is preserved as parkland, as are Hawaii's remaining wetlands and mountainous interior. Land use issues are a hot item in today's Hawaii.

Forests contain dozens of ecosystems. Hawaii's forests are divided into dryland, medium-wet, and rainforests. Before humans came to Hawaii, dryland forests covered the leeward side of the larger islands and nearly all of Lanai and Kaho'olawe.

Ancient Hawaiians cleared much of this land for agriculture; later settlers finished the job. Today, dryland forests are rare. Researchers believe that in the past, the islands were wetter, with extensive dryland forests producing and holding moisture.

Medium-wet forests, growing between 2,000 and 9,000ft (600 and 2,700 meters), have the largest number of native tree species of all ecosystems in Hawaii, including the rainforests, which grow in the elevation zone just above the medium-wet forests. Hawaii's rainforests receive at least 100ins (254cm) of rain per year. During the winter, clouds often engulf these forests, producing thick, cool mists. The two native trees seen most often in both types of forests are *koa* and *'ohi'a lehua*, which support Hawaii's famous forest birds, the honeycreepers and their relatives.

Above the forests are alpine zones where few plants grow. Some desert-type plants like Hawaii's famous silverswords thrive in these high, dry, alpine areas, along with some insects. In some of these alpine areas, on Hawaii Island's Mauna Loa and Maui's Haleakala, for example, snow sometimes falls in winter.

PLANTS AND ANIMALS

The Hawaiian Islands began as barren lava rock, thousands of miles from the nearest land. Today the islands are lush with plants and teem with animal life; some of these are native, but most have been introduced by people.

Hawaii's native species are the plants and animals that managed to establish themselves without human interference. This colonizing of the islands was a slow process. If today's Hawaiian islands are between 1 million (Hawaii Island) and 7 million (Kauai) years old, then only one plant needed to establish itself every 15,000 years to account for today's mix of native plants. The best places to see these plants and animals are in Hawaii's national parks, wildlife refuges, and the state's marine conservation districts, where all reef-life is protected from fishing.

Most marine life encountered is native, or endemic, except for several species of snappers, imported by the state from Tahiti in the 1950s as game fish. All sea turtles in Hawaii are native, and are endangered and protected by law. It is illegal to ride or chase these harmless creatures.

Hawaii's only native land mammal is the hoary bat. Because of their night-time habits and secretive natures, bats are extremely difficult to find, even for researchers.

Native marine mammals include whales, dolphins, and monk seals. These are also protected by federal laws. Perhaps the greatest success story is that of the humpback whale, which once was endangered but now is thought to be thriving to the point where researchers are considering removing it from the endangered species list. On the flipside, with only about 1,300 of them left, Hawaiian monk seals are in extreme danger of extinction. If you see one resting on a beach, which is normal behavior for them, back off quietly and consider it a lucky day.

Only a few of the flowers and trees along Hawaii's highways are native. Seven kinds of hibiscus are native, but with 200 species of hibiscus in the world and more than 5,000 hybrids, the ones you see are often not Hawaii originals. Pandanus, also called screwpine or *hala*, are roadside native trees. *Koa* (popular for furniture) and *'ohi'a lehua* are native trees common to parks and preserves. Since many of their seeds float, beach plants are often native, including beach morning glories and beach *naupaka*, or thick green bushes with white flowers.

Bamboo forest in the Na Pali Coast State Wilderness Park, Kauai.

INTRODUCED SPECIES

By AD 500, Polynesians had brought with them the plants and animals they needed to live in their new home. Although keeping these species alive through such voyages was a tricky business, the immigrants managed to shuttle at least 27 kinds of plants and several kinds of animals – some wanted, some not – to Hawaii.

Even though this happened centuries ago, these species are considered alien because humans had a hand in their introduction. As a result, a few plants and animals that many might think of as native to Hawaii are actually aliens, introduced by those early settlers. Some common plants on this list are coconut palms, bananas, bamboo, ginger, breadfruit, taro, sweet potatoes, yams, mountain apples, and bottle gourds.

Candlenut trees, called *kukui* in Hawaiian, were also introduced, but this is still Hawaii's official state tree, partially due to the fact that the nut had so many uses in early Hawaii. The meat could be burned for light or ground up for seasoning food. The nut itself was used for body adornment. *Kukui* products are still common: the oil from the nuts is used in cosmetics, and the nuts themselves are polished to make necklaces and bracelets. It's easy to spot the abundant *kukui* trees in a forest: their leaves, which look as if they've been dusted with flour, are very pale next to others.

Sugar cane is another introduced Polynesian plant. Ancient Hawaiians used it as a sweetener, for food during famines, and as medicine. The leaves were used for hats and thatching. For decades, sugar cane was Hawaii's leading crop. It is still grown today; one acre (0.5 hectare) of land yields more than 11 tons (9,900kg) of cane, giving Hawaii the highest yield per acre in the agricultural world. In recent years a number of corporations (and

Green turtle at Carlsmith Beach, Hilo, Big Island.

⊙ HAWAIIAN GOOSE

One of the most famous animal stories in Hawaii is that of the *nene*, or the Hawaiian Goose. Believed to have descended from the Canada Goose, the official state bird is endemic to Hawaii and is believed to have first landed on Hawaii 500,000 years ago. By the mid-1900s, the *nene* was once endangered due to hunting and predation (by mongooses and other critters). State-led conservation efforts in the last 20 years have succeeded in rehabilitating the species significantly, but it is still considered the rarest goose on Earth. The animals can be spotted in the wild on Hawaii Island and Maui; there also is a healthy population at the Honolulu Zoo.

wealthy individuals) have tried to burn sugar cane as an alternative energy source, but potential environmental ramifications have hindered widespread adoption of these efforts. Generally speaking, high overhead and steady competition from other sweeteners have caused a dramatic and continuing decline in the Hawaiian sugar cane industry overall.

THE POST-CONTACT ONSLAUGHT

Hawaii's landscape changed forever when the first Polynesian explorers landed with their plants and animals, but that was only the beginning. Since Cook's arrival, plants and animals have streamed into the islands from all over the world. Today, many of these are more common than native or Polynesian-introduced species.

As these aliens often out-compete or eat native species, the flood of introductions is causing the extinction of many endemic plants and animals. Hawaii has the dubious distinction of having more endangered plant and animal species than any other American state. This can be attributed partly to its isolation, as a lack of natural enemies allowed more species to adapt and survive here than elsewhere.

Obviously, introduced species aren't all bad. Exotic plants provide Hawaii with stunning flower *lei*, sweet-smelling gardens, and highways lined with color, which comes from bougainvilleas and plumerias, native to tropical America. Other common aliens are ironwood and silk oaks from Australia, banyan trees from Asia, and Cook's pines from the South Pacific Cook Islands. Orchid growers, especially on Hawaii Island, have made Hawaii world-famous for orchid hybrids. Hawaii has just three native orchids, a minute number compared to the 30,000 species that make up the entire family.

Many food plants associated with Hawaii are foreign, including coffee (Africa), pineapples (Brazil), mangos (India), papaya (tropical America), and lychee (China).

Many alien animals, however, are not welcome: pigs, goats, sheep, and wild cats have all caused environmental disasters. Mongooses, for example, were imported by sugar growers to eat rats, but preferred native birds and their eggs. It was realized too late that mongooses hunt during the day, while rats are active at night. Only Kauai remains mongoose-free, and it therefore holds the largest population of birds.

Some non-native creatures, such as mynah birds and red-crested cardinals, are welcome, but state officials guard against pests such as snakes, particularly the brown tree snake from Guam, which has virtually extinguished avian life there. (The snakes hitchhike in the wheel wells of commercial and military aircraft flying to Hawaii from Guam.) Strict laws have been largely successful: outside the zoo, only a few illegal snakes have been found. However, there is growing concern about the brown tree snake.

Finally, perhaps the most egregious evidence of humans impacting upon the marine ecosystem off the shores of the Hawaiian Islands is the Great Pacific Garbage Patch. This is a constantly spinning mass of marine debris in the North Pacific;

much of the debris is plastic that cannot always be seen by the naked eye. Apart from the obvious threats to birds, sea mammals, and turtles from plastic bags and packaging, tiny pieces of plastic can block sunlight from reaching plankton and

---

Common Hawaiian plants like coconut palms, bananas, sugar cane, and breadfruit were actually early imports.

Nene goose on Big Island.

algae below. These both play a crucial part in the food web; if their numbers dwindle this will have a knock-on effect on their predators, their predators' predators and so on. The Ocean Cleanup, a nonprofit aiming to remove 90 percent of the Great Pacific Garbage Patch by 2040, has developed technologies to clear the floating trash. The team creates artificial coastlines where there are none, driving the garbage into a long U-shaped barrier and removing it from the water. The plastic is then recycled and turned into items like sunglasses (products.theoceancleanup.com). However, unless humans pay more attention to how they dispose of their waste, the Great Pacific Garbage Patch will keep growing every year with potentially disastrous consequences.

Vintage 1950s tourist map of the islands.

DECISIVE DATES

150,000 BC
Diamond Head forms through crack in the emerged reef of Oahu.

AD 200–500
First settlers arrive in Hawaii, probably from the Marquesas Islands.

800–1200
Polynesian pioneers arrive, this time from Tahiti.

c.1750
Kamehameha (the Great) born on Hawaii Island's northernmost point.

THE MODERN ERA

1778
Captain James Cook encounters Hawaiian Islands, and names them Sandwich Islands, after his patron, the Earl of Sandwich.

1779
Cook killed in a skirmish with Hawaiians.

1790–1
Kamehameha I begins unification of the Hawaiian Islands by conquering Maui and Lanai.

"The Death of Captain James Cook, 14 February 1779" by Johann Zoffany (1794).

1812
Sandalwood trade booms.

1819
Kamehameha I dies in Kailua, on Hawaii Island. His son, Liholiho, becomes Kamehameha II, and paves way for the introduction of Christianity in the islands by abolishing the ancient *kapu* system.

WESTERN INFLUENCES

1820
The first contingent of Protestant missionaries arrives in Hawaii. The kingdom's capital and royal court are moved to Lahaina, on Maui.

1825
Whaling industry begins 40-year boom.

1835
First Hawaiian sugar plantation established at Koloa, Kauai.

1842
Kawaiaha'o Church dedicated in Honolulu.

1845
Hawaii's capital moved back to Honolulu from Lahaina. First legislature in Hawaii convenes.

King announces plans for constitutional government.

1848
Kamehameha III enacts Great Mahele, dividing land among the crown, chiefs and commoners.

1852
The king unveils new constitution.

1869
"Big Five" company Alexander & Baldwin founded.

1872
Kamehameha V dies, ending the dynasty. He leaves no heir.

1873
Lunalilo elected king.

1874
After Lunalilo dies, Kalakaua is elected king. New monarch visits Washington, DC, to push for a reciprocity treaty with US.

1878
Thousands of immigrant plantation workers arrive, primarily from Portugal and Asia.

1887
Kalakaua signs Bayonet Constitution, which limits his power.

1889
Robert Wilcox leads unsuccessful revolt against opponents of the king.

1891
Kalakaua dies in San Francisco. His sister, Lili'uokalani, is named queen.

END OF THE MONARCHY

1893
Anti-royalists launch successful coup. Self-proclaimed provisional government is established.

1894
Provisional government declares itself to be the Republic of Hawaii.

1895
Supporters of Lili'uokalani stage a counter coup, but are defeated.

1898
President William McKinley signs legislation to annexe Hawaii.

1900
Hawaii becomes territory of the United States. Construction of naval base at Pearl Harbor begins.

1902
First transpacific telegraphic cable linking Hawaii and California is laid.

1903
Prince Jonah Kuhio Kalaniana'ole begins term as Hawaii's delegate to Congress.

1912
Hawaii's premier surfer, Duke Kahanamoku, wins Olympic gold medal in swimming.

1917
Queen Lili'uokalani dies.

1922
James Dole's Hawaiian Pineapple Company buys island of Lanai.

1929
Inter-Island Airways (now Hawaiian Airlines) starts passenger service between islands.

1936
Pan American Airways launches transpacific passenger service to Hawaii.

1941
Japanese fighter planes bomb Pearl Harbor, propelling the United States into World War II.

STATEHOOD

1959
Hawaii becomes 50th state.

1986
Hawaii's first ethnic Hawaiian governor, John Waihe'e, takes office.

1990s
Resort development takes off along Oahu's Waikiki Beach, and on Maui, Kauai, and Hawaii Island.

2002
Former Maui mayor Linda Lingle, a Republican, becomes Hawaii's first female governor. She is re-elected in 2006.

2006
Del Monte ceases operating in Hawaii, leaving Dole as the island's only pineapple producer.

2008
Barack Obama, a native of Hawaii, elected President of the United States. He is re-elected in 2012.

2011
Opening of Aulani in Oahu's Ko 'Olina resort area signifies Disney's entry into Hawaiian resort market.

2012
Larry Ellison, CEO of Oracle Corporation, buys 98 percent of the island of Lanai for a reported $600 million.

2013
State legislature legalizes same-sex marriage.

2016
Donald Trump is elected the 45th US president. Japan's PM Shinzo Abe visits Pearl Harbor and apologizes for the Japanese attack in 1941.

2017
HI-SEAS Mission, a NASA-funded eight-month research study simulating life on Mars is conducted on top of Mauna Kea volcano, a sacred site in Hawaiian culture. After much protest, a controversial Thirty Meter Telescope is built on top of the volcano.

2018
Kilauea volcano erupts violently, destroying around 700 homes and upending thousands of lives.

2020
The global coronavirus pandemic reaches the US on January 20, with former President Donald Trump declaring a public health emergency on January 31. On March 6, Hawaii's first case of Covid-19 is confirmed in Oahu. On May 25, George Floyd is killed by a police officer in Minneapolis, sparking civil rights protests across the US, including Hawaii, and all around the world.

2021
Democrat Joe Biden is inaugurated as the 46th US president, and Kamala Harris is sworn in as vice president, making history as the first woman, first Black person and first South Asian American in the role.

Waikoloa petroglyph field,
Big Island.

BEGINNINGS: ANCIENT HAWAII

Thousands of centuries passed after the Hawaiian Islands' creation before the first life took root. People, however, arrived just 15 or so centuries ago.

The Hawaiian Islands have existed for millions of years: culturally, however, they are relative newcomers to the modern world as humans arrived only 1,500 years ago. Those first humans, ancient seafaring Polynesians from the Marquesas and the other islands around Tahiti (more than 2,000 miles south of Hawaii), came en masse, probably in search of a better life.

These island people made the journey in seaworthy, double-hulled canoes embellished with 'aumakua – carved images of their family gods. In the years that have followed, research-ers have not been able to pinpoint specifically what prompted them to make the trip, or why they went in the direction they did. Perhaps they followed the migrating speckled plover, which headed north every spring. As for why they came, some have postulated that they may have been seeking refuge from persecution and conquering enemies, escaping the pressures of overpopulation, or simply following curiosity about what lay beyond the horizon.

These islanders – who represented nearly 1,000 islands overall – were but the last chapter of an island-hopping migration of peoples that had begun thousands of years earlier, probably in Southeast Asia. By AD 400, Marquesan canoes had sailed as far east as Easter Island, 2,500 miles (4,000km) away. In time they also reached New Zealand and Hawaii; recently archeologists have even found proof that they reached the Americas, albeit too late to have any significant cultural input.

IN THE STARS

The first Polynesians to reach Hawaii, located in latitudes high above the familiar stars, had not just ventured into the unknown, but had, in the

A helmeted, tattooed warrior in a feather cape, drawn by a French artist in 1819.

words of contemporary American author and ecologist Kenneth Brower, literally "left their universe." Instead of relying on navigational instruments and charts using latitude and longi-tude and the tools upon which European sailors had come to rely, they used an internal naviga-tion system programmed by intuition, knowl-edge, and experience. The Polynesian navigator counted on an eclectic mix of information and clues gained from studying the behavior of birds, dolphins, and the colors of the ocean and the clouds.

Most obvious, of course, were the stars. The early Polynesians did not use just one star, or even a dozen stars. They used hundreds of stars that were woven into a memorized tapestry of mnemonic chants that detailed hundreds of known course settings throughout the Pacific.

Based on observational and astronomical data accumulated over the years, it seems that Polynesians made the incredible 2,000-mile (3,200km) journey to Hawaii by fixing on two key stars – Sirius and Arcturus. Astronomers at the Bishop Museum in Honolulu note that "Sirius, the brightest star in the sky, passed almost directly over Tahiti and Raiatea (also called Hawa'iti). The present position of Sirius with

DISCOVERY OF HAWAII

The first discoverers and settlers of Hawaii are believed to have arrived sometime between AD 200 and 500. Evidence of Marquesan landfalls in Hawaii has been confirmed by carbon dating, and by comparison of fishhooks and adzes found in Hawaiian and Marquesan sites dating from around the same period. These new Hawaiians lived in isolation for several centuries, but sometime between 800 and 1200, other Polynesians arrived from Tahiti. Some researchers believe there were only a few voyages between Tahiti

Priests row across Kealakekua Bay for rituals surrounding first contact with Westerners, sketched by an artist with Captain Cook.

respect to the equator has changed very little from that of the days of Polynesian voyaging. Arcturus, called Hokule'a by the Hawaiians and noted for its bright redness off the Big Dipper's handle, presently passes over the northern end of the island of Hawaii. At the time of the great voyaging it passed over the island of Kauai.

Some of the most skilled Polynesian navigators did not use the stars at all. Perhaps because their boats were considerably smaller than the large European sailing ships, the Polynesians "felt" the ocean more, sensing its subtle moods and messages. They felt the ocean, literally, in the direction of swells and the subtle interference of waves reflected off distant islands.

and Hawaii. Others argue there were numerous voyages over a period of two centuries.

Scholars have speculated that this second wave of Polynesians subjugated the earlier Marquesans as slaves, or perhaps drove them farther north in the Hawaiian chain until they were completely eliminated. When the Tahitian migration ended, the newcomers lived in isolation for several centuries, developing into the Hawaiian culture that would later greet Captain Cook.

Conquered Marquesans may have been the *manahune*, or *menehune*, mentioned in early Hawaiian and Tahitian chants. The term *manahune* was used derisively in the Tahitian homeland to refer to slaves or plebeian castes, but its meaning changed through the centuries to mean, probably sarcastically, the mysterious gnomes supposed in Hawaiian folklore to inhabit remote corners of the islands. (The little gnomes have become quite a large part of modern Hawaiian folklore, especially on Kauai.)

"OFFSPRING OF TAHITI"

The Marquesans and Tahitians brought with them a similar language, as well as foods, myths, traditions, and gods. It was the Tahitian, however, who is credited with bequeathing the name "Hawaii,"

A gourd helmet with foliage and tapa (bark cloth) strip decoration.

which was first given to the largest of the islands, now commonly called Hawaii Island, and later to the complete chain of islands. As the Polynesian bard Kamahualele chanted centuries ago, "Behold Hawaii, an island, a people/The people of Hawaii are the offspring of Tahiti."

Sir Peter Buck, the eminent half-Maori ethnologist who once served as the Bishop Museum's director, explained the origin of the word Hawaii in his book, *Vikings of the Pacific*, published in 1938. He noted that in ancient times "the headquarters of the Polynesian main body was established in the largest island of the leeward group of Tahiti, named Havai'i after an ancient homeland."

As Tahiti-based fleets set out to settle the Society Islands, Samoa, Tonga, Fiji, Hawaii, and New Zealand, they established colonies often named after their home island. Dialectal differences resulted in today's place name variations. An even more persuasive Hawaii–Tahiti relationship is exemplified by the ancient name of a channel located south of Maui, between the islands of Lanai and Kaho'olawe. The channel's Hawaiian name is Kealaikahiki. By substituting the letter *k* in the word with *t*, the word *te-ala-i-tahiti* is formed, which translates as "the pathway to Tahiti," or "the pathway to foreign lands."

ANCIENT WAYS

Most of what we know of ancient Hawaiian life is from poetic oral traditions, known as *mele*. In these *mele*, the Hawaiians' *kupuna*, or ancestors, passed on to their descendants all they knew of their history. Various aspects of life, from the trivial to the momentous, were reported in this unwritten literature, which consisted of family genealogies, myths, and day-to-day accounts of human experiences.

Other insights about early Hawaii come from the initial observations made by foreign explorers such as James Cook, George Vancouver, and Otto von Kotzebue. Additionally, there are the important memoirs of early Hawaiian scholars, notably John Papa Ii (1800–70), Samuel Kamakau (1815–76), Kepelino Keauokalani (1830–78), and David Malo (1793–1853).

Another source has been the antiquities and folklore collected by Abraham Fornander

⊘ VOYAGES OF THE HOKULE'A

In the constellation Boötes, the star Arcturus is a zenith star for Hawaii, meaning that it passes directly overhead daily. In Hawaiian, the star is called *Hokule'a* – star of gladness. In the 1970s, a Polynesian-style voyaging canoe was built to recreate the journeys of ancient Polynesians to Hawaii. It was named *Hokule'a*. Since then, *Hokule'a* has made several successful voyages between Hawaii and southern Polynesia. *Hokule'a* was joined in the 1990s on expeditions by a sister canoe, *Hawai'iloa*. From 2014 to 2017, *Hokule'a* made a journey around the world. When not out exploring, it is berthed at Honolulu's Polynesian Voyaging Society.

(1812–87), a surveyor, editor, and judge. Fornander, who was married to a Hawaiian woman, spoke and wrote the Hawaiian language fluently. He wrote a history of the islands entitled *An Account of the Polynesian Race: Its Origins and Migrations*. He also collected and translated many Hawaiian chants into English. According to these chroniclers, the people of Hawaii developed one of the most complex non-technological cultures ever encountered by early Europeans.

Early Hawaiian culture operated within systematic laws known as *kapu*, the Hawaiian

Sometimes the unfortunate *kauwa* were marked by tattoos on their foreheads, and they were summarily conscripted as sacrificial victims by the priestly *kahuna*.

Under this hierarchy, the tightly circumscribed *kapu* and bloodlines could not be crossed. A typical penalty for a *kapu* violation was execution by stoning, clubbing, or strangulation; violators might also be buried or burned alive. Sometimes a *kapu*-breaker was singled out as a convenient sacrificial victim for a god, but usually he was sacrificed as a lesson to oth-

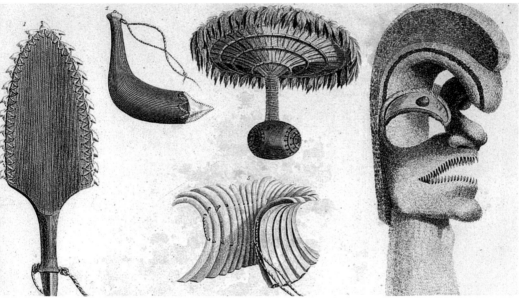

Articles of ceremony from early Hawaii.

version of the Tahitian word *tapu*, from which the word "taboo" originates. At the time of the first contact with Europeans, Hawaiian society was feudal and defined mostly by territory, with two or three *mo'i*, or kings, contending for control of each island. Ranking below the kings were hereditary groups of *ali'i*, or nobles. The *ali'i were* supported by *kahuna*, a prestigious group including priests, healers, and astrologers. Lower down was a class of craftsmen and artists, *kanaka wale*, who made the canoes, calabashes, and *lei* (garlands). This class also included fishermen and hula dancers. The labor and working class, *maka'ainana* or commoners, worked the land. At the very bottom were the social outcasts, the slaves or *kauwa maoli*.

ers. The Hawaiian historian David Malo wrote that a person could be put to death for allowing his shadow to fall upon the house of a chief, or for passing through that chief's stockade or doorway, or for entering the house before changing his *malo* (loincloth). He also could be executed because he appeared before the chief with his head smeared by mud. Other common *kapu* declared that women could not eat pork, coconuts, bananas, and shark meat, nor could they eat with men.

Certain seasons were established for the gathering or catching of scarce plants or animals for food, probably as conservation measures. Sometimes sporting chiefs declared certain surfing-spots *kapu* for their own exclusive use. Some *kapu* were implemented by Machiavellian chiefs, priests or influential court retainers under the guise of religion, or to tyrannically oppress a person or group of people. Many of the laws, however, were simply to protect resources and assure social stability.

Kapu violators had a place where they could seek sanctuary, whatever their crime. These places of refuge, called *pu'uhonua*, had to be reached by the transgressor before he was caught. The odds, of course, were against the transgressor. A good example of a *pu'uhonua*

walls made of large river-rounded lava stones. In ancient times, they housed *kapa*-covered oracle towers, sacrificial platform-altars, carved stone and wooden sculptures, images of gods made of thatch and feathers, sacred stones, rough-hewn monoliths, groupings of wood and stone sub-temple structures, and often a disposal pit for decayed human, animal, or plant offerings.

The most complex temples were those built by Hawaiian chiefs to initiate a war. These *heiau wai-kaua* (war temples), also called *luakini*, were kept spiritually "alive" by periodic human sacrifices.

An 1873 engraving of female surfers.

is located on a lava promontory at *Pu'uhonua O Honaunau National Historical Park*, on Hawaii Island's Kona coast. This *kapu* system affected every aspect of Hawaiian life, from birth to death, until it was abolished in 1819 by King Kamehameha II. But until its abolition, *kapu* protected the powers of Hawaiian kings.

WORSHIP

Hawaiians generally worshiped privately and at small shrines they built in their homes or outdoors, but the focal points of most major religious observances were large open-air temples known as *heiau*. Ruins of these *heiau* can be seen throughout Hawaii. In most cases, what remains today are rudimentary platforms, terraces and

Only *ali'i* were allowed access to the *heiau*. Once it had been decided to wage war, and appropriate sacrifices had been made to Ku, the war god, the high chief would call for his *kilo lani* (astrologer) to determine the most auspicious day to do battle. Exceptional power might be elicited from the gods by sacrificing an enemy chief at the *luakini*.

WAR AND ARTS

Given the generally clannish and feudalistic structure of ancient Hawaiian society, wars were frequent. Periodic and courtly sham battles were held between friendly chiefs to keep young warriors prepped and alert. This system of forearming and forewarning was reminiscent of European days of chivalry.

The ritual aspects of Hawaiian wars quickly gave way to brutality. There might be some opening decorum, gladiator-style, in which two renowned warriors would fight to the death in front of opposing armies. But more often

> A chief's feather cloak could require some 450,000 feathers plucked from an estimated 80,000 birds.

Admiring a temple's carved deities.

than not, the two armies would meet on an impromptu or chosen battleground, usually during daylight hours and following an exchange of verbal taunts and insults, commence battle.

Common Hawaiian weapons included spears up to 18ft (5 meters) in length, shorter javelins, assorted daggers (some lined with shark teeth), stone-headed clubs, serrated shark tooth clubs, a variety of carved wood and stone weapons, slingshots, strangling cords, and any and all objects (rocks, boulders, branches) that could be spontaneously introduced into the fray by resourceful warriors.

But life in ancient times was not an endless cycle of war-making, oppression, and workaday drudgery. Hawaiians developed unique forms of recreation, including such diversions as kite-flying, puppet theater and staged dances, numerous games of skill and chance, archery, tobogganing on *holua* sleds that were raced down specially prepared hillside runways, and surfing, known as *he'e nalu* or "wave sliding."

The Hawaiians also created the most exquisite variety of fine artwork and personal adornments found anywhere in Polynesia. Wood and stone sculpture was graphic and bold, while Hawaii's delicate featherwork is still considered to be the finest example of this art to be found. James Cook, in describing Hawaiian featherwork, observed that "the surface might be compared to the thickest and richest velvet." His lieutenant, James King, suggested that the "feathered cloak and helmet... in point of beauty and magnificence, is perhaps nearly equal to that of any nation in the world."

It would be impossible today to duplicate one of these cloaks, because most of the birds whose feathers were plucked for use have since become extinct. In old Hawaii, the king commissioned specially selected groups of royal feather-pluckers who stalked and snared their preferred prey with nets and long sticky wands. Most of the birds were released after the desired feathers had been removed.

Hawaiian *kapa*, the soft bark-cloth fashioned from paper mulberry, also represents a major artistic achievement. Strips of bark were soaked, then beaten until smooth and paper-thin. The cloth was then decorated by bamboo stamps with intricate designs carved on them, inked by dyes made from the leaves, bark, fruit, and roots of various native plants.

Perhaps the most diverse art practiced was in the form of necklaces, headbands, and anklets made of flowers, nuts, seeds, shells, ivory, teeth, turtle shells, and human hair. Tattooing, too, was popular, often as an expression of mourning. Both men and women tattooed their bodies with a variety of bright designs: some were of a topical nature, but there were also repetitious, geometric motifs. These tattoos were created with small sharp needles made of fish and bird bones, or shells.

Tattooing was condemned by the missionaries and had largely disappeared until the late 1980s, when it was revived as an art form and as a way of asserting native Hawaiian identity.

HAWAIIAN GODS

Polynesians brought with them to Hawaii steadfast belief in four major gods; around these deities belief in all other higher beings revolves.

From their South Pacific homelands, early Polynesian seafarers brought north with them the foods that had sustained them back home. By doing so, they also brought to Hawaii the great gods of Polynesia: Kane, Ku, Lono, and Kanaloa.

Polynesian gods were never distant and abstract. Rather, they moved through the waters and on the earth, and they could take on many forms, including plants. For instance, by bringing taro, one of the god Kane's forms, to Hawaii, the Polynesians carried with them Kane himself. Kane, the supreme god, was the procreator, the ancestor of all chiefs and commoners, the male power who dwells in eternity – the god of sunlight, water, forests. Kane was not fond of human sacrifices. An owl was one of his assumed forms.

Hawaiians prayed to Ku for rain and growth, and for successful fishing and sorcery, but he was best known as a patron god of war. Resplendent images of Ku, whose combative title was "The Island Snatcher," were carried on the war canoes of Kamehameha the Great. According to oral traditions, these fearsome images – wrought of red i'wi feathers embellished with mother-of-pearl eyes and mouths of jagged dog teeth – would utter dreadful cries during battle.

Lono was a god of thunder (lono means "resounding"), clouds, winds, the sea, agriculture, and fertility, but his personage could assume many forms, including a fish or a man-dog being. Hawaiians never appealed to Lono with human sacrifices. Most notably, he was honored during the makahiki harvest festivals of November, December, and January, when his image was carried by chiefly retainers on their tribute-and-tax-collecting tours of the islands.

It was during makahiki that Captain James Cook's arrival on Hawaii Island was greeted joyously by Hawaiians gathered at Kealakekua Bay. Some theorize the Hawaiians mistook his visit for the prophesied return of Lono.

Kanaloa, lord of the ocean and the ocean winds, was often embodied in the octopus and squid. He was a companion of Kane, and according to some, the two traveled together, "moving about the land and opening spring and water holes for the benefit of men."

HIERARCHY OF DEITIES

Coming to Polynesia from distant, unknown places, these four gods had been created before all other gods. They created the universe from the earth, symbolized as a calabash. By tossing the calabash's cover skyward, the sky, sun, and moon were formed. Seeds in the calabash became stars. The pantheon of Hawaiian deities is vast, including the lesser specialized gods, such as Pele, the volcano goddess, and Laka, goddess of hula.

Wooden image of Kakailimoku, the war god.

For the contemporary traveler to Hawaii, Pele is the best known of the lesser gods. As the fire goddess, she is responsible for the Kilauea eruptions. A common misconception is that Pele created the Hawaiian Islands. The islands had already surfaced when Pele, driven by wanderlust, arrived from Tahiti in a great canoe provided by the god of sharks. From Ni'ihau, she traveled down the island chain looking for a suitable home, which was within active volcanoes.

On Hawaii Island, she sought out the reigning fire god, Aila'au, hoping to settle in with him. But he had heard of her power and the blazing firepits she dug. As she approached Kilauea, he ran away, leaving her to build a soaring palace of fire that endures in legend and in periodic eruptions on Hawaii Island to this day.

ARRIVAL OF CAPTAIN COOK

Captain James Cook was noted for his sensitivity to the cultures he encountered during his global explorations. Still, after his arrival, Hawaii changed immensely.

Hawaii's modern era began in 1778, amid excitement and terror, when Hawaiians on the island of Oahu saw two strange, white-winged objects moving at sea. These "floating islands," as the Hawaiians were to describe them, were the British ships HMS *Resolution* and HMS *Discovery*, commanded by Captain James Cook.

ONE OF A KIND

En route from the South Pacific to the north – and, it was hoped, an elusive Northwest Passage – Cook and his crew, which included an astronomer and artist assigned to the expedition by the British Admiralty, had accidentally become the first known non-Polynesians to land on the Hawaiian Islands. It was a formidable find, the last significant land on Earth to be found by Europeans.

In his ship's log, Cook later suggested that finding Hawaii was "in many respects the most important discovery made by Europeans throughout the extent of the Pacific Ocean." Cook marveled at the existence of the remote Polynesian settlements: "How shall we account for this nation spreading itself so far over this vast ocean...?" Cook decided to name this chain of isles the Sandwich Islands, in honor of Cook's patron, the Earl of Sandwich, First Lord of the Admiralty.

Oahu was the first island to be sighted, but Cook passed by and continued on to the northeast, making landfall on January 21, 1778 at Waimea, on Kauai's west coast, after a long search for safe anchorage. After five days of replenishment and sightseeing, strong winds at night blew his ships away from Kauai toward the smaller island of Ni'ihau. There, Cook's men received salt and yams from the islanders

The British navigator James Cook.

⊘ WERE THE SPANISH FIRST?

Spanish ships may have landed in Hawaii up to two centuries before Cook. Historians point to artifacts, including a chart of the northern Pacific that marked the track of the round trip between the Philippines and Acapulco taken from a captured Spanish galleon by the British in 1742. The map showed islands in approximately the same latitude as Hawaii.

Also, feather cloaks and helmets – not found elsewhere in Polynesia – with a Spanish look and usually of red and yellow, the royal colors of Spain, were found in Hawaii. Furthermore, early Western visitors reported island residents with distinctly Caucasian features.

in exchange for goats, pigs, and the seeds of melons, pumpkins, and onions. Western flora and fauna were thus introduced.

Also introduced, against Cook's explicitly posted orders, were syphilis, gonorrhea, and other European diseases. All too aware of the effects of introduced diseases on indigenous peoples, Cook had told his men clearly that no Hawaiian women were to be allowed on board the ships, nor any person "having or suspected of having the venereal disease or any symptoms thereof, shall lie with any woman" under threat of severe lashing at the ship's masthead.

Thomas Edgar, master of the *Discovery*, said his men employed every devious scheme possible to get women on board the ships, even "dressing them up as men." But he noted also that the Hawaiian women "used all arts to entice them into their houses and even went so far as to endeavour to draw them in by force."

THE RETURN VISIT

In February, Cook left Hawaii to continue his search for the Northwest Passage, taking his two ships far above the Arctic Circle. As winter again approached, Cook returned to Hawaii, sighting Maui in November. For two months, the *Discovery* and *Resolution* charted the islands, first Maui, then Hawaii Island. Coming around Hawaii Island's southern tip from the east, Cook anchored along the Kona coast in a bay called Kealakekua, the "pathway of the god." It was exactly one year since his first landfall in Kauai.

If Cook was impressed a year earlier by the way Hawaiians on Kauai had prostrated themselves in his presence, he must have been even more impressed by his reception at Kealakekua Bay; Cook's second coming was monumental. He arrived at a propitious time: the *makahiki* celebration, an annual tribute to the god Lonoi-kamakahiki – and some researchers believe that Cook's auspicious arrival was identified by the Hawaiians as Lono's return. Consequently,

Engraving showing Cook receiving an offering.

⊙ THE HAOLE ARRIVE

Many Hawaiian scholars have opined about the day that Captain James Cook first arrived in Hawaii. Samuel M. Kamakau, a 19th-century Hawaiian author and historian, had this take: "The ship was first sighted from Waialua and Wai'anae (on Oahu) sailing for the north. It anchored at night at Waimea, on the island of Kauai. A man named Moapu and his companions who were fishing with heavy lines saw this strange thing move by and saw the lights... they hurried ashore and hastened to tell Ka'eo and the other chiefs of Kauai about this strange apparition.

"The next morning the ship lay outside Ka'ahe at Waimea. Chiefs and commoners saw the wonderful sight and marveled at it. Some were terrified and shrieked with fear. The valley of Waimea rang with the shouts of the excited people as they saw the boat with its masts and sails shaped like a gigantic stingray. One asked another, 'What are those branching things?' and the other answered, 'They are trees moving on the sea.' A certain *kahuna* named Kuohu declared, 'That can be nothing else than the *heiau* of Lono, the tower of Keolewa, and the place of sacrifice at the altar.' The excitement became more intense..."

Some say natives, who had gathered to honor the god Lono were so convinced that he would return during the festival held in his honor, that they considered Cook to be the god immediately.

Cook was afforded the greatest welcome ever accorded a mortal in Hawaii.

One of Cook's lieutenants estimated that 10,000 Hawaiians turned out in canoes, on surfboards, swimming in the bay, and waiting on shore to greet the return of Lono. Cook wrote, "I have nowhere in this sea seen such a number of people assembled in one place; besides those in the canoes, all the shore of the bay was covered with people, and hundreds were swimming about the ship like shoals of fish." John Ledyard, an American adventurer who had signed on board the *Resolution* as corporal of the marines, reported later that two officers counted from 2,500 to 3,500 canoes afloat in Kealakekua's waters. Ledyard and others also described unusual white *kapa* (bark cloth) banners held aloft on crossbars – an ancient symbol of Lono – which resembled the ships' masts and sails. Ledyard wrote that when Cook went onshore, the masses of Hawaiians "all bowed and covered their faces with their hands until he was passed."

There were extravagant ceremonies held in Cook's honor, including one at a sacred temple, or *heiau*. Cook and his men tried their best to please the Hawaiians with tours of their ships, a flute and violin concert, and a fireworks display. All the while, Cook readied his ships for a voyage to Asia, and after two weeks, they set sail. But three days later, just off Hawaii Island's North Shore, a fierce winter storm damaged the *Resolution's* foremast. Cook returned to Kealakekua to make essential repairs to his boat.

DEATH OF COOK

Cook now found that the *makahiki* festival at Kealakekua was finished, and because of a *kapu* put on Kealakekua Bay by King Kalaniopu'u, the area was nearly deserted. Those Hawaiians who remained were not as generous in their tribute, and in fact were surprised that a god's property could be badly damaged within his own domain.

The Hawaiians grew increasingly bold, taking objects from the ships that pleased their fancy, particularly items made of metal. When they seized the *Discovery's* cutter, Cook went ashore with nine marines to take Kalaniopu'u hostage in exchange for return of the boat,

a strategy that had worked before on other Pacific islands. Not on this occasion. A violent scuffle broke out, and a large party of more than 200 Hawaiian warriors attacked Cook's landing party. Five of the marines managed to escape, but four others, as well as Cook himself, died. The British ships fired on the Hawaiians, who retreated.

Two delegations of concerned Hawaiians later returned parts of Cook's body "cut to pieces and all burnt," wrote James King, Cook's second lieutenant. One bundle of Cook's bones, wrapped

Bewohner der Sandwich-Inseln.

Image of the islands' inhabitants, by Karl Joseph Brodtmann.

in fine *kapa* and a cloak made of black and white feathers, included "the captain's hands (which were well known from a remarkable cut), the scalp, the skull, wanting the lower jaw, thigh bones and arm bone; the hands only had flesh on them, and were cut in holes, and salt crammed in; the leg bones, lower jaw and feet, which were all that remained and had escaped the fire, he said were dispersed among other chiefs."

What remained of Cook was buried at Kealakekua Bay, and in late February of 1779, the *Discovery* and *Resolution* set sail, passing Maui, Molokai and Oahu before anchoring again briefly at Waimea, on Kauai.

Portrait of Queen Liliʻuokalani, 1891.

THE HAWAIIAN MONARCHY

The monarchy of Hawaii began with Kamehameha the Great, who united the Hawaiian Islands. It ended with the overthrow of Queen Lili'uokalani.

All told, Hawaii had eight main monarchs between 1795 and Hawaii's designation as an American territory in 1900.

KAMEHAMEHA I (1795–1819)

Often mentioned in the logs and diaries of visiting ships' captains and merchants was Kamehameha, which means "the lonely one." A distinguished warrior and one of King Kalaniopu'u's nephews and subordinate chiefs, Kamehameha (pronounced *ka may-ha may-ha*) had impressed Cook at Kealakekua Bay. Kamehameha was a careful observer of the *haole* (Caucasians). He had been wounded by a gun on the beach when Cook was killed, and it was evident to Kamehameha that one man with a small brass cannon could have a great advantage over several warriors with clubs and spears. By 1789, Kamehameha's own large double canoe was carrying a swivel gun mounted on a platform strapped across the hulls.

A 10-year civil war involving Kamehameha and others erupted on Hawaii Island in 1782. When the timing seemed astrologically and militarily propitious, Kamehameha conquered Maui and Lanai in 1790, then fought to keep Maui again a few years later. Perhaps his toughest battle was against Keoua, his chief Hawaii Island rival.

Kamehameha took no chances against Keoua. He built the immense Pu'u Kohala *heiau* (temple) to his war god near Kawaihae in Kohala – it still stands – and invited Keoua to meet him there. When he arrived, Kamehameha had him killed. Kamehameha was now king of all of Hawaii Island. He recaptured Maui, then Molokai. In the meantime, civil war had erupted on Oahu, and Kamehameha took advantage

One of the few paintings made of Kamehameha while he was alive.

of the disorder to land his fleet there, at the foot of Diamond Head in 1795. In a display of military strength, his warriors drove Oahu's defenders into Nu'uanu Valley and over the edge of Nu'uanu Pali, a precipitous cliff. With Oahu's conquest, and the ritual sacrifice of its king, Kalanikupule, to Kamehameha's war god, Kamehameha became monarch of all of Hawaii, except Kauai and Ni'ihau, more than 70 miles (110km) west of Oahu.

In both 1796 and 1809, Kamehameha assembled invasion fleets destined for Kauai and Ni'ihau. In 1810, Kauai's king peacefully yielded his throne. The islands thus finally became united under a single ruler, Kamehameha the Great.

Although Kamehameha retained the traditional ways, such as the *kapu*, he also learned from the Europeans whose ships he supplied with provisions. Hawaii's sandalwood proved a lucrative trade for Kamehameha, and he directed commoners by the thousands to harvest it for shipment to Asia. Exports continued until there were no more sandalwood trees in the islands.

, Kamehameha the Great died after a long illness in 1819, at his royal compound Kamaka Honu – the Eye of the Turtle – in what is now Kailua on Hawaii Island. He was about 63 years old. So that nobody could defile them or use their powerful *mana* (spirit), Kamehameha's bones were hidden in a still-secret location somewhere on the Kona coast.

KAMEHAMEHA II (1819–24)

Kamehameha's son and successor, Liholiho, was not a strong and commanding ruler like his father. But Ka'ahumanu, the favorite of Kamehameha the Great's many wives, was intelligent, fearless, and powerful. Upon Kamehameha's death, she made it clear to Liholiho that it was his father's wish that she be the *kuhina nui*, the joint ruler or queen regent of Hawaii.

One of Ka'ahumanu's first actions was to abolish the ancient *kapu* system. Urged on by Ka'ahumanu, Liholiho sat down with his mother, Keopuolani, and Ka'ahumanu at a feast, violating the *kapu* that prohibited men and women from eating together. Ka'ahumanu and Liholiho then ordered that all the *heiau* and carved wooden idols be destroyed. The social and cultural shock to Hawaiians was enormous, leaving an overwhelming spiritual vacuum.

The vacuum didn't last long. The first party of New England missionaries arrived in 1820 aboard the American brig *Thaddeus*, ready to fill the religious void. Had the timing of the *kapu* collapse and the arrival of Christian missionaries not been so coincidental, the history of Hawaii could have been very different.

Although Ka'ahumanu and Liholiho had reservations about these overdressed *haole*, they let the American missionaries preach at Kailua-Kona and Honolulu for a one-year trial. The missionaries never left, and their descendants garnered land and power.

The English had retained an interest in Hawaii since Cook's first contact, and in 1822 Liholiho received a gift from King George IV: a small schooner named the *Prince Regent*. Delighted, Liholiho left Hawaii the next year on a British whaling ship to visit King George and negotiate a treaty. Liholiho and his entourage were royally feted in London, but before he could meet with King George, he and his queen, Kamamalu, caught the measles and died. Liholiho designated his younger brother Kauikeaouli as his logical successor.

KAMEHAMEHA III (1825–54)

The early years of Kauikeaouli – Kamehameha III – would better be called the reign

Queen Ka'ahumanu with a servant.

⊙ CIVILIZED MISSIONARIES

Reverend Hiram Bingham, whose grandson was credited with "discovering" Machu Picchu for the Western world, led the first group of Christian missionaries to Hawaii and wrote of his followers' impressions: "The appearance of destitution, degradation, and barbarism among the chattering, and almost naked savages, whose heads and feet, and much of their sunburnt skins were bare, was appalling. Some of our number, with gushing tears, turned away from the spectacle. Others, with firmer nerve, continued their gaze, but were ready to exclaim, 'Can these be human beings? Can such things be civilized?'"

of Ka'ahumanu, since Kauikeaouli was only 10 years old when his brother died. As *kuhina nui*, Ka'ahumanu exerted a strong influence on both the boy king and the Hawaiian people, most of whom were still disoriented and adrift after the demise of the *kapu* system.

Half a year after Liholiho left on his ill-fated trip to England, Ka'ahumanu had announced a system of civil laws obviously based on the Congregationalist missionaries' teachings. In fact, the Congregationalists had cultivated considerable spiritual and political influence over Ka'ahumanu, eventually converting her to Christianity. Ka'ahumanu became one of the Congregationalists' most enthusiastic converts. Another convert to Christianity was an *ali'i* peer, the Hawaii Island high chiefess Kapi'olani.

In 1824, Kapi'olani (not to be confused with her niece and namesake, the future Queen Kapi'olani) hiked to the mouth of Halema'uma'u in the Kilauea caldera on Hawaii Island. There, at the edge of the fire goddess Pele's domain, Kapi'olani defiantly renounced her. She lived to tell the tale, and at the Hilo Congregationalist mission, 90 impressed Hawaiians instantly became new converts.

Encouraged by the royal support, missionaries built churches and schools throughout the islands. Even more, as "messengers of Jehovah," the missionaries used their court influence to veil Hawaiians with everything Puritan. Bare skin on women in any degree – much less nudity – was condemned, and women were draped in dresses mostly ill-suited to the tropics. The ancient and sacred hula, which combined dance and poetry, was outlawed as lewd and lascivious.

Equally high on the agenda was putting the Hawaiian language into Romanized script. The missionaries' intent in doing so was evangelical, no doubt, but teaching Hawaiians to read and write gave them a new tool with which to communicate their own histories and thought. This was especially important as the missionaries had suppressed traditional storytelling methods like the hula.

When Ka'ahumanu died in 1832, Kamehameha III took full control of the government in a reign noted for a couple of frivolous early years of horseracing, gambling, drinking, and dancing. His half-sister, Kina'u, the *kuhina nui* successor to Ka'ahumanu, managed state matters during his bouts with the bottle. The missionaries

continued to consolidate power, accepting government appointments.

In the mid-1820s, just as the sandalwood trees had all but disappeared in the islands, whaling became Hawaii's major source of revenue, with Honolulu and Lahaina among the Pacific's most important ports. Whaling kept Hawaii's economy above water for over 30 years. At its peak in 1846, 429 ships were anchored in Maui's Lahaina Harbor.

The missionaries, of course, protested the extracurricular activities of sailors on liberty.

Hawaii's royal coat-of-arms engraved on the Queen's piano in Washington Place, Honolulu.

Attempts by the missionaries to quench liquor and prostitution were not well received, and the homes of several preachers in Lahaina were bombarded with cannon by angry sailors from aboard the safety of anchored ships.

Perhaps Kamehameha III's most significant act was an edict issued in 1848, which became known as the Great Mahele. Under subtle pressure from missionary advisers and businessmen, the king divided Hawaii's land ownership – previously the pleasure of the royalty – among the monarchy, government, and common people, thus allowing ordinary Hawaiians to own property for the first time.

Two years later, foreigners also were permitted land ownership. Within a few years, the *haole* had accumulated large estates; by 1886, about two-thirds of all government lands sold had been bought by resident *haole*. Hawaiians, unfamiliar with land ownership, had done little to thwart the foreigners' acquisitions.

By the late 1850s, whales had been hunted nearly to extinction, petroleum and coal were replacing whale oil, and the United States was sinking into a civil war. The boom days of the Hawaiian Islands were over.

Hawaii's business and political interests turned from whaling to a new commodity,

in 1852, followed over the decades by Japanese, Portuguese, Filipinos, Norwegians, Germans, Koreans, Puerto Ricans, Spaniards, and Russians. A significant percentage of Hawaii's ethnic mix today descends from those early immigrant laborers.

Before the 30-year reign of Kamehameha III was over, the king had established a supreme court, an upper house of royalty, and a lower house of elected representatives. Kamehameha III had no children and named a nephew, Alexander Liholiho, as his successor.

View of Honolulu from the harbor, c.1854.

sugar. During California's gold rush in 1849, a handful of small sugar planters in Hawaii had made great profits when Kaleponi – California – turned to Hawaii for its sugar supply. Sugar's potential looked sweet, especially for those with the land under the cane. Whereas whaling had been mostly a merchants' boom, sugar would be a land barons' boom. But sugar plantations are labor intensive, and the local pool of laborers was small. More pragmatically, Hawaiians saw little appeal in the low-paying, backbreaking work of harvesting sugar cane, especially as the islands offered plenty of traditional foods.

For sugar to become a major industry in Hawaii, thousands of laborers needed to be imported. The first group of 293 Chinese arrived

KAMEHAMEHA IV (1855–63)

Alexander Liholiho – the grandson of Kamehameha the Great – had a certain dislike for America, and during his short reign, he was to shift Hawaii closer to the British Empire both in spirit and in policy. Educated by Americans at an elite royal school, Kamehameha IV and a brother had visited Europe and America in 1849 and 1850. Their experiences in Europe, especially England, were enjoyable and enriching. Their experiences in America were not.

Today, Alexander Liholiho is remembered for his concern for Hawaiians. One surviving legacy is the Queen's Medical Center, established by him and his wife, Queen Emma, in 1859 to care for sick and destitute Hawaiians, many of whom were still suffering from introduced European diseases.

In 1863, after the death of his son, Kamehameha IV died (at the age of 29) during an asthma attack.

KAMEHAMEHA V (1863–72)

A believer in the strong, autocratic style of Kamehameha the Great, Lot Kamehameha, an elder brother of Kamehameha IV, refused to take an oath to uphold the liberal constitution of 1852. He believed that it weakened the powers

Kamehameha V.

of the Hawaiian monarchy, making it vulnerable to overthrow by non-royalists, a forethought that later turned out to be true.

In 1864, Lot Kamehameha declared a special convention to revise the constitution. This convention accomplished nothing, so the king then offered a new constitution that abolished the matriarchal office of *kuhina nui*, set up a one-chamber legislature for nobles and elected representatives, and decreed that persons born after 1840 be required to pass literacy tests and meet certain property qualifications before being allowed to vote or serve in the legislature. His act was in effect a bloodless but effective coup d'état. This strengthening of the monarchy led to increasing resentment among

non-royalists – mostly foreign businessmen – and added fuel to the fire that would later bring down the monarchy.

A bachelor, Lot left no heir and named no successor. When he died at the age of 42, the 77-year-long dynasty of Kamehameha the Great at last ended.

WILLIAM LUNALILO (1873–4)

Under the constitution of 1864, the legislative assembly unanimously elected Prince Lunalilo as king in 1873. It was a popular decision with the Hawaiians, who had already voted for him a week before. As popular as Lunalilo – or Prince Bill – was with the people, he was ineffective in leadership and was thought to have a drinking problem. Thirteen months later he died without an heir. The kingdom's legislative assembly once again went about the sticky business of electing a new sovereign.

KALAKAUA (1874–91)

> A train conductor in New York mistook the future Kamehameha IV for a servant and ordered him out of the railroad car. That memory of America lingered long.

There were two contenders for the throne: David Kalakaua, who had lost to Lunalilo in the previous election, and Queen Emma, widow of Kamehameha IV. After a spirited campaign, the assembly handily elected Kalakaua as king of Hawaii in 1874. Kalakaua's ancestors had been high chiefs on Hawaii Island.

Ruling with a flourish and style that earned him the nickname "the Merrie Monarch," Kalakaua ignored the calls for annexation by the US and devoted his energy to fashioning his kingship in the courtly tradition of European monarchs. He built himself the magnificent 'Iolani Palace; became the first monarch to circumnavigate the globe; and presented gala horse races, grand balls, and old-style Hawaiian feasts. During his reign, Kalakaua openly clashed with educators and Christians about restoring Hawaii's rapidly disappearing cultural traditions.

In 1874, the same year he ascended the throne, Kalakaua traveled to Washington, DC, hoping to negotiate a reciprocity treaty with the US. He and his entourage were grandly received by President Ulysses S. Grant and a joint session of Congress. Newspaper reporters described the state banquets arranged for Kalakaua as the most lavish ever seen in the nation's capital. Kalakaua subsequently received strong personal support from Grant.

By the following year, the US Senate approved a treaty giving Hawaii "favored nation" duty con-

Coronation of Kalakaua in Honolulu.

cessions and thus eliminating tariffs on sugar. While the treaty was a triumph for the new king, it also gave America a lock on the islands, presaging its future interest in Pearl Harbor as a military base, and preventing Kalakaua from using Hawaii's location to gain concessions from Britain or France.

Perhaps most importantly for Hawaii's immediate future, the treaty gave the sugar growers increased economic confidence and security. And, as would later become clear, the agreement gave the growers disproportionate political and social leverage, eventually weakening the Hawaiian monarchy's power.

A string of scandals began to taint Kalakaua's reign, much to the self-righteous delight of the foreign business community. In 1887, an armed insurrection led by a *haole* political group called the Hawaiian League forced Kalakaua to accept a new so-called "Bayonet Constitution" that seriously constrained his powers. This new constitution required that voters own at least

> *Queen Emma's backers protested at Kalakaua's selection, and a free-for-all fight took place inside and outside the courthouse.*

$3,000-worth of property or have an income of at least $600 a year, requirements that effectively eliminated most Hawaiians from the political franchise. Power conclusively shifted to Hawaii's land-owning and predominantly white minority.

Two years later, a fiery part-Hawaiian revolutionary named Robert Wilcox staged a counter coup against the businessmen. He and about 150 armed followers loyal to the kingdom swashbuckled their way past the King's Guards and occupied 'Iolani Palace. But Wilcox's coup d'état failed miserably. Within hours, he and the other revolutionaries were flushed out with rifle fire and crude dynamite bombs laced with twenty-penny metal spikes. Seven of his men were dead and another 12 wounded.

For the remainder of his reign, Kalakaua was, for the most part, a figurehead monarch. In 1891, while visiting California in an effort to restore his failing health, Kalakaua died in a San Francisco hotel suite. Before leaving Hawaii, Kalakaua had appointed his sister, Princess Lydia Kamakaeha Lili'uokalani, heir to the throne, as regent during his absence. She became Hawaii's first and only reigning queen.

LILI'UOKALANI (1891–3)

Lili'uokalani was a staunch royalist. Right from the start, she made it clear that she planned to restore monarchical power and the rights of native Hawaiian people. Weary of the plodding cabinet government created by the Bayonet Constitution of 1887, she announced in 1893 that she would issue a new constitution placing power firmly back in the hands of the monarchy.

Pro-annexation, anti-royalist forces planned to overthrow the monarchy and support annexation negotiations with the United States. In January 1893, they launched their revolt after first enlisting John B. Stevens, the US minister in Hawaii. An ardent supporter of the pro-annexation movement, Stevens ordered the landing of Marines from the visiting gunship USS *Boston*, ostensibly to protect American lives and property – but without authorization from Washington. That afternoon, some 160 armed Marines positioned artillery pieces and Gatling guns at strategic points in Honolulu, and by the next day, "without the drawing of a sword or the firing of

King Kalakaua, Hawaii's last king.

a shot," a self-proclaimed government led by Sanford Dole was in power. Lili'uokalani had no choice but to abdicate her throne.

She believed that the American government, learning of the coup, would reinstate the monarchy. She was right – sort of. Unlike his predecessor, newly elected President Grover Cleveland did not support the coup, and he dispatched a special investigator to Honolulu to investigate. The investigator arrived in Hawaii to find American flags flying above Hawaii's public buildings. He ordered the flags to be taken down and the Marines withdrawn. He reported to Cleveland that "a great wrong has been done to the Hawaiians." Cleveland sent a message to Congress stating that the unauthorized use of American

troops in Hawaii was "an act of war against a peaceful nation." Congress, lobbied by the sugar interests, disagreed.

In 1894, the provisional government established itself as the Republic of Hawaii. Sanford Dole was named president. President Cleveland sent a representative to Hawaii seeking the reinstatement of Queen Lili'uokalani, but Dole and his cabinet refused to step down. Lili'uokalani and her supporters planned a counter-coup, to be led by the indefatigable Robert Wilcox. The government arrested the royalists, including Queen Lili'uokalani, for treason. The queen denied guilt, but bombs and arms were found in her Washington Place garden.

Lili'uokalani was placed under house arrest and a week later she gave up the throne. She was found guilty of treason and sentenced to five years of hard labor and fined $5,000. The penalties were never enforced, but she remained imprisoned at 'Iolani Palace until later that year.

FULLY ASSIMILATED INTO THE US

In November 1897, Cleveland lost the US presidential election to William McKinley, and in 1898 McKinley signed annexation papers. Two years later, Hawaii was an American territory. Sanford Dole was its first territorial governor. Lili'uokalani and Dole publicly reconciled in 1911 at the opening of the Pearl Harbor naval base. In 1917, during World War I, Hawaii's last monarch raised the American flag over Washington Place for the very first time. Seven months later, she died at the age of 79.

⊘ HISTORICAL HINDSIGHT

In the 1890s, right around the time that Hawaii achieved statehood, two different leaders had two similar perspectives of Hawaii. First, President Grover Cleveland wrote in his memoirs: "Hawaii is ours. As I look back upon... this miserable business and as I contemplate the means used to complete the outrage, I am ashamed of the whole affair." Next, Queen Lili'uokalani wrote in her memoirs: "Overawed by the power of the United States... the people of the Islands have no voice in determining their future, but are virtually relegated to the condition of the aboriginals of the American continent."

MODERN HAWAII

First it was sugar that defined Hawaii's economy.
Pineapples came along and helped out, as did the military.
Now, tourism is the state's financial anchor.

At the start of the 20th century, it looked as though the schemes of the business and land barons had finally come to pass. Hawaii became an American territory in 1900; the governor and judges were now appointed by the American president. Sugar was soon joined by a new commodity, pineapples, when James Dole (a relative of Sanford Dole) began marketing Hawaii-grown pineapples successfully on the US mainland. Hawaii would soon become the world's major supplier of the fruit.

THE RISE OF SUGAR

With Sanford Dole leading the territorial government, just about all of the new territory's banking, commerce, and transportation remained under the continuing control of five large *haole* corporations built largely on sugar: Castle and Cooke, Alexander and Baldwin, C. Brewer, Theo H. Davies, and American Factors (now called Amfac). By intention and default, the so-called "Big Five" controlled Hawaii's politics and government.

Sugar's future remained of paramount importance. Because it was now part of the US, Hawaii was classified a domestic producer and thus no longer subject to import tariffs. Greater profits could be anticipated, and the plantations could grow. But expansion of the sugar plantations required yet more labor, and the companies had to import more workers to do the job.

Before, as an independent kingdom and republic, there had been no restrictions on immigration to Hawaii, and so the sugar barons had brought in tens of thousands of workers from Asia, first from China and then from Japan. Later, workers came from Portugal, Puerto Rico, Korea, and the Philippines.

Sanford Ballard Dole, c.1900.

But now, as an American territory, immigration quotas were determined in Washington. Immigration from Asia was curtailed. With their traditional labor sources evaporating, Hawaii's sugar plantations were nevertheless in luck with a new source: the Philippines, under the American flag since 1898.

At this time, Hawaii was very much a Republican territory, governed by an entrenched oligarchy of businessmen intent on preserving their power. Hawaii was a place of well-defined social hierarchies. White men owned the plantations and held supervisory positions, while immigrant laborers ranked low. The first generation of immigrant laborers, indentured and mostly from Asia, buttressed this rigid plantation hierarchy.

THE NEW AMERICANS

As Hawaii swaggered into the 20th century, something happened that had not been anticipated at all. Those first-generation Chinese, Japanese, and Filipinos who had worked hard and quietly on the plantations decided to stay in Hawaii after their labor contracts ended. They had children, and these plantation babies were by birth American citizens. Unlike their parents, they were not foreigners, nor were they newcomers, nor strangers in a strange land. Hawaii was their home.

Congress made it legal for workers to organize into unions and engage in collective bargaining.

WORLD WAR II

Early on Sunday morning, December 7, 1941, two waves of Japanese aircraft – 360 planes in all – dropped below cloud cover and attacked every major military installation on Oahu. The surprise attack devastated the US Pacific fleet: 2,323 Americans were killed while Japanese casualties numbered fewer than 100. Most of the ships in the harbor were severely damaged if not sunk.

Pineapples and plantation workers, c.1910.

> *Japan had been expanding its control in Asia. Now the Pacific was next, including Pearl Harbor, home of the US Pacific fleet since 1908.*

As this second generation of Asian immigrants grew up, the power of the Big Five corporations, Republican politicians, and missionary landowners was challenged, their footing further undermined by an economic depression that boosted the confidence of labor movements. In 1935, 10 years after a violent strike by cane laborers in Hanapepe, Kauai, left many Filipino workers dead, legislation passed by the US

Some 68 Oahu residents were killed or injured. Japanese submarines sank cargo and passenger vessels in local waters. They also surfaced to shell Hilo, Nawiliwili, and Kahului harbors.

The same day as the attack on Oahu, President Franklin Roosevelt declared war on Japan. Later in the morning, Hawaii was placed under martial law. The state remained under martial law until 1944, during which time military courts completely replaced all civilian jurisdiction in Hawaii. The US Supreme Court ruled after the war that this was an unconstitutional move.

At the beginning of the war, the largest ethnic group in Hawaii were the *nisei*, of Japanese ancestry. On the mainland, Americans of Japanese ancestry (AJAs) were confined in desert internment camps, a policy that was entirely racial and not substantiated by claims of national security. (Americans of German and Italian ancestry were, in contrast, left alone.)

In Hawaii, the *nisei* were far too prominent to be confined, not only because they were a majority percentage of Hawaii's population, but also because they were a major thread in Hawaii's social and cultural fabric.

Eventually, AJAs of military age were permitted to enlist in the army; after the war, returning home to Hawaii, many AJAs used veterans'

different incoming group of territorial legislators – half of whom were AJAs – and who were supported by labor unions.

PUSH FOR STATEHOOD

Between 1903 and 1957, 22 bills addressing statehood for Hawaii failed Congressional votes in Washington. Unlike mainland areas annexed as territories, there had been no provisions in Hawaii's territorial legislation for eventual statehood. And in any case, territorial status had suited the sugar interests just fine.

US Navy battleships being attacked at Pearl Harbor.

benefits to pay for college, turning later to law and politics and becoming the core of another shift in Hawaii's structure.

After the war, a succession of workers' strikes established unions among Hawaii's major political and economic forces. They solidified their power in 1952 with a six-month work freeze on Hawaii's docks that nearly devastated the territory's economy, which was almost completely dependent on shipping. Hawaii's business and political *ancien régime*, however, were sore and sour losers, accusing the unions of being part of the Marxist plague. However, the Republican Party, which had been entrenched since well before anyone alive could remember, was knocked out of power in 1954 by a decidedly

But in 1934, Congress had given Hawaii's sugar barons a kick in the *'okole* (buttocks) by grouping Hawaii along with foreign producers of sugar. Exports to the mainland plummeted. Statehood would be necessary to sustain Hawaii as a leading sugar producer. The Big Five and other interests pushed for statehood and eventually overcame Congressional reluctance. It has been suggested that southern congressmen were against admitting Hawaii as a state dominated by non-Caucasians.

A deal was finally struck linking Hawaii and Alaska for statehood, and in 1959 Hawaii became the 50th American state. Statehood was ratified by Hawaii's voters by 17 to 1. Only the precinct of Ni'ihau, the privately owned island off Kauai, peopled by native Hawaiians, voted against it. Statehood was one of those historical pivots, like Cook's visit and the overthrow of Lili'uokalani, that irrevocably changed Hawaii's destiny and direction. At the time of statehood,

> *In the 1950s, Hawaii's activist unions were accused of being revolutionary tools of an unproven Communist conspiracy.*

the tallest building in Hawaii was the 10-story-high Aloha Tower, and Waikiki was peppered here and there with just a few hotels. Defense and agriculture, primarily sugar and pineapples, were Hawaii's two main sources of revenue.

That same year, a regular commercial jet service was inaugurated by Qantas between Australia, Hawaii, and San Francisco, cutting travel time to California from nine propeller hours to less than five hours by jet. A few months later Pan Am connected Honolulu with the Pacific Coast and Tokyo, Japan.

John Burns, Delores Martin, Henry Jackson and Governor William Quinn celebrate Hawaiian statehood.

⊘ HAWAII BY AIR

Air transport between the islands of Hawaii arrived in 1929, when Inter-Island Airways, now Hawaiian Airlines, connected the archipelago with amphibious aircraft. Five years later, the new airline started to run regular mail routes between the islands.

The first flight between Hawaii and another destination beyond the island chain had almost been completed four years earlier when a US Navy seaplane coming from California ran out of fuel 300 miles (480km) from Hawaii. Just two years later, the first civilian flight to reach the islands similarly ran out of fuel on its journey, and crashed into a mesquite tree on Molokai.

A more reliable air connection with the US mainland was established in April 1935, when a 19-ton Pan Am Clipper landed at the fleet air base in Pearl Harbor, completing an "exploratory" flight from San Francisco that took 19 hours and 48 minutes.

Seven months later, a second Pan Am aircraft touched down with a cargo of mail, then continued an island-hopping route to Manila, creating the first Pacific air connection between North America and Asia. Less than a year later, the *Hawaii Clipper* skimmed across Pearl Harbor's waters with a cargo of seven paying passengers – a new kind of tourist with money to spend.

The commercial jet's ability to maintain a constant turnover of visitors made mass tourism a very promising enterprise. The jets brought increasing numbers of visitors, and the once-stately, low-rise Waikiki hotels soon found themselves surrounded, and dwarfed, by bigger and taller hotels.

In the neighboring islands, too, agricultural land was converted into resort developments, especially on Maui and Kauai. On Hawaii Island, vacation resorts were built on barren lava. Former sugar-plantation workers became hotel employees.

Hawaii's urban center since the end of whaling, Honolulu simply exploded as new mainlanders and businesses arrived. Some peripheral neighborhoods expanded in population by up to 600 percent. And in the areas where it couldn't spread out, Honolulu shot up in wall-to-wall office buildings and high-rise condos. Small, quiet rural towns – Kailua, Kane'ohe, Mililani, Hawaii Kai, Makakilo – turned into bedroom communities for Honolulu-bound commuters.

In the early 1980s, tourism overtook government and military spending in economic importance. Agriculture slipped to a distant third. Some of the lost agricultural revenues were replaced by the exponential growth of *pakalolo*, or marijuana, cultivation, which illegally flourished in Hawaii's forests, sugar cane fields and backyards. Since then, an aggressive eradication effort, involving aerial herbicide spraying, has cut production substantially.

ASIAN INVESTMENT

In the 1980s, Hawaii's tourism entered a period of unparalleled expansion, fueled in part by the triumph of plastic money over cash. Additionally, an influx of Asian capital, mostly from the over-heating Japanese economy, prompted a building boom that extended beyond Waikiki to the Neighbor Islands. Huge "fantasy resorts," developed to suit upscale tastes, became the new paradigm. Designed to keep visitors and therefore money on the property, the resorts themselves, not Hawaii, became the destination.

By the late 1980s, Japanese investors had injected $15 billion into Hawaii's economy. The Japanese bought heavily into hotels and resorts, acquiring 30 percent of all hotel rooms in Hawaii, and 70 percent of those that cost over $100 a day. There was some backlash against such a concentration of foreign ownership. But the Japanese kept the hotels under American management – thus

successfully deflecting the worries of labor unions and local residents – and spent tens of millions of dollars to upgrade tired hotel properties. Throughout the islands, hotel standards increased.

While immense profits were made in the 1980s by some Hawaii residents with upscale property to sell, many others were pushed out of their homes and neighborhoods where families had lived for generations. When low-income retired people started being evicted from apartments they had rented for years, Hawaii's welcome of the yen wavered.

Honolulu in the 1950s.

The infusion of yen into Hawaii finally skidded to a halt in the early 1990s, when the over-leveraged Japanese investors lost their shirts as Japan's stock markets and real estate markets crashed. The subsequent downturn in Hawaii saw property values plummet, thereby aggravating economic instability.

LAND ISSUES

Today about half of Hawaii is owned by the state, county, and federal governments. Of the remaining land, three quarters is owned by a collection of fewer than 40 owners, mainly descended from the early Protestant missionary families with names like Bishop, Campbell, and Wilcox. These private landowners collectively own 60 percent of Molokai, and 40 to 50 percent of Oahu, Maui, Hawaii Island, and Kauai. Nearly all of Lanai and Ni'ihau are privately owned by single people or families. Land ownership in Hawaii involves both "fee simple" purchase, whereby the land is included in a real-estate transaction, and leasehold, in which the land is held for a set period of time, generally ranging from 20 to 50 years. Many of Hawaii's larger hotels have been built on leased land, particularly those on Maui and in Honolulu.

Through the 1970s many private homes and condominiums were also built on leased land,

Pineapple field on Oahu.

All of Hawaii's shoreline up to the high-tide mark is public property and must be accessible to the public.

although since that time, the land beneath most of these homes and apartment buildings has been sold to homeowners and converted to fee simple ownership.

The heady swirl of money and resort development during the 1980s rekindled concerns about the land, and about Hawaii's priorities. The state's over-heated real-estate market peaked in the early 1990s and then stagnated, along with the

state's economy. The question of land, unfortunately but perhaps inevitably, has the potential to polarize and divide ethnic interests in the islands.

HAWAIIAN SOVEREIGNTY

In 1993, the land issue came to the forefront during a four-day centennial remembrance of Queen Lili'uokalani's overthrow. With 'Iolani Palace covered in black bunting, it was certainly not a time of celebration and festivities. Then Governor John Waihe'e, the state's very first governor of Hawaiian ancestry, issued executive orders that only the Hawaiian flag, not the American one, should fly over state office buildings during the four days of remembrance.

There is no dispute that the overthrow of Queen Lili'uokalani was illegal under international law. In fact, the sovereignty of the islands had earlier been recognized by both the United States and the European powers. The immediate events of the overthrow were orchestrated by local businessmen and a representative of the United States whose actions, which included the dispatch of American troops from a visiting ship to sustain the coup, were taken without the authorization of the American president. This was sustained by congressional inaction.

On the centennial of the overthrow of the Hawaiian monarchy in November 1993, the then President Bill Clinton formally apologized on behalf of the US government for its role in the 1893 coup in Hawaii.

THE RESURGENCE OF TOURISM

In 2002, former Maui mayor Linda Lingle was elected as Hawaii's first Republican governor for 40 years, as well as the first-ever woman governor. Although Democrats continue to have overwhelming majorities in both chambers of the state legislature, Lingle was re-elected as governor in 2006 by the largest margin in Hawaiian history.

Lingle earned much of her reputation as a champion of tourism on Maui, helping to spearhead the apparent recovery of Hawaii's tourist industry from its 1990s downturn. However, visitor numbers were dealt a further body blow by the terrorist attacks of September 2001. For a nerve-wracking couple of years, American travelers in particular seemed reluctant to brave the long flight from the mainland. More recently, however, the figures have first matched and then exceeded previous record levels.

Perhaps the most significant changes have been on Oahu, where Waikiki, which had fallen rather behind the times and become a little seedy, has determinedly set about re-branding itself as a classy, upscale destination. Modern tower-blocks are replacing the small-scale, family-run places that were the last remaining vestiges of the 1950s and 1960s, with the extravagant Trump International Hotel, at the heart of the Waikiki Beachwalk development, typifying the new era with its emphasis on luxury individually owned condos.

The construction boom has been present on other islands, too. On Maui, both the Wailea and Ka'anapali Beach areas have expanded in recent years; on Hawaii Island, the South Kohala resort area has grown as well. Even on Lanai, development is picking up; when Larry Ellison bought the island for (a reported) $600 million, he promised to invest another (reported) $500 million in the island's infrastructure.

Perhaps the biggest impact of new resort construction in Hawaii has been reinvestment in some of the islands' older resorts. To compete with the newcomers, more "veteran" properties have consistently upgraded their facilities to remain at the very highest international standard. Among the wave of facelifts is a light refresh of lifestyle hotel Waikiki Beachcomber by hospitality giants Outrigger, who look set to next wave their wand over the Sheraton Kona Resort & Spa in Kailua-Kona after buying the 509-room behemoth in 2020.

However, despite this boom in infrastructure the irony is that from a social perspective, Hawaii is experiencing an escalating problem of homelessness. The current governor of the islands, David Yutaka Ige, a Democrat of Japanese descent elected in 2014, even had to declare a state of emergency. After Washington DC, Hawaii had the joint largest number of homeless people per capita in the US in 2020, along with New York and California. Since then, the government has closed down dozens of unauthorised encampments, and enforced measures and programs aimed at providing permanent housing and assistance. Although the problem has not disappeared, a significant progress has

Souvenirs of former US president Barack Obama, who was born in Honolulu.

been made to improve living conditions for the island's homeless community.

In 2020, the coronavirus pandemic swept across the world. The first US case of Covid-19 was confirmed in Washington state on January 21, and the virus reached Hawaii on March 6 when the first case was recorded in Oahu. With approximately 88,000 cases and 1,000 deaths at the time of writing, Hawaii has seen relatively low Covid numbers compared with other US states. It maintained some of the strictest travel measures of any state, and today it has eased restrictions to allow vaccinated travelers to visit. Each county can impose its own limits, so check before you travel at www.hawaiicovid19.com/travel.

⊘ A HAWAIIAN PRESIDENT

When Barack Obama was elected 44th President of the United States in 2008, he not only became the nation's first-ever African-American president, but also became the nation's first ever president born in the state of Hawaii. Obama was born in Honolulu, and during his two terms he made many aspects of Hawaiian culture part of his presidential persona. For starters, he spoke publicly about his love for the sweet snack, shave ice. He also popularized the "shaka" sign, a greeting popular in Hawaiian surf culture that means, essentially, "Hang Loose." When he visits Oahu, he has been known to frequent the restaurants of Kapahulu on the outskirts of Waikiki.

Cliff jumping at Waimea Bay, Oahu.

HAWAII'S PEOPLE

With Native Hawaiians originating from as far afield as Asia, Europe, North America, and the South Pacific, the state has an extraordinary ethnic and cultural mix.

The entire United States is rich with diversity, and Hawaii best illustrates this cultural fusion. Over the decades, Hawaii has received waves of immigrants from various cultures. Except for the Native Hawaiians, who were here first, and the Caucasians, who came to convert or build business empires, or in later years to settle in "paradise," most of Hawaii's ethnic groups came to work on sugar cane or pineapple plantations and stayed to raise families. According to US Census Bureau statistics, Asians make up about 37.6 percent of the state's nearly 1.4 million people, Caucasians follow with about 25.5 percent, then the Native Hawaiians (or other Pacific Islanders) at just over 10 percent. The rest comprise people who identify themselves as having a mixed-race background, or those who identify as Hispanic, Latino, and African-American.

THE HAWAIIANS

Indigenous Hawaiians are now among the most inconspicuous people walking the streets of Hawaii. In the century following first contact with Europeans, most of Hawaii's native people died from epidemics of introduced diseases: cholera, influenza, mumps, measles, whooping cough, and smallpox. Gonorrhea caused sterility; syphilis resulted in stillbirths.

The statistics astound. Hawaii's aboriginal population had shrunk from an estimated 300,000 at the time of Captain Cook's 1778 visit to about 40,000 in 1893, when the Hawaiian monarchy was overthrown. And many of those 40,000 were *hapa*-Hawaiian, or part-Hawaiian. By the mid-19th century, a hauntingly intangible but real disease killed many more thousands of Hawaiians: sheer psychological depression. *Na*

In a glassblower's workshop in the town of Lahaina, Maui.

kanaka ku'u wale aku no i ka 'uhane – The people freely gave up their souls and died.

Given the degree of inter-racial mixing over the past two centuries, it's difficult to know how many full Hawaiians remain. According to state health department estimates, there are approximately 9,000 Hawaiians of unmixed ancestry, fewer than one percent of Hawaii's total population, including military. Those of partial Hawaiian ancestry number roughly 130,000. The most Hawaiian of islands is Ni'ihau, a privately owned island off Kauai's west coast with a population of about 130 – all Hawaiian. Molokai has the next largest percentage of part Hawaiians – about 40 percent of its population. Lanai, another mostly privately owned island, is next with just under 10 percent.

The Hawaiians have made a comeback, it might be argued, by marrying into other racial groups and thus sustaining some of the blood lines. Equally if not more important is the revival of the Hawaiian culture, nearly extinguished by Protestant missionaries in the 19th century.

A *malihini*, or newcomer, might point out that part-Hawaiians are also part something else, but part-Hawaiians, whatever their other ancestry, almost unanimously think of themselves as

Shopping at the T. Komoda Store & Bakery in Makawao, Maui.

Hawaiian first. It's a point of pride, if not of status, to be a *keiki o ka 'aina*, a child of the soil.

Many Hawaiians embrace this pride in a variety of ways. For some, it might be speaking a Hawaiian version of the English language known as pidgin. For others, it might be participating in cultural events such as hula or falsetto contests – both of which harken back to a simpler time in Hawaii's history. Still others staunchly support sovereignty; some going so far as to be distrustful of and spiteful toward Caucasians. Granted, most of the biggest divisions between locals and migrants from the mainland play out in schoolyards. Still, in some communities, there is definitely anti-outsider sentiment that runs deep.

THE CHINESE

"The ball at the Court House on Thursday night last, given to their majesties the King and Queen by the Chinese merchants of Honolulu and Lahaina, was the most splendid affair of its kind ever held in Honolulu... We have heard but one opinion expressed by those present (which includes all Honolulu and his wife), and that was that the Celestials have outshone the 'outside barbarians' in fete-making for the throne."

According to this newspaper report, the party hosted by Chinese business leaders in 1856 to honor the marriage of King Kamehameha IV and Queen Emma took Honolulu by storm.

At the time of the ball, Hawaii's Chinese community numbered maybe 600 people. It marked the entry of local Chinese into the highest circles of society. The king was so pleased that one of the Chinese sponsors married the foster sister of the future King Kalakaua, later becoming the first and only full-blooded Chinese to be appointed to the Hawaiian royal court.

Hawaii's Chinese didn't always have it so good. In the 1890s, jealous American businessmen, in an attempt to restrict the inroads that enterprising Chinese were making into local commerce, initiated legislation that restricted the freedom of Chinese immigrant laborers. Nevertheless, over the decades the Chinese have become one of Hawaii's most prominent, influential, generous, and financially successful ethnic groups. They and the Japanese represent the biggest players in the Asian immigration boom that Hawaii has experienced since the turn of the millennium.

From the sandalwood trade of the early 1800s, the Chinese were well acquainted with Hawaii, known to them as Tan Heung Shan, or the Country of the Fragrant Tree. The first Chinese laborers arrived here in 1852, about 300 workers from Guangdong and Fujian provinces in southeastern China. Before they left China, they had signed five-year contracts promising them $36 a year, sea passage, food, clothing, and housing.

Many of those first Chinese were intent on finishing their contracts and returning to China with money. Others married local women and, with their savings, set up shops in Honolulu and Lahaina, the boomtowns of the mid-1800s. The Chinese often found a niche in retail, especially as they were not welcome in the sugar industry except as laborers.

Most Chinese who used to live in Honolulu's so-called Chinatown (near the harbor) left Downtown long ago, taking their new-found affluence to other, ritzier, sectors of the community, especially after World War II. But a few persistent old-timers stayed behind, where they still mind Hong Kong-style acupuncture clinics, market food stalls, noodle factories, and restaurants.

It was in Chinatown where Honolulu schoolmates Ho Fon and Dr Sun Yatsen met to plan a Chinese revolution. Dr Sun Yatsen, considered

southeasterly approach, rather than the standard northwesterly. The reason: the emperor's pilots wanted to avoid flying over Pearl Harbor and subjecting him to reminders of the war fought in his name 35 years earlier. Meeting him at the airport was an *aloha* delegation that included three US congressmen of Japanese descent, the Japanese-American governor of Hawaii, and an American of Japanese ancestry, then president of the University of Hawaii.

Along the highway from the airport to Downtown and Waikiki, Hirohito and his entourage

Vendor at Hilo Farmers' Market, on the Big Island.

the father of modern China by both Communist and Nationalist Chinese, founded his original revolutionary group in Honolulu in 1895. That secret society, first known by the Chinese-Hawaiian name Hsing Chung Hui (Revive China Group) was crucial to the future success of China's revolutionary movement against foreign powers. Because Chinese patrons in the islands contributed generous support to Dr Sun's cause, Hawaii became known in some Chinese circles as the cradle of the Chinese republic.

THE JAPANESE

When Hirohito, the late Emperor of Japan, arrived in Hawaii in 1975, his aircraft landed at Honolulu International Airport from a

⊘ THE REAL CHARLIE CHAN

During the 1910s and 1920s, downtown Honolulu was the stomping ground of Chang Apana, a Hawaiian-Chinese police detective. Known to the local Chinese as Kana Pung, Apana retired in 1932 after 34 years of distinguished service. At his funeral the following year, the Royal Hawaiian Band marched in his cortege.

Apana was the inspiration for Charlie Chan, a fictional character from American writer Earl Derr Biggers. In 1925, with the publication of Biggers' novel *House Without a Key*, the whimsical Inspector Chan assumed a place in fictional history. Biggers wrote many installments of *The Adventures of Charlie Chan*.

TRADITIONAL BELIEFS

Tradition is alive and well in Hawaii. Spiritual beliefs inform everyday life, and many ancient rituals are still in practice today.

A woodcarver.

Even though Hawaii has stormed into the 21st century, some of its belief systems are still just as traditional as they were hundreds of years ago; and many of its inhabitants are markedly superstitious. In Hawaiian tradition, for instance, the land, or *'aina*, is mother. *'Aina* literally means "that which feeds." The land doesn't belong to people; Native Hawaiians, or *kanaka maoli*, as they call themselves, belong to it and are part of it. If separated from the land, Hawaiians and their culture tend to drift and lose meaning. The sheltering home, the trees outside, the earth beneath – all are alive and aware.

The shapes of the clouds, the cries of birds at night, the sounds of waves on the reef – all have messages for the Hawaiian people. Hawaiian tradition involved constant communication with other living beings, with the land, rocks, clouds, sea, and spirits of ancestors.

PRESERVING CULTURAL TRADITIONS

Beyond *'aina*, a number of key concepts have evolved as critical aspects of preserving cultural traditions. No. 1 on the list: spiritual power, or *Mana*. *Mana* can come from a number of places. One source is rank at birth. *Ali'i* (royalty) are born with more *mana* than commoners. Higher-born *ali'i* have more *mana* than lesser-born.

The other source is training: a skilled carver, fisherman, chanter, navigator, physician, or dancer gradually acquires this kind of *mana*, as ability is refined. These skills require long apprenticeship. They also require protection; one's specialized knowledge shouldn't be too readily shared with others lest its power be diminished. Most skills incorporate the notion of *Huna* – certain confidential, secret aspects of the skill. According to tradition, this requires the understanding of how numerous forces interact, the maintenance of certain kinds of protocol, and the observance of strict forms of behavior.

THE RIGHT WAY

At all levels of society, *kanaka maoli* believe in balance and protocol. Preparing and consuming a meal has to be done in a certain way. Preparations for the treatment of someone who is ill, such as the gathering of *la'au lapa'au* (medicinal plants), must be completed at a certain time of day with certain rules, prayers, and thoughts. Chants, dances, and rituals have to be conducted impeccably. There is a right way to do everything, and even the smallest daily activity is enmeshed in a web of belief and practice.

The chants used in ritual, prayer, and hula, if the words and songs are uttered properly, carry with them considerable power. Hawaiians don't merely petition the gods and hope they'll act; Hawaiians participate by their way of asking. The belief, the ritual, and the result all become one process. And prayers are two-way communications between humans and gods. Responses are received and interpreted in whatever form they may come: patterns in the fire, images in a dream, a sudden gust of wind, a grumble of thunder, a thought that seems to come from nowhere. But of course, nothing comes from nowhere; everything has causes and exists for a reason.

rolled past dozens of businesses with Japanese names, fleets of fishing sampans wriggling with fresh tuna for Hawaii's sashimi-crazy households, and opulent Buddhist and Shinto temples and shrines. To say that the Japanese have succeeded in Hawaii is an understatement. From World War II until the present day, their political and social power has been considerable.

This Japanese rise to prominence began with humble origins. It wasn't until 1868, during the first year of Japan's reformist Meiji Era, that an "official" group of immigrants from Japan put into Hawaii. These *gannenmono*, or first-year men, arrived at Honolulu on board the British sailing ship *Scioto*. Carrying three-year laborer contracts, all were quickly assimilated into local plantations, earning about 12 cents a day or, according to one account, about twice what they could make in Japan. By 1885 that income quadrupled to about 50 cents a day.

Strict emigration laws in Japan, however, made it difficult for more Japanese to come to Tenjiku, or the Heavenly Place, as Hawaii also came to be known. A little diplomacy was called for on this matter. So in 1881, King Kalakaua visited Japan on the first leg of a royal tour around the world. He initiated treaty discussions with the Japanese and actively pursued the Japanese immigration issue until it was given sanction. In 1885, a group of 943 immigrants – 676 men, 159 women, and 108 children – arrived in Honolulu.

Life was often miserable in the plantation camps, but Japanese continued to arrive in ever increasing numbers. By 1900, there were 61,000 Japanese workers and dependants in the islands, or more than twice the number of Hawaiians, Caucasians, or Chinese in Hawaii. Until the mid-1970s, the Japanese remained Hawaii's largest ethnic group.

The Japanese, like nearly all of Hawaii's non-*haole* laborers, suffered from racial and economic prejudices under Hawaii's plantation elite. And when Japan attacked Pearl Harbor, local Japanese-Americans were forced into internment camps on the mainland.

In Hawaii, where Americans of Japanese ancestry (AJAs) made up 40 percent of the population in the early 1940s, internment of all AJAs was out of the question. But under martial law, Japanese language schools and radio stations

were shut down; Buddhist, Shinto and Zen temples were closed; and Japanese newspapers were strictly censored. Still, not a single case of Japanese-American disloyalty or sabotage occurred during the war.

Regardless of ethnic background, nearly everyone in Hawaii lives a little bit of the Japanese lifestyle, knowingly or not. Few are the homes where shoes aren't removed before entering, and many are the *kama'aina* (long-time residents) who order sushi or sashimi without thinking twice. All residents of Hawaii are

Baristas give a "shaka" at Grandma's Coffee House in Kula, Maui.

very much at home with things Japanese. The thump of *mochi* pounding or of drums for the Buddhist *bon odori* that honors souls of the dead are common sounds in Hawaii's diverse neighborhoods. Even Spam is most commonly eaten Japanese-style – in a form of sushi known as Spam *musabi*.

THE FILIPINOS

The first Filipinos to call Hawaii home were acrobats and musicians who swept into Honolulu after a performing tour of China and Japan. In true Filipino spirit, they set to work entertaining Oahu's residents for two weeks in 1888 while waiting for their ship to San Francisco.

The Filipino troupers pleased their Hawaiian audiences, and the spell of Hawaii upon the performers was even more potent: so much so that when sailing time came and their manager refused to pay their salaries until arrival in San Francisco, they returned to their lodgings and took up their abode in Hawaii. Four of the 12 young men found immediate employment in the Royal Hawaiian Band of King Kalakaua.

It is the sugar industry more than anything that gets the credit for making Hawaii the largest Filipino community in the world outside the Philippine archipelago. Immigration of Filipinos as laborers began in 1906 with the arrival of 15 Filipino laborers to work on a sugar plantation. For the next 40 years, Filipinos poured into Hawaii at a pace exceeded only by Japanese.

More than 125,000 Filipinos were recruited by the labor-hungry sugar companies, mostly in northern Ilocos. Of them, however, only 10,000 were women, and another 7,000 children. Not keen on being bachelors, about half of the men returned home to find wives and begin lives anew with money earned in the fields. Most who

Home Maid Bakery in Wailuku, Maui.

⊘ GOING FOR BROKE

Despite internment during the war, second-generation *(nisei)* Japanese-Americans still volunteered by the hundreds for the army. The government finally created an all-*nisei* unit in 1942: the 100th Battalion. A year later, a larger unit was formed: the 442nd Infantry Regiment. Both were sent to Italy in 1944, where they were nicknamed, "Go For Broke."

Fighting in Italy and France, the *nisei* units won an impressive seven presidential unit citations and 6,000 individual awards, the most highly decorated unit in the American military during World War II. Their casualty rate was over three times the military's average.

remained in Hawaii either married women from other ethnic groups or endured an extended if not eternal bachelorhood.

Tired of the plantation hierarchy and inequalities, the Filipinos organized into labor unions. The Filipino Federation and Labor Union, for example, was well organized and actively agitating for employee benefits as early as 1919. And although some of their early labor-management confrontations ended in violence, death, and defeat, *bum-by* (by-and-by), to use a favorite Filipino expression, their tenacity and eventual successes nurtured a collective dignity. Eventually, unions attained legal status and protection.

Filipino celebrations follow Roman Catholic observances, including an exotic candlelight festival held every spring on the Feast Day of Santa Cruz. The biggest annual event is the June Fiesta Filipina, which takes place at various locations throughout the islands. You'll find people in traditional garb enjoying Filipino music and food.

Filipino cuisine hasn't captivated island palates as have the cuisines of Korea, China, Thailand, Vietnam, and Japan. But for complete menus à la Manila or Zamboanga, stroll into one of several eateries around Honolulu and wish the proprietor a sincere *mabuhay* (hello).

THE KOREANS

"In Hawaii you rarely ever see a group of Koreans, but you see a Korean in every group." This comment by a Honolulu-born Korean businessman is a contemporary comment on Hawaii's highly mobile and adaptable Korean community.

Unlike the more clannish Japanese and Chinese, Hawaii's 20,000-plus Koreans have rapidly fanned out into society; their "out-marriage" rate, for example, has been as high as 80 percent for both men and women, an inter-racial marriage statistic second only to part-Hawaiians. In the United States, Honolulu is second only to Los Angeles in the number of native-born Korean residents. Both long-established and recently immigrated Koreans have capitalized on their verve, ambition, and versatility to achieve business and social successes in Hawaii. Their overall education and income levels, for example, are the highest per capita of any ethnic group in Hawaii. Whether in the land of Morning Calm or in Hawaii, Koreans are a down-to-earth lot, who speak their minds and tend to be more direct in their communication than their Asian neighbors. Since Korea was opened to the West, they have been dubbed the Irish of Asia: being highly sociable people, they enjoy a drink or two.

They've adapted well to Hawaii, but many of their traditions elude the younger generation. *Halmoni* (grandmothers) who first came to Hawaii as "picture brides" still try to arrange marital matches in the traditional Korean way, but second- and third-generation children usually have other ideas. The *haraboji* (grandfathers) still gather at community centers to spend long hours deep into clacking rounds of an ancient Korean board game, *changgi*, or Korean chess.

In the islands, probably the most popular nickname for Koreans is *yobo*. Literally, *yobo* means "my dear" and is a way of addressing one's husband or wife. It is also the informal equivalent of "hello" or "hey there," when used to catch one's attention. Early Korean immigrants would address one another as *yobo-seyo*, or simply *yobo*, which is not quite as polite. This term stuck as an island nickname.

Koreans first arrived as laborers in 1903. Over the next two years, more than 7,000 Koreans, most of them young men (10 for every Korean woman), signed up to work in Hawaii. But in 1905, Korea's emperor cut off all labor emigration after hear-

Inside St Francis Church in Kaluapapa, Molokai.

ing that Korean laborers had been mistreated on hemp plantations in Mexico. Not until the Japanese annexed Korea in 1910 and allowed a thousand Korean "picture brides" to join their "picture grooms" did Korean immigration to Hawaii resume.

After Japan invaded Korea, Hawaii became a source of pro-Korean revolutionary support. In fact, most Korean social societies still in Hawaii began as anti-Japanese and restore-the-homeland groups, and some of them are highly secretive. Dr Syngman Rhee, an American-educated diplomat, turned to Koreans in Hawaii for revolutionary support against the Japanese occupation. After Japan's defeat in World War II, Dr Rhee returned to Korea triumphant as the first president of the Republic of Korea. Following a

Korean military coup d'état that deposed him in 1960 at the start of his fourth term, he fled to Hawaii, dying in exile in 1965.

THE SAMOANS

Samoans were later arrivals to the Islands, coming from the six isles that make up the territory of American Samoa, an 80-sq-mile (200-sq-km) group located about 2,600 miles (4,200km) due southwest of Honolulu.

Some 500 Samoans had trickled into Hawaii after World War I, the majority of them to join a

special council called a *fono*. At these councils, the chiefs establish policy, mediate in the case of intra-Samoan grievances, and, if they feel a Samoan problem requires government attention, draft mutually agreed-upon statements for the appropriate outside individual or agency.

Most Samoan gatherings, however, are of a more celebratory nature: a wedding, or the investiture of a new chief, or Flag Day, an annual holiday that celebrates the raising of the American flag over Eastern Samoa in 1899. As part of this celebration, out come the

Playing chess by the waterfront on Front Street in Lahaina, Maui.

Mormon community based in La'ie, on Oahu's Windward Shore. In 1952, after Samoan immigration to America was liberalized, a group of 900 Samoan men, women, and children – about half of them Samoan-American navy men and dependants being transferred to Pearl Harbor – boarded a navy transport ship and set off for the Hawaiian Islands. At the time, these emigrants from American Samoa represented 6 percent of American Samoa's total population.

Perhaps out of all the local Asian-Oceanic ethnic groups, Samoans have best retained their traditional cultural touchstones. When a Samoan "community" problem arises, elected chiefs, some of whom represent the various expatriate Samoan clans in Hawaii, call a

kava cups and the colorful *lava-lava* sarongs and *puletasi* dresses, and the finely woven *lau hala* mats to be spread out on the ground. Joined by expatriates from Tonga, Fiji, Tahiti, and the Marquesas, the Samoans get together in fine *fia-fia* (feasting) fashion – *fa'a Samoa*, the Samoan way.

THE CAUCASIANS

As some Hawaiians explain it, their ancestors called the first Europeans *haole* because they could not believe that men with such pale skins and frail bodies could be alive. *Haole*, from *ha*, which means breath or the breath of life, connects with *ole*, which connotes an absence of the breath of life or, more simply, without life.

Samoan Americans have become quite successful in sumo wrestling, especially in Japan. Some have even become Japanese citizens.

Originally applied to any outsider, *haole* now refers to Caucasians, sometimes with neutral meaning, occasionally with negative meaning. Since the time of Cook, it has been fashionable in Hawaii for both *haole* and non-*haole* to put down *haole*.

For many years, the term was more of a slur than a synonym for Caucasian. *Haoles*, whether a *malihini* (newcomer) or *kama'aina* (long-time resident, old-timer), are now one of the fastest-growing ethnic groups in the islands and are vying against residents of Asian descent as the islands' main political force.

Since World War II, most *haole* coming to the islands more or less assimilated into the local lifestyle and rhythms, or at least made an attempt to. In recent years, however, new arrivals sometimes seem more interested in fashioning Hawaii into their own image of a paradise, or at least bringing a West Coast (from where a good percentage originate) attitude with them. It is not a new phenomenon. Since the first Polynesians arrived, every group has brought cultural baggage.

One distinct *haole* group that deserves special mention is the Portuguese, or *Portagee* in the local pidgin dialect, who immigrated in large numbers when Hawaii was still a kingdom, mostly to work in the cane fields. As early as 1872, there were perhaps 400 or so Portuguese in Hawaii, mostly sailors who had left whaling ships for life on land. These Europeans were well received by both Hawaiians and *haole* merchants and planters, so in 1878 the Hawaiian government and sugar barons conducted an official labor recruitment campaign in Portugal's Azores and Madeira islands. Twenty years later, almost 13,000 Portuguese had made the rough voyage to the Hawaiian Islands, which, with their volcanic soils, offered very similar conditions for agriculture.

Many became *luna*, or foremen, on the sugar plantations, gaining a mid-level power foothold much more quickly than the Asian immigrants

who worked alongside them. By the 1930s, the Portuguese community had a territorial supreme court chief justice, a territorial secretary and an acting governor, and the Catholic vicar apostolic of the Hawaiian Islands.

The Portuguese also introduced a small four-stringed instrument, known as the *braquino* or *cavaghindo* in Portugal, which became the *'ukulele* in Hawaiian. The Hawaiian word *'ukulele* literally means "leaping flea," and the story goes that it came from the nickname of Edward Purvis, an English expatriate who arrived in Hawaii

Everything's OK for this couple on the Big Island.

in 1879. Purvis made friends with newly arrived Portuguese immigrants, and he soon learned to play the *braquino* with entertaining finesse. Purvis was small in stature and quick with his hands, so his Hawaiian friends nicknamed him *'Ukulele*, the Leaping Flea.

Local Portuguese, although more than two generations removed from the old country, still celebrate Portuguese traditions and religious festivals. A series of post-Easter *festas* are known as the Seven Domingas, or Holy Ghost festivals. During the seven weeks of *festa*, families participate in prayer and celebration. Traditional delicacies are prepared, such as *pao dolce* (sweet bread) and hot fried *malasadas* (a delicious light Portuguese donut).

📷 ANCIENT WAYS AND PLACES

While the Westernization of the Hawaiian islands has been thorough, ancient ways are still available to explore.

The arrival of Europeans in Hawaii sparked a process that sociologists call "dualism," in which two distinct cultures and economies exist simultaneously. While Western processes and values eventually supplanted those of traditional Hawaii, one still may witness the ways and places of old Hawaii even today.

Archeologists, anthropologists, and sociologists have undertaken reconstructions and preservation of sacred temples and villages. Some of these sites: Pu'ukohola, Lapakahi, and Pu'uhonua 'O Honaunau, all on Hawaii Island; Kane'aki and Pu'u O Mahuka *heiaus* (temples) on Oahu; Pi'ilanihale Heiau, *in the Kahanu Garden* on Maui; and 'Ili 'ili 'opae Heiau on Molokai.

LIFE IN ANCIENT TIMES

In ancient Hawaii, the *'aina*, or land, was considered the property of the gods, held in trust by a chief or king. He allocated land to support the *ali'i* (royalty), who allowed *maka'ainana* (commoners) to cultivate it. The commoners, protected by the *ali'i*, turned over food grown to the *ali'i*.

The land itself was divided into wedge-shaped parcels called *ahupua'a*, which usually extended from the coastline up into a mountain valley.

Life during these times was satisfactory, but it wasn't especially idyllic. Warfare was common, and commoners had to be careful not to violate *kapu* (see page 36). A person always could find safety in a *pu'uhonua*, a place of refuge. Here, absolution by a *kahuna*, or priest, cleansed transgressions or assured sanctuary.

Polynesian statues of gods in the Honolulu Museum of Art.

Carved wooden ki'i at the Hale o Keawe Heiau (temple), Big Island.

Craftsmen still carve the fearsome sacred images called ki'i akua.

Ancient petroglyphs on Lanai.

Royal stones and petroglyphs

In central Oahu are the birth stones of Kukaniloko, which have been sacred to Hawaiians as far back as the 1100s.

The wives of high-ranking chiefs gave birth on the stones' gently curved surfaces. Attendant chiefs, high priests, and physicians would gather in a ceremony marked by chants and offerings. The *ali'i* child would be named and the umbilical cord – *piko* – would be cut.

Hawaiians would place the severed *piko* in a hole carved into the rock, essentially a simple petroglyph, or *kaha ki'i*. *Piko* were put where *mana*, or spirit, was strong, such as at Kukaniloko. It was hoped that the child might be influenced by the *mana*, and maybe even absorb some of it. Sometimes a representation of the family's *'aumakua* (family or personal god) would be carved into the rock adjacent to the *piko* hole.

On Hawaii Island, the Kona and Kohala districts offer several easily accessible petroglyph sites, such as at Puako. As most of them are at ground level, take extreme care and don't walk on top of them.

Tapa, or cloth made from bark, was used for clothes.

Pu'ukohola Heiau National Historic Site protects the ruins of Pu'ukohola Heiau, a major ancient Hawaiian temple on the Big Island.

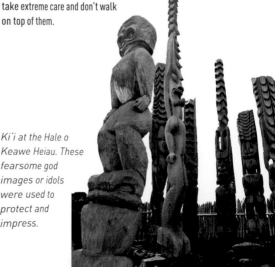

Ki'i at the Hale o Keawe Heiau. These fearsome god images or idols were used to protect and impress.

Ziplining with Kolekole Falls in the background, Big Island.

OUTDOOR ACTIVITIES

With countless trails, hundreds of thousands of acres of jungle, miles upon miles of coastline, and great dirt roads, Hawaii is one big playground for outdoor adventure-seekers.

If you like the outdoors, there's never a shortage of things to do in Hawaii. Hiking, bicycling, surfing, snorkeling, diving, swimming, stand-up paddleboarding, kayaking, outrigger canoeing, wildlife-watching, paragliding, horseback riding, ziplining, deep-sea fishing, and off-roading are just some of the outdoor activities available here. You can careen down the flanks of a volcano by bike, ride a motorcycle on one of the curviest roads in America, or kitesurf into the teeth of strong trade winds. Because none of the islands is very big, you can wake up early and enjoy two or three of these pastimes in a day. And you can still be home before dinner.

Many visitors come to Hawaii to sip Mai Tais in a chaise lounge near a resort pool. A growing number of other visitors fly to the islands exclusively to enjoy all of the outdoor recreation the islands have to offer. These travelers rarely leave disappointed.

HIKING

To put it simply, Hawaii is a hiker's paradise. Local groups estimate the state boasts more than 3,000 miles (4,828km) of hiking trails. Options range from easy to moderate to challenging, catering to all levels.

Some of the trails have reputations that precede them. The 11-mile (18km) Kalalau Trail, for instance, along the Na Pali Coast on Kauai, is considered one of the best backcountry hikes in the United States, and usually requires two or three overnights to get from the trailhead near Keʻe Beach to the Kalalau Valley. Another epic tromp: the trail to Koko Head, on Oahu. It's not the length of this trail that presents a challenge for hikers (it's only 1.5 miles/2.4km long). Instead, it's the elevation gain: the trail

Surfing at Hoʻokipa Beach, Maui.

includes more than 1,000 steps as it climbs 1,600ft (488 meters).

Elsewhere – and on other islands – hiking is less about the trails themselves and more about the journey. On Maui and Hawaii islands, just about any hike on national park land will be fulfilling. On Molokai, especially in Kalaupapa National Historical Park, hiking (you must go with a guide) is almost always part of an immersive learning experience. On Lanai, in places like the fire-red Garden of the Gods, you can feel as if you are on another planet.

BICYCLING

Another great way to experience the Hawaiian countryside: by bike. Once considered an alternative sport, the bicycling community in Hawaii has grown rapidly over the last ten years, and has gotten to the point where most of the major cities and towns have at least one bike shop.

There are benefits to seeing sights via bicycle. For starters, admission to national parks is cheaper, and admission to state parks is free. Second, since all of the islands were volcanoes at one point, most roads have incline, meaning that using a bike likely will provide quite a work-out. Finally, this mode of transport produces no greenhouse gases, which means that it's the more environmentally friendly choice. One word of caution: the majority of rides must occur alongside automobile traffic, which sometimes can be a problem for families with little children.

For those who prefer to just do downhill on a bike, outfitters near Haleakala National Park, on Maui, run trips during which participants quite literally careen down roads that hug the side of the volcano. Most of these trips are offered just after sunrise and guaranteed to get the adrenaline pumping.

Hiking the Hanakapi'ai Falls trail in the Hanakapi'ai Valley, Kauai.

⊙ HIKING KAPALUA

Even Hawaii's ritziest hotels and resorts such as the Kapalua Resort, in the westernmost corner of West Maui, have hiking trails. Here, since the late 1990s, officials have invested big bucks in creating and maintaining a trail system worth exploring. The crown jewel of this system is the grueling 6-mile (10km) Mahana Ridge Trail, which connects the Maunalei Arboretum with D.T. Flemming Beach Park. Kapalua also has built a short boardwalk trail that traces the contours of the coastline on resort land. On a clear day, this pathway is a great spot from which to watch the sunset; time your walk to coincide with dusk.

SURF'S UP

The Hawaiian Islands are considered the birth-place of modern surfing, which makes Hawaii a great place to hang ten.

Accomplished surfers gravitate toward the best of the "Big Wave" surfing destinations: the North Shore of Oahu and Peahi (or Jaws), on the northern shore of Maui. Amateurs usually opt for calmer spots: Waikiki Beach on Oahu, Poipu Beach on Kauai, Kahalu'u Beach Park near Kailua on Hawaii Island, and off Lahaina on Maui. Surf schools operate in all four of these latter spots; average lessons last 1–2 hours and cost anywhere from $95 to $150. (However, instructors do not guarantee you'll be able to get up on the board after one class!)

There are other ways to get your surf on in Hawaii. Stand-up paddleboarding, an ancient activity that Polynesian fishermen likely used to spear fish hundreds of years ago, has enjoyed a spike in popularity in recent years, and today is one of the most favored sports in Hawaii. Other forms of surfing (kitesurfing and windsurfing) are harder to come by but available to thrill-seekers who wish to seek them out. Then, of course, there's bodyboarding, which just about anyone can do on just about any beach with sand and the smallest of waves.

WILDLIFE-WATCHING

The waters surrounding the Hawaiian Islands teem with life. Naturally, then, Hawaii is a great place to observe some of these creatures and critters in their natural environments.

Perhaps the most common wildlife-watching activity is snorkeling – it's cheap, it's easy, and the water is clear enough to do it just about anywhere (provided the seas are calm). Resort areas on Maui, Oahu, Kauai, and Hawaii Island all offer some degree of snorkeling off the beaches right in front of the hotels. For even better experi-

Take a jeep on the 4WD trail to the Garden of the Gods rock formations, on Lanai.

In 2011, Hawaiian pro surfer Garrett McNamara set a world record when he rode a wave measuring a gobsmacking 78ft (23.77 meters) high at the Portuguese resort town of Nazaré. Six years later, Brazilian Rodrigo Koxa nudged up the mark to 80ft (24.38m). In 2020, 18-year-old Portuguese surfer António Laureano claimed to have conquered a 101.4ft (30.9m) behemoth – the holy grail of surfing – though measurements hadn't been made official at the time of writing.

ences, check out Hanauma Bay on Oahu, or hop aboard a charter from Ma'alea Harbor to Molokini, a tiny atoll between Maui and Kaho'olawe.

Snorkeling might be the most common form, but the most popular wildlife-watching activity takes place every winter, when humpback whales migrate to Hawaii from Alaska to mate, and birth and rear their young.

The whale-watching is best in the 'Au'au Channel between Maui and Lanai; on any given day, you might spot 20–30 whales less than five minutes from shore. Two- and four-hour boat trips are available from Lahaina Harbor and Ma'alea Harbor between December and April.

Finally, you've always got to be on the lookout for two of Hawaii's most endangered (and, therefore, most loved) animals: Hawaiian Monk Seals and Hawaiian Green Sea Turtles. These critters can appear on any beach at any time, but they seem to show up with frequency on beaches along the North Shore of Oahu, especially in summer.

DEEP-SEA FISHING

It should come as no surprise that the Hawaiian Islands represent one of the best deep-sea fishing destinations anywhere in the world – after all, the rocks are surrounded by water.

the Pacific Ocean. That said, most of the Hawaiian Islands offer a variety of options for horseback riding, and the activity is a great way to get to know the land.

Without question, the best place to ride is Maui, where, in the cowboy town of Makawao, outfitters such as Triple L Ranch Maui lead visitors on one-hour and half-day excursions a few times every week. Also of note here is the annual rodeo (Makawao Stampede) on July 4; the event draws thousands of people from the local community and is fun for everyone, even those who don't ride.

Kayakers at Rainbow Falls, Wailuku River State Park, Big Island.

The best fishing in the islands is from charter trips on which attendants bait your line and help you remove all of the fish you've caught. These sorts of trips leave from just about every major harbor, including Hilo (on Hawaii Island), Ma'alea (on Maui), and others. No experience is necessary for these kinds of outings, but it does come in handy if you know your way around a ship. And if you're a total pro, consider entering the Hawaiian International Billfish Tournament, held every summer on Hawaii Island.

HORSEBACK RIDING

No matter how many times you do it, it is always exhilarating and mind-boggling to find yourself riding a horse across volcanoes in the middle of

Horseback riding tours also are available on Hawaii Island, in both the North Kohala and Waimea areas, and on Oahu, at private ranches with lots of land to explore. On Molokai, mules (part horse, part donkey) are a key part of one of the tours you can take to explore Kalaupapa National Historic Park.

OFF-ROADING

Undeveloped and underdeveloped parts of Hawaii offer great terrain on which to go off-roading. In some cases, this means taking a Jeep or 4x4 out for a spin; in other cases, it means climbing aboard a dirt bike and kicking up some dirt.

Among the best places to go off-roading in the Hawaiian archipelago is Lanai. The island offers nearly 400 miles (644km) of dirt roads to explore by

Whale researchers know humpback whales come to Hawaii to mate and birth their young, but they have never witnessed whales mating or giving birth.

Jeep. The dirt road of the Munro Trail climbs up to the 3,370ft (1,027-meter) peak of Lanaihale, where, on a clear day, the view of the open ocean is spectacular. Two trips from Lanai City also are worth mentioning: the road through the lush Kanepu'u Preserve, on the north side of the island; and the bumpy ride to Shipwreck Beach, from which you can see an oil tanker that ran aground in the 1940s.

Other islands offer off-roading experiences that require ATVs. On Kauai, many of these tours follow old sugar cane access trails to remote locations that have served as backdrops for major Hollywood movies. On Hawaii Island, ATV tours of the Waipi'o Valley include descending a treacherous dirt road into the valley, and lead participants through lush jungle down below.

Outfitters on all four of the main islands also offer dirt-biking tours. On Maui, some of these outfitters take customers along the "Back Road to Hana," a ride that is bumpy but beautiful. On Hawaii Island, near Hilo, customers can rent bikes (or bring their own) and zip and zoom around a course on the slopes of Mauna Loa.

OTHER ADVENTURE SPORTS

Just about all of the Hawaiian Islands have reefs worth diving. One of the best: Kealakekua Bay, about 40 miles (64km) south of Kailua, on Hawaii Island. Here, calm waters teeming with marine life provide the perfect backdrop to get up close to dozens of different kinds of tropical fish. Within the bay you can also kayak or take a boat ride to the seaside memorial of Captain James Cook, the British Explorer who discovered the Hawaiian Islands in 1778.

Ziplining has become another big draw on the islands, with a number of zipline "parks" sprouting up since 2008. On Maui, Maui Zipline and Skyline Hawaii have spectacular zipline courses. On Kauai, a number of outfitters offer similar adventures; one, near Lihu'e, combines ziplining with inner-tubing down the open-air canals of a former sugar cane plantation.

Kayaking is prevalent around Hawaii, as well. In most cases, visitors are kayaking in the open ocean; because of the elevation associated with most of the rivers in the Hawaiian Islands, it's basically impossible to paddle very far up or down these waterways. When kayaking, the more protected the water, the better. This is what makes paddling near Wailea and Ka'anapali on Maui so popular; especially in the morning, the ocean is as calm as a bathtub.

To experience rougher waters, try outrigger canoeing. In many ways, this sport is quintessentially Hawaiian: it mimics the very same way Polynesians traveled from one island to another,

Tandem paragliding over Kula, Maui.

hundreds of years ago. Hawaiians take their outrigger canoeing very seriously, regularly competing in races that stretch for hundreds of miles. You also can get a taste of outrigger canoeing along Waikiki Beach, or in Lahaina Harbor on Maui.

Finally, paragliding has become a more popular option for visitors to Hawaii in the most recent part of the 21st century. Almost all of these flights happen "in tandem," which means that visitors must go with a guide essentially attached to them at all times. The presence of a stranger doesn't diminish the impact of the experience at all; as beautiful as the Hawaiian Islands are from the ground, they are even more beautiful from above.

Hula lessons at Kualoa Ranch on Oahu.

MUSIC AND HULA

The missionaries nearly erased the ancient forms of music and dance from the islands. Thankfully, they did not succeed.

Few other types of music have girdled the earth more smoothly, more often, and more completely than Hawaiian music, and few musical genres have remained so popular with so many for so long. Say "Hawaiian music" to a banker in Bangkok, an army captain in Amsterdam, or a housewife in Minneapolis, and all get the same romantic, dreamy look. They're thinking of swaying palms and hips, the sultry slack-key guitar, a tremulous falsetto voice, and the sassy plunky-plunkiness of a 'ukulele.

Hawaii has been described as a melting pot, historically quick to accept whatever comes to its golden shores. Nowhere is this phenomenal rate and degree of cultural assimilation more apparent than in the music.

MUSICAL LEGENDS

In ancient times, Hawaiian music sounded simpler, consisting of long, monotonous chants recited either without accompaniment or against a percussive background of drums made from coconut trees, gourds, bamboo rattles and pipes, sticks, and pebble castanets. The ritualistic aspects of the music were complex and played a vital part in daily life and a significant role in religious beliefs and services. Chants, for example, were the means of establishing contact between humans and gods.

In the 1800s, Christian missionaries from New England had an impact on Hawaiian music, too. These devout and dedicated settlers built churches amid the Hawaiian huts, held services, and sang hymns. Hawaiians had never heard melody and four-part harmony before, and they collected by the hundreds outside the small churches to listen to these exotic combinations. Thinking that the quickest way to a

Playing the 'ukulele.

Hawaiian's soul might be through the ears, the missionaries enrolled the Hawaiians in church choirs. Progress was slow; the broader tones required by church hymns were new to Hawaiians, so songs had to be learned by rote as the missionaries sang the hymns, called *himeni* by the Hawaiians, over and over and over again, and the Hawaiians copied as best they could.

OUTSIDE INFLUENCES

Hawaiian music's other most dominant influence came in the form of a single man and reflected a Hawaiian king's wish to be Westernized. King Kamehameha V decided that he wanted a royal band like those in Europe, and so the brisk, mustachioed Heinrich Berger was imported from Germany in 1868 to be bandmaster. Berger, who is known today as the father of Hawaiian music, served as director of the Royal Hawaiian Band from 1872 until 1915. During this time, he conducted more than 32,000 band concerts, arranged more than 1,000 Hawaiian songs, and composed 75 original Hawaiian songs, including several still popular today.

He also reversed the traditional order of the *mele*, or song, by composing the music before the words. Hawaiians began doing the same, and before the 1870s ended, they were compos-

From Madeira came a small, four-stringed instrument called the *braquino*, or *cavaquinho*. It was brought to Hawaii by laborers imported to work in the sugar cane fields, in 1878. As with so much else in Hawaiian musical history, there is disagreement as to how the *braquino* became *'ukulele*, which, in Hawaiian, roughly translates as "leaping flea".

Scholars also continue to argue about who invented the steel guitar. Some say a Hawaiian student discovered the sound in the 1880s when he dropped his pocket knife upon the strings

Engraving of locals dancing, 1822.

ing lyrics and music simultaneously. Heinrich Berger also served as inspiration and teacher for two generations of Hawaiian musicians, some of whom later went on to local, if not national or international, stardom.

Other influences arrived: the guitar, for instance, was brought by early whalers or perhaps by traders from Mexico and California, but not, as is popularly believed, by Mexican cowboys, who arrived later in the early 1830s. In time, the traditional style of playing changed as the Hawaiian musicians loosened their strings, and tunings became whatever the player wished them to be. This style of playing came to be known as *ki ho'alu*, or slack key, and is as uniquely Hawaiian as flamenco is Spanish.

of a guitar, and holding it there with one hand, plucked the strings with the other, moving the steel knife to "slide" the sound.

Others think the inventor once visited India, where he could have seen a stringed instrument, the *gottuvadyam*, played in a similar fashion. While the steel guitar has since been much identified with country-and-western music, it remains the single most identifiable part of the Hawaiian instrumental sound.

ROYAL INSPIRATION

The descendants of the ancient *ali'i* ruling Hawaii in the final years before annexation to the United States were among the most talented and prolific composers of song that the island culture ever produced. The best known of these was King David Kalakaua, a complex and jovial man whose reign was also an inspiration for a genuine renaissance of music and dance.

Kalakaua was a gifted politician, world traveler, and patron of the arts. He promoted the 'ukulele and steel guitar, and formed his own musical group, entering into competitions with relatives and friends. He collected the legends and myths of Hawaii into a definitive and literate book, and co-wrote with Heinrich Berger Hawaii's national anthem, "Hawaii Pono'i," a

His sister, Lili'uokalani played a major part in the history of Hawaiian music, too, composing a song that has been a certifiable "hit" for almost a century: "Aloha 'Oe."

The sound of Hawaiian music changed again after Lili'uokalani's kingdom was made a territory of the United States. This focused mainland interest toward Hawaii, and in 1915 a group of Hawaiian musicians, singers, and dancers were the runaway sensation of the Panama-Pacific International Exposition in San Francisco, sparking a craze that swept North America and spread to Europe.

Henri Berger, at the front, and the Royal Hawaiian Band, 1889.

The Royal Hawaiian Band is still going strong after all these years, appearing in several public concerts each week, notably at noon nearly every Friday at the 'Iolani Palace Coronation Stand (see page 116).

song that's still sung at ball games and public assemblies. The hula, long suppressed by the Christian missionaries, was revived under his personal direction. Much music is played every year on November 16, Kalakaua's birthday; the state's biggest hula competition also takes place on Hawaii Island every year around that time.

Even if most of those new songs had little to do with true Hawaiian musical tradition, the influence was immediate and significant. The craze propelled authentic Hawaiian musicians across America for many years. They, in turn, accepted the phony Hawaiian songs to satisfy requests, eventually turning them into Hawaiian "classics." At the same time, they began arranging traditional, more authentic Hawaiian songs with the newly popular jazz beat that they heard everywhere they went.

In Hawaii, the first hotels were going up in Waikiki, and dance bands were formed for the growing number of tourists. Ragtime, jazz, blues, Latin, and foxtrot rhythms were interspersed with Hawaiian themes and English lyrics. The purists were appalled, as always, but by 1930

Hula dancers were popular in vaudeville. They were called "cootch" dancers because many non-native performers adapted the movements lasciviously.

the *hapa-haole* (halfCaucasian) song was an entrenched and accepted part of Hawaiian music, soon to become a staple on what was eventually the most widely heard radio program in the world. In 1935, Hawaii's music caught the ears of

The most important figure among those responsible for keeping the flame of traditional Hawaiian music alive during this time was the slack-key guitarist Gabby Pahinui. He made his first solo recording, "Hi'ilawe," in 1947, and in the late 1950s formed the Sons of Hawaii group with 'ukelele virtuoso Eddie Kamae, a keen musicologist who hunted out long-forgotten Hawaiian-language songs from all the islands. In the early 1970s, their reunion album, "The Folk Music of Hawaii," was hugely influential among younger musicians, many of whom

Hula dancers perform at the Kuhio Beach Hula Show in Waikiki, Oahu.

the mainland's West Coast listeners via "Hawaii Calls," a radio program broadcast from under a banyan tree in Waikiki Beach and other exotic locales. Today, many of the more than 300 Hawaiian musicians who were on that radio program are legends of the state's musical past, among them Danny Kaleikini, Alfred Apaka, and Benny Kalama.

TRADITIONAL SOUNDS REVITALIZED

The period from 1930 to 1960 is regarded as Hawaiian music's "golden age," as the music of the islands circled the world on television and in radio and film. Crooners such as Kui Lee and Don Ho emerged as top Hawaiian stars, rendering songs such as "One Paddle, Two Paddle," "Days of My Youth," and "I'll Remember You."

began to write their own songs, celebrating the poetic resonance of the Hawaiian language and also addressing contemporary social realities.

During this so-called "Hawaiian renaissance," all the traditional Hawaiian arts experienced a rich revival, as islanders with Hawaiian blood discovered a renewed sense of ethnic awareness and pride. Many were influenced by the cultural changes taking place in the rest of the United States, and some of the Hawaiian music of the era, it has to be said, sounds awfully like Californian-style rock.

However, there was also a great resurgence of interest in the more traditional Hawaiian sounds. As Moe Keale, who also played 'ukulele with the Sons of Hawaii, put it, "Music is not something you just hear with your ears. It's something you hear with your heart. I can tell when Hawaiian music is being played right, because it makes me cry."

Gabby Pahinui left the Sons in the mid-1970s, and, thanks in part to his collaborations with guitarist Ry Cooder, went on to achieve international acclaim before his premature death in 1980. Meanwhile, new stars were emerging in Hawaii, such as guitarist Keola Beamer, who honed his techniques on an album called "Hawaiian Slack Key in the Real Old Style." Beamer says, "There's

'Ukulele shop on Kalakaua Avenue in Honolulu.

Bing Crosby introduced two songs in the 1937 movie Waikiki Wedding. One of them, "Sweet Leilani" won an Oscar, so Hollywood began churning out musical romances.

---

power in our music which is drawn from the environment. If you sit and watch a waterfall or listen to the trade winds for a while, you begin to feel a rhythm. You can be far away from Hawaii and hear a song and instantly be transported."

Among other new names on the scene were the Sunday Manoa, who included the Cazimero brothers; Hui Ohana, a trio featuring Ledward

and Nedward Ka'apana and Dennis Pava'o; Palani Vaughan; and a young group from Gabby's hometown of Waimanolo, Oahu – the Makaha Sons of Ni'ihau, featuring the brothers Skippy and Israel Kamakawiwo'ole.

By the early 1990s, Hawaiian music was at the forefront of the political struggle for Hawaiian sovereignty. Dennis Pava'o recorded the popular "All Hawaii Stand Together," but it was Israel Kamakawiwo'ole, by then a solo artist and universally known as "Iz," who gave the movement its greatest anthems, in the form of songs like "Hawaii 78." Morbidly obese and plagued by the chronic health problems that had already killed his brother – whose weight is said to have exceeded a phenomenal 1,000lbs (454kg) – but blessed with a voice of astonishing power and delicacy, Iz became a much-loved superstar. He died in 1997, and was honored with a state funeral. His legacy was albums such as "E Ala E," and, especially, "Facing Future," which was still high in the world music charts a decade after his death, while his million-selling medley of "Somewhere Over The Rainbow/What A Wonderful World" has become a staple of Hollywood soundtracks.

FALSETTO TRADITION

Women have always played a crucial role in Hawaiian music. Queen Lili'uokalani composed many of the islands' most enduring classics, while chanter/dancer Edith Kanaka'ole was the 20th-century's greatest repository of the Polynesian heritage. Female vocalists have been especially significant as performers of the unique Hawaiian tradition of falsetto singing, which is characterized by audible breathing for extra effect. Lena Machado, known as "Hawaii's Songbird," championed the form from the 1930s until the 1960s, while Auntie Genoa Keawe, who first recorded in the 1940s and established her own record label, was still performing regularly in Waikiki well into her 80s before passing away aged 90. The latest divas in the genre are Amy Hanaiali'i Gilliom, known for her entertaining live performances with guitarist Willie K, and Molokai's Raiatea Helm. Popular falsetto vocal groups include the trio Na Leo Pilimehana, responsible for albums like "Anthology I" and "Colours," and Na Palapalai. It's worth mentioning too that there have been some fabulous male falsetto singers, such as Bill Lincoln Ali'iloa, and the phenomenal Mahi Beamer.

HAWAIIAN MUSIC TODAY

New generations of young entertainers continue to emerge, sending out Hawaiian vibes to the mainland, Japan, and beyond, combining music with showmanship that draws on early Hawaiian traditions. On stage, composer, chanter, dancer, and singer Keali'i Reichel stands bare-chested, hair streaming about his shoulders, carved bone fishhook nestled at his neck. His body tattoos run from his ankle to disappear under his brief *malo* (loincloth). In the bright spotlight, he sings in sweet, resonant tones, switching from ballads

Kaumakaiwa; and the *ukulele* prodigy Jake Shimabukuro.

RETURN OF HULA

There was a time in Hawaiian history when entering a *halau* (hula school) was equivalent to entering a monastery. Today, the hula is both a spiritual and an artistic expression of Hawaiian culture.

Legends say that the goddesses of dance were Laka and Hi'iaka. (If not actually worshipped, both are still revered today.) At first, both men

Keiki (children) hula dancers.

like "Ku'u Pua Mae 'Ole" (about lasting romance and calming waters), to a poetic chant "Maika'i Ka 'Oiwi O Ka'ala" with *ipu* (gourd) accompaniment.

Singer/songwriter Jack Johnson, who lives on the North Shore of Oahu, attracted a huge following among the surfer set, and now has a mass popular appeal. In recent years, singer-songwriter Bruno Mars has done Hawaii proud; Mars was born and raised in Honolulu and performed in various musical venues there throughout his childhood before moving to Los Angeles. Other names to watch out for these days include Keola Beamer, a slack-key artist from Maui (and cousin of Mahi Beamer); the duo Hapa, who, as their name suggests, consist of a *haole* and a native-Hawaiian; Edith Kanaka'ole's great-grandson

and women performed the dance, but only men could perform the hula during temple worship services. It was believed that by pantomiming an action, that action could be controlled in the future. Thus there were many dances for desired events, such as a successful hunt, fertility, or other successes. The hula later engulfed all of Hawaiian society and became many things – teaching tool, popular entertainment, and a basic foundation for *lua*, an art of self-defense promoted by the Hawaiians. As the dance became widespread and society increasingly complicated, wars and governing duties kept the men too busy for the years of training required to be a performer. Thus, the women began to share equally in the performance of the hula.

Hula was banned in the beginning of the 19th century; by the 1850s it had nearly disappeared. Forty years later, by the time King Kalakaua revived the sacred dance, a great deal of the art of hula had already been lost forever.

Today, hula has regained much of its serious heritage. Contemporary students heed ancient ritual religiously, although they are not asked to give up sex in order to be a hula performer, as was true in ancient times. Different *halau* compete fiercely; hula masters, or *kumu hula*, are revered figures. And with the male hula now in

the same month, the Prince Lot Hula Festival is played out under the giant monkey pod trees of Moanalua Gardens. At Princeville, Kauai, local entertainers meet mainland musicians at the Prince Albert Hula Festival every May. On Maui, the Na Mele O Maui Song Contest and Hula Festival takes place annually in Ka'anapali, while Molokai's Ka Hula Piko Festival is celebrated each May close to hula's supposed birthplace, near Maunaloa. If you are in Hawaii when any of these events is being celebrated it will be well worth attending.

Hula dancers at the May Day festival.

a period of rich revival, the dance has become a symbol of the islanders' newly rediscovered sense of Hawaiian identity.

HULA EVENTS

Hawaii's most prestigious hula event is the Merrie Monarch Festival, which pays homage to King David Kalakaua, Hawaii's last king. It has been held every April since 1964 at the Edith Kanaka'ole Stadium in Hilo. The highlight of the week-long festival, which includes a parade and musical celebrations, is the two-day competition of *kahiko*, or ancient hula, and *'auwana* or modern hula.

Every island has its signature hula events. On Oahu, the Queen Lili'uokalani Keiki Hula festival draws 500 children to perform every July, and in

⊘ HITTING THE BIG TIME

Despite centuries of culturally significant songs, Hawaiian music officially 'arrived' in 2005 with the creation of a Grammy for the Best Hawaiian Music Album of the year. In the first few years, awards were doled out to Charles Brotman, Tia Carrere, George Kohumoku, Jr., and others. The Academy retired the award in 2011; instead introducing the Best Regional Roots Music category as a catchall for Hawaiian, Native American/First Nation, polka, Cajun and zydeco music. Singer-songwriter Kalani Pe'a is the only Hawaiian musician to have won the award – twice, in fact. His debut album, *E Walea*, scooped the accolade at the 59th Annual Grammy Awards in 2016, followed by *No 'Ane'i* in 2018.

LEI

Flower necklace *lei* once were sacred symbols, but today are used to convey *aloha* and respect.

Lei, necklaces made from flowers, have a colorful history in Hawaii. In ancient times, *they* were offered to the gods during sacred dances and chants. Today they are draped around the necks of grooms and prom escorts.

Lei are made of flowers, leaves, shells, and paper. There are six basic *lei*-making techniques. If a *lei*-maker uses *wili paukuku*, she is winding roses and begonias in a certain style. *Humuhumu* is a *lei* sewn onto a backing. *Wili* is a *lei* that is wound or twisted, *hili* is braided with leaves, and *haku* is braided with flowers. *Kui* is strung on a thread.

Before needle and thread were introduced to Hawaii, stiff grass blades from the Nu'uanu Valley were used as needles, and strands of banana bark were utilized as string. For the more elaborate feather *lei* reserved for the royalty of old Hawaii, strips of *olona* bark were twisted into a cord that was flexible and strong.

Prices may range today from less than $5 up to $50 for the fragrant *maile* and multiple strands of pikake. Many *lei*, like the woven ginger *lei* or the complex maunaloa orchid *lei*, are intricate works of art. Others, such as a simple plumeria *lei*, can be strung by anyone with a needle and thread.

Makers of lei produce hundreds, if not thousands, of lei daily for the islands' tourism industry. Most common is the plumeria lei.

Rosettes for the winners of the wili-style (a corkscrew-type twist used to make the lei) May Day contest. Competitors need to be able to describe the types of flora used.

The hula, both traditional and modern, uses lei as an important adornment. Often in hula, lei are not made from flowers, but leaves and other parts of flora considered to impart importance.

Leis at the grave of Father Damien at St Philomena Church in Kalawao.

Draped by aloha and respect

In Hawaii, a *lei* is a special symbol or gift given as a sign of respect, welcome (or departure), or good feeling. *Lei* are also draped over the statues or images of important people in Hawaii's history.

Each island has its own special material for making *lei*. The delicate orange *'ilima* blossom represents Oahu. Feathery red lehua blossoms from gnarled *'ohi'a* trees symbolize the island of Hawaii. Pink *lokelani* (an introduced Castilian rose) make up Maui's *lei*, while Molokai is adorned by silver-green leaves from the *kukui* tree and decorated with tiny white blossoms.

Oblong leaves and dark berries from the *mokihana* tree are fashioned into a *lei* for Kauai. On Lanai, *lei* are woven from slim strands of *kauna'oa*, an orange, mossy beach vine. Even uninhabited Kaho'olawe has a *lei* from *hinahina*, a beach plant with narrow green leaves and little white flowers. Ni'ihau is the only island not represented by a flower, but by shells: the rare and very tiny *pupu* that are treasured by *kama'aina* as much as valuable gems.

Beautiful haku lei, made by twining or braiding foliage into a bouquet. Nearly any flower or nut can be fashioned into a lei, including bougainvillea, ginger, and plumeria with its luscious scent.

Making leis at a stand in Honolulu.

Lei made of plumeria flowers, of which the yellow and white version is the most common.

AN ECLECTIC CUISINE

With ethnic influences from Polynesia, Asia, Europe, and North America, Hawaii's cuisine is among the world's most eclectic.

Island menus read like a United Nations lunch order: sushi, pasta, crispy *gau gee*, *kim chee*, tortillas, tandoori chicken, Wienerschnitzel, spring rolls – you name it, they eat it in Hawaii. Within a relatively small geographical area, visitors find a universe of dishes served in surroundings both down-home and haute, from casual eateries that serve two scoops of rice for a "plate lunch," to candlelit corners with chateaubriand and chocolate mousse on the menu.

FOOD FROM ALL OVER

Hawaii has many to thank for its diverse culinary landscape. Chinese immigrants, for instance, taught islanders that rice goes just as well with eggs at breakfast as it does with lunch and dinner. Supermarkets of all stripes stock supplies of cilantro, lemongrass, and ginger, and restaurants turn out everything from Mandarin, Sichuan, and Cantonese to Mongolian barbecue and stir-fry. For an energizing assault on the senses, make a beeline for a house of *dim sum*, where waitresses load your table with little plates of bite-sized dumplings until hands are held up in surrender.

From the Japanese came the gifts of *shoyu* (soy sauce), *sashimi* (thinly sliced raw fish), and *tempura* (deep-fried vegetables and meats, introduced to Japan from Portugal, actually). Almost every street has at least one sushi bar for swigging *sake* while chefs with lightning-fast hands fashion edible fantasies out of rice, seafood, and *wasabi* (hot green-horseradish). Japanese culinary sensibilities are best summed up by the *bento*, a lunch box with tidy compartments for morsels of chicken, shrimp, pork cutlets, fishcake, pickled plums, rice, and other artful treats.

Fruits at Hilo Farmers' Market.

Wafts of garlic and grilled specialties lure hungry diners through the doors of Hawaii's Korean restaurants, which generally assume the form of Formica-tabled eateries. Therein await *kim chee* (pickled vegetables), *kalbi* (marinated short ribs), *jun* (foods fried in an egg batter), and the musical *bi bim bap*, which is a bowl of rice, with vegetables, fried egg, and a sweet sauce.

A more recent influx of people from Thailand has introduced spring rolls, *mee krob* (noodle salad), and a coconut-milk/hot pepper-flavored dish called Evil Jungle Prince, best followed by Thai iced tea with sweetened condensed milk. Vietnamese food – less spicy than Thai – is particularly popular for its *phô*, a broth with noodles and beef or chicken slices. Portuguese influence makes itself known in *pao dolce* (sweet bread), chorizo (spicy sausage), *vinha d'alhos* (marinated meat), and a robust bean soup, while from the Philippines comes *lumpia* (fried spring rolls),

> *A staple of the traditional diet, poi is a thick, viscous paste-like food. It is made from the taro root, light purple in color, and often served in knotted plastic bags.*

and Chinese workers in simple, single-walled wooden houses. The Chinese built community cookhouses, the Japanese added mom-and-pop tofu factories. People grew their own *bok choi* and lemongrass in backyards.

CELEBRATING REGIONAL CUISINE

The most recent take on island food is called Hawaii Regional Cuisine – a variation of what's known elsewhere as Pacific Rim Cuisine or New Australian Cuisine. This movement gained momentum in 1992, when a dozen curious, crea-

Harvesting taro, which grows in paddy fields.

pancit (noodles, vegetables, and pork), *pork guisantes* (pork rump), *bagoong* (fish sauce), and *bitsu bitsu* (sweet potato scones).

Stir into this pot the creativity of classically trained chefs from France, Switzerland, Germany, North America, and Italy who have been imported to work in some of Hawaii's upscale restaurants. The state's continental ideas of the 1970s have evolved into today's more health-conscious cooking, but without too much effort you can still find an authentic veal *scaloppini* or a slab of salmon drenched in dill sauce.

Inevitably, the blending of cooking styles occurred in Hawaii's plantation villages. When Japanese contract laborers were imported in the 1880s, they lived side-by-side with Hawaiian

tive, and congenial chefs began getting together to share their ideas as well as their wish lists for a wider variety of fresh produce and other more varied ingredients. In the kitchens of their own elegant restaurants, their sous-chefs and *garde-mangers* were feasting on interesting, flavorful treats they had learned to make at home.

Alan Wong was one of the 12. He says the diversity of Hawaii's food is inextricably linked to its cultural history: "While I was growing up in Hawaii, my grandfather cooked Chinese and my mother cooked Japanese, but she mingled in flavors of Filipino, Chinese, Japanese, and Hawaiian dishes."

The growth of Hawaii Regional Cuisine has made a difference on Hawaii's culinary scene.

Today, any number of farmers are growing crops to the specifications of chefs who visit the fields and make known what they want for their own restaurants. Tomatoes are vine-ripened; arugula and baby lettuces fill upcountry fields on Maui and the Big Island. Several hotels grow their own fresh herbs, while a number of hotels in Waikiki have their own rooftop hydroponic gardens, and at least one Maui resort harvests fresh tropical fruit and other produce from an organic garden that surrounds its parking lot.

A host of professional chefs were inspired by the daring dozen, and Hawaiian Regional Cuisine has become a palate-pleasing password even beyond island shores. Names such as Sam Choy and Roy Yamaguchi, both of whom own several restaurants, have published cookbooks, and hosted their own television cooking shows, have become synonymous with Hawaiian cooking. The current pantheon of greats includes George Mavrothalassitis, Peter Merriman and Daniel Thiebaut, each with their own signature restaurants. More recently, "Top Chef" runner-up Sheldon Simeon, Ed Kenney, Jon Matsubara, and Hisashi Uehara were added to that list.

PASSION AND PINEAPPLE

Local products have become as intrinsically linked to Hawaii's lifestyle as the ebbing and flowing of the tides. Residents and visitors alike have easy access to an abundance of fresh fruit, and we're not just talking pineapple and coconut. Equally common are the apple banana, the golden papaya, the pungent *liliko'i*, and the guava, a yellow, lemon-sized gem with a shockingly pink interior.

The lychee, prized for its juicy white flesh, can be spotted hanging in grape-like clumps on trees in Manoa Valley, while *poha* (cape gooseberry) thrives on bushes near Kilauea Volcano. The markets of Honolulu's Chinatown district are a good source of these and lesser-known fruits, like the tamarind, kumquat, starfruit, *rambuton* (sweet white fruit in a red, spiky shell), and *cherimoya* (with tart white flesh).

Visit Hawaii during the summer and you'll discover the joys of the mango. When mango trees start to blossom in May, it's as big a deal as seeing the first whales of winter. By July, the fruit is weighing down the branches, and neighbors distribute free bags of sweet, juicy mangos.

Each island also is known for certain naturally occurring "specialties." Think of a papaya and one thinks of the prolific trees of Puna on Hawaii Island. Onions conjure up images of cool upcountry Kula on Maui, where the sweetest variety is grown. Guava thrives in Kilauea on Kauai, and Molokai is known for its sweet potatoes, while fresh fish are pulled from the waters round all the islands.

OCEAN HARVESTS

What is harvested by land is matched by the bounty of the sea. The king and queen of

Seafood at Mama's Fish House in Paia, Maui.

Hawaiian fish are the *mahimahi* (dolphin fish) and *'opakapaka* (pink snapper), but *ulua* (jack crevalle), *ono* (wahoo), *ahi* (yellow-fin tuna), *onaga* (red snapper) and *tako* (octopus), which is served raw and marinated as *poke*, are equally memorable, whether blackened Cajun-style or baked in wafer-thin layers of crisp phyllo pastry. In the world of aquaculture, Hawaii Island, Kauai, and North Shore of Oahu are creating miniature ocean tanks and fishponds teeming with prawns, lobsters, abalone, and other delicacies.

Called *'opihi*, limpets are Hawaii's signature mollusk but are rarely found on restaurant menus. Locals have been known to scamper crab-like across shorelines, hanging on when the big waves roll in (not recommended; deaths are reported each year when waves overpower harvesters), in order to pick a bunch of quarter-sized shells off the lava rocks.

PERFECTION ON A PLATE

Hawaii's homegrown extends to grain-fattened beef, grass-fed lamb, and free-range game. *Paniolos* (cowboys) on Maui and the Big Island saddle up in the pre-dawn mist to round up the beef that ends up on dinner plates. Ni'ihau is promoting its own special grade of lamb. Lanai axis deer has become a popular entrée laced with plum sauce, and Molokai venison makes for a tasty stew or toothsome sausage.

If all this choice sounds a little overwhelming, start with the basics. Try a "plate lunch" – the statewide institution defined by a few simple elements. You'll get a paper plate loaded with "two scoop rice," plus a mound of heavily may-onnaised macaroni salad. Order one with *teri-yaki* beef, breaded pork or chicken *(katsu)*, fried fish, or Spam, an unexpected passion among local people.

Stopping by Local Boys Shave Ice in Kihei, Maui.

⊘ FOR THE LOVE OF SPAM

Spam has a special place in the Hawaiian diet; it is sometimes referred to as the "Hawaiian Steak." Residents of the islands consume more Spam per capita than any residents of any other place in the US. This popularity can be attributed in part to the military; in the years that followed World War II, the meat product was used as a substitute for fresh meat, and, gradually, surplus supply of it made its way into native diets. Today in the islands, the canned meat is most commonly eaten atop a rectangle of rice and bound with a piece of nori seaweed. The resulting sushi-like creation is called Spam musubi.

OTHER TASTY GOODIES

There are other tasty treats to sample in Hawaii. On hot days, try a shave ice, a snowcone soaked in neon-colored tropical syrups like mango, guava, and coconut, and one of former US President Barack Obama's favorite treats. Those in the know order it with vanilla ice cream and sweet azuki beans on the bottom.

Additional snacks have a decidedly Asian flare. Try *manapua*, the tennis ball-sized steamed Chinese dumpling filled with pork or curried chicken. Enjoy a bowl of *saimin*, an Asian noodle soup topped with an encyclopedia of garnishes like sliced *char siu* (roast pork), fishcake, and green onions. Or pick up a bag of crack seed (preserved and flavored fruits), pickled plums, and *pipi kaula* (beef jerky).

The lu'au predates the modern dinner dance. And it's a great way to get a quick perspective on local culture.

Traditionally, the lu'au is a festival of food and dance, an amalgamation of Hawaiian culture unlike any other. These days, however, most of the lu'aus you'll discover will be the commercialized variety, complete with the comic hula and Mai Tais. While purists may find this a shallow version of the real thing, the imu ceremonies, hula, Hawaiian music, kalua pig and other culinary specialties, and good cheer are all rooted in Hawaiian tradition. If you can let go of prejudices about "authenticity," you're very likely to have a really good time.

HISTORIC FEASTS

These modern lu'aus emerged from the aha'aina, or feasts of old, when women dined separately from men and were prohibited from eating some of the choicest of lu'au fare. Finally, after 1819, when Liholiho (King Kamehameha II) abolished the old kapu (taboo) system of restrictions, lu'aus became a lively tradition enjoyed by all.

Today, the heart of any lu'au, commercial or private, continues to be the preparation and unearthing of the imu. Current lu'au food is reasonably authentic, except for such items as macaroni and potato salads or teriyaki-beef, which were added to suit all tastes.

You'll still find pig roasted to juicy tenderness in the imu (hole-in-the-ground oven. filled with koa wood and heat-retaining rocks that continue to cook after the wood has burned off) accompanied by poi, sweet potatoes, marinated lomilomi salmon with chopped tomatoes and onions, and sometimes 'opihi, a Hawaiian shellfish plucked from wave-washed rocky shorelines and eaten raw as a special delicacy. For uninitiated taste buds, it's best to sample poi with salty kalua pork or lomilomi salmon to enhance the flavors and textures.

Many lu'aus ladle out chicken long rice, a dish of chicken cooked with translucent noodles made of rice flour and garnished with green onions. Frequently you'll find laulau, little green bundles of taro leaf, which taste like spinach, steamed with pork and fish. For dessert, coconut cake is a new addition, but haupia, a coconut-milk pudding, has long been served as a sweet finale.

ISLAND ENTERTAINMENT

The entertainment at one of these modern feasts is like taking a mini-tour through the island cultures

Preparing the pig, the staple of lu'aus.

of Hawaii, Tonga, Samoa, New Zealand, and Tahiti. Hawaii's contribution includes the haunting chants that perpetuate the genealogies and legends of the past, as well as the graceful hula. Some lu'aus, including the one at the Polynesian Cultural Center on Oahu, include pageantry with participants dressed like early Hawaiian royalty.

Whether visitors will get their money's worth from a commercial lu'au, which could range in price from $60 up to $125 per person, depends upon the individual, and the lu'au. If you are ready to throw yourself into the spirit of the night by donning your most colorful aloha shirt, taking off your shoes, and getting up on stage to learn a Tahitian tamure while your traveling companions cheer, and if you find unfamiliar foods intriguing, you'll have a good time. Lu'aus range from tacky to traditional, and you'll just have to look around for your style.

HAWAII ON SCREEN

With lush valleys, mind-bending waterfalls, and tropical paradise around every corner, Hawaii has become a darling of Hollywood.

You can't really blame Hollywood producers for falling in love with Hawaii. Between lush valleys, swaying palm trees, white sand beaches, and tropical vistas, the islands offer more authentic paradise than any studio set. Starting with a pair of one-reelers in 1913, more than 100 films have been shot in the islands since the 1950s, and countless other television shows have been filmed there, as well. Some islands, such as Kauai, are more famous than others. But all of the Hawaiian Islands wear the spotlight well; over the years Hawaii has become known as "Hollywood's Tropical Back Lot."

What makes Hawaii so appealing to producers and directors? Its versatility, for one. Hawaii has the ability to morph easily, making the audience believe it is anything from a South Pacific beach to a South African village to an exotic Peruvian rainforest.

The islands also are renowned for great weather and spectacular light – both of which are important considerations when filming for movies or TV. Another reason Hawaii is a big draw is that the islands beckon movie stars; if celebrities know a production is being shot in Hawaii they are that much more likely to sign up. Finally there's cost. You might think filming on location in a tropical paradise is expensive, but the truth is that tax breaks and other incentives make the endeavour almost as affordable as shooting in a studio back on the mainland. Add to this the only state-owned and -operated film studio in the country and a growing list of production facilities, an experienced pool of crew and talent, a comprehensive local inventory of state-of-the-art equipment, a well-established one-stop process for state film permits, and a film-friendly government and community, and it's no wonder Hawaii has said "Aloha" to so much film production over the years.

Jurassic Park used locations on Oahu and Kauai.

⊘ HAWAII THE CHAMELEON

Tropical jungle is tropical jungle, all over the world. For this reason, over the years Hollywood studios have not only depicted Hawaii as Hawaii in film; they also have used parts of the lush archipelago as other tropical destinations, including the Amazon, Africa, and more. Perhaps the most famous example of Hawaii on location was the 1995 film, *Outbreak*. In this gripping thriller, Kamokila Hawaiian Village, a throwback-type attraction along the Wailua River on the east side of Kauai, was turned into the African village where a deadly airborne virus that threatened civilization began.

THE BIG SPLASH

A number of small movies were filmed in Hawaii between 1913 and 1950, including *Bird of Paradise* in 1932 and *Waikiki Wedding*, with Bing Crosby, in 1937. Still, Hawaii's real Hollywood boom started following World War II. Perhaps the film that put the islands on the map was the original Hollywood adaptation of *From Here to Eternity*, starring Burt Lancaster, Frank Sinatra, Montgomery Clift, and Deborah Kerr. This movie dealt with a sensitive subject: the Japanese bombing of Pearl Harbor,

Burt Lancaster and Deborah Kerr in the beach scene filmed on Oahu in From Here to Eternity (1953).

on Oahu, in 1941. Still, thanks in part to a racy on-screen kiss between Lancaster and Kerr (and Oscars for Best Picture and Best Director), the movie became an instant classic, and remains one of the film industry's greatest accomplishments today.

Among directors, *From Here to Eternity* changed the landscape, opening up Hawaii as a destination for on-location spots. Over the next decade, dozens of films were filmed in Hawaii, including *Blue Hawaii* and *Girls! Girls! Girls!*, both starring Elvis Presley. In the second half of the 1960s, as the film and television industries entered their respective heydays, more and more Hollywood studios saw Hawaii as a viable option for authentic, on-location tropical shoots. The islands' life in pictures had begun.

KAUAI IN THE SPOTLIGHT

Since then, if the Hawaiian Islands have had a "star" in Hollywood, it would have to be Kauai. Perhaps it's the remote location. Perhaps it's the green forests. Perhaps the island has captured more directorial imaginations than any other. Whatever the reason, Kauai has appeared on the silver screen (and the small screen) more than any other Hawaiian Island.

Fantasy Island; *Pirates of the Caribbean*; *Six Days, Seven Nights*; *Voodoo Island*; and *South Pacific* all are films that were at least partly on Kauai. Old buildings in the town of Hanapepe reportedly inspired backdrops for the Disney movie *Lilo & Stitch*. In recent years, the Garden Isle also has been a backdrop for the television show *Lost*; the George Clooney film, *The Descendants*; and *The Hunger Games: Catching Fire*. Clooney's film in particular has turned at least one destination into a veritable tourist goldmine; because the Tahiti Nui restaurant and bar in Hanalei has a cameo in the film, fans have lined up to dine and/or drink there ever since.

OTHER ISLANDS TAKE CENTER STAGE

Other Hawaiian Islands have had their proverbial 15 minutes of fame, as well. On Oahu, between 1968 and 1980, Honolulu and Waikiki Beach were the inspiration behind the original Hawaii police show *Hawaii Five-O* (and a recent remake of the same show). Another popular television show filmed on Oahu: *Magnum P.I.*, with Tom Selleck. More recently, 2019 war drama *Midway* was shot in Honolulu among other filming locations, while 2021 fantasy action movie *Godzilla vs. Kong* was filmed in downtown Honolulu, at Manoa Falls and on the *USS Missouri* in Pearl Harbor.

Oahu also has seen its share of surfing movies (most notably *North Shore* and *Blue Crush*), and war movies including *Pearl Harbor*. Turtle Bay Resort, on the North Shore, was the setting for the 2008 romantic comedy *Forgetting Sarah Marshall*. And Kualoa Ranch has provided the backdrop for a number of films, including *Jurassic Park*, *Jurassic World* and *50 First Dates*.

The ranch now offers private bus tours on which visitors can get an inside look at filming sites; the experience has become quite popular among fans of *Lost*. The island was also the setting of the romantic comedy *Aloha* (2015), starring Emma Stone, Rachel McAdams, and Bradley Cooper, as well as *Big Eyes*, based on the true story of painter Margaret Keane.

Maui has appeared in many films and TV series over the years, too. Lahaina took center stage in Clint Eastwood's *The Devil at 4 O'Clock*, and some of the island's beach locales were

television. Hawaii Island has provided backdrops for *Waterworld* and *Planet of the Apes*, while Lanai appears in a modern version of Shakespeare's *The Tempest*, starring Helen Mirren. New Lanai owner Larry Ellison has said he will try to bring more film crews to that island in the coming years.

CELEBRATING FILM ON HAWAII

Hawaii is not only a destination for on-location filming these days; it also has become a destination for festivals that celebrate films in

George Clooney in The Descendants, filmed on location in Hawaii and based on a novel by a Hawaii resident.

front and center as backdrops in movies such as *Just Go With It* and *Pirates of the Caribbean: At World's End*. *Baraka*, a 1991 documentary about life as humans (and, for the film geeks, shot in 70mm film), opened with an eerie shot from inside the crater atop Mount Haleakala. HBO satirical comedy-drama The White Lotus was a hit not just for its astute social commentary but also its idyllic scenery. The TV show, starring Connie Britton, Jennifer Coolidge, Alexandra Daddario and Fred Hechinger, was set in an exclusive Hawaiian resort called The White Lotus – the Four Seasons Resort Maui, in fact, at Wailea.

Other islands in the Hawaiian archipelago have had less of a role in modern film and

general. With this in mind, a number of towns across the islands now sponsor annual film festivals through the year. Some of the largest of these parties include festivals on Maui and Hawaii Island and in Oahu. Many of these festivals screen independent movies; in 2017, for instance, the Maui Film Festival (www.mauifilmfestival.com) premiered Big Wave Project – A band of Brothers documenting the life of surfers who ride the world's biggest waves.

Film buffs also might enjoy attending the Hawaii International Film Festival (www.hiff. org), an annual event held every November on Oahu, Big Island and Kauai, celebrating new and emerging cinema talents in the Asia-Pacific region.

Surfers at Waipio Bay in Waipio Valley, Big Island.

Riding mules in Kalaupapa, Molokai.

Waikiki Beach with Diamond Head volcanic cone in the background in Honolulu, Oahu.

Hanakapi'ai Falls in the Hanakapi'ai Valley, Na Pali Coast State Wilderness Park, Kauai.

INTRODUCTION

They're part of the same archipelago, but each of the Hawaiian Islands has its own personality, history, and vibe.

Road sign on Kamehameha Highway near Hale'iwa town, Oahu.

Geologically speaking, the islands have all been cut from the same cloth; the volcanic vent that continues to make Kilauea erupt on Hawaii Island was responsible for the genesis of all Hawaii's islands. Since this creation, however, each one has developed differently. Here's a look at the islands from southeast (youngest) to northwest (oldest).

Hawaii Island, previously known as the Big Island, is, well, big – the biggest of all eight, actually. And it's getting bigger every day that Kilauea erupts. Against the backdrop of these explosions, the rest of the island operates quietly; more than half of the island is farmland. The island chain encompasses 6,423 sq miles (16,635 sq km) of land area. Hawaii Island is twice the area of all the others combined.

Next up is Maui where the residents like to say, "Maui no ka oi," which translates into "Maui is the best." And the island certainly is awesome. Whether you're visiting the beaches of Ka'anapai, the jungles of Hana, or the slopes of Mount Haleakala, the spectacles are sure to impress.

Kaho'olawe, once a testing site for weapons, is now a nature reserve closed to visitors. Neighboring Lanai, once covered in pineapples, is emerging as a luxury tourist destination – a great spot to get away from the world. The same can be said for Molokai, which is the most undeveloped of the islands and, as a result, is perhaps the most "authentic" of the bunch.

Then, of course, there's Oahu, the most populous island. *Waimanalo Beach Park, Oahu.* The party rages nonstop on Waikiki Beach, and Honolulu is the seat of the state's government. Beyond this metropolis, however, the island boasts lush mountains, great surf, and cultural sites, including Pearl Harbor.

On Kauai, the "Garden Isle," nature has shaped the land as she has wished; cutting into the island at Waimea Canyon and wearing it down into beautiful bluffs along the Na Pali Coast. In between is some of the most pristine paradise on Earth; no wonder Oscar Hammerstein immortalized the spot in "South Pacific." Finally, is Ni'ihau, a lush island only open to native Hawaiians.

Eight islands, eight completely different personalities. Together, they comprise the Hawaii of today. This diversity only makes the local culture richer – and more fun to experience and explore.

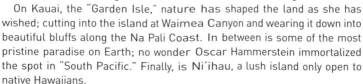

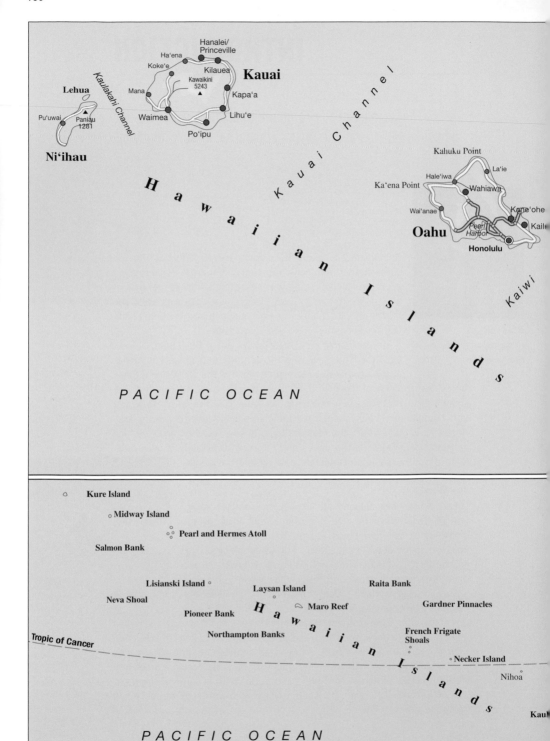

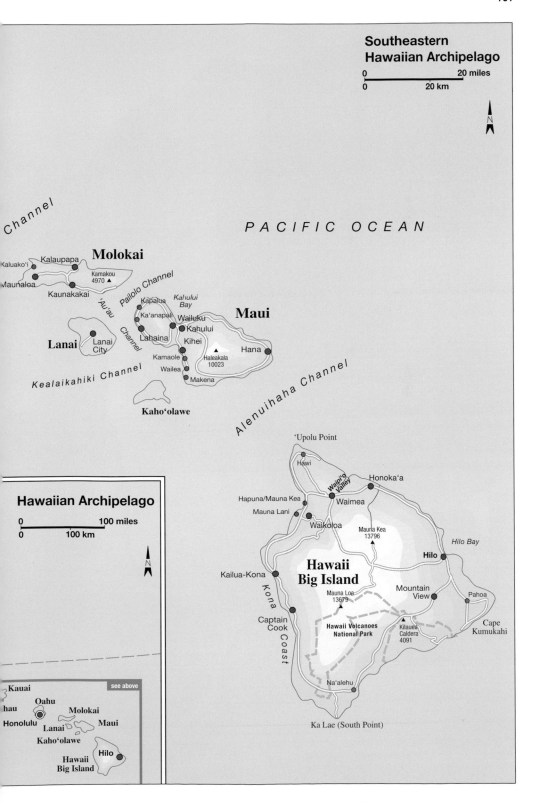

Southeastern Hawaiian Archipelago

0   20 miles
0   20 km

N

PACIFIC OCEAN

Channel

Molokai

Kaluako'i   Kalaupapa

Maunaloa

Kaunakakai

Kamakou
4970 ▲

Pailolo Channel

'Au'au

Kapalua

Kahului Bay

Ka'anapali   Wailuku

Maui

Lanai

Lanai City

Lahaina   Kahului

Kihei

Channel

Kamaole

Wailea

Haleakala
10023 ▲

Hana

Kealaikahiki Channel

Makena

Kaho'olawe

Alenuihaha Channel

'Upolu Point

Hawi

Waipi'o Valley

Honoka'a

Hapuna/Mauna Kea

Waimea

Mauna Lani

Waikoloa

Mauna Kea
13796 ▲

Hilo Bay

**Hawaii
Big Island**

Hilo

Kailua-Kona

Mauna Loa
13679 ▲

Mountain
View

Pahoa

Kona Coast

Captain
Cook

**Hawaii Volcanoes
National Park**

Kilauea
Caldera
4091

Cape
Kumukahi

Na'alehu

Ka Lae (South Point)

Hawaiian Archipelago

0   100 miles
0   100 km

N

Kauai

Oahu

hau   Molokai

Honolulu   Lanai   Maui

Kaho'olawe

Hawaii
Big Island

Hilo

see above

At Kualoa Ranch on Oahu.

OAHU

The most populous of the Hawaiian Islands also is the most visited – with good reason: Honolulu is a happening place, and the North Shore's beaches are among the most picturesque in the world.

Waikiki Beach in Honolulu.

Scour the globe and you won't find another island quite like Oahu. Its varied attractions include dense rainforest in the center of the island, monstrous surfing waves on the North Shore, a multi-billion-dollar skyline at Waikiki, lively Honolulu, colorful history, epic hikes, volcanic craters, and a Disney resort. Pre-pandemic, more than 75,000 visitors would explore the island every day, coast to coast, tip to tip, from Wai'anae in the west to Hale'iwa in the north, Pearl Harbor and Waikiki in the south, and Makapu'u in the east.

"O'ahu" is said to mean "the gathering place," and there is no doubt that Oahu plays that role today. Its 950,000-plus residents make up around 65 percent of the state's population. Honolulu is the seat of island and state government, and is the longest city in the world; because the city and county of Honolulu are one and the same, the metropolis extends 1,400 miles (2,250km) northwest up the Hawaiian chain to Kure Atoll, near Midway Island.

Honolulu proper lies on Oahu's southern coast, backed up against the Ko'olau Range. Its two best-known neighborhoods, downtown Honolulu, and Waikiki, 3 miles (5km) to the east, hold almost all its facilities and attractions for tourists. Waikiki is virtually a separate destination in itself, and

Ko 'Olina Golf Club in Kapolei.

many visitors to Hawaii never leave it except to reach the airport on the other side of Honolulu. The truth is that there is much more to Oahu than this famous beach. On the other side of the Ko'olau Mountains is the windward side, which is green and wet. Life slows down along the North Shore, whose waters are placid in summer but violent in winter with surfing's best waves. On the south coast to the west of Honolulu and Waikiki is Pearl Harbor, encircled by military bases and housing. Farther to the west are the Ko 'Olina resort area, the 'Ewa plains and the sunny Wai'anae coastal valleys, probably Oahu's most "local" area. You can experience five or six microclimates in a day, all without ever leaving Oahu.

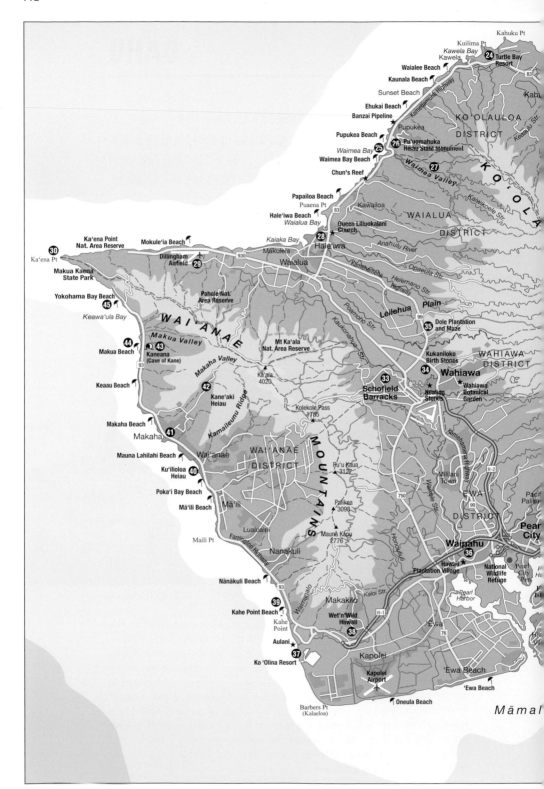

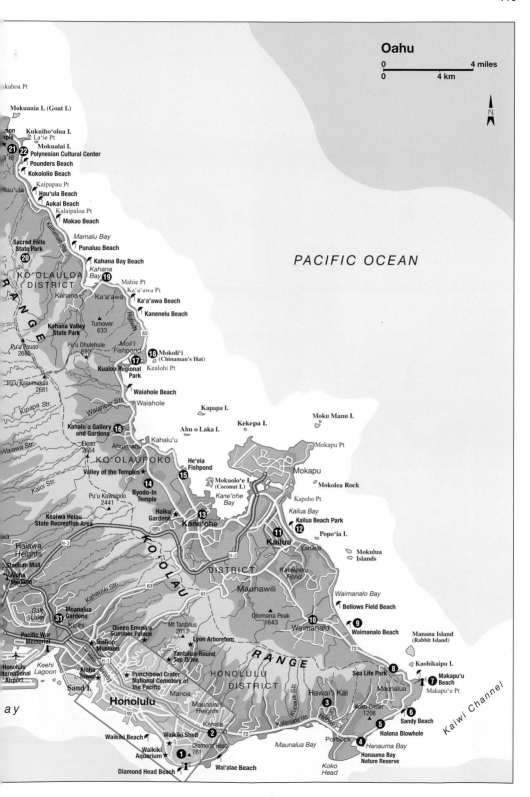

Oahu

| 0 | | 4 miles |
| 0 | | 4 km |

N

kahoa Pt

Mokuauia I. (Goat I.)

Kukuiho'olua I.
La'ie Pt
21 22 Mokualai I.
Polynesian Cultural Center
Pounders Beach
Kokololio Beach

Kaipapau Pt
Hau'ula Beach
Aukai Beach
Kalaipaloa Pt
Makao Beach

Mamalu Bay
Sacred Falls
State Park **20** Punaluu Beach

KO'OLAULOA
DISTRICT
Kahana Bay Beach
Kahana
Bay **19**
Mahie Pt
Ka'a'awa Pt
Kahana Ka'a'awa Beach
Kanenelu Beach

Turnover
633
Kahana Valley
State Park
Pu'u Ohulehule
690
Pu'u Pauao
2685
Moli'i
Fishpond **18** Mokoli'i
17 (Chinaman's Hat)
Kualoa Regional
Park Kealohi Pt

Pu'u Kaaumakua
2681
Kipapa Str.
Waiahole Beach
Waiahole Str.
Waiahole

Kapapa I.
Ahu o Laka I.
Kekepa I.
Moku Manu I.

Kahalu'u Gallery
and Gardens **16**
Waiawa Str. Eleao
2664
Ahuimanu
Kahalu'u
Kaloi Str. KO'OLAUPOKO
He'eia
Fishpond
Valley of the Temples ★ **15**
14 Mokapu Pt
Byodo-In
Temple Mokapu
Pu'u Kawaipoo
2441 Mokulo'e I.
(Coconut I.)
Kane'ohe Mokolea Rock
Bay
Kapoho Pt
Keaiwa Heiau
State Recreation Area Haiku
Gardens **13**
Kailua Bay
Kailua Beach Park
11 **12** Popo'ia I.
Kane'ohe

Haiawa
Heights **11**
Kailua
Stadium Mall
Aloha
Stadium Lanikai Mokulua
Islands
DISTRICT
Kahauiki Str. Kaelepulu
Pond
Salt
Lake Maunawili
Moanalua
Gardens
Kalihi 63
Pacific War **31**
Memorial 61 Waimanalo Bay
Bellows Field Beach
Queen Emma's
Summer Palace Mt Tantalus Olomana Peak
2013 1643 **10**
Bishop Lyon Arboretum Waimanalo **9** Waimanalo Beach
Honolulu Keehi Museum
International Lagoon Waimanalo Manana Island
Airport Aloha Tantalus-Round (Rabbit Island)
Tower Top Drive RANGE
Sand I. Punchbowl Crater HONOLULU Kaohikaipu I.
National Cemetery of
the Pacific DISTRICT **8**
Manoa Sea Life Park **7** Makapu'u
Beach
ay 92 Maunalua Makapu'u Pt
Maunalani
Heights Hawai'i Kai **3**
Honolulu Koko Crater **6**
Kahala 1208 **5** Sandy Beach
Waikiki Beach 72 Halona Blowhole
Waikiki Shell **2** Kalaniana'ole Koko Crater
Diamond Head
Waikiki 761 Portlock **4** Hanauma Bay
Aquarium **1** Hanauma Bay
Nature Reserve
Diamond Head Beach Wai'alae Beach Maunalua Bay Kaiwi Channel
Koko
Head

PACIFIC OCEAN

KO'OLAU RANGE

Kailua

Kipapa Str.

Kalaniana'ole Hwy

Statue of King Kamehameha I by Thomas Ridgeway Gould in front of the King Kamehameha V Judiciary History Center.

HONOLULU

A cosmopolitan metropolis in the middle of the Pacific Ocean. Sure, it seems strange. But that's what makes Honolulu worth a visit.

Honolulu – the name rolls off the tongue like a soft wave breaking off Waikiki. There's no mystery about its origin: *hono*, a bay, and *lulu*, protected. It explains why Honolulu has been the commercial, political, and cultural center of the Hawaiian Islands since the 1800s. Until Pearl Harbor was made navigable in the mid-19th century, Honolulu Harbor was the largest protected body of water within 2,000 miles (3,200km) of Hawaii.

Three miles (5km) west of the beaches of Waikiki, downtown Honolulu is a walker's delight. A stroll through Downtown with its grid of side streets, shops, oddball bars, and historic buildings can consume hours or days. The key to unlocking Honolulu is to treat it not like a city, but like the real gem that it is. You're on Hawaiian time now, so take it slow and easy.

PALACE IN PARADISE

Grand old **ʻIolani Palace** ❶ (364 S. King Street; tel: 522-0822; www.iolanipalace.org; Tue–Sat 9am–4pm) is the only royal palace on US soil. It was built in a Victorian-era architectural style called American Composite or American Florentine. Completed in 1882 during King Kalakaua's reign, the palace took over three years and $350,000 to finish.

King Kalakaua and his successor-sister, Queen Liliʻuokalani, lived in the palace, holding royal court from 1882 until 1893, when a group of American businessmen staged a coup d'état and abolished the monarchy. ʻIolani – Hawaiian for heavenly hawk – was renamed the Executive Building after the monarchy's overthrow, but the humiliation did not end there. In 1895, following a futile counter-revolution led by royalists, Liliʻuokalani was convicted of misprision of high treason and was returned to ʻIolani Palace, where

Main attractions
ʻIolani Palace
Honolulu Museum of Art
Chinatown
Foster Botanical Gardens
Aloha Tower
Aina Moana State
  Recreation Area
Ala Moana Shopping
  Center

Maps on pages 112, 116, 136

Gallery of 18th-century European art at the Honolulu Museum of Art.

she spent most of the year living alone on the second floor of the building, under house arrest as a prisoner of the provisional government.

The palace was used as a capitol for the provisional, territorial, and state governments of Hawaii. In 1969, the state legislature and administration moved out of the palace and into the new capitol building and grounds just *mauka* (toward the mountains) of the palace. The state and a private non-profit-making group then began a $6-million effort to restore the palace to its former splendor. Original furnishings were tracked down and recovered and the palace proper now glows as it did when Kalakaua and Lili'uokalani hosted formal banquets and grand balls. This includes Corinthian columns, etched-glass door panels, chandeliers, the mirrored and gilded Throne Room, and the spectacular three-story *koa* (an indigenous hardwood) stairwell with carved balusters. Also back in operation are the first flush toilets known to have been installed in any palace anywhere in

the world, and Hawaii's first internal telephone and electric-light systems. A worthwhile museum of royal Hawaiiana is housed in the basement.

On the palace grounds are some other intriguing sites. The **Coronation Pavilion** was built in 1883 for King Kalakaua and Queen Kapi'olani's coronation. The stand's foundation was rebuilt in 1919, but the copper dome is the original and now plays host to free public music concerts (every Friday at noon) by the Royal Hawaiian Band (www.rhb-music.com).

The **'Iolani Barracks** is a stone structure that served as headquarters and home to the Royal Household Guards from 1871 until the overthrow of the monarchy. The small building now includes a gift shop, a screening room, and the palace ticket office.

The **Royal Burial Ground and Tomb** is an inconspicuous, grass-covered mound surrounded by *ti* plants in the Diamond Head *makai* (towards Diamond Head and toward the ocean) corner. It was the site of the first Royal Mausoleum, built in 1825 to house

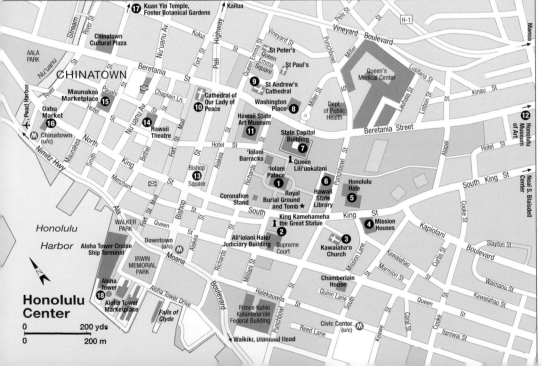

the remains of King Kamehameha II and Queen Kamamalu, who died of measles when they visited England in 1823. Later Hawaiian *ali'i* (royalty) were also buried there. But in 1865, with the tomb overcrowded with royal remains, all were moved to a new Royal Mausoleum in Nu'uanu Valley.

On the *makai* side of King Street, across from 'Iolani Palace, is the **King Kamehameha the Great Statue** ❷. Although this heroic bronze probably bears little resemblance to Kamehameha the Great, it's a Honolulu monument and a prime spot for camera-wielding tourists. The statue shows the king holding a barbed *polulu* (spear) in his left hand as a symbol of peace and his right arm outstretched in a welcoming gesture of *aloha*. Hanging from the king's shoulders is a large feather cloak and on his head is a *mahiole*, or feather helmet. Around his loins and chest he wears a feather *malo*, or loincloth, and a sash. When the Hawaiian kingdom's 1878 legislature commissioned this statue, King Kalakaua chose John Timoteo Baker, a local businessman, to serve as its primary model, as he was the most handsome man in court circles. Baker was mostly Anglo-Saxon, and only about one-quarter Tahitian. Photos were taken wearing ancient clothing, and these plus copies of painted likenesses of Kamehameha were sent to Thomas B. Gould, an American sculptor in Florence. Unveiled during Kalakaua's 1883 coronation, the statue is a copy of the original, which is located in Kapa'au, on Hawaii Island.

Behind the statue is the old **Judiciary Building** (tel: 539-4999; Mon–Fri 8am–4pm; free), originally designed by Australian architect Thomas Rowe to be King Kamehameha V's palace. The king's household plans changed, however, and after the building was completed in 1874, it was used instead as a courthouse and legislative building. The building – also known as Ali'iolani Hale (*hale* means house, and *ali'iolani* translates as "chief of heavenly repute") – is now home to the state's supreme court and the Judiciary History Center (www.jhchawaii.net).

Every June, the Kamehameha Festival opens with a colorful lei-draping ceremony at the bronze statue of King Kamehameha I, with lei up to 18ft (5 meters) long.

The grounds of 'Iolani Palace.

Kawaiaha'o Church.

KAWAIAHA'O CHURCH

Towards Diamond Head up King Street from the Judiciary Building is Hawaii's most famous Christian structure, **Kawaiaha'o Church** ❸ (www.kawaiahaochurch.com). On Sunday mornings, or when the church's Hawaiian choir is in rehearsal, the royal palms and hala trees in its grounds seem to sway with the lyrics of *"He A-kua he mo-le-le"* – "God is Holy," or *"E Ha-wai-i e ku'u o-ne ha-nau e,"* the opening words of "Hawai'i Aloha," which translates as, "Oh, Hawaii, my own birthplace, my own land."

For years this was the gathering place of missionaries and Christian Hawaiian *ali'i*. Even today, the church often serves as a meeting place where matters of serious Hawaiian interest are discussed. Designed by Reverend Hiram Bingham, who led the first Congregationalist mission to Hawaii in 1820, Kawaiaha'o Church was constructed in the late 1830s and early 1840s of some 14,000 large coral blocks cut from nearby reefs. Although the present Kawaiaha'o structure was dedicated in 1842, it was preceded by four thatched churches also built under Bingham's direction, the first in 1821.

Kawaiaha'o, the "water used by Ha'o," was named after an ancient sacred spring that still flows in the church grounds. The grounds also hold a cemetery for early missionaries and faithful Hawaiian members of the congregation. It is estimated that as many as 2,000 Hawaiians were buried here in the 1800s, many the victims of diseases unwittingly introduced by the early sailors and settlers. Missionaries and their descendants were buried at the back of the church, while native Hawaiians and others were segregated in death on the harbor-side of the church.

One Hawaiian, who received special exemption from Kawaiaha'o's congregation: King William Lunalilo, the popular "Prince Bill," whose Gothic tomb stands just to the right of the churchyard's main entrance. Lunalilo, who died in 1874 after a one-year reign, requested on his deathbed that he be buried "among his people" at

Kawaiaha'o, away from the "clannish" Kamehameha kings and queens who rested in vaults at the Royal Mausoleum in Nu'uanu.

It was at **Likeke Hale**, an adobe schoolhouse built on Kawaiaha'o's grounds around 1836, that early Congregationalist missionaries taught Hawaiian children the *palapala*, or Bible, and literature in general. Built of mud, limestone, and coral, the schoolhouse is the only survivor of the many adobe structures that were constructed during the early 1800s. It is still used today for Sunday-school classes and smaller church meetings.

MISSION HOUSES MUSEUM AND AROUND

Across from the schoolhouse is the yard where the missionaries lived, prayed, and printed the first of their many 19th-century publications. Now a museum complex, the **Mission Houses ❹** (553 S. King Street; tel: 447-3910; www.missionhouses.org; Tue–Sat 10am–4pm; hourly tours 11am–3pm) rank among the oldest

surviving Western-style structures in Hawaii.

The main white Frame House still stands as it was the day it was erected in 1821 of New England timbers, which were cut and fitted in Boston and shipped to Hawaii aboard the brig *Thaddeus*. It is the oldest wooden house in Hawaii, and was for many years home to several prominent missionaries. The Coral House, where the first printing in the north Pacific was made, was built in 1823. A third building, the Chamberlain House, used as a storehouse and home for the mission's purchasing agent, was built in 1831. All three structures belong to the Hawaiian Mission Children's Society, an exclusive *kama'aina* (long-time residents') club made up of missionaries' descendants. If you fail to coincide with a guided tour of the actual houses, you can settle instead for the museum in the separate visitor center.

From the front entrance of Kawaiaha'o Church, across King Street is **Honolulu Hale ❺**, the city's California-Spanish-style city hall built

The Frame House at the Mission Houses Museum.

Tomb of King Lunalilo at Kawaiaha'o Church.

Statue of Queen Lili'uokalani, Hawaii's last monarch, near the State Capitol Building.

Washington Place.

in 1927. Adjacent is a red-brick structure in a burst of Americana with white pillars, opposite the Mission Houses, which was dedicated in 1916 as the Mission Memorial Building to honor the original New England missionaries. Since 1947, it's been used as a city hall annex. 'Ewa (to the west) is the Greco-Roman **Hawaii State Library** ❻ (478 S. King Street; tel: 586-3500; www. librarieshawaii.org; Mon, Tue & Sat 9am–4pm, Thu 9am–7pm, Fri 11am–4pm; free), which has an extensive Hawaiian and Pacific Isles collection. Built in 1911–2, it was restored and modernized in the late 1980s.

STATE CAPITOL AND SURROUNDINGS

Behind 'Iolani Palace is contemporary Hawaii's center of power – the **State Capitol Building** ❼, dedicated in 1969 and completely renovated in the mid-1990s. The structure's architectural lines were designed to suggest Hawaii's volcanic and oceanic origins. Its high and flaring support pillars represent royal palms. Paneling made of

koa in offices and conference rooms gives the structure a distinctly Hawaiian touch. On the *makai* (ocean) side of the building stands a majestic, bronze **statue of Queen Lili'uokalani**, the last monarch of Hawaii (see page 50). An outstretched hand holds fresh flowers, placed there daily by admirers and supporters.

On the *mauka* (mountain) side of the capitol, along Beretania Street, fly the American and Hawaiian flags, and a blue, red, and starred governor's flag. Visitors to the islands are sometimes surprised to see the British flag in the upper left corner of Hawaii's red, white, and blue flag, designed in 1816 for Kamehameha the Great. It is thought that this flag includes the Union Jack out of consideration for the British sea captain George Vancouver, who presented Hawaii with its first flag when Kamehameha temporarily placed his islands under the protection of Great Britain. Other historians say Kamehameha adopted the Jack-and-Stripes flag so that Hawaiian ships at sea would look both American and

British, thereby discouraging pirates from pillaging his kingdom's vulnerable vessels.

On the same side, take a moment to study the bronze **sculpture of Father Damien** (formerly Joseph De Veuster), the self-sacrificing priest who lived and died among sufferers of leprosy (now called Hansen's disease) at Kalaupapa, Molokai in the 1870s–80s. This blockish statue, created by Venezuelan sculptor Marisol Escobar, is a duplicate of one that stands in Statuary Hall at the US Capitol building in Washington, DC. Unveiled in 1969, the statue ignited controversy because the bold and tragic likeness was based on a photograph taken of the priest shortly before he died in 1888; a sufferer of the disease, his formerly handsome features were grossly disfigured. Controversy regarding the statue has subsided, but Escobar's Damien remains a powerful artistic statement, and a telling memorial.

The official residence of Hawaii's governor is a white Greek Revival mansion on Beretania Street, **Washington Place**  (320 Beretania Street; tel: 536-8040; www.washingtonplacefoundation. org; tours by appointment only; free). It was built in 1846 for American sea captain John Dominis. His daughter-in-law, Lydia Kamakaeha, lived here between her marriage in 1862 and her accession to the throne as Queen Lili'uokalani in 1891, and returned just two years later following the overthrow of the Hawaiian monarchy. Washington Place remained a center of courtly social proceedings until Lili'uokalani's death in 1917, at the age of 79, and the deposed queen regularly sang her own compositions for visitors at the massive *koa* grand piano in her Music Room. The current governor, Neil Abercrombie, lives in a separate new building in the grounds.

Peek in next door at **St Andrew's Cathedral**  , (www.cathedralhawaii.org), a Gothic Revival structure built at a snail's pace between 1867 and 1958 of imported English sandstone. Another block 'Ewa (west) up Beretania Street is the **Cathedral of Our Lady of Peace** (www.cathedralofourladyofpeace.com),

In the central courtyard at the Honolulu Museum of Art.

Impressionist and Post-Impressionist gallery at the Honolulu Museum of Art.

○ Fact

Just *mauka* (toward the mountains) of Nimitz and 'Ewa (west) of Chinatown is an area called Iwilei (pronounced ee-vee-lay), formerly the locale of the Dole Pineapple Cannery. Hawaii's once prosperous pineapple industry is in decline, however, and the operation shut down in the early 1990s. Attempts to keep the site going as a tourist attraction soon fizzled out.

built by Roman Catholic missionaries from France. This coral building at the top of the Fort Street Mall was dedicated in 1843. Father Damien was ordained here in 1864.

The historic Richards Street YMCA building, immediately west of 'Iolani Palace across Richards Street, now houses the **Hawaii State Art Museum** ⑪ (250 Hotel Street; tel: 586-0300; www.hisam.hawaii.gov; Mon–Sat 10am–4pm; free). This highlights the state's impressive collection of art, purchased over a 25-year period as part of the Art in Public Places program. Exhibits are loosely divided between large-scale landscapes and natural-history displays in the eastern wing, and quirkier multi-media works in the western wing.

HONOLULU MUSEUM OF ART

Down Beretania Street from Washington Place and the Capitol, towards Diamond Head, is the superb **Honolulu Museum of Art** ⑫ (900 Beretania Street; tel: 532-8700; www.

honolulumuseum.org; Thu & Sun 10am–6pm, Fri & Sat 10am–9pm). Housed in a magnificent Japanese-influenced former private home, built in 1927, the academy holds galleries of Asian and Western art, plus inner courtyards rich in flora and sculpture. There are works by Modigliani, Picasso, Gauguin, Van Gogh, Monet, and Rodin, and some fascinating displays on how Hawaii has been depicted, and imagined, by the rest of the world. The true highlight of the museum, however, is one of the finest Oriental collections in America, including a wonderful range of artifacts from ancient China, statues and religious carvings from throughout Southeast Asia, and the writer James Michener's collection of Japanese woodblock prints.

BIG BUSINESS AND WEALTHY FAMILIES

Anchoring Downtown is **Bishop Square** ⑬, a refreshing plaza with bubbling fountains at the intersection of Bishop and King streets. Named after Charles Reed Bishop, who established both the

Dim sum in Chinatown.

Bishop Estate and the Bishop Museum, **Bishop Street** contains the graciously porticoed suites of the "Big Five" *kama'aina* corporations – conglomerates built on sugar in the 19th century by business and missionary families.

Today, a bronze statue of the royalist Robert Wilcox shares their turf. Every Friday is Aloha Friday, when nearly every man on the street – Big Five type, banker, or otherwise – wears an aloha shirt. A necktie on Friday is truly an odd sight, as is a sports coat or sweater.

Be sure to check a special events listing before heading downtown. You just might be able to catch a show at the historic **Hawaii Theatre** ⑭ (1130 Bethel Street; tel: 528-0506; www. hawaiitheatre.com), located at the corner of Bethel and Pauahi streets, two blocks *'Ewa* (west) of Bishop Street. The 1,400-seat theater, which opened in 1922 and closed in 1984, was reopened in 1996, restored to its original glory: gold metallic leaf adorns the columns and grillwork moldings inside the theater; the lobby has new marble floors and counters. Lionel Walden's *Glorification of the Drama*, a stunning mural that presides over the proscenium arch, has been fully restored. Today, the theater showcases a wide range of musical and theatrical acts.

CHINATOWN AND HOTEL STREET

Historic buildings vie with rising glass towers throughout Honolulu. Perhaps the most interesting of the historic structures outside of the capitol district are in an area near the harbor. This brick-built neighborhood is a pleasant four-block stroll from the Federal Post Office Building, down Merchant Street, Honolulu's old "Financial Boulevard." Many of the old structures in this area escaped the demolition ball: some have been carefully restored, while others add a somewhat seedy edge to parts of Chinatown.

Between Bethel Street and Nu'uanu Avenue, two immense stone lions flank **Hotel Street** to announce **Chinatown**, an area bounded by the harbor waterfront, Nu'uanu Avenue, and Beretania and River streets. In the late 1860s,

Chinatown market.

Aloha Tower.

Chinese plantation workers, after paying off their indentured labor contracts, gathered here and established new lives.

Chinatown comes into its own in a medley of Asian markets, noodle factories, shops, and art and antique galleries. Side streets cutting across Hotel Street and extending from King Street to Beretania Street tempt the curious. The **Maunakea Marketplace** ⑮ (1120 Maunakea Street; daily 5.30am–4pm) is a modern, open plaza nestled amid the old – look for the clock tower with Chinese numbers. Down on King Street, toward the waterfront, the **Oahu Market** ⑯ is an early-morning hubbub of mongering and bargaining.

Hotel Street ends at River Street, which parallels the lower **Nu'uanu Stream** descending from the Ko'olau Mountains. On the *mauka* (mountain) side of Chinatown, on Vineyard Boulevard, is the **Kuan Yin Temple** ⑰, where Buddhist and Daoist images gleam and a 10ft (3-meter) statue of Kuan Yin, the Buddhist goddess of mercy, dominates the cityscape.

A quiet respite can be found beneath hardy tropical trees in the spacious **Foster Botanical Gardens** (tel: 522-7066; daily 9am–4pm) on Vineyard Boulevard, just beyond the Kuan Yin Temple. Several plants, such as the fragrant and ever-blossoming cannonball tree, are the only specimen of their genus and species in Hawaii.

ALONG THE HARBOR

Toward the waterfront, Fort Street Mall empties into **Ala Moana Boulevard**, an oceanside artery that starts as Nimitz Highway near the Honolulu International Airport and turns into Ala Moana (Ocean Street) when it reaches Downtown. Near here stood the old "fort" – Ke Ku Nohu, c.1816 to 1857 – that gave Fort Street its name. Cross Ala Moana and hop on the elevator to the top of the **Aloha Tower** ⑱ (observation deck daily 9am–5pm; www.alohatower. com; free) for views that span Downtown, with Waikiki to the east and the Wai'anae Mountains to the west. This pleasing 1925 structure is only 10 stories high – or 184ft (56 meters) – but it

⊘ "BOAT DAYS"

As recently as the 1950s, Aloha Tower smiled down upon Hawaii's famous "Boat Days," when luxury Matson liners would arrive and depart at piers 10 and 11 in a flurry of flowers and *hapa-haole hula*. On and off the ships would go huge steamer trunks and travelers in white linen suits and ribboned hats. At pier side, local boys would dive for coins tossed into the water. Something of that spirit has returned as increasing numbers of cruise ships make Honolulu port-calls, with Boat Day arrivals reinstituted in the process. The half-hour long mix of hula, music, confetti launches and waterboat displays provides a festive atmosphere, with Aloha Tower as the centerpiece of an open-air shopping, restaurant, and entertainment complex (www.alohatower.com). For the Boat Day schedule, call 528-5700.

was once the tallest building in Hawaii. It is now dwarfed by the skyscrapers of downtown Honolulu.

TOWARD 'EWA

From Aloha Tower, heading *'Ewa* (west) along the Nimitz Highway leads towards the airport and *'Ewa*, while traveling *Diamond Head* on Ala Moana Boulevard leads to Waikiki. Nimitz Highway is an unattractive gateway to Waikiki, a mess of traffic amid light industry and warehouses – an unfortunate introduction to Oahu's beauty, partly revealed on the crowded H-1 Freeway that also links the airport to Waikiki.

TOWARD WAIKIKI AND DIAMOND HEAD

Along Ala Moana Boulevard, past the **Prince Kuhio Kalaniana'ole Federal Building**, the harbor and ocean disappear behind walls and buildings, including Restaurant Row, where a theater complex plays art films not offered elsewhere in Hawaii.

A mile or so farther on there's **Kewalo Basin ⑲**, where Honolulu's fishing fleet returns with the day's catch, and which serves as a departure point for coastal cruises and sport fishing excursions. Opposite Kewalo Basin and on the other side of Ala Moana Boulevard, is **Ward Village Center**, a popular shopping mall , with restaurants and movie theaters.

On the *makai* (ocean) side, just past Kewalo Basin, begins the **Ala Moana Beach Park ⑳**, 100 acres (40 hectares) of open space and beaches with good swimming and decent surfing beyond the reef. The adjacent artificial peninsula, known locally as **Magic Island ㉑**, or **Aina Moana State Recreation Area**, is popular with joggers, cyclists, skaters, and walkers. Created by infilling a coral reef, this spot was originally intended as the site for a collection of new luxury hotels, but they were never built, and instead it holds a peaceful little sand-fringed lagoon.

Directly *mauka* (towards the mountains) from Ala Moana Beach Park you come to the **Ala Moana Shopping Center ㉒** (www.alamoanacenter.com), the world's largest open-air shopping mall, crammed with more than 350 stores, eateries, and services. The huge modern development is four stories tall, and holds a roster of top-name luxury retailers that includes the likes of Chanel, Dolce&Gabbana, Prada, and Valentino.

On the extreme Diamond Head end of Ala Moana Beach Park, a bridge rises over the **Ala Wai Canal** and leads into Waikiki. The Ala Wai is a favorite training area for outrigger canoe paddlers. On the west side of the canal rises the Modernist Hawaii Convention Centre; to the east looms the first of Waikiki's highrises.

Oceanside, there are dozens of spindly sailing craft at the **Ala Wai Yacht Harbor** (http://alawaiharbor.com) and yacht basin, towered over by the Prince Waikiki Resort (www.princeresortshawaii.com) and Renaissance Ilikai (www.ilikaihotel.com) hotel.

◉ DISCOVERING HONOLULU HARBOR

European explorers didn't find Honolulu Harbor for more than 14 years after Captain Cook's arrival in 1778. But in late 1792 or early 1793, Captain William Brown, then busy in both the Pacific Northwest–China fur trade and a new Hawaiian gun trade, accidentally came across a nameless inlet. He described it in his logbook as "a small but commodious basin with regular soundings from 7 to 3 fathoms clear and good bottom, where a few vessels may ride with the greatest safety." Brown named it Fair Haven, which in an unusual reversal was translated into Hawaiian to become "Honolulu."

While Oahu's chiefs had always preferred Waikiki, with the arrival of sailing vessels and a new concept called money, other *akamai* (smart) Hawaiians, including Kamehameha, began moving to Honolulu's harbor. In Kamehameha's hands, Honolulu became the most important stopover point in the mid-Pacific ocean, with hundreds of ships making use of the harbor every year. Although Kamehameha returned to Hawaii Island around 1812, he closely monitored commerce at Honolulu until his death in 1819, as did his sons, Kamehameha II and Kamehameha III. Later, during the whaling era, the Kamehamehas moved Hawaii's capital to the booming town of Lahaina, on Maui. Eventually the Hawaiian elite recognized that the future would play out in Honolulu, and in 1845, Kamehameha III returned to Honolulu where he declared it the capital of the Hawaiian Kingdom in 1850.

Waikiki Beach with Diamond Head in the background, Honolulu.

WAIKIKI

Crystal-clear water, fine white sand, and a host of luxurious hotels nearby; to many, Waikiki Beach might just be the best beach on Earth.

At 500 acres (200 hectares) in size, Waikiki covers less than 1 percent of Oahu's land area, yet it pumps more than $5 billion into Hawaii's economy annually, representing about 42 percent of the state's total tourism dollars. It provides about 40,000 jobs tending to Oahu's almost 500,000 monthly visitors, while somehow finding the room to house its 25,000 residents. In 2020, the coronavirus crisis, however, sparked a serious decline in tourism and the annual number of visitors fell dramatically. The following year, though, Hawaii's tourism industry thankfully appeared to pick up again.

World-famous **Waikiki Beach**, actually a series of connecting beaches – Sans Souci, Queen's Surf, Kuhio, Waikiki, DeRussy, and Duke Kahanamoku – extends for more than a mile in a crescent of sand. The city has spent millions upgrading the Waikiki beachfront promenade, adding landscaped gardens, statues, historic story boards, and tourist facilities. Additional upgrades to Kapi'olani Park, Fort DeRussy, and along the Ala Wai Canal have greatly enhanced Waikiki's appeal, with extensive redevelopment to the heart of Waikiki, along Lewers Street, and Kalakaua and Kuhio avenues. The central showpieces of all this revitalization are the Beach Walk development on Lewers Street and the Trump International Hotel Waikiki (www.trumphotels.com/waikiki).

Early Hawaiians named this 1.5-mile (2.5km) -long coastal strip *Waikiki*, or spouting water, because its inland section was a wetland nurtured by mountain streams and springs. As early as the 1400s, Hawaiians capitalized on this water with a sophisticated irrigation system that fed aquaculture ponds and taro fields.

Until the 1920s, when completion of the Ala Wai Canal diverted water from the swamps and created dry land for future hotels, Waikiki's somewhat smelly interior was still a boggy place of fish ponds, taro patches, and

Main attractions

Waikiki Beach
Royal Hawaiian Hotel
US Army Museum
Kapi'olani Park
Honolulu Zoo

Map on page 130

Waikiki.

"If anyone desires such old-fashioned things as lovely scenery, quiet, pure air, clear sea water, good food, and heavenly sunsets hung out before his eyes...I recommend him cordially to the Sans Souci," wrote author Robert Louis Stevenson, pictured above in Honolulu.

Looking northwest along the beach at night.

rice paddies populated by quacking waterfowl and other damp creatures. The area's beaches, coconut groves, and fish-rich reefs, however, have long made this area a favorite spot among *ali'i*, or the Hawaiian royalty. All Hawaii's royals had homes here, as did the island's ruling chiefs before them.

TRANSPORT LINKS AND TOURISTS

In the 1860s, a dirt road was built to link Waikiki's cool surf with hot and dusty Honolulu. Two decades later, a mule-drawn omnibus began making daily round trips to Waikiki; by 1888, a regular tram service was initiated, which was motorized in 1895. Most visitors stayed with friends or in one of downtown Honolulu's hostelries – notably the long-gone Hawaiian Hotel – until the 1880s and early 1890s, when a few Waikiki homes and cottages were converted into guest houses.

In 1884, Allen Herbert opened one such guest house near Diamond Head and named it **Sans Souci** (in French this means "without a care"), and later hosted

the noted Scottish author Robert Louis Stevenson. To this day, the "heavenly sunsets" that Stevenson loved take place off Sans Souci Beach, where the New Otani Kaimana Beach Hotel (www.kaimana.com) has replaced Stevenson's bungalow.

REMINDERS OF THE PAST

Once home to Oahu's chiefs, today's Waikiki offers intriguing hints of its past. Take, for example, the **Stones of Kapaemahu Ⓐ**, four imposing boulders at Kuhio Beach adjacent to the Honolulu Police substation. Approach the stones with respect, because, according to Hawaiian oral traditions, they possess the *mana*, or spiritual powers, of four *kahuna* – priests or wizards – who were renowned throughout Polynesia for their wisdom and healing abilities. These four wizards – Kapaemahu, Kahaloa, Kapuni, and Kinohi – came to Oahu from Tahiti in the 16th century, then left. A metal plaque notes that "before vanishing, the wizards transferred their powers to these stones."

Close by is the bronze **Statue of Duke Kahanamoku Ⓑ**. The statue includes a bronze surfboard representing Duke's

Ⓞ NEVER-ENDING SANDPIT

It's no secret that Honolulu's Waikiki Beach is one of the most heralded beaches in the world. But with constant use, rising sea levels, and the consistent battering from seasonal storms, fighting erosion has proven to be a challenging task. In response to the situation, the state government in 2012 allocated $2.5 million to pump sand from offshore to fill in the beach. In just a year, the controversial project added a 37ft (11-meter) band of sand to a small stretch of beach from Kuhio Beach north to the Royal Hawaiian hotel. Sand replacement will be needed every few years, something experts consider "mission critical." After all, without the beach itself, what would Waikiki really be? What's more, portions of the seawall tracing Halekulani waterfront are crumbling away due to erosion. Sections, awash with sand and seawater, are closed to the public.

classic 24ft (7.5-meter) -long *koa* board. Short boards are the norm today, but some of the old long boards still in use can be found nearby in storage racks wedged between the Moana Hotel and the Honolulu Police substation. Duke Kahanamoku was a swimming world-record holder in three Olympics. He also brought surfing into the modern age, introducing Hawaii to the rest of the world. Beach boys here still paddle oversized surfboards out to surf spots like Queens, Populars, or Canoes.

A block beyond Duke is a statue of Prince Kuhio, royal champion of Hawaiian rights in the US Congress for 20 years after annexation. A statue of King Kalakaua graces Gateway Park, at the *'Ewa* (west) end of Waikiki. A statue of his niece, Princess Kaiulani, is located on the street that bears her name, while statues of Mahatma Gandhi and Queen Kapi'olani are to be found in Kapi'olani Park.

The section of beach fronting the statue of Prince Kuhio is known as Kuhio Beach. Almost entirely enclosed by stone breakwaters, the inshore waters here offer Waikiki's safest swimming, and are therefore good for families. On Tuesday, Thursday and Saturday evenings at dusk at the beachside hula stand at Kuhio Beach, the lighting of torches begins an hour of music and dance. On select evenings, movies are shown beachside at the Kalakaua entrance to Kapi'olani Park.

THE FIRST LUXURY HOTEL

Since the mid-1950s, hotels in Waikiki have risen in escalating waves of concrete and steel, a Great Wall of Waikiki. At last count, there were more than 30,000 hotel rooms in Waikiki. However, for most of the 20th century, three Waikiki hotels anchored the beach, luxurious locales that are still regarded with respect by *kama'aina* (long-time residents) who knew them way back when.

The **Moana Surfrider, A Westin Resort & Spa** © (www.marriott.com),

on the beach along Kalakaua Avenue near the Duke Kahanamoku statue, is the *tutu-kane*, or granddaddy, of them all. At its center is Hawaii's first luxury hotel, the **Moana**, which is what it is commonly called even today.

Opened in 1901 and geared to steamer-set tourists, it offered 75 rooms, Hawaii's first electric elevator, and a 300ft (90-meter) wooden pier with a bandstand at its far end; unfortunately, the pier was dismantled in 1930.

In 1918, two wings were added, forming the **Banyan Courtyard**, which is still popular today for its ambiance and nightly music beneath a majestic banyan tree planted in 1885. It now stands at 75ft (23 meters) high. Another extension was added in 1952, and in 1969 the **Surfrider Tower** was built.

From 1935 to 1972, the Moana's Banyan Courtyard was known internationally as the favorite home of *Hawaii Calls*, a Hawaiian music program hosted by Webley Edwards (1902–77), who had previously been a World War II news correspondent, and the first to announce the attack on Pearl Harbor

⊙ Tip

If you are renting a car, be aware that Honolulu's roads can be a little confusing. Entrances and exits for the H-1 freeway defy logic – they often don't come in pairs – and the routes into Waikiki are very convoluted and fussy.

Statue of Duke Kahanamoku, often referred to as the father of modern surfing, in Waikiki.

on air. *Hawaii Calls* was once regarded as the most widely listened-to radio show on earth. Some 1,900 shows, broadcast by as many as 600 different radio stations around the world, were broadcast live from Hawaii.

Today, the Westin Resort & Spa comes under the Marriott umbrella, with a luxurious spa, clutch of restaurants and bars, and oceanside pool (though some of the newer, uninspired rooms feel as though they could be in any Westin). Its wine and piano bar, Vintage 1901, located in the historic wing of the hotel, has become one of the swankiest spots in all of Honolulu.

THE ROYAL HAWAIIAN

When the Matson Navigation and Territorial Hotel companies unveiled the $4-million, shocking pink **Royal Hawaiian Hotel** ❶ (www.royal-hawaiian.com) in 1927, Honolulu's *kama'aina* elite shifted their focus from the Moana to this Moorish-Spanish-style structure just down the beach. Social Honolulu and San Francisco were positively atwitter as the Royal Hawaiian's completion date

neared. An advance *Honolulu Advertiser* story promised that the Royal's opening would be "one of the greatest social events in the history of Hawaii...." And indeed it was; 1,200 guests turned out to witness a "semi-barbaric pageant" produced by Princess Abigail Kawananakoa, the hotel's first official guest and wife of the late Prince David Kawananakoa. From the Royal's pink balcony, the princess hand-directed the movement of a fleet of 15 outrigger canoes and dozens of Hawaiians in warrior regalia, a re-staging of the 1795 landing at Waikiki by Kamehameha.

During the next 15 years, the six-story, 400-room Royal Hawaiian became the place in Hawaii where the Hollywood likes of Mary Pickford, Douglas Fairbanks, Al Jolson, and Ruby Keeler joined various Duponts, Rockefellers, Fords, presidents, and royalty over green turtle soup Kamehameha, and medallions of sweet breads Wilhelmina, in the tapestry-filled Persian Room.

With bush-jacketed bellhops tending to guests' needs, the Royal cruised

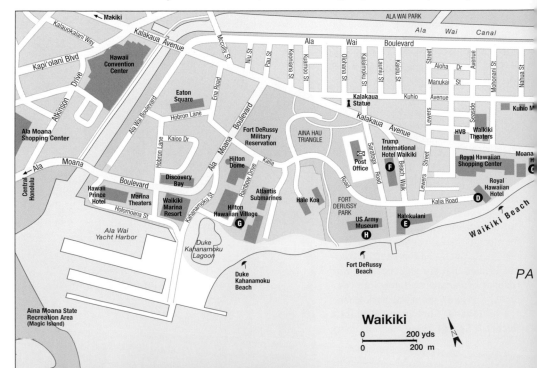

Waikiki

0   200 yds
0   200 m

through the Great Depression. But in 1941, World War II hit Pearl Harbor, and barbed wire was rolled across the sands of Waikiki. So the Royal mothballed its tapestries and was leased to the US Navy until 1945. Postwar, the Royal prospered once again and in 1959 was purchased by Sheraton, which, in 1975, sold it to the Japanese conglomerate, Kyoya. Today, however, it is another Marriott big-hitter, this time coming under the Luxury Collection Resort branch of the behemoth's portfolio.

THE HOUSE BEFITTING HEAVEN

The **Halekulani** ❻ (www.halekulani. com), 'Ewa (west) along the beach, was another pioneering hotel in Waikiki, where in the early 1900s, American author Jack London drank hard, chain-smoked, and spun stories on his typewriter. It was here, too, that writer Earl Derr Biggers created the fictional detective Charlie Chan. The Halekulani's bar, The House Without A Key, takes its name from the title of the first Charlie Chan novel, published in 1925. Opened in 1907 as the Hau Inn, the original five bungalows of the Halekulani ("The House Befitting Heaven") were eventually replaced with 453 modern but exquisite rooms (some of Waikiki's finest) in wings terraced back from the beach. Today, the five-star hotel's peaceful vibe, Italian-glass tiled pool, and award-winning dining offer unrivalled luxury. A quartet and hula dancer perform nightly under the beachside banyan tree. With one of Waikiki's superlative trademark sunsets as a backdrop, and no cover charge for a stage-front table, it's the perfect way to round off a day in paradise.

MORE STAYS IN PARADISE

The newest luxury kid on the block along Waikiki is the **Trump International Hotel Waikiki** ❻ (www.trumphotels.com/waikiki), a 2009 condo-hotel 'Ewa (west) along the beach from Halekulani and kitty-corner from the US Army Museum. When the 462 units went on sale in 2006, they sold out in one day for a total of $700 million. Real

The Royal Hawaiian Hotel.

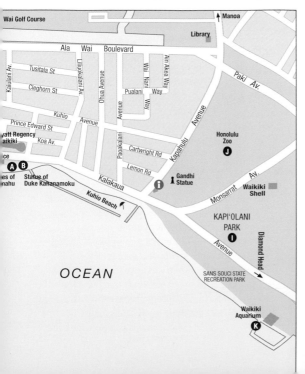

DUKE KAHANAMOKU

One of Hawaii's great names, the legendary Duke Kahanamoku managed to literally swim his way into the history books.

In his lifetime, he was an Olympic champion, a Hollywood celebrity, a local sheriff, and one of Hawaii's pre-eminent ambassadors of goodwill. Duke Kahanamoku's most enduring legacy, however, lives on through thousands of surfers in Hawaii and all around the world. Through it all, Kahanamoku was first and foremost a beach boy. He helped popularize surfing in places like California, Australia, and New Zealand. Kings and queens once governed Hawaii's lands, but it was a Duke who ruled its ocean waves.

A full-blooded Hawaiian, Duke Paoa Kahanamoku was born in Honolulu in August 1890. The Kahanamoku family moved to Waikiki three years later, and the young Duke was never far from the beach he would help make famous. In 1911, in his first timed swims, he broke three free-style world records at Honolulu Harbor. Kahanamoku, in fact,

Duke surfing at Waikiki Beach in 1929.

shattered the 100-meter record by 4.6 seconds. When word was sent to Amateur Athletic Union (AAU) officials in New York, they replied sternly, "Unacceptable. No one swims this fast!"

A year later, at the Summer Olympics in Stockholm, Kahanamoku made believers the world over by capturing the gold medal in the 100-meter free-style, and a silver medal as part of the American 200-meter free-style relay team. The handsome Olympic star became an international celebrity. In the 1920 and 1924 Olympics, Kahanamoku again came home a medalist.

LIFE AFTER GOLD

In the 1920s, Kahanamoku tried his hand at acting. In all, he appeared in nearly 30 movies, sharing the screen with Hollywood giants like Dorothy Lamour, Ronald Coleman, and another Duke, John Wayne.

Kahanamoku's most impressive performance, however, came in 1925, when he used his longboard to rescue eight drowning men off Newport Beach, in California. The local police chief called his act of heroism "the most superhuman rescue act and the finest display of surfboard riding that has ever been seen in the world."

After returning to Oahu, he married Nadine Alexander in 1940 (who died in 1997 at the age of 92). Kahanamoku was elected Honolulu's sheriff and was re-elected 12 times, finally giving up his office in 1960 when the position was abolished.

In January 1968, Kahanamoku suffered a heart attack in the parking lot of the Waikiki Yacht Club and died at the age of 77. An estimated 10,000 people attended his funeral at Waikiki Beach. From outrigger canoes, family and friends scattered his ashes in the waters off Waikiki Beach. Reported the *Honolulu Star-Bulletin*: "There is a strange sound in the booming surf in Waikiki today, like the anguished cry of a mother at the loss of her favorite son."

In 1990, on the centennial anniversary of his birth, an imposing bronze statue of Kahanamoku, sculpted by local artist Jan Fisher, was unveiled at Waikiki Beach. Some beach boys lament the fact that the statue is facing *mauka* (the mountains) instead of the ocean. Perhaps only the Duke could safely ignore the rule of the surf never to stand with one's back to the ocean.

estate experts say it was the fastest real estate sale in history.

At the far western end of the Waikiki Beach Waterfront, golden Kahanamoku Beach, once the home of the eponymous legendary surfer's family, is now dominated by the mighty towers of the **Hilton Hawaiian Village** G (www.hiltonhawaiian-village.com). At the landscaped Ala Moana gateway you won't be able to miss the larger-than-life depictions of hula dancers. Take the time to wander through the Village's landscaped grounds, enjoying the collection of rare birds and the king's ransom of giant *koi* (Japanese carp). Beachside, look up at the 30-story rainbow murals (the largest in the world) that make the Rainbow Tower a Waikiki landmark. On Friday nights there's an hour-long show of music and dance and a grand fireworks finale.

Near the Hilton Hawaiian Village, at 252 Paoa Pl, is a base of operations for **Atlantis Submarines** (tel: 800-973-9800/381-0237; www.atlantisadventures.com/waikiki), which offers fabulous underwater excursions to submerged shipwrecks a mile or so offshore.

US ARMY MUSEUM

A short walk east of the Hilton, the oceanfront **US Army Museum** H (Fort DeRussy on Kalia Road; tel: 438-2825; www.hiarmymuseumsoc.org; Tue–Sat 10am–5pm; free) displays an array of interesting warfare artifacts including weapons of ancient Hawaii, the American Revolution, Spanish–American War, World Wars I and II, and the Korean and Vietnam wars.

Even for the pacifist, this is an interesting and underrated museum, located inside Battery Randolph, a massive bunker built in 1911 with walls on its seaward side made of 22ft (7-meter) -thick concrete. When the military tried to demolish the foothall-field-size bunker in the late 1960s, they couldn't do it – hence the museum.

The battery had two disappearing 14in (35cm) shore guns, cut up in the late 1940s, capable of firing a 1,600lb (726kg) shell 14 miles (22km) out to sea. Today, the museum has an extensive archive that boasts information about every military unit that has served in Hawaii since 1898.

Waikiki Beach and Diamond Head. The latter's distinctive uplifting shape came from the steady trade winds 150,000 years ago that piled erupting ash higher on the ocean, or leeward, side of the tuff cone.

Moana Surfrider Hotel.

The Aquarium in Kapi'olani Park.

Learning to surf.

KAPI'OLANI PARK

Kapi'olani Park , a complex of beaches, grassy picnic and play areas, amphitheaters, jogging courses, gardens, a zoo, and aquarium, at the eastern end of Waikiki, was dedicated on June 1, 1877, Kamehameha Day, as Hawaii's first public park. Opening day was celebrated with a slate of high-stakes horse races held on a new track laid out just below Diamond Head. (The park's Kamehameha Day races in the early years of the 20th century were outlawed by temperance and anti-gambling forces.) King Kalakaua named the park after his wife.

Today Kapi'olani Park remains one of Oahu's favorite recreational areas, and whether you're seeking tennis, soccer, kite-flying, surfing, or long tranquil walks under monkeypod and ironwood trees, you'll find it here.

Kapi'olani Park is also the finishing point for one of the running world's biggest and best-known marathons. The Honolulu Marathon (www.honolulu-marathon.org) takes place each December and draws competitors from around the world. The race, which was first run here in 1972, draws more than 33,000 runners annually, many of them from north Asia, and particularly Japan, where marathon-running has become extremely popular.

Across the street at **Queen's Surf Beach** – Lili'uokalani's beach house once stood here – beach boys gather for volleyball, and to listen to impromptu conga drum, guitar, and flute concerts held under a banyan tree, especially at sunset. The nearby **War Memorial Natatorium**, built to commemorate World War I veterans, was dedicated in 1927 as a world-class swimming facility. Although the pool, long in a state of disrepair, was approved for an $11-million restoration program in the 1990s, that plan drew substantial opposition from the community and sparked legal challenges. In 2019, talks resumed over plans to renovate the war memorial and reopen it as a saltwater pool, with estimations that repairs would cost $25.6 million. However, whether this idea ever gets off the ground is anyone's guess.

Also nearby is **Kaimana Beach**, a sandy beach that is popular among locals. The beach also was the endpoint of the first submarine communications cable between Hawaii and California. The first telegraphic message over that cable was sent on January 1, 1903, from Henry Ernest Cooper to President Theodore Roosevelt.

ZOO AND AQUARIUM

At the **Honolulu Zoo**  in Kapi'olani Park (tel: 971-7171; www.honoluluzoo. org; daily 10am–3pm), you can enjoy the typical antics of assorted primates, lions, elephants, giraffes, and hippos. The zoo is the only place in Hawaii where you can see a live snake: there are no wild snakes in Hawaii and strict control is maintained on their import to keep it that way.

Except for sea birds, virtually all the birds you will see nowadays in Hawaii are introduced species. Ironically, then, the zoo is probably the only place a visitor to Oahu – and most residents, as well – can see indigenous mountain birds, including the exquisite 'apapane (Hawaiian honeycreeper) at the Manyara Bird Sanctuary and the South American Aviary. It's also one of the few places that you are guaranteed to see a nene.

The Tropical Forest section here is filled with flowering plants, trees and gardens, and there is a Children's Zoo where youngsters can pet a llama or touch a monitor lizard. Over the past decade or so, the zoo has made significant improvements, including the opening of the expansive African Savanna exhibit.

Yet more exotic creatures can be found just a few minutes away at the small **Waikiki Aquarium ⓚ** (2777 Kalakaua Avenue; tel: 923-9741; www.waikikiaquarium.org; daily 9am–4.30pm), established in 1904. Affiliated with the University of Hawaii since 1919, the Waikiki Aquarium is the third-oldest aquarium in the United States.

Probably the rarest inhabitants here are the monk seals; along with the hoary bat, these creatures are the only two mammals known to have been native to Hawaii when the first Polynesian settlers arrived. There are also some fascinating exhibits on the nautilus and the spawning of the mahimahi, perhaps the most popular fish for eating in the Hawaiian Islands.

If you are more interested in local art than flora and fauna, there is plenty around if you know where to look. Not far from here, at the Waikiki branch of First Hawaiian Bank (2181 Kalakaua Avenue; www.fhb.com) you will find the huge fresco mural Early Contacts of Hawaii with Outer World, by Jean Charlot.

If you're still feeling energetic after all this activity, it's possible to continue walking around the front of Diamond Head and into Kahala. There are spectacular views from Diamond Head Road overlooking the ocean, and the beach at Diamond Head Beach Park is a nice spot for a picnic. The loop from Kuhio Beach Park is about 4.5 miles (7km), so be sure to take plenty of water.

> **⊙ Fact**
>
> In 1927, world swimming records were set at the Waikiki Natatorium, a Beaux-Arts public pool that was a World War I memorial, west of Kapi'olani Park, by Buster Crabbe and Johnny Weissmuller, the future Hollywood Tarzan.

Outrigger canoes mingle with beach parasols on Waikiki Beach.

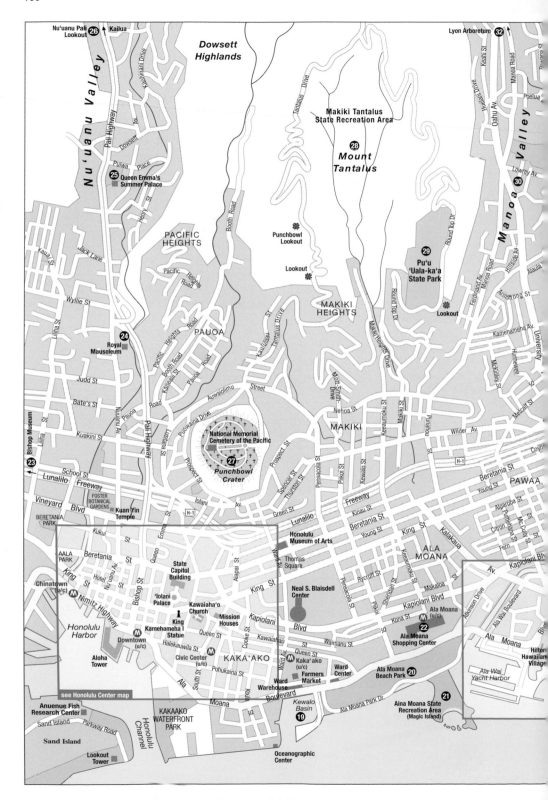

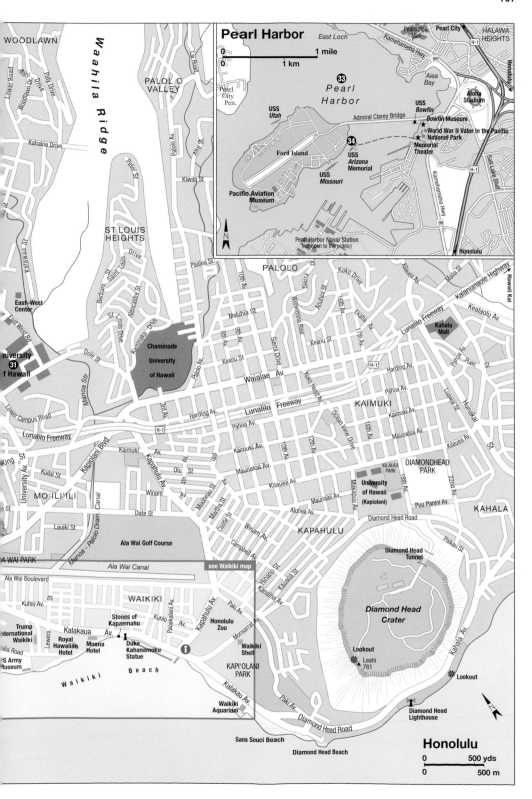

WOODLAWN

W a a h i l a R i d g e

PALOL O VALLEY

 St LOUIS HEIGHTS

Kahaloa Drive

Kaimuki Dr.

Lower Road

Lower Road

Woodlawn Dr.

Paki Drive

East West Rd

East-West Center

University of Hawaii

Dole St.

Lower Campus Road

Lunalilo Freeway

Manoa Str.

King St.

University Av.

Kuilai St.

MO'ILI'ILI

St.

Kapiolani Blvd

A WAI PARK

Ala Wai Boulevard

Kuhio Av.

Trump International Waikiki

US Army Museum

Kalakaua

Royal Hawaiian Hotel

Moana Hotel

Stones of Kapaemuhu

Duke Kahanamoku Statue

W a i k i k i   B e a c h

Lauiki St.

Date St.

Winam

Kapiolani Ave.

WAIKIKI

Kuhio Av.

Paoakalani Av.

Kapahulu Av.

Paki Av.

KAPI'OLANI PARK

Waikiki Aquarium

Sans Souci Beach

Diamond Head Beach

Ala Wai Golf Course

Ala Wai Canal

Manoa - Palolo Drain Canal

see Waikiki map

Stones of Kapaemahu

Honolulu Zoo

Waikiki Shell

Monsarrat Av.

Kalakau Av.

Kapahulu Av.

Kanaina Av.

Kauloa St.

Hinano St.

Paki Av.

Campbell Av.

Winam Av.

Castle St.

Makua St.

Maluhia St.

8th Av.

9th Av.

Keanu St.

Palolo Av.

Ahe St.

Kiwila St.

Peter St.

10th Av.

Sierra Drive

Sierra

Wilhelmina Rise

Anuhea St.

Koko Head Av.

Koko Drive

16th Av.

17th Av.

Ekaha Av.

Harding Av.

Pahoa Av.

Keanu St.

Waialae Av.

Lunalilo Freeway

Harding Av.

Kaimuki Av.

Maunaloa Av.

Kilauea Av.

Maunalei Av.

Alohea Av.

KAIMUKI

KAPAHULU

Ocean View Drive

12th Av.

10th Av.

9th Av.

4th Av.

3rd Av.

Olu St.

Winam Av.

Kamailkai Av.

Kilauea Av.

DIAMONDHEAD PARK

KILAUEA PARK

University of Hawaii (Kapiolani)

Puu Panini Av.

Makapuu Av.

8th Av.

22nd Av.

KAHALA

Diamond Head Road

Diamond Head Tunnel

Diamond Head Crater

Lookout

Leahi 761

Lookout

Diamond Head Lighthouse

Paikau St.

Kahala Av.

Kalanianaole Highway

Kealaolu Av.

Pahoa

Pueo

Iliwai St.

Hunakai

St.

Kilauea Av.

Kahala Mall

Hawaii Kai

Lunalilo Freeway

PALOLO

Paalea St.

Kiekie Av.

Malia Av.

Chaminade University of Hawaii

PALOLO

Pearl Harbor

0 ————————— 1 mile
0 ————————— 1 km

East Loch

Pearl Harbor

Pearlridge Mall

Pearl City

HALAWA HEIGHTS

Kamehameha Hwy

Honolulu

H-1

99

Aiea Bay

Aloha Stadium

Salt Lake Blvd

Kamehameha Hwy

H-1

99

Pearl City Pen.

USS Utah

Ford Island

Pacific Aviation Museum

USS Missouri

USS Arizona Memorial

Admiral Clarey Bridge

USS Bowfin

Bowfin Museum

World War II Valor in the Pacific National Park

Memorial Theater

Pearl Harbor Naval Station (not open to the public)

Honolulu

33

34

N

Honolulu

0 ————————— 500 yds
0 ————————— 500 m

The WWII battleship
USS Missouri.

GREATER HONOLULU

Outside Waikiki, away from the hustle and bustle of Downtown, Honolulu features mind-bending history, pristine valleys, and much more besides.

What can loosely be called Greater Honolulu stretches for around 15 miles (24km) along Oahu's southern shoreline. Its single most attractive feature has to be its physical setting, squeezed between the ocean and the soaring Ko'olau Mountains. Although the sharp, green-velvet ridge of the *pali* (cliffs) is often just three miles from the beach, the mountains are repeatedly indented by lush valleys. Several such valleys cradle characterful city neighborhoods, like Kalihi, Nu'uanu, and Manoa. Two major roads cross the mountains close to Downtown, the Likelike and Pali highways, while a meandering 8-mile (13km) route along Tantalus and Round Top drives enables visitors to enjoy some superb rainforest scenery.

Of course the biggest draw to this area is Pearl Harbor – named for the pearl oysters once found here – a cemetery and historic site that pays homage to those who lost their lives during the Japanese attack of Oahu on December 7, 1941. Few military memorials in the world offer the type of perspective that this one does.

BISHOP MUSEUM

Greater Honolulu is also home to the world's greatest repository of Pacific and Polynesian artifacts: the **Bishop Museum ㉓** (1525 Bernice Street; tel:

847-3511; www.bishopmuseum.org; daily 9am–5pm). Anchoring the working-class neighborhood of Kalihi, around 2 miles (3km) northwest of Downtown, the museum tells a colorful story of the history of the Hawaiian Islands, with exhibits showing how the region became a state. It is considered one of America's most important multi-disciplinary museums, a Smithsonian Institution in microcosm.

The museum was established in 1889 by Charles Reed Bishop as a memorial to his wife Bernice, a

Main attractions
Bishop Museum
Soto Zen Mission of Hawaii
Nu'uanu Pali Lookout
Lyon Arboretum
Pearl Harbor

Maps on pages 112, 136

Bishop Museum.

Fact

The Bishop Museum also manages off-site attractions: a planetarium and astronomical observatory, the Falls of Clyde, and a four-masted sailing ship in Honolulu Harbor.

princess and the last of the Kamehameha family. Today, with the help of grants and a steady endowment, the facility maintains natural history collections of nearly 20 million animal and plant specimens. Among the highlights of its central building, the cavernous *koa*-paneled Hawaiian Hall (1903), are carved and feathered icons, capes, and many other remnants of pre-contact Hawaii; brilliant regalia from the time of Kamehameha the Great; the monarchical crowns, thrones, and court costumes used in 'Iolani Palace by King Kalakaua and his sister, Queen Lili'uokalani; and important pieces reflecting the experiences of Hawaii's many immigrant groups. The renovated Pacific Hall incorporates artifacts, photographs, and storytelling to take a broader look at island people from all over the Pacific.

Further galleries explore specific points in Hawaiian history, such as immigration, plantation-era island life, and the push for statehood. Across the lawns, a modern building, the Richard T. Mamiya Science Adventure Center,

Interior of Bishop Museum.

explains volcanology and Hawaiian natural history in an entertaining and kid-friendly way. Throughout the month, the museum hosts classes in a variety of aspects of Hawaiian culture, teaching visitors everything from hula to *lei*-making, basket-weaving, and more. It also has a small on-site café and the J. Watumull Planetarium, which offers a choice of shows mostly dedicated to Hawaii, notably one on the traditional Polynesian means of navigation that helped to find the way from Tahiti to Hawaii.

OAHU CEMETERY

Nearby is the old **Oahu Cemetery**, where many names of rich or famous *haole* residents can be seen on tombstones. One in particular merits the attention of serious American sports fans: the layered, pink granite tomb with the inscription, "Alexander Joy Cartwright Jr. Born in New York City April 17, 1820. Died in Honolulu July 12, 1892." This austere monument, located at the center of the cemetery, marks the remains of the man who

many believe to have invented modern baseball. After setting down the rules of the game – the first baseball contest played under Cartwright's rules took place in 1846 in Hoboken, New Jersey – Cartwright drifted west and eventually ended up in Hawaii. He founded Honolulu's first volunteer fire department and served as its fire chief from 1850 to 1859.

A few hundred yards/meters farther up Nu'uanu Avenue is the **Royal Mausoleum** ㉔ (2261 Nu'uanu Ave; Mon–Fri 8am–4.30pm; free), where the bodies of Kamehameha II, Kamehameha III, Kamehameha IV, Kamehameha V, Kalakaua, Queen Lili'uokalani, and other members or favored friends of those royal Hawaiian families are buried. The only two Hawaiian monarchs not buried here are King Lunalilo, who at his own request was buried in the grounds of Kawaiaha'o Church, and Kamehameha the Great, whose bones were hidden away in a secret burial place on Hawaii Island. The mausoleum, which lies on a 3-acre (1-hectare) site chosen by Kamehameha V, was prepared in 1865 to replace an overcrowded royal burial tomb on the grounds of 'Iolani Palace.

QUEEN EMMA'S SUMMER PALACE

Half a mile (1 km) up the Pali Highway from its intersection with Nu'uanu Avenue stands **Queen Emma's Summer Palace** ㉕ (2913 Pali Highway; tel: 595-3167; www.daughtersofhawaii.org; Mon–Sat 9am–4pm, Sun 10am–3pm, tours Mon–Sat free with admission). This royal bower with a ginger- and *ti*-lined driveway was built in the late 1840s and later sold to John Young II, an uncle of Queen Emma and son of Kamehameha the Great's chief *haole* adviser, the Englishman John Young. Queen Emma and Kamehameha IV in turn bought it from Young and named it Hanaiakamalama, "the foster child of the moon," after a favorite Hawaiian demi-goddess.

Until Emma's death in 1885, the royal family used this home as a summer retreat, salon, and courtly social center. In 1890, the summer palace was bought

Queen Emma's Summer Palace.

by the Hawaiian government. The Daughters of Hawaii organization, a non-profit founded by women who were daughters of American Protestant missionaries, has maintained it as a museum since 1915.

The palace's rooms have been restored with many of the royal family's belongings. Among the items are a spectacular triple-tiered *koa* sideboard of Gothic design presented to Emma and Kamehameha IV by Britain's Prince Albert, the husband and consort of Queen Victoria; a heavy gold necklace strung with tiger claws and pearls given to Emma by a visiting maharajah; and various opulent wedding and baby gifts, which were given to the royal family by Queen Victoria, who was godmother to Emma's son, the Hawaiian Prince Albert. Among the most fascinating Hawaiian pieces is a stand of feather *kahili* (royal standards) in the queen's master bedroom. Behind and around the corner from the palace, off Pu'iwa Road, is a lovely little retreat, Nu'uanu Valley Park, favored by lovers and daydreamers who like to lounge under its gigantic trees.

NU'UANU

Just a half-mile or so inland from Chinatown (along Nu'uanu Avenue), and a mile east of the Bishop Museum, near the foot of the Pali Highway, **Nu'uanu** is perhaps Honolulu's prettiest valley. Even the name is beautiful – Nu'uanu, meaning the "cool height." There was no doubt among early *haole* settlers that Nu'uanu was the best place to live. Nu'uanu was the first suburb in which they built their Victorian mansions with broad *lanai*, and where they planted the monkeypods, banyans, Norfolk Island pines, bamboo, eucalyptus, African tulips, and golden trees that now tower over the valley's indigenous ferns, hibiscus, *koa*, and ginger. Many of these estates are still occupied by wealthy missionary descendants, but most have been sold or leased to institutions, churches, or Asian consulates.

Before exploring the valley's lush rainforest, listen for the "oms" vibrating out of the beautiful **Soto Zen Mission of Hawaii** (1708 Nu'uanu Avenue), a duplicate of a major Buddhist *stupa* at Bodhgaya, India, where Gautama

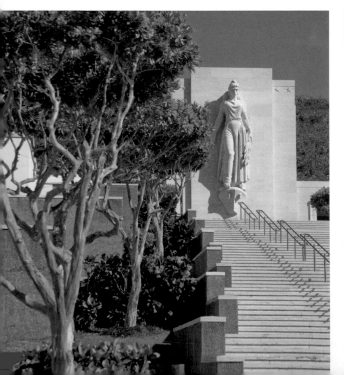

National Memorial Cemetery of the Pacific.

⊘ THE HAWAIIAN RAILWAY

In the heyday of the sugar cane industry, railroads were a popular way of transporting the product – and the people who harvested it – around each of the Hawaiian Islands. Today, however, the only railroad still operating on Oahu is the 'Ewa Train (www.hawaiianrailway.com), which departs from the Hawaiian Railway Society's headquarters in 'Ewa, just outside of Honolulu, and runs to Nanakuli, about seven miles (11km) away. The train runs every Saturday at 3pm and every Sunday with departures at 1pm and 3pm; each journey includes a historical narrative delivered by a volunteer. The Society also operates the only railroad museum in Hawaii; a small affair with artifacts and photographs from yesteryear. The on-site gift shop has a surprisingly large collection of Oahu Railway & Land Company branded merchandise.

Buddha gave his first sermon. This temple's towers would appear most at home on a Himalayan crag, but a few Japanese influences – gardens of tinkling water, sand, and bonsai – give its authenticity away. Built in 1952, the temple is somewhat similar to an even larger shrine, the nearby and hard-to-miss **Honpa Hongwanji Mission** (1727 Pali Highway; www.hongwanjihawaii.com), which was built in 1918 to commemorate the 700th anniversary of the creation of the Shin Buddhist sect.

Nu'uanu Pali Drive winds through the hanging vines, bamboo, wild ginger, jasmine, and cool air in two separate sections, east of the Pali Highway inland from Queen Emma's Palace. Along this wending path you'll spot stately mansions hidden away in the bushes, and, on rainy days, dozens of tiny waterfalls run wherever wrinkled Ko'olau ridges let them flow. **Waipuhia Valley Falls**, on the left side of Nu'uanu Valley just before you reach the Pali Lookout, is nicknamed "Upside Down Falls" because its waters are often blown straight back up a cliff and turn into mist before they can reach the precipice below. Waipuhia means "blown water."

The **Nu'uanu Pali Lookout** ㉖, just off the Pali Highway, is one of the most popular scenic attractions on Oahu, offering panoramic views of the *pali* (cliffs) and the Windward Coast. Gale-force winds rush up this Ko'olau palisade and literally stand one's hair on end. The view from the lookout is spectacular: sawtooth peaks rise like a great rampart, with lush flatlands facing a sea of all shades of blue.

Several spectacular trails start to the left of the lookout, including one atop an abandoned stretch of the old Pali Highway. From here, the Pali Highway continues down to the windward side and the bedroom communities of Kailua and Kane'ohe.

PUNCHBOWL CRATER AND THE NATIONAL MEMORIAL CEMETERY

Another iconic Honolulu experience includes two areas above town

View from Nu'uanu Pali Lookout.

between Nu'uanu and Manoa valleys, Punchbowl and Mount Tantalus. **Punchbowl Crater** , once a site of human sacrifices, was known to Hawaiians as Puowaina, or "the hill for placing [of sacrifices]." Like Diamond Head and Koko Head craters to the east, Punchbowl emerged during an eruption phase about 150,000 years ago. It was pushed upward by volcanic action through a vast coral plain that had built up around this side of the Ko'olau Mountains.

Today, Punchbowl is the site of the **National Memorial Cemetery of the Pacific,** (www.cem.va.gov/cems/nchp/nmcp. asp; daily 8am–6pm; free), where more than 40,000 war veterans and family members are buried. The small, flat, white headstones, set level with Punchbowl's expanse of grass, stretch across the crater's 112-acre (45-hectare) floor.

Perhaps the most famous person buried here was Ernest Taylor "Ernie" Pyle (1900–45), not a conventional war casualty but a journalist whose ability to write about the average foot-slogging GI during World War II made him one of the most widely read combat correspondents, and earned him the Pulitzer Prize in 1944. The following year, he was killed by Japanese gunfire on a small Pacific islet. Pyle's burial here was allowed because he had served in the US Navy during World War I. More than 60 years after his death, cemetery officials have estimated that as many as 50,000 people a month visit his grave.

TANTALUS

From Punchbowl's mountain-side entrance, Puowaina Drive crosses a bridge over Prospect Street and drifts along a steep valley through Papakolea, one of Oahu's few Hawaiian homestead communities. At the top of Puowaina Drive, turn right onto Tantalus Drive, a winding mountain road that twists and turns through some of Oahu's largest *kama'aina* estates. **Mount Tantalus** has some of the coolest and most panoramic vantage points on this side of the island. You can hike one of the marked trails near the mountain's 2,013ft (610-meter) peak into groves of bamboo and fern. At the top, Tantalus Drive connects with Round Top Drive, which descends down the ocean side to Makiki and Punahou.

There are at least a dozen knockout viewpoints on Tantalus, but locals agree that the best one, a panorama extending from Diamond Head to Pearl Harbor and the Wai'anae Mountains, is from **Pu'u 'Ualaka'a State Park** , (www.hawaiistateparks.org), on Tantalus's Diamond Head flank.

A few hairpin turns below this peak is a straight stretch of Round Top Drive beside a lava rock wall, with an unobstructed postcard view of Diamond Head, the University of Hawaii, and broad Manoa Valley.

MANOA

Manoa Valley , meaning "vast," has long been preferred by islanders as a

Bamboo trail around Mount Tantalus.

residential refuge from the heat and hassle of Honolulu's coastal flatlands. Indeed, residents of both Manoa and Nu'uanu consider their valleys the closest one can get to Eden – both are verdantly green and consistently wet – and still manage to be near shopping centers and bus routes.

At the mouth of this easy-going valley is the center of higher education in Hawaii, the large **University of Hawaii** ③ Manoa campus, attended by some 18,000 full-time students (www.hawaii. edu; tours Mon, Wed and Fri; www. hawaii.edu/campuscenter). This institute has the academic and post-adolescent aura typical of any university in the world, except that its student body, like Hawaii itself, is generally more diverse and casual – loud T-shirts, shorts and sandals – and more ethnically mixed than the typical US university campus. The university's sports teams are nicknamed the Rainbow Warriors.

At the **East–West Center** (www. eastwestcenter.org) – a federally funded institute on the university campus that promotes understanding in the Pacific

Basin – are a Thai pavilion personally presented and dedicated by King Bhumibol Adulyadej of Thailand in 1967; a Center for Korean Studies building hand-painted in the busy and intricate style of Seoul-area Yi dynasty palaces; and the center's main building, Jefferson Hall, which is fronted by large Chinese dog-faced lions and backed by a Japanese garden rich in sculptured grass, bonsai trees, and a lily pond full of nibbling koi carp.

ARBORETUM AND FALLS

Half a mile or so beyond Punahou School and beyond the university is the junction of Manoa and East Manoa roads. Branching left, Manoa Road leads to the back of the valley and the University of Hawaii's **Lyon Arboretum** ③ (3860 Manoa Road; tel: 988-0456; www.manoa.hawaii.edu/lyonarboretum; Mon–Fri 8am–4pm, Sat 9am–3pm; free), established in 1907. Nearly 6,000 plants grow on the arboretum's 120 acres (48 hectares), on land rising from 300ft (90 meters) to 1,800ft (550 meters) above sea level. Tropical and

The red cap cardinal is native to South America but was introduced to Hawaii in the 1930s.

The USS Arizona Memorial.

⊘ ORIGINS OF A MONUMENT

The USS *Arizona* Memorial grew out of a wartime desire to establish some sort of memorial at Pearl Harbor to honor those who died in the attack. Suggestions for such a memorial began in 1943, but it wasn't until 1949, when the Territory of Hawaii established the Pacific War Memorial Commission, that the first real steps were taken to make it a reality. Initial recognition came in 1950 when Admiral Arthur Radford, Commander in Chief, Pacific, ordered that a flagpole be erected over the sunken battleship USS *Arizona*. On the ninth anniversary of the attack, a commemorative plaque was placed at the base of the flagpole.

President Dwight D. Eisenhower, who helped achieve Allied victory in Europe during World War II, approved the creation of the Memorial in 1958. Its construction was completed in 1961 with public funds appropriated by Congress and private donations. The Memorial was dedicated in 1962. According to its architect, Alfred Preis, the design of the Memorial, "Wherein the structure sags in the center but stands strong and vigorous at the ends, expresses initial defeat and ultimate victory....The overall effect is one of serenity. Overtones of sadness have been omitted to permit the individual to contemplate his own personal responses...his innermost feelings."

Commissioned on December 7, 1942, the USS Bowfin was later mothballed in the Middle Loch of Pearl Harbor until it was brought out of retirement.

The University of Hawaii's Manoa campus, in the Manoa Valley.

native Hawaiian plants, conservation biology, and Hawaiian ethnobotany are the major themes here.

Nearby, cool **Manoa Falls**, accessed via a steep trail that climbs through spectacular rainforest for just under a mile, is fed by 160–200ins (4,065–5,080mm) of rain a year (and is a haven for insects; bring repellent and wear long sleeves).

PEARL HARBOR

One of the major reasons why the US annexed Hawaii, at the end of the 19th century, was to acquire control of **Pearl Harbor ㉝**. This vast inlet, at the heart of Oahu's southern coast, is the finest harbor for 2,000 miles (3,200km) in any direction. As the base of the US Pacific Fleet, it became the target of the notorious Japanese surprise attack on the morning of December 7, 1941. Denounced by President Roosevelt as a "date which will live in infamy," it immediately precipitated US entry into World War II.

Japanese torpedoes and dive-bombers, launched from an armada 200 miles (320km) northwest, destroyed a total of 18 warships that day. Their most famous victim is now the focus of the **USS _Arizona_ Memorial ㉞** (tel: 422-0561; www.nps.gov/perl; visitor center daily 7am–5pm; shuttle boats run 8am–3pm, weather permitting; to reserve tickets and book tours visit www.recreation.gov). US Navy boats ferry a constant stream of visitors to stand on the dazzling white platform that straddles the wreck of the USS _Arizona_, still visible, indeed still leaking oil, where it sank beneath the waters, carrying almost 1,200 of its crew to their deaths.

Designed by Honolulu architect Alfred Preis, the memorial was made possible in part by a benefit concert staged in 1961 by Elvis Presley, as his first public performance after leaving the US Army. It's the most popular free attraction on Oahu, with more than a million visitors annually – some 4,000 daily – so reserving online is advised to avoid at best a long wait or at worst the attraction being fully booked. The visitor center has an interesting museum

and good bookshop to keep you occupied should you need to wait.

USS *BOWFIN* AND USS *MISSOURI*

A few minutes' walk from the USS *Arizona* Memorial visitor center, across the parking lot, brings you to the privately operated **USS *Bowfin* Submarine Museum & Park** (tel: 423-1341; www.bowfin.org; daily 7am–5pm). Would-be submariners and the curious can check out defused torpedoes, and descend into and walk through a completely refurbished World War II diesel-electric submarine, the USS *Bowfin*, which is credited with sinking 44 ships in nine patrols, many of them well inside Japanese waters.

Shuttle buses run from the *Bowfin* across a slender road bridge to reach Ford Island, which is otherwise barred to non-military personnel. Their destination is a decommissioned World War II battleship, moored a short way along from the USS *Arizona* Memorial – the **USS *Missouri*** (tel: 973-2494; www.ussmissouri.org; daily 8am–4pm).

Known affectionately as the "Mighty Mo," this was the last battleship ever built by the US, in 1944, and was retired in 1992. You can visit the *Missouri* by yourself or take one of the guided tours – the 35-minute "Mighty Mo Tour" swings by the site of the surrender that ended World War II, while the 75-minute "Heart of the Missouri" tour ventures down the longest and widest passage on the ship. Whichever tour you choose to sign up to, the highlight will undoubtedly be the precise spot on deck where Japan's surrender was signed in Tokyo Bay in September 1945.

Another monument, considerably lower in profile and cost, can be found on Ford Island alongside the rusting hulk of the USS *Utah*. Civilians, however, can visit the site only if they are accompanied by a member or dependent of the United States military. At neighboring **Hickam Air Force Base**, you'll discover a plaque marking the spot where the *Apollo 11* astronauts first touched earth after their walk on the moon in 1969.

USS Bowfin.

Inside the USS Arizona Memorial.

SOUTHEAST OAHU

Beyond Diamond Head, Oahu becomes a mix of lush jungle, dense neighborhoods, and, of course, pristine beaches.

Main attractions

Diamond Head
Koko Head Trail
Hanauma Bay
Makapu'u Point and
  lighthouse
Waimanolo Beach

Map on page 112

This is the part of Oahu where the city gives way to the country, where it appears humans have remembered that nature is in charge. The most noticeable landmark is mighty Diamond Head, which towers to the east of Waikiki and is the most conspicuous of the chain of ancient volcanic cinder cones that rise from the coastline. Rent a car and drive beyond Honolulu's most luxurious residential neighborhoods to some dramatic beaches and scenery, including the popular snorkeling site of Hanauma Bay, the hiking trails of Makapu'u, and the

soft sand of Waimanalo. As you go, take advantage of the many pull-outs – these are here for slower cars to allow faster traffic to pass, but they also are the perfect excuse to stop and enjoy the view.

DIAMOND HEAD

You can actually drive into the extinct volcanic tuff cone of **Diamond Head ❶** (www.dlnr.hawaii.gov/dsp/parks), and hike up the inner walls to its sea-side rim 761ft (231 meters) above the beach. It's well worth the short but steep hike. The view of Waikiki and Oahu's South Shore is one of the island's best, and atop one of the abandoned World War II gun emplacements there is a comfortable picnic spot. The crater's interior and exterior slopes are part of the 500-acre (200-hectare) Diamond Head State Monument. Inside the crater there's a visitor center, as well as civil defense and National Guard facilities, and an air traffic control facility of the Federal Aviation Administration.

Diamond Head is a nickname given the crater in 1825 by British sailors who mistook worthless calcite crystals found on its slopes for diamonds. Its original Hawaiian name was Lae'ahi, which means "brow" (lae) of the yellow-fin tuna ('ahi). Hawaiian legends say that the fire goddess Hi'iaka, Pele's younger sister, noticed the resemblance between Diamond Head's profile and that of the 'ahi and named it Lae'ahi. In later years this

On the trail to Diamond Head.

was shortened by map-makers to Leahi. Its steep slopes were favored for *holua* sliding, a tropical form of tobogganing over dry ground.

Long before this tuff cone became Hawaii's most famous landmark, Lae'ahi was the site of the Papa'ena'ena *heiau*, an important temple. According to historical accounts, some of the last human sacrifices ordered by Kamehameha the Great took place at this *heiau* following the decisive Battle of Nu'uanu Valley, in 1795. Early descriptions indicate that the *heiau* was located below Diamond Head's jutting brow. A lovely estate called La Petra, now the Hawaii School for Girls, is built on the site.

KAHALA AND HAWAI'I KAI

Beyond Diamond Head, at the eastern end of the H-1 highway, stands the high-priced neighborhood of **Kahala** ❷. Following Hawaii's statehood in 1959, this part of the island became increasingly residential as Honolulu proper began running out of living space. Today, Kahala is one of Oahu's most desirable neighborhoods. At the end of ritzy Kahala Avenue is the Kahala Hotel & Resort (www.kahalaresort.com). Built in 1959, the hotel has become the Hawaiian escape for those with money and status. A walk along Kahala Beach toward Diamond Head leads past immaculate beachfront estates. In the other direction is the Wai'alae Country Club (www.waialaecc.com).

Further along Kalaniana'ole Highway, toward Oahu's southeastern tip, is the sprawling **Hawai'i Kai** ❸, created by the late billionaire industrialist Henry J. Kaiser during the early 1960s. The development included converting Kuapa, once Hawaii's largest fishpond, into a marina for Kaiser's master-planned suburb, now home to more than 30,000 people. Check out the variety of water activities, from parasailing to snorkeling, offered by Hawaii Water Sports Center, located in Hawai'i Kai's Koko Marina complex (tel: 395-3773; www.hawaiiwatersportscenter. com); they will take you out into the neon-blue waters of Maunalua Bay. Once past Hawai'i Kai the Kalaniana'ole Highway cuts over a saddle ridge at **Koko Head**, yet another cinder cone, named either

Tip

The drive between Hanauma Bay and Sandy Beach is stunning but challenging; the road is narrow and twisting, with many blind spots so keep your eyes on the road if you are driving.

View of Waikiki from the summit of Diamond Head.

Hawai'i Kai marina.

for the striking red earth common in the area or for the blood *(koko)* of a man bitten by a shark long ago. Koko Head also boasts one of the toughest summit trails anywhere in Hawaii; a hike that includes more than 1,000 wooden steps.

HANAUMA BAY AND SANDY BEACH

Even beach-loving tourists who otherwise never leave Waikiki during their entire trip emerge at least once to make the pilgrimage to gorgeous **Hanauma Bay ❹** (Hanauma Bay State Park; tel: 396-4229; https://hanaumabaystatepark. com; Wed–Sun 6.45am–4pm). Famed since Elvis Presley's 1961 movie *Blue Hawaii* as Oahu's premier snorkeling spot, Hanauma is also exceptionally pretty in its own right. Its name, meaning "curved bay," is an understatement. Cradled in what remains of an eroded extinct volcanic tuff cone, the bay is inhabited by enough protected but bold Hawaiian fish to seduce any snorkeler.

Snorkeling heaven at Hanauma Bay.

Daily visitor numbers are carefully regulated to minimize environmental harm – if you arrive any later than 9am you may

not be allowed in – and the entire site remains closed every Tuesday. Snorkeling equipment is available for rent, and all visitors are obliged to watch an educational film. No food or water is sold at the beach, but if you bring your own supplies this is a great place to spend the whole day.

After Hanauma Bay, the feeling of a city evaporates. At the next cliffside turn, *makai* (the ocean side) of Koko Crater, tourists wait at a parking lot lookout to hear the **Halona Blowhole ❺**, a lava formation that emits a geyser-like wheeze when incoming sea swells push up through its underwater entrance.

Appropriately, *halona* means "peering place." Just along the coast, before you round Makapu'u Point to Oahu's windward side, is **Sandy Beach ❻**, a local favorite for bodysurfing, people-watching, and, in season, an occasional whale sighting. If you go, watch those waves – in winter, they're lethally dangerous to all but experts.

MAKAPU'U

Continue northward from Sandy Beach along winding Kalaniana'ole Highway

and watch for **Makapu'u Beach Park ❼**, which is bounded by rough open seas, sheer lava-rock cliffs, and hill-sized dunes. Makapu'u is prized for its bodysurfing waves. Lifeguards are stationed on the beach.

The rocky summit on the right is **Makapu'u Point**, where a white lighthouse is perched on the craggy black-lava palisade. A paved road leading up to the lighthouse is closed to automobiles but is accessible by foot; the view of the coastline is well worth the easy hike.

On Makapu'u's *mauka* (mountain) side sits **Sea Life Park ❽** (www.sealifeparkhawaii.com). Among the highlights is a 300,000-gallon (113,562-liter) Hawaiian reef tank, filled with sharks, rays, sea turtles, and teeming with fish of every color. The park also maintains a wildlife rehabilitation unit, and is called upon when marine animals are found in distress.

WAIMANALO

If you are looking for a beach with plenty of empty space, an awesome mountain *pali* (high-cliff) backdrop, and warm waters to soak in, **Waimanalo Beach ❾** has few

Body boarding at Sandy Beach.

peers, but it's one of those gems that are often overlooked by visitors. **Waimanalo ❿** is as local a town as anywhere in Hawaii, a place where the rural Hawaiian lifestyle is sustained. Perhaps the area's most notable resident was Gabby Pahinui (1921–80), a slack-key guitarist and one of Hawaii's finest musicians. Another famous son of Waimanalo is Chad Rowan, born here in 1969, a sumo star who fought in Japan under the name Akebono (Sunrise). In 1993, he became the first *gaijin* (foreigner) ever to ascend to the rank of *yokozuna*, or grand champion, in sumo.

Beyond Waimanalo and **Bellows Air Force Station** (www.bellowsafs.com) rises 1,643ft (499-meter) **Olomana**. Named for a giant who jumped from Kauai to Oahu, Olomana casts morning shadows over **Maunawili**, an emerald vale where two parting lovers inspired Queen Lili'uokalani to write her timeless song *Aloha 'Oe*. Just minutes past Maunawili's pastures and farms are Oahu's second and third most populated towns – Kailua and Kane'ohe (see page 153) – which unfurl in a hybrid of modern suburbia and natural setting.

Coastline near Halona Blowhole.

⊘ HIKE TO THE RIM

The hike to the rim of Diamond Head is, without question, the most popular (and most accessible) hike on the island of Oahu. Though the trail isn't long – most reliable GPS units clock it at less than 2 miles (3km) – the way to the top is almost entirely uphill, climbing 560ft (170 meters) from the trailhead. The hike begins on pavement, then switches to dirt and follows some switchbacks to a flight of stairs. From there, head through a tunnel and up more stairs before reaching old bunkers at the top. At this point, if you're not too winded, climb atop the bunkers for a 360-degree view of the island, the ocean, and Waikiki Beach. Another tip: bring sunscreen and lots of water, as there is almost no shade at all along the way.

Touring the Hakipuʻu Valley in a 6x6 Swiss Pinzgauer from Kualoa Ranch.

WINDWARD OAHU

Lush, verdant mountains and valleys are the result of heavy winds and rain on the eastern coast of Oahu. Amid all this green, there's plenty to marvel at.

In Hawaii, the "windward" side of each island is the side that is blitzed by wind and rain every winter. The result is forests like the ones that appeared on the television series *Lost*. On Oahu, this stretch begins near the beginning of the majestic **Ko'olau Mountains**. Like a massive curtain that parts now and then to expose lone spires, fluted columns, crystal falls, and deep green valleys, these sheer cliffs dwarf everything in their vicinity. Ko'olau wears, as the Hawaiians like to poetically say, *lei i ka noe*. (mist as a *lei*); on and on the mountains stretch, from Makapu'u in Southeast Oahu nearly to the North Shore, encircling enchanting towns such as Kailua in between.

KAILUA

Take the Pali Highway up from Honolulu, and, dropping down the sheer flank of the Ko'olau Mountains beyond the Nu'uanu Pali Lookout, you will reach Oahu's second largest town, **Kailua ⓫**. This unremarkable suburb has become famous because it is where former President Obama and his family celebrate Christmas, but the area also is known for the famous banyan tree on the corner of Oneawa Street and Ku'ulei Road. If you're entering **Kailua** around sunset, pass by the tree and witness the wonderful sight of scores of mynah birds gathering to roost for

Outrigger at Lanikai Beach, Kailua.

the night, kicking up a squawking fuss. Of course the beaches in this area are top-notch, too.

A fine beach stretches the length of **Kailua Bay**, and the most convenient access to this swathe of sand is at **Kailua Beach Park ⓬**. (Some locals might argue that beaches at Kalama and Lanikai are just as good.) The choppy water just off these beaches often is the site of international windsurfing competitions. Beyond the surfsails, beyond the breaking waves, sit a number of small sanctuary islands named the Mokuluas and

Main attractions
Kailua
Kane'ohe Bay
Kualoa Regional Park
Kualoa Ranch
Polynesian Cultural Center

Map on page 112

Popo'ia. All of them are easily swimmable from Kailua Beach Park.

KANE'OHE

North of Kailua, Kane'ohe ⑬ is a bedroom community for Honolulu and the nearby marine base, with residential subdivisions that hug shimmering **Kane'ohe Bay** and the *pali* (steep cliffs). The large Kane'ohe Marine Corps Air Station (www.mcbhawaii.marines.mil) dominates scenic Mokapu Peninsula. Just offshore, Mokuolo'e, better known as Coconut Island, is the site of the Hawaii Institute of Marine Biology (www.himb.hawaii.edu), run by the University of Hawaii.

Stunning Kane'ohe Bay is a popular recreation area, protected by outlying reefs and good for most watersports. Several catamarans offer day trips to the bay's central sandbar. Kane'ohe means "bamboo husband." One interpretation says that a woman of ancient times compared the cruelty of her husband with a sharp bamboo knife; others suggest the name refers to one of his physical attributes.

Cultural attractions in the area include the serene **Byodo-In Temple** ⑭ (47-200 Kahekili Highway; tel: 239-8811; www.byodo-in.com; daily 8.30am–5pm), a termite-proof, cement replica of Kyoto's famous Byodo-In Temple of Equality. It is the major structure in the **Valley of the Temples Memorial Park** (www.valley-of-the-temples.com). A 7-ton bronze bell, a 2-acre (0.8-hectare) reflecting lake, peacocks, swans, ducks, tranquil meditation niches, and tinkling waterfalls enhance its imported architecture.

Of cultural and historical importance is a series of ancient fishponds that pepper windward shores north of Kane'ohe. The splendid **He'eia Fishpond** ⑮, on the Kane'ohe side of **Kealohi Point**, is Oahu's biggest. It has a wall 12ft (3.6 meters) wide and 5,000ft (1,500 meters) long, and once enclosed an area of 88 acres (35 hectares). Visiting the site provides perspective on exactly how big fishpond operations were back in the heyday. A restful stop here also provides a good opportunity for personal

Byodo-In Temple.

⊘ ROYAL GETAWAY

In past centuries, the beauty of the windward city of Kailua drew vacationing Hawaiian royalty. These days, at least some of that appeal is back: former US President Barack Obama and his family have celebrated Christmas and New Year in the area every year since 2008. The American "royals" have spent most of those years in the same 5,000-sq-ft (465-sq-meter) beachfront home that rents for $4,500 per night. Because the house is white, locals have dubbed it the "Winter White House." Obama's draw to the place goes back decades; he spent time in Kailua as a child and apparently always had wanted to return with his own family to enjoy what is now a chic resort town with a laid-back vibe and a sandy beach that some claim to be Hawaii's best.

reflection; something about the site today seems almost sacred in nature.

Another worthwhile stop is **Kahalu'u Gallery and Gardens** ⑯ (47-754 Lamaula Road; tel. 239-8146; www.kahaluugalleryandgardens.com; Sat–Mon by appointment 10am–4pm), one of the oldest art galleries in Oahu and set among lush gardens and tropical forest. The permanent exhibition showcases paintings, photographs, sculptures, ceramics, and jewelry. You can also visit a small museum devoted to the founder of the gallery, Hiroshi Tagami.

KUALOA: PARK AND RANCH

At **Kualoa Regional Park** ⑰, heads usually crane seaward for lingering looks at a small, distinct island known to Hawaiians as **Mokoli'i** ⑱ (which means the little *mo'o*, or lizard). Long ago, the conical island was nicknamed Chinaman's Hat. At low tide, one can easily wade out on the reef to this island (reef shoes are recommended), bask under palm trees, and photograph the graceful Hawaiian stilts *(ae'o)* and frigate birds *(iwa)* that soar overhead. On shore, the 124-acre (50-hectare) **Moli'i Fishpond**, easy to spot with a 4,000ft (1,200-meter) -long retaining wall, has been in cultivation for 800 years. This is also a very good place to see endangered Hawaiian waterfowl. Kualoa has long been sacred to the ancient Hawaiians and was favored as a royal residence.

Inland is the **Kualoa Ranch** (tel: 237-7321; www.kualoa.com), the largest of the few working cattle ranches still left on Oahu. The enterprising owners have developed it as a film location, notably for *Lost* and *Jurassic Park*, and as a popular tourist destination, offering activities like horseback riding, snorkeling, and jet-skiing at the beach park just across the street, plus helicopter tours that take in this spectacular stretch of coast and mountains. Equally impressive is a sailing trip in a catamaran to Kane'ohe Bay's sweeping sandbar. Set in the middle of the bay's waters and backed by the towering *pali*, this is Hawaii at its most beautiful. For information call Captain Bob's Picnic Sail (tel: 942-5077; www.captainbobspicnicsail.com).

> **⊙ Fact**
>
> Oahu once had nearly 100 fishponds used by Hawaiians to grow seafood. Now, only five are left intact. Four are on this Windward Coast: He'eia (north of Kane'ohe), Kahalu'u, Moli'i (off Kualoa Point), and Huilua (Kahana Bay). The fifth is at Oki'okiolepe, in Pearl Harbor.

On the beach looking towards Kualoa.

KAHANA AND HAU'ULA

Beyond Ka'a'awa is Mahie Point, which overlooks the *hala* (screwpine) groves, reedy lagoons, and whistling ironwood that rim the silent beauty of **Kahana Bay** ⑲. Off the point, there is a rock formation at the Point called **Kauhi**, better known as Crouching Lion.

Kahana Bay itself shelters a fine beach of grayish sand, while the valley behind, which is still farmed in the traditional manner by native Hawaiians, offers a couple of good hiking trails.

Straw baskets bulging with plump papayas, avocados, and Chinese bananas hanging inside weathered wooden stands compete with shell chandeliers for the traveler's dollar along this stretch to **Hau'ula**. Further hiking trails enable adventurous walkers to explore the hillsides behind the little residential community of Hau'uh.

One place trails no longer go is **Sacred Falls State Park** ⑳, which is known as **Kaliuwa'a Falls** in Hawaiian. Due to a landslide that claimed eight lives in 1999, the trail to Kaliuwa'a has been closed indefinitely. Now, for those intent on getting back to see the area, the only option is a helicopter tour.

POLYNESIAN CULTURAL CENTER AND ENVIRONS

Three miles (5km) north of Hau'ula is **La'ie** ㉑, a predominantly Mormon community that's home to the Hawaii campus of Brigham Young University, as well as the chaste-looking **Mormon Temple**, built in 1919 by descendants of missionary Mormons living in this area since 1864. The temple is closed to non-Mormons; however, its visitor center is open to all.

La'ie is very much on the tourist map, thanks to the **Polynesian Cultural Center** ㉒ (tel: 1-800-367-7060; www.polynesia.com; Mon, Tue & Thu–Sat 12.45–9pm, Hukilau marketplace 11am–9.30pm; villages 12.45–5.30pm), which manages to educate more than a million visitors each year about the history and culture of the Pacific islands, despite its decidedly theme-park presentation.

Your hosts are native islanders whose enthusiasm and warmth are

Horseback trekking through Kualoa Valley scenery.

infectious, and the activities range from the serious to the comical, with plenty to keep you occupied and entertained. There are boat rides, luaus, and even an IMAX theater that adds a high-tech element to the experience.

The center's main shows – performed nightly by young Mormon students from Fiji, Samoa, Tahiti, Tonga, the Marquesas, New Zealand, and Hawaii – are designed, according to brochures, to give visitors a "pure cultural view of Polynesia." Exactly how much you pay for the experience depends on which of the many possible packages, including meals and shows, you choose to buy, but it can easily run into hundreds of dollars. The center runs special buses from Waikiki if you'd rather not drive.

Just north of the cultural center is **La'ie Point**, at the end of Anemoku and Naupaka streets and where windward waters running hard from the north pound two little offshore isles – **Kukuiho'olua** and **Mokualai** – with a frightening and beautiful force, especially in winter.

Kahuku ㉓ is an ex-plantation town where the only landmark is a former sugar mill (it closed in 1971). The site is now a rather run-down shopping mall, though sadly its towering chimney stack, deemed a health and safety hazard, had to be demolished in 2004. Here you will discover a place where workers' cafés, grocery stores, karate *dojo,* and tiny homes survive much as they did when residents awoke to the mill's morning steam whistle. A walk around this village, where ferns and orchids hang in bleach-bottle planters, is a pleasant way to spend a morning and usually highly rewarding.

Aquaculture is very big business in the Kahuku area. Shrimp, shellfish, and edible seaweed are all cultivated in large ponds that flank the James Campbell National Wildlife Refuge (www.fws.gov/refuge/james_campbell).

Roadside stands offer the freshest and best catches of the day's harvest; if you drive past one, don't fret, as you likely will pass about six more before leaving the region.

Students from the University of Hawaii perform a traditional Samoan dance on a canoe at the Polynesian Cultural Center.

NORTH SHORE

Home to some of the best and most hallowed breaks in the world, Oahu's sleepy North Shore is where serious surfers go to catch some serious waves.

Main attractions

Ted's Bakery
Waimea Bay
Hale'iwa
Pu'uomahuka Heiau
State Monument

Map on page 112

Both figuratively and literally, the North Shore is as far away from Waikiki as one can get without leaving Oahu. On the map, it's clear on the other side of the island. It's also got a totally different vibe; life here is just slower. And that's the appeal.

The first major landmark encountered on the North Shore, continuing from the windward side, is the **Turtle Bay Resort** ㉔ (www.turtlebayresort.com), on a dramatic point extending into the ocean, with dramatic vistas of storms and waves. A few miles farther, the

world's finest surfing waves crash onto offshore reefs and sandbars: Sunset, Rocky Point, Banzai Pipeline, Waimea Bay, Chun's Reef, Hale'iwa, and Avalanche. Each of these spots corresponds to a pocket beach off the main road. In summer, the beaches are ideal spots to witness Hawaiian Monk Seals or green sea turtles in the wild (just don't get too close). Year-round, **Ted's Bakery** (www.tedsbakery.com), across the street from Sunset Beach, is a great place to grab a coffee and a slice of coconut cream pie.

Calm in summer and for much of the year, **Waimea Bay** ㉕ hosts monster waves when the North Shore feels the fury of winter storms in the Arctic that drive rough seas toward Hawaii. In December 1969, more than 30 homes between Kahuku Point and Hale'iwa were reduced to tinder as monstrous 50ft (15-meter) waves pounded the North Shore. The most jaded surfer will agree that a tubing, top-to-bottom wave off one of those reefs generates enough adrenaline to keep anybody going through at least a few nervous lifetimes, especially when Waimea Bay is breaking with waves so big that hundreds of people line the road like spectators at a gladiator show. The waves are so thunderous that the ground trembles underfoot. Only the

The Banzai Pipeline reef break is off Ehukai Beach.

best surfers paddle out toward the 20 to 30ft (7- to 10-meter) winter swells lifting like glossy black holes on the blue-gray horizon.

A good place to take in Waimea Bay, most of the North Shore, and the distant Wai'anae Mountains is from the 17th-century **Pu'uomahuka Heiau State Monument** ㉖ (http://dlnr.hawaii.gov/dsp/parks), on a 250ft (75-meter) bluff above the **St Peter and Paul Church**. To get there, turn off from the main road onto Pupukea Road, at the fire station and supermarket.

At the very top of the bluff, on a marked side road, is an ancient *heiau*, or temple. It is one of Oahu's largest, and Hawaiians still leave offerings for the gods, usually lava stones wrapped in *ti* leaves, on its walls. It was known as Pu'uomahuka, the hill of escape, although historically not for some. In May 1792, two crew members (some accounts say three) of Captain George Vancouver's ship HMS *Daedalus* were offered in sacrifice at this *heiau* after being captured while filling water barrels at the mouth of the Waimea River.

During that period, the Hawaiians had an insatiable desire to procure guns and ammunition.

When Vancouver was informed of what had happened, he pledged to track down and punish the culprits, and eventually he did. Three Hawaiians were executed with a pistol by their own chiefs in full view of islanders and crewmen. There is some debate as to whether the trio were the actual offenders. Some historians believe Oahu's wily ruler, Kahekili, rounded up three innocent people and "sacrificed" them to assuage the British captain. Whatever the truth may be, the *heiau* is a somber, foreboding place.

Where Waimea River enters Waimea Bay, on the *mauka* (mountain) side of the road, just east of the beach park, look out for the entrance to **Waimea Valley** ㉗ (59-864 Kamehameha Highway; tel: 638-7766; www.waimeavalley.net; daily 9am–4pm, summer until 5pm). This 1,800-acre (728-hectare) botanical garden used to be run as a theme park, but now serves as a nature preserve. Shady trails leading well over

Waimea Falls.

Lush vegetation in the nature preserve of Waimea Valley.

a mile back into the lush valley, and culminating at a spectacular waterfall, enable visitors to enjoy more than 6,000 varieties of native and imported plants, many of which have magnificently colorful flowers.

SUMMER AND SHAVE ICE

Farther westward along the North Shore's surfing grounds, a small cement bridge funnels traffic over a little stream into **Hale'iwa** ㉖ (House of the Frigate Bird), an arty and funky outpost – but the biggest town on this side of Oahu – where people of all ethnic backgrounds and lifestyles mingle. An eclectic mix of trendy cafés, art galleries, independent boutiques, and shops mix with remnants of the old plantation days. No visit to Hale'iwa would be complete without a stop at Matsumoto General Store (66–87 Kamehameha Highway; www.matsumotoshaveice.com; daily 10am–6pm), famous for shave ice in a rainbow of flavors, complete with azuki beans and ice cream at the bottom.

Hale'iwa.

A mid-summer visit to Hale'iwa coincides with the height of the Japanese *Obon* season, when the **Hale'iwa Jodo Mission** has its annual lantern festival, *toronagashi*, with dozens of flickering lanterns – each a farewell light for an ancestor's spirit – floating on the dark sea to the east side of **Kaiaka Bay**. Hale'iwa also hosts the **Hale'iwa Arts Festival** in July, a celebration that offers a hometown glimpse into Hawaiian culture.

NORTHWEST OAHU

From Hale'iwa, continue south down the Kamehameha Highway through central Oahu and back to Honolulu, or head farther east past taro and banana patches to the old plantation town of Waialua.

Beyond Waialua, on the *mauka* (mountain) side of Farrington Highway, is the **Hawaii Polo Club** (www.hawaii-polo.org), where visiting teams from around the world battle through chukkas of polo against local pony teams (most Sundays from March to August); bring a picnic and settle in for a languid afternoon.

Farther down the road is the **Dillingham Airfield** ㉙, where Honolulu Soaring (tel: 637-0207; www.honolulusoaring.com) take to the skies alongside the 2,000ft (610-meter) -high Wai'anae *pali*. The more courageous can test their mettle with a skydive with Skydive Hawaii (tel: 637-9700; www.hawaiiskydiving.com), which also departs from Dillingham. At the end of the road beyond Mokule'ia, a leafy foot trail continues to **Ka'ena Point** ㉚, the westernmost tip of Oahu where the Hawaiians believed the souls of the dead departed to the afterlife.

The surrounding area is now a protected wildlife conservation district. Beyond, on foot, is the element-lashed Wai'anae Coast. In winter, waves as high as 50ft (15 meters) have been witnessed off Ka'ena Point. No one has surfed them. Yet.

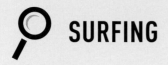

SURFING

Surfing is said to have started in Hawaii, and it makes sense that the sport has established itself as the unofficial pastime of the island chain.

Surfing is as much a part of Hawaiian culture as hula, *lu'aus* and *'ukulele* music. Some historians believe that a primitive form of surfing originated somewhere in the Pacific around 2000 BC. It is likely that when the first Polynesians migrated to the Hawaiian Islands around AD 400, they were already well versed in the sport.

Early Hawaiians called surfing *he'e nalu*, which literally translates as "wave sliding." Hawaiian chants dating from the 15th century recount surfing exploits, indicating that *he'e nalu* had become so developed that competitions were held among famous surfers, usually royalty, or *ali'i*. These were widely heralded affairs, sometimes pitting chiefs against each other; crowds of supporters would indulge in high-stakes gambling by placing property bets on a favored wave rider.

One Hawaiian legend tells the story of Kawelo, whose wife was taken by his brother, the ruling chief 'Aikanaka. Full of anguish, Kawelo was plotting his revenge when he suddenly noticed a crowd gathered on the beach, enjoying *he'e nalu*. Overcome with desire, Kawelo at once forgot completely about his wife and 'Aikanaka and headed straight for the beach to engage in his favorite pastime. No wonder one long-time surfer says, "Perfect waves are miracles. When they come, everything else stops, including romance."

WAVES OF CHANGE

Gone are the days when *ali'i* rode on large *koa* boards weighing 150lbs (70kg). Also gone are early 20th-century Waikiki-style boards made of California redwood. And just as extinct are the balsa "pig boards" that were popular in the early 1950s. Thanks to modern technology, today's surfboards are made of foam and fiberglass, and can weigh less than 5lbs (2kg). The serious surfer today maintains not just one surfboard, but an all-purpose "quiver" of boards, ranging in function and size. Short-boards are slightly more than 6ft (2 meters) in length, while long-boards (more buoyant and stable, they permit the surfer to perform more creative maneuvers) are about 9ft (3 meters) in length. – one that cannot begin without the proper training. Visitors to Hawaii usually sign up for some sort of lessons; there are a handful of surfing instruction schools on Oahu. If you are especially confident and have plenty of time to kill, you can usually get informal lessons from willing beach boys in Waikiki.

For those who just want to watch, the best time to be a spectator of big-wave surfing is in November and December, when the Vans **Triple Crown of Surfing** (www.vanstriplecrownofsurfing.com) is held on Oahu's North Shore. The Triple Crown consists of three separate competitions featuring professional surfers from around the world. Binoculars are a critical tool to help watch the events unfold.

Surfing at Waipi'o Valley on the Big Island.

Taro, a Hawaiian staple crop, grows at Hawaii Plantation Village in Waipahu.

CENTRAL OAHU AND THE WAI'ANAE COAST

Wedged between the mountains of the old Wai'anae and Ko'olau volcanoes, central Oahu is an eclectic mix of resort living, farmland, ancient sites, and untamed wilderness.

There's something for everyone in central Oahu: resorts, golf courses, farmland, ancient sites, stellar beaches, and miles upon miles of open space. Hotels in the Ko 'Olina resort area – especially Disney's Aulani – have become some of the most popular on the entire island, and many travelers like stopping at the Dole Plantation for some pineapples on the drive to the North Shore. The US military also has quite a presence. In short, the area might be the most eclectic portion of the entire island. Which is precisely why so many visitors like it so much.

ANCIENT MOANALUA

Just off the H-1 freeway is **Moanalua Gardens ㉛**, a tranquil retreat graced with huge, umbrella-like monkeypod trees. A popular picnic spot and site of July's Prince Lot Hula Festival, the gardens (www.moanaluagardens.com; temporarily closed at the time of writing) are privately owned but are open to the public. A country home built by Kamahameha V in Victorian style with Chinese accents graces the setting. Behind is **Moanalua Valley**, an even more spectacular wilderness area where there are tall white hibiscus trees shading a stream, and Hawaiian petroglyphs and an ancient medicinal pool surrounded by colorful morning glories, gardenias, ferns, and

On the Farrington Highway heading for Ka'ena Point State Park in Wai'anae.

fragrant vines. The valley is now owned by the state, which has pledged to ensure continued access for hikers.

ALOHA STADIUM

Also off the H-1 as you approach Pearl Harbor, you'll easily spot the 50,000-seat **Aloha Stadium ㉜**, Oahu's prime but plagued-by-rust outdoor venue for major sports and special events like the annual State Fair. The stadium was built in 1975 and can be realigned into baseball or football configurations. Concession workers here sell Chinese

Main attractions
Aloha Stadium Swap Meet
Dole Plantation
Aulani
Makua Beach
Ka'ena Point

Map on page 112

Fact

'Aiea, Honolulu, is the only town or city in the United States whose name is made up entirely of vowels.

crack seed and *saimin* noodles along with the usual hot dogs and burgers.

Aloha Stadium's parking lot doubles as the site for one of Oahu's biggest attractions, when some 30,000 residents and visitors flock to the **Aloha Stadium Swap Meet** (tel: 486-6704; www.alohastadium.hawaii.gov; Wed & Sat 8am–3pm, Sun 6.30am–3pm). Here are rows upon rows of vendors hawking everything from *aloha* shirts to zucchini.

Just *mauka* (toward the mountains) of the stadium is **Stadium Mall**, a retail complex, unremarkable except that it is home to **The Ice Palace** (tel: 487-9921; www.icepalacehawaii.com; temporarily closed for renovations at the time of writing), a popular ice-skating venue that occasionally hosts hockey competitions.

Beyond the stadium lie the east, middle, and west lochs of Pearl Harbor (see page 146) and the towns of 'Aiea, Pearl City, and Waipahu, largely bedroom communities for Honolulu.

CENTRAL PLATEAU

On the drive north and inland on the H-2 freeway, Oahu's central plateau rises gradually until it reaches the **Schofield Barracks 🔞** army post and **Wahiawa**, the highest residential community on Oahu. Wahiawa ("Place of Noise") can be bypassed altogether by staying on Highway 90, which separates the town from Schofield Barracks. But military enthusiasts will enjoy a stop at Schofield's **Tropic Lightning Museum** (tel: 655-0438; Tue–Fri 10am–4pm; free), which houses artifacts, photographs, and archival materials documenting the history of Schofield Barracks and the famed "Tropic Lightning" 25th Light Infantry Division.

Others, more interested in a place of quiet than a place of noise, might care to stop in Wahiawa to take a look at the visually unspectacular **Healing Stones**. The stones sit on a simple altar inside a concrete shelter on California Street. Until the late 1920s, pilgrims regularly visited these stones, which, according to legend, were two sisters from the island of Kauai who were petrified by greater powers. Other myths attribute alternative origins to the stones but, whatever the explanation, they are still thought to emanate healing powers. Offerings are regularly left here. Also in Wahiawa is the **Wahiawa Botanical Garden** (1396 California Avenue; tel: 621-7321; daily 9am–4pm; free).

BIRTH STONES

On the north side of Wahiawa, to the left of Kamehameha Highway and just beyond Whitmore Avenue, are sacred stones of a different sort. These are the **birth stones of Kukaniloko 🔞**. This eucalyptus-fringed clearing in a pineapple field has been venerated by Hawaiians as far back as the 12th century. The wives of high-ranking chiefs bore their children on the gently curved surfaces of these stones. Attendant chiefs, high priests, and physicians would gather around the newborn infant and, during an impressive ceremony marked by great drum rolls, chants, and offerings, the royal child would be named and the umbilical cord cut and ritually hidden away.

Dole Plantation's pineapple maze.

From this open-air site, to the west in the direction of the Wai'anae Range, you can look up the side of Leilehua Plain to the broad **Kolekole Pass**, which was used by low-flying Japanese bombers as a convenient cover and western approach for their sneak attacks on Schofield Barracks and adjacent **Wheeler Army Air Field**. In 1969, when the joint American-Japanese movie *Tora! Tora! Tora!* was being filmed, the sight of Japanese Zeros, Kates and Vals roaring through Kolekole and raining simulated bombs and machine-gun fire on Schofield Barracks and Wheeler Air Force Base produced a chilling sense of *déjà vu* for anyone who had been here during World War II.

PINEAPPLE WORLD

Although the Dole company no longer grows pineapples on Oahu on a significant commercial scale, its former headquarters, just north of Wahiawa, have been converted into a flourishing tourist attraction known as the **Dole Plantation** ㉟ (Kamehameha Highway; tel: 621-8408; www.doleplantation.com; daily 9.30am–4.30pm; free but entrance fee to specific attractions). The central building is a large store that sells all kinds of pineapple-related products, along with coffee, Hawaiian plants, and T-shirts displaying the company logo. There's a little yellow train, the Pineapple Express, which makes regular 20-minute tours of the fields, accompanied by a helpful narrative. There is also what's claimed to be the world's largest maze (it was featured in the 2001 edition of the *Guinness Book of World Records*), an intricate tangle of hedgerows with six distinct "centers," and more than 10,000 colorful plants, including varieties of hibiscus, the state flower.

WAI'ANAE COAST

The Wai'anae Coast is perhaps the most misunderstood and maligned area of Oahu. It is true that this 20-mile (32km) coastline is hotter, dustier, and drier than the rest of the island. And with the exception of the Ko 'Olina Resort (www.koolina.com) at the southern end, it lacks the usual tourist attractions. But dig deep, and you'll find that West Oahu has considerable

> **Tip**
>
> Throughout the islands you will encounter *lei*- or *ti*-covered objects at sacred sites. These are religious offerings of Native Hawaiians and should be left undisturbed. They are not tourist souvenirs.

Sampling the goods at Dole Plantation.

PINEAPPLES

Europeans first came across pineapples in South America and the West Indies. Quickly adopted as a crop, they were transplanted throughout the world, and were reportedly grown in Hawaii as early as 1813. However, the commercial selling of pineapple in Hawaii did not begin until 1899, when an Oahu-born entrepreneur called James D. Dole planted 60 acres (24 hectares) of Wahiawa land with the fruit. Two years later, Dole organized the Hawaiian Pineapple Company, and by 1906 he had begun building a pineapple cannery at Iwilei, near Honolulu Harbor. Dole's father was a cousin to Sanford Dole, president of the Hawaiian Republic from 1893 to 1900 and one of the group of businessmen and landowners who were responsible for overthrowing the monarchy in Hawaii.

Plantation-era living room at Hawaii Plantation Village.

Hawaii Plantation Village.

natural and cultural beauty to offer a respectful and adventurous traveler.

Question any long-time resident of Nanakuli, Ma'ili, Wai'anae, or Makaha about the West Side, and they may just spend hours explaining why it's paradise: "It's the closest thing to an unspoiled Hawaiian place on this island," says a truck driver from Lualualei. A Nanakuli elder states flatly that "You've never been to a real *lu'au* until you've been to a big one on this side." Indeed, wedding or first-birthday *lu'aus* (see page 95) on this side of the island are legendary, remembered by participants by the number of *kalua* pigs and kegs of beer consumed during celebrations.

Just over 35,000 people live along Wai'anae's jagged shorelines and dry mountain slopes. Before the arrival of Captain Cook, the west coast of Oahu was a major center of Hawaiian civilization, probably because of the rich fishing grounds in the clear offshore waters between Nanakuli and Ka'ena Point. It was here, according to oral traditions, that the demigod Maui lived and first learned to make fire after he arrived in Hawaii. Also along this coast, several myths refer to the infamous man-pig Kamapua'a, renowned throughout Hawaii as a god who both charmed and harassed mortal worshipers with his capricious antics.

Just past Pearl City and a quick dash off the H-1 Freeway, lies the town of **Waipahu** , which is over a century old. Until the mid-1970s, it was devoted to growing sugar cane, but today employment is provided by other industries, such as tourism and leisure.

The past is still celebrated at **Hawaii Plantation Village** (tel: 677-0110; www.hawaiiplantationvillage.org; Mon–Fri 9am–2pm, guided tours on the hour). Plantation-era houses reveal the diverse cultures of eight ethnic groups in Hawaii that were a part of the sugar industry's century-long flowering. Guided tours of the 3-acre (1.2-hectare) site are offered.

THE SOUTHWEST CORNER

The **Ko 'Olina Resort** 37 has the requisite golf course plus a spa and a series of beach-lined lagoons. Anchoring the resort is **Aulani** (www.disneyaulani.com), the biggest and most popular: a Disney resort that blends the familiar faces of Mickey Mouse, Minnie Mouse, Donald Duck, and the gang with a Hawaiian motif. The resort is popular among Disney devotees, especially since the characters are omnipresent. The resort also has one of the best spas outside of Waikiki.

Also worth exploring is the **Marriott's Ko Olina Beach Club** (www.marriott.com) perched on one of the lagoons and white-sand beaches. Film buffs will recognize the hotel from *Blue Crush*, a 2002 surfing movie starring a young Kate Bosworth. Several large *lu'aus* (feasts) are held adjacent to the resort (there's a bus link to Waikiki). Each Wai'anae coast beach has its own character and devotees. 'Ewa Beach Park, for example, is famed for its abundance of *limu* (also called *ogo* in Japanese), or edible seaweed.

Just outside Ko 'Olina is **Wet'n'Wild Hawaii** ❸ (400 Farrington Way; tel: 674-9283; www.wetnwildhawaii.com; opening times vary), with 25 acres (10 hectares) of water-slides and wave pools. Favored by surfers, **Kahe Point** ❸ is a beach past Ko 'Olina, opposite an electric power plant on the main road, which parallels the western coastline. This spot is called the Kahe Point Beach Park, but locals call it Tracks because remnants of the old narrow-gauge train tracks still run parallel to the highway traveling northward.

Ku'ilioloa Heiau ❹, on the extreme fingertip of Kane'ilio Point on the south side of Poka'i Bay, is surrounded by water on three sides. This *heiau*, or temple, of coral and lava rock was built in the 15th or 16th century in honor of Ku'ilioloa, a giant dog that often protected travelers in the area.

Protection by giant dogs was appreciated here. This area is said to have been populated in ancient times by cannibals preying on passers-by. According to J. Gilbert McAllister, who wrote a 1933 Bishop Museum survey entitled *Archaeology of Oahu*, these highwaymen apparently hid behind high ridges and ambushed unwary victims who came their way. The largest town on this coast, Makaha, meaning fierce or savage, takes its name from these marauders.

"For many years these people preyed upon the traveler," McAllister wrote, "until at one time men from Kauai, hairless men *(olohe)* came to this beach. They were attacked by these cannibals but defeated them, killing the entire colony. Since then, the region has been safe for traveling."

MAKAHA: COAST AND VALLEY

Several reefs and points of land along this coast have long been favored as surfing spots, but perhaps the most famous is Kepuhi Point in **Makaha** ❹, where the annual Makaha International Surfing Championships were once held. In recent years, an oldie-but-goodie surfing event at Makaha has caught the fancy of wave-riding old-timers: the annual Buffalo's Longboard Contest, which began in 1978. Makaha Beach commander Buffalo Keaulana and other

⊙ Tip

The Wai'anae Coast has developed a reputation for not embracing tourists. Break-ins of parked rental cars underline this impression. Still, if you behave respectfully you may find yourself liking this part of the island and its residents best of all.

Makaha Beach.

kama'aina (long-time residents) organized it to renew interest in the style of surfing that was in vogue during the 1950s and 1960s.

Wander into the back reaches of **Makaha Valley** to the impressive **Kane'aki Heiau** ㊷, which has been restored by the National Park Service, Bishop Museum, and the Makaha Historical Society. This 17th-century *heiau*, one of the best-preserved on Oahu and tucked away in a spectacular setting alongside Makaha Stream, was rebuilt entirely by hand, using indigenous *pili* grass, *'ohi'a* timber and lava stones much as they were utilized by ancient craftsmen. To get there, head up into Makaha Valley toward the Sheraton Makaha Golf Club and continue through the golf course to the gate for Mauna 'Olu Estates. Unfortunately, the site was closed at the time of writing due to safety reasons.

KANEANA AND KEAWA'ULA BAY

Another famous site you can walk into is about 3 miles (5km) north of Makaha: **Kaneana** ㊸, the Cave of Kane. Although this cave is 100ft (30 meters) high in places and about 450ft (135 meters) deep, it is not a lava tube. Rather, it was carved out by the sea 150,000 years ago. According to legend, this cave was occupied by a fierce character, Kamohoali'i, who was able to alternate at will between being a human and a shark. Kamohoali'i had a fondness for human flesh, so in his guise as a mortal, he would periodically jump on people and drag them into this cave for dinner. Eventually, this human disguise was discovered and Kamohoali'i fled into the sea, but he was captured and destroyed by vengeful Makua residents.

Makua Beach ㊹ is the photogenic area where much of the epic motion picture *Hawaii*, based on James Michener's eponymous novel, was filmed in 1965. Film producers recreated an entire set on this beach representing the old Maui whaling town of Lahaina. That set has long since been carted away, but the spectacular backdrop remains.

Moments later, Farrington Highway ends and briefly becomes a modest road that terminates at **Keawa'ula Bay** ㊺, a bodyboarding spot known as **Yokohama Bay**. This sandy playground received the Japanese name at the turn of the 20th century when the Oahu Railway train between 'Ewa and Hale'iwa would stop here to let off Japanese fishermen, who favored the fishing at Keawa'ula.

Beyond Yokohama Bay, the landscape turns into a jangle of black lava, thorny scrub brush, and sand dunes at **Ka'ena Point**. Like an arrow, Ka'ena points slightly to the northwest and the island of Kauai. It can be traversed on foot or bicycle – but not by car. Continuing farther on and around Ka'ena Point leads to the North Shore. Ka'ena Point is now a state wildlife preserve, home to nesting albatross, the occasional Hawaiian Monk Seal, and rare flora.

Ka'ena is said to be named for the brother or cousin of Pele, the fire and volcano goddess, and ancient Hawaiians were reluctant to cross it, for it was a place from which souls departed the earth – the good to the right, and the not-so-good to the left.

View towards Yokohama Bay from Ka'ena Point State Park.

THE LEEWARD ISLANDS

Oahu County continues west from Honolulu, encompassing thousands of miles and dozens of islands where nature reigns supreme.

For most travelers, Honolulu ends at the sharp, beaky tip of Ka'ena Point on northwest Oahu. Unknown to many, however, including most Honolulu residents, is that Honolulu is the most far-flung city in the world. The city's jurisdiction not only includes Oahu, but also dozens of smaller points of land that stretch some 1,400 nautical miles (2,200km) to the northwest.

These shoals, atolls, and desert isles have names like Nihoa, Necker, French Frigate Shoals, Gardiner Pinnacles, Maro Reef, Laysan, Lisianski, Pearl and Hermes Reef, and Kure Island. The better-known Midway Islands are also within Honolulu's sprawling city limits, but they were placed under military jurisdiction at the start of the 20th century. Some 2,000 US Navy personnel and dependants – as well as hundreds of thousands of goony birds – live at Midway, but the other islets are uninhabited, except for Tern Island at French Frigate Shoals, which supports an airstrip and Loran navigation station maintained by the US Coast Guard. Midway, partially converted to ecotourism in the 1990s, is currently closed to the public and only available for activities connected with nature conservation and airfield operations.

Collectively, these islands are often referred to as the Leeward Islands, although, officially, they are the Northwestern **Hawaiian Islands Marine National Monument**. Eight of these islands and reefs have been combined to form the Hawaiian Islands National Wildlife Refuge.

WILDLIFE HAVEN

Largely because of their remoteness, these isles are a favorite breeding ground of the Hawaiian Monk Seal, an endangered species. This sea mammal prefers solitude over congregating in groups, hence the name "monk" seal, and can grow to over 7ft (2 meters) in length and weigh nearly 500lbs (230kg).

Each spring, adult green sea turtles – Hawaiians called them *honu* – migrate to the wildlife refuge, where the females lumber ashore to lay eggs. The turtles can grow up to 4ft (1.2 meters) in length and weigh up to 400lbs (180kg). They are known to bask on the beach on these uninhabited Hawaiian islets, an activity rare among sea turtles. The monk seals and green sea turtles are federally protected and should not be disturbed.

Among the interesting birds that populate these islands and excite ornithologists are Hawaiian noddy terns, sooty terns, red-footed and blue-faced boobies, Laysan albatrosses, shearwaters, frigate birds, wandering tattlers, Pacific golden plovers, Laysan honey eaters, bristle-thighed curlews, and Laysan teals (said to be the rarest ducks in the world). Nihoa, also known as Bird Island, has several endemic species including the Nihoa Millerbird and the Nihoa Finch.

For biologists, the region also has become a special spot for observing rare bivalves, mollusks, and other forms of simple sea life. Today it is considered the foremost place for spotting nudibranchs, a hard-to-find cousin of the snail.

A Laysan albatross nests on Sand Island, part of Midway Atoll National Wildlife Refuge on Midway Atoll.

Waterfalls near the Hana Highway.

Front Street in Lahaina.

MAUI

With resorts aplenty, remarkable beaches, and one of the largest volcanoes on Earth, Maui is a mix of natural beauty and manmade elegance.

If the Hawaiian Islands had a prom, Maui would be crowned queen for all it has to offer. The island's economy is growing more quickly than the economies on other islands, and it has weathered the recession better than anywhere else in Hawaii. Resorts are swanky and full. Humpback whales visit every winter like clockwork. And the beaches one is more spectacular than the next. Together with Lanai and Molokai, the other islands that comprise Maui County (also known as Greater Maui), the center of the Hawaiian archipelago is by far the most exciting part these days.

In ancient times, Maui was a strong and stable island kingdom. Then, in the late 1800s, the Maui town of Lahaina was capital of the newly united Hawaiian kingdom. Nowadays, Maui sustains itself with three basic industries: tourism, sugar cane production and information technology. The island also has spawned a variety of cutting-edge businesses, including floriculture (the growing of flowers) and wind energy.

For a relatively small island – if it were square, it would only be 27 miles (43km) on each side – Maui possesses an amazing natural diversity. The island is composed of two entirely different volcanic masses. The island of Maui is dominated by a single landmark – mighty Haleakala that makes up Eastern Maui. This massive dormant, three-sided shield volcano – capped with a Manhattan-sized *caldera*, a national park, and a space-age research facility – offers the adventure of lofty, sometimes snowbound, heights. It's also a great place from which to watch the sun rise.

Surfers at Ho'okipa Beach Park, Paia town.

West Maui is anchored by the island's older and second volcano: Komohana (or, depending on whom you ask, Kahalawai). Adding to this diversity are two other neighboring islands that comprise the County of Maui – Molokai and Lanai. Together with uninhabited Kaho'olawe, this row of sheltering islands forms one side of the 'Au'Au Channel, which protects Maui's dry shores from the open ocean and creates a haven for humpback whales.

People visit Maui for all of these reasons: the beaches, the watersports, the glamour, whale-spotting, and the scenery. Of course they also come for the golf and resorts – some of which rank among the best in the world. As the island grows, though, locals are increasingly concerned about water, traffic, and overcrowding.

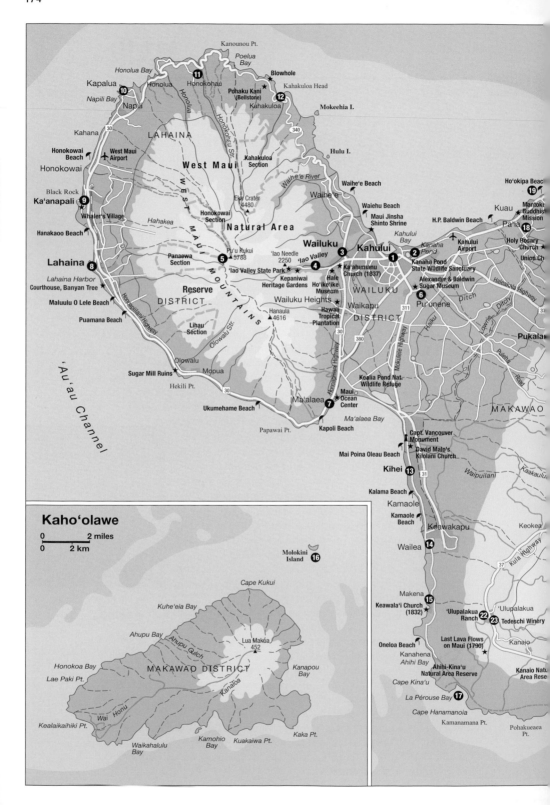

Kanounou Pt.

Poelua
Bay

Honolua Bay

Kapalua

Napili Bay

11 Honokohau

Honolua

10

Napili

Pohaku Kani
(Bellstone)

Blowhole ★

Kahakuloa Head

12

Kahakuloa

Mokeehia I.

Kahana

30

L A H A I N A

Honokohau
Str.

Hulu I.

Honokowai
Beach

West Maui
Airport

West Maui

Kahakuloa
Section

Honokowai

West Maui

Waihe'e River

Waihe'e Beach

Black Rock

W E S T

Ka'anapali

9

Whaler's Village

Hahakea

Honokowai
Section

Natural Area

Waihe'e

Waiehu Beach

Waiehu Beach

Maui Jinsha
Shinto Shrine

H.P. Baldwin Beach

Ho'okipa Beach

19

Kuau

Mantoki
Buddhist
Mission

Hanakaoo Beach

M A U I

Pu'u Kukui
5788

5

'Iao Needle
2250

'Iao Valley

3 Kahului

Kahului
Bay

Kanaha
Pond

2

Kahului
Airport

Pa'ia

18

Holy Rosary
Church

Lahaina

8

Lahaina Harbor
Courthouse, Banyan Tree

M O U N T A I N S

Panaewa
Section

'Iao Valley State Park

4

Ka'ahumanu
Church (1837)

1

Kanaha Pond
State Wildlife Sanctuary

Union Ch

Maluulu O Lele Beach

'Au'au Channel

Reserve

D I S T R I C T

Kepaniwai
Heritage Gardens

Hale
Ho'ike'ike
Museum

W A I L U K U

Alexander & Baldwin
Sugar Museum

6

Pu'unene

Haleakala Highway

Puamana Beach

Lihau
Section

Honoapiilani Highway

Olowalu Str.

Wailuku Heights

Hanaula
4616

Waikapu

Hawaii
Tropical
Plantation

D I S T R I C T

30

311

380

Mokulele Highway

Haiku

Lowrie
Ditch

Ditch

Pukala

Sugar Mill Ruins

Olowalu

Mopua

30

Hekili Pt.

Ukumehame Beach

Ma'alaea

7

Maui
Ocean
Center

Honoapiilani Highway

Kapoli Beach

M A K A W A O

Papawai Pt.

Ma'alaea Bay

Capt. Vancouver
Monument

David Malo's
Kilolani Church

Mai Poina Oleau Beach

Kihei **13**

31

Waipuilani

Kaakauu

Kalama Beach

Kamaole

Kamaole
Beach

Keawakapu

Keokea

37

Kula Highway

Wailea **14**

Makena

15

Keawala'i Church
(1832)

'Ulupalakua
Ranch **22**

'Ulupalakua

23 Tedeschi Winery

Oneloa Beach

Kanahena
Ahihi Bay

Ahihi-Kina'u
Natural Area Reserve

Last Lava Flows
on Maui (1790)

Kanaio

Kanaio Natu
Area Rese

Cape Kina'u

La Pérouse Bay **17**

Cape Hanamanoia

Kamanamana Pt.

Pohakueaea
Pt.

Kaho'olawe

0 ——— 2 miles
0 ——— 2 km

Molokini
Island **16**

Cape Kukui

Kuhe'eia Bay

Ahupu Bay

Ahupu Gulch

Lua Makua
452

Kanapou
Bay

Honokoa Bay

Lae Paki Pt.

M A K A W A O   D I S T R I C T

Wai Honu

Kanaloa

Kealaikahiki Pt.

Waikahalulu
Bay

Kamohio
Bay

Kuakaiwa Pt.

Kaka Pt.

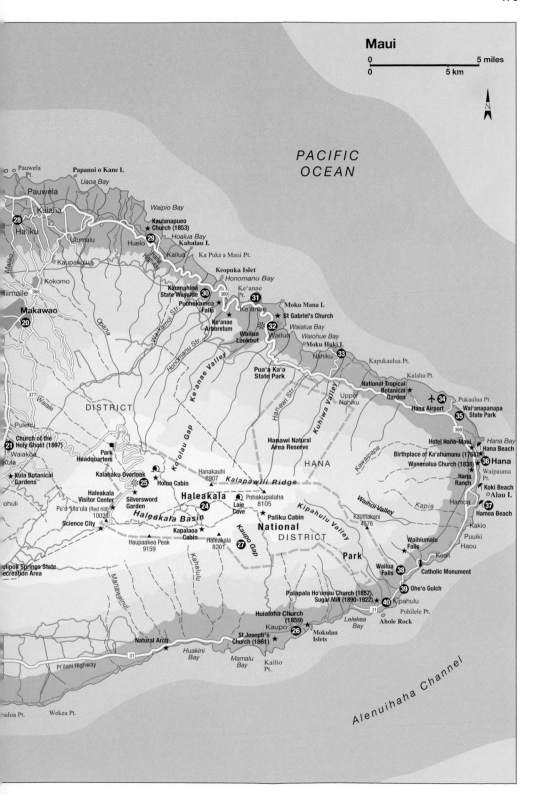

Maui

0 — 5 miles
0 — 5 km

N

PACIFIC
OCEAN

Pauwela
Pt.
Papanui o Kane I.
Uaoa Bay
Pauwela
Kuiaha
(28) Ha'iku
Ulumalu
Waipio Bay
Kaulanapueo
Church (1853)
(29) Huelo
Hoalua Bay
Kahalau I.
Kailua
Ka Puka a Maui Pt.
Kaupakulua

Keopuka Islet
Honomanu Bay
Kaumahina
State Wayside (30)
Ke'anae
Pt.
(31)
Ke'anae
Moku Mana I.
St Gabriel's Church
Puohokamoa
Falls (360)
(32)
Ke'anae
Arboretum
Wailua
Lookout
Wailua
Waialua Bay
Waiohue Bay
Moku Huki I.

Makawao
(20)

Kokomo
Kaupakulua

Miimaile 365

Ka'anae
Waiale
377

DISTRICT

Church of the
Holy Ghost (1897)
(21)
Waiakoa
Kula Botanical
Gardens

Park
Headquarters
Kalahaku Overlook
(25) Holua Cabin
Hanakauhi
8907
Kalapawili Ridge

Nahiku
(33)
Kapukaulua Pt.

Kalahu Pt.
National Tropical
Botanical
Garden
Upper
Nahiku
(34)
Pukaulua Pt.
Hana Airport
(35)
Wai'anapanapa
State Park

Hana Bay
Hotel Hana-Maui
Hana Beach
(360)
Birthplace of Ka'ahumanu (1768)
(36) Hana
Wananalua Church (1838)
Waipauma
Beach
Hana
Ranch
Koki Beach
Alau I.
(37)
Hamoa Beach

Haleakala
Visitor Center
Pu'u 'Ula'ula (Red Hill)
10023
Science City
Silversword
Garden
Haleakala Basin
(24)
HALEAKALA
Pohakupalaha
8105
Laie
Cave
Paliku Cabin
Kapalaoa
Cabin
Haupaakea Peak
9159
Haleakala
8201
(27)
Kaupo Gap
National
DISTRICT
Park
Kaumakani
4576
Kipahulu Valley
Waihoi Valley
Kapia
Hamoa
Kakio
Puuiki
Haou
Koali
Waihiumalu
Falls
Wailua
Falls (38)
Catholic Monument
(39) Ohe'o Gulch
Kahalulu
Manawainui
Haleakala

Palapala Ho'omau Church (1857),
Sugar Mill (1890-1922)
(40) Kipahulu
Puhilele Pt.
Lelekea
Bay
Ahole Rock

Olipoli Springs State
Recreation Area

ohuli

Natural Arch
Pi'ilani Highway
(31)
Huakini
Bay
Huialoha Church
(1859)
Kaupo
St Joseph's
Church (1861)
(26)
Mamalu
Bay
Kailio
Pt.
Mokulau
Islets

Wekea Pt.
naloa Pt.

Alenuihaha Channel

West Maui mountains in ʻIao
Valley State Park, near Wailuku.

CENTRAL MAUI

The urban center of Kahului anchors the isthmus connecting the island's two volcanoes. But it is the sun and surf of the west coast – and Lahaina's whaling history – that seduce visitors.

Think of Maui like a suspension bridge; the volcanoes rise like supports on either end, and sloping farmland stretches in between. This farmland – technically it's an isthmus – is the island's prime agricultural region, and was created when the Haleakala volcano filled in the gap between it and the much older West Maui volcano. This farmland isn't the brazen money-maker that it used to be, but the production of both pineapples and sugar cane remains important here today.

KAHULUI

Kahului ❶, Maui's deep-water port on the north side and the site of the island's primary airport is the island's commercial hub, with shopping malls, a community college, and the **Maui Arts and Cultural Center** (Kahului Beach Road; tel: 242-7469; www.maui-arts.org). Created by an heroic grass-roots fund-raising campaign, the center includes the elegant, 1,200-seat Castle Theater, several smaller performance spaces, an amphitheater, and an art gallery, and public installations by local artists.

Kahului is important for another reason; just off the highway between the airport and downtown Kahului is **Kanaha Pond State Wildlife Sanctuary ❷**, the state's most important

A charter boat docks at Ma'alaea harbor in Wailuku.

waterfowl sanctuary and the home of several species of native birds. Three indigenous species in particular make the pond particularly worthwhile given their relative rarity on other islands: the Hawaiian Coot, the Hawaiian Duck, and the Hawaiian Stilt.

WAILUKU

Wailuku ❸ is perched in the western foothills above Kahului like an older and wiser sibling. Once centered around a now-defunct sugar mill, Wailuku is the seat of the Maui County

Main attractions

Maui Arts & Cultural
  Center
Hawaii Nature Center
'Iao Needle
Home Maid Bakery
Maui Ocean Center

Map on page 174

⊙ Eat

Every morning, **Home Maid Bakery** (1005 Lower Main Street; tel: 244-7015; www. homemaidbakery.com; daily 5am–8pm) cooks up dozens upon dozens of fried and sugar-coated dough balls dubbed *malasadas*. These treats are a throwback to the Portuguese part of the island's history; today they are among the most popular baked goods on Maui.

government, administering not only Maui, but the islands of Molokai, Lanai, and the contentious but uninhabited Kahoʻolawe.

In Wailuku's historic district in the heart of town is **Kaʻahumanu Congregational Church**, built in 1876 of white-painted wood and plastered stone to honor Queen Kaʻahumanu, who played an important role in establishing Christianity in the islands. The church is often closed except when services are being held, but if you attend one of the services you will hear hymns sung in the Hawaiian language.

An early example of Western architecture touched with Hawaiian influences is the stone- and timber-built **Bailey House** (tel: 244-3326; www.maui-museum.org; Mon–Sat 10am–4pm), a small museum operated by the Maui Historical Society. The structure was built in 1841 for Edward Bailey, headmaster of the former Wailuku Female Seminary. The museum conveys the spirit of missionary life and exhibits paintings of old Maui by Bailey himself.

WEST MAUI MOUNTAINS

Beyond Wailuku at the end of the road are the wet, lush remnants of the West Maui crater and **ʻIao Valley ❹** (pronounced *ee-ow*, meaning "cloud supreme"). At the valley's mouth is **Kepaniwai Heritage Gardens**, a country park with gardens and pavilions representing the many ethnic groups that have settled in Maui. It was established in counterpoint to an historic and vicious Hawaiian battle waged in the area; during the battle of ʻIao Valley, Kamehameha's forces pushed Maui warriors back into the valley and slaughtered them, choking the river with their lifeless bodies. Kepaniwai means "water dam."

Next to Kepaniwai is the **Hawaii Nature Center** (tel: 244-6500; www. hawaiinaturecenter.org), an environmental education project with particular emphasis on informative programs for children. The Interactive Science Arcade offers 30 hands-on natural history exhibits and daily guided nature hikes in the afternoons.

Making malasadas (fried, powdered pastries) in Wailuku.

⊙ MAUI FOOD TRUCKS

It didn't take long for the food truck craze to make its way from the mainland to Maui, arguably the hippest of the eight major Hawaiian islands. Today, trucks congregate near the harbor in Kahului and the church in downtown Wailuku. While there are about a half-dozen decent choices across the island, locals swear by two trucks in particular: Dinos Gourmet On-The-Go, which sells sandwiches with fried meat, pasta dishes, and excellent garlic fries; and the Geste Shrimp Truck, which specializes in shrimp dishes (and a delicious crab macaroni salad), all day long. Prices at both trucks might seem high to food truck devotees, but consider the portions: In both cases, for $12–30, you get enough food for a weekend. Expect lines during lunch on weekdays: this is food worth sinking some teeth into.

Farther up, the scenic road ends in **'Iao Valley State Park** (www.dlnr.hawaii.gov/dsp/parks), a lush mountain terrain dominated by **'Iao Needle**, the exposed core of an old cinder cone that rises 1,200ft (365 meters) above the stream at its base. There is a parking lot at the end of the road, and a tree-lined path leads down to the trickling stream and up to various sheltered spots offering stunning views across the emerald green valley.

Surrounding this compact, spectacular valley are the imposing 5,788ft (1,764-meter) walls of **Pu'u Kukui** ❺, the summit of the eroded remains of the West Maui volcano and one of the wettest places in the islands, with more than 400ins (10,000mm) of rain annually. The summit is a natural wonderland, as it has one of the greatest selections of native species in Maui, but unfortunately it is totally inaccessible to visitors.

ON THE ISTHMUS

Just to the east of Kahului is the old plantation town of **Pu'unene** ❻ and a sugar mill that is still in operation. The former plantation manager's house next to the mill has now been converted into the **Alexander & Baldwin Sugar Museum** (tel: 871-8058; www.sugarmuseum.com; Mon–Thu 10am–2pm), with working exhibits and an informative look at the lives of early migrant laborers toiling on Hawaii's sugar plantations.

On the south side of the central isthmus is **Ma'alaea** ❼, a small coastal village and boat-speckled harbor, and a departure point for fishing and whale-watching charters, with one of the best surf breaks on the island. Ma'alaea's star attraction, though, is the **Maui Ocean Center** (tel: 270-7000; www.maui-oceancenter.com; daily 9am–5pm), a brilliantly designed aquarium dedicated to the Hawaiian marine environment. Exhibits are captivating and include a gigantic walk-through open-ocean tank where all kinds of sea life glide past – and over – you, a turtle pool, and a touch pool. The displays of live coral, some of which are illuminated, are also worth a look.

⊙ Fact

If the heat and slow traffic get to you, especially on the cliffside highway into Lahaina, try and spot the remnants of the old stagecoach road, which parallels the highway in some places; the trip to Wailuku used to take all day.

'Iao Needle.

WEST AND SOUTH MAUI

Most of Maui's resorts are clustered in the south and the west, making these parts of the island prime spots for golf, beaches, and good eats.

⊙ Main attractions
Lahaina
Whale-watching (Lahaina and Wailea)
Ka'anapali
Whaler's Village shopping center
Kapalua Beach

Maps on pages 174, 183

Maui's most protected beaches are on its south and western shores. Naturally, then, these are the places where, in the 1960s and 1970s, resort development happened first. Since then, resort communities have sprouted in places such as Wailea, Ka'anapali and Kapalua. Along the way, the historic whaling village of Lahaina has evolved to become perhaps the island's most sophisticated and visitor-friendly tourist town. It's worth noting that humans aren't the only visitors who enjoy these parts of this great island; humpback whales do,

too. Every winter, these marine mammals migrate to Hawaii from Alaska to mate, birth, and rear their young. Watching the leviathans is quite an experience – and, at least between the months of December and April, something you simply cannot avoid.

LAHAINA

After Honolulu, **Lahaina ❽**, on the western coastline of West Maui, is Hawaii's best-known town, partly for the nearby beaches of Ka'anapali, partly for its history, and nowadays for its party atmosphere.

The city has quite a history. In the early 1820s, King Kamehameha III made Lahaina the capital of his kingdom, and it remained so until 1845. By then, New England whaling ships had begun visiting. Missionaries followed in 1823, sponsored by Queen Keopuolani, mother of Kamehameha II and Kamehameha III. She helped the missionaries establish a grass church called Waine'e, the site of today's Waiola Church. Keopuolani is buried at the site, on Waine'e Street in Lahaina.

By the 1840s, Hawaii had become the principal forward station of the American whaling fleet. All the actual hunting of whales took place in the northern Pacific; humpback whales were never the prey. Lahaina was a favorite port-of-call because of its protected offshore

Front Street, Lahaina.

waters in **'Au'au Channel** that are sheltered by nearby Molokai and Lanai. The whaling ships have long disappeared from Lahaina, but this waterfront town, once a magnet for whalers and seamen on shore leave, continues to preserve the lively spirit and look of the salty 1800s – although sometimes with a decidedly commercial or Hollywood veneer. It's a superb walking town, nonetheless, compact and manageable for any traveler.

The heart of Lahaina lies along **Front Street**, between Shaw and Papalaua streets, parallel to the waterfront. The narrow streets that Mark Twain and Herman Melville walked are now lined with cafés and restaurants (some perched over the water in weathered buildings), art galleries, T-shirt boutiques, and fashionable shops. In 1962, the town was designated a National Historic District, and since then, the Maui County Historic Commission and the non-profit Lahaina Restoration Foundation (www.lahainarestoration.org) have worked to encourage the preservation of older buildings and the construction of harmonious new ones. The result is a blend of seaport nostalgia and contemporary living (peppered nonetheless with some gaudy schlock), found nowhere else in Hawaii.

EXPLORING THE TOWN

The **Pioneer Inn Ⓐ**, built on the harbor in 1901 and wedged between Wharf and Front streets, is nothing if not nostalgic. On its walls are fading photographs of early ships and sailors, whaling equipment, and other memorabilia, including the original house rules: "Women is not allow in you (sic) room; if you burn you bed you going out; only on Sunday you can sleep all day." Downstairs is a veranda restaurant and a popular and noisy bar. The former inn has been meticulously restored and adapted by the Best Western hotel chain.

Kamehameha's Brick Palace once stood nearby; it is thought to have been Hawaii's first Western-style building. Built around 1798 of locally produced brick, it was commissioned by Kamehameha the Great, using the labor of two ex-convicts from a British penal colony in Australia. Unfortunately, all traces of the ruins have now disappeared.

Wo Hing Society Temple, Lahaina.

HUMPBACK WHALES

Humans aren't the only mammals to visit Maui with regularity; every winter, thousands of humpback whales descend on the island, too.

The humpback whales that visit Hawaii each winter spend their summers in Alaska, where the rich waters fatten the whales with krill, a type of shrimp. Around November, the whales start heading for Hawaii's warmer waters, where they mate and give birth. By the end of May, they have disappeared again.

Scientists believe that at least 10,000 humpback whales make the journey to Maui; they have no idea how many of these animals pass through the 'Au'au Channel in any given season. What they do know is that the number of whales that winter in Hawaii is steadily increasing each year; great news for a population once feared to be headed to extinction (and one that, technically, still sits on the endangered species list).

Of the behavior displayed by the humpbacks, breaches (where the whale jumps out of the water), are the most spectacular to watch; between January and March, you can do so from most of the waterfront cafés

Breaching humpback whale.

in Lahaina and on Ka'anapali. Whales also can be seen from charter boats – many of which are available for hire out of Lahaina and Ma'alaea harbors. Most of these boats are inflatable speedboats; some have fiberglass hulls. If you opt for this method of whale-watching, don't expect to get too close; federal and state laws require whale-watchers in Hawaii to keep a distance of 300ft (90 meters), and the law is strictly enforced. (That said, there is no law prohibiting whales from checking out boats of their own accord.)

Other types of behavior one can witness off Maui are flipper-slapping, spyhopping (poking a head above the surface), and lobtailing (slapping the tail flukes on the surface of the water). Each fluke is unique, a whale "fingerprint." Researchers photograph the flukes to track the mammals.

SONG OF THE HUMPBACKS

Female humpbacks spend most of their time in Hawaii being mothers or being pursued by males. Scientists believe that when in Hawaiian waters, males attract females to areas called arenas by singing. (Not all whale species, however, have songs; and not all humpback songs are about attracting females – males also sing in other social situations.) It is not known whether the information contained in the songs is simple or complex. What is known is that during the winter season, males repeat the song in a precise sequence and that, over time, the whale song changes and evolves.

The songs are composed of thematic sets sung repeatedly in a specific order. The average song session lasts maybe a quarter of an hour, although they have been known to last as long as 22 hours. Whale songs sound like creaks and groans of different lengths in many pitches. Because sound travels well underwater, it's easy to hear these enchanting tunes if the whales are singing nearby.

When the humpbacks leave Hawaiian waters in spring, the singing stops, to resume again the following winter in almost exactly the same spot in the song as where they broke off months earlier. Humpbacks in Hawaii sing the same evolving song as humpbacks in Mexico; some scientists believe this indicates communication between regional whale "cultures."

In a plaza next to the Pioneer Inn is the expansive **Banyan Tree**, planted in 1873 by the town sheriff. It is the largest known banyan tree in the islands: more than 60ft (18 meters) high and covering 0.6 acres (0.25 hectares) with its canopy. Next to it is the old courthouse building, now an art gallery and information center. Opposite the Pioneer Inn on Front Street is the **Baldwin Home B** (tel: 661-3262; www.lahainarestoration.org/baldwin-home-museum; Wed–Sat 10am–4pm, Fri until 8pm). Formerly the home of Dwight Baldwin, a Protestant medical missionary, it was a focus of Lahaina missionary life in the mid-19th century. The home has been fully restored and is now a museum.

Hale Pa'ahao C ("Stuck-in-Irons House"; daily 10am–4pm; free) is the old prison, located a few blocks up – where else? – Prison Street. It's a worthwhile stop just for its cool, quiet courtyard. Step inside one of the whitewashed cells and imagine a confined life in paradise. The prison had inmates convicted of the usual perfidy, including some convicted of "furious riding" – 89 in 1855 but just 48 in 1857. In that same year, one person was imprisoned for "neglect of parent to send children to school."

A few blocks to the east is **Malu'uluolele Park**, once a pond with an island where Maui chiefs lived. Kamehameha III enjoyed showing visitors the ornate coffins and burial chamber embellished with mirrors, royal feather standards, and velvet drapes. A well-known *mo'o*, or lizard god, inhabited the pond. Today, the place is a ball park.

Farther north along Front Street, the **Wo Hing Society Temple D** (tel: 661-3262; www.lahainarestoration.org/wohing-museum; Wed–Sat 10am–4pm) is a fascinating museum of early Chinese life in the islands. The early 1900s-era building was a cultural and social home for Chinese immigrants, mostly male and single. In the former cook house next door, old Thomas Edison movies are projected amongst the pots and pans. At the north end of Front Street is the seaside **Jodo Mission Buddhist Cultural Park**, with the largest Buddha outside of Asia.

Lahainaluna High School E is located up Lahainaluna Road and behind the now

Inside the Wo Hing Society Temple on Front Street.

Ka'anapali Beach.

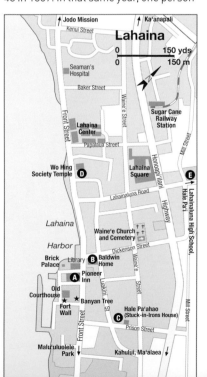

Lahaina

0   150 yds
0   150 m

Jodo Mission
Ka'anapali
Kenui Street
Seaman's Hospital
Baker Street
Waine'e Street
Front Street
Sugar Cane Railway Station
Lahaina Center
Papalaua Street
Honoapi'ilani
Mill Street
Wo Hing Society Temple D
Lahaina Square
E
Lahainaluna Road
Lahainaluna High School
Hale Pa'i
Highway
Lahaina
Waine'e Church and Cemetery
Harbor
Dickenson Street
Brick Palace
Library
Baldwin B Home
Waine'e Street
A Pioneer Inn
Old Courthouse
Banyan Tree
Fort Wall
Lua kini St.
Hale Pa'ahao (Stuck-in-Irons House) C
Front Street
Prison Street
Mill Street
Malu'uluolele Park
Kahului, Ma'alaea

defunct Pioneer Sugar Mill. It opened as a general academic school in 1831 under the name "Lahainaluna Seminary." This is the oldest American high school west of the Rockies. Californians once sent their children here rather than to the East Coast schools, which ran the risk of Indian attack. The original printer's shop, **Hale Pa'i** (tel: 661-3262; www.lahainares-toration.org/hale-pai-museum; Mon–Wed 10am–4pm and by appointment with 48h notice), is where the first Bible in the Hawaiian language was published.

KA'ANAPALI

When the **Ka'anapali Resort** ❾ began to be developed during the early 1960s, less than 5 miles (8km) north of Lahaina, Maui entered the global tourist industry, starting the expansion that has since doubled the island's population. This complex of hotels, shopping centers, golf courses, and condominiums also lays claim to what some people consider to be Hawaii's finest beaches: two 1-mile (1.6km) -long stretches of sand separated by a promontory made of lava rock. Hotels line both stretches,

though the less-urbanized North Beach is slightly less built up.

The **Whaler's Village** shopping center (www.whalersvillage.com) is home to many international top-brand stores and a smattering of Hawaiian artisans' shops, along with a handful of restaurants and bars. Its greatest attraction, in fact, is its beachfront location just steps from the ocean – the ideal spot for sunset-gazing, drink in hand.

A rebuilt 1890s-vintage sugar cane train, the **Lahaina Ka'anapali Railroad** (tel: 667-6851; www.sugarcanetrain.com), puffs over a 6-mile (10km) route between Lahaina and Ka'anapali, transporting tourists through the cane fields (from the end of November until Dec 25th at 6.30 and 8pm). Narrow-gage tracks follow the haul-line road that was used by the Pioneer Mill until the early 1950s.

The first of Ka'anapali's hotels, the Sheraton Maui, opened in 1963, sits at the northern end of Ka'anapali Beach at a rocky point called **Black Rock**, or **Pu'u Keka'a** ("The Rumble"). This *'uhane lele*, or sacred place, was where the souls of the dead departed for ancestral spirit

Whaler's Village shopping center.

worlds. Whether you are staying at one of the Ka'anapali deluxe resorts lining the beach – which include the Hyatt Regency Maui, Westin Maui, and Maui Marriott – or not, enjoy a walk along Ka'anapali Beach, timed to coincide with the sunset, if possible, for the spectacular, torch-lighting, cliff-diving ceremonial that ends the Ka'anapali day.

NORTHWARD

From Ka'anapali, Honoapi'ilani Highway passes through **Honokowai**, **Kahana**, and **Napili**, a clustering of condos and apartment hotels. Just beyond Napili Bay is **Kapalua Resort ⑩**, renowned for its golf courses (the best in Hawaii; www.kapalua.com) and beautiful setting at the base of the West Maui Mountains offering the islands best views and trails, along with its luxury accommodations The Ritz-Carlton, Kapalua.

Beyond Kapalua, the road arcs eastward over the northern end of the West Maui Mountains, passing the beach at the **Honolua/Mokule'ia Marine Preserve**, a hugely popular surfing destination that is also great for snorkeling (visited by catamaran). Park roadside (the long line of cars makes the site obvious) and it is then only a short hike down to the beach.

Situated nearby is the small bay of **Honokohau ⑪**. Beyond the Marine Preserve, the landscape becomes wilder, with beautiful panoramic coastal and mountain views. Although the road has some rough stretches (not suitable for large rental cars), it is possible to travel all the way to **Wailuku**. Make sure you stop in the rustic town of **Kahakuloa ⑫**, a scenic rural enclave where taro is still grown and the lifestyle is quintessentially Hawaiian.

SOUTH MAUI

In the past 25 years, the area known as South Maui has come to rival West Maui as the island's main resort destination. The name is somewhat misleading; South Maui is not along the island's southern coast, but at the foot of the west-facing slopes of Haleakala. This region is nothing like as green as West Maui, in fact it used to be a virtual desert, but what it lacks in scenic

One of Kapalua Resort's golf courses.

beauty it makes up for in reliable sunshine, and, crucially, sheltered sandy beaches. Roughly half of Maui's guest rooms are now located in the neighboring communities of Kihei and Wailea, which are not so much towns as simply elongated strips of low-rise hotels, condos, and restaurants.

KIHEI

Stretching for seven miles (11km) along the shoreline of Ma'alaea Bay, **Kihei** ⓭ consists largely of endlessly repeated condominium rentals and shopping centers with little aesthetic appeal. They are at least here for a good reason: the adjacent beaches are actually quite decent, and offer spectacular sunset views and whale-watching during winter months. Some of the best deals in accommodations can be had here. Broadly speaking, the more northerly beaches, where the swimming is poor, are mainly used by windsurfers heading out into the sheltered waters of the bay, while the further south you go, the better the beaches become for bathing.

WAILEA AND MAKENA

Immediately south of Kihei lies the far more upscale resort of **Wailea** ⓮, home to a succession of glorious crescent beaches – Wailea and Polo beaches are the best of all – a fancy, luxury-oriented shopping mall, and several extravagant oceanfront hotels (including the Grand Wailea, the Four Seasons, Maui and the Fairmont Kea Lani.) As elsewhere throughout Hawaii, you don't have to be a hotel guest here to visit any beach you like. Higher up the landscaped slopes of Haleakala, there are five 18-hole golf courses.

South again from Wailea, little **Makena** ⓯ had only one hotel until 2016, the Makena Beach and Golf Resort, which was closed and then bulldozed in 2018. Plans are underway to build a luxury condo complex – the Makena Golf and Beach Club – complete with golf course, beach club and posh residences (www.makenagolfandbeachclub.com.) Makena did at least exist before the tourist boom, so it retains one or two vestiges of the past, in the shape of the pretty Keawala'i Church, and the remains of its former

⊙ THE MAUI FOOD SCENE

When Sheldon Simeon nearly won "Top Chef" Season 10 in 2012, the national spotlight shone brightly on Lahaina, where Simeon used to work (he now has opened his own restaurant, Tin Roof, in Kahului) as chef at Star Noodle, an Asian restaurant. The attention on Hawaii's culinary prowess was long overdue; for years, South and West Maui have boasted some of the most celebrated chefs in the islands – chefs whose expertise, flair, and gourmand creations are so great, diners often travel great distances to taste the fruits of their labor. Like the treats from chef Tylun Pang at Ko, in Wailea or the sushi masters at Sansei in Kapalua. There are so many delicious food options in this part of Hawaii that one could make an entire trip based solely around eating.

Molokini island.

harbor. There's yet another lovely beach in front of the closed resort, but the finest of all South Maui's beaches lies another mile (0.5km) farther south. Known to everyone as "Big Beach," but officially named both Oneloa Beach and Makena State Park, this magnificent 1-mile (0.5km) -long expanse of broad golden sand is a wonderful place for walking and taking pictures, but unless you're an expert boogie-boarder the waves are too dangerous for swimming.

MOLOKINI AND KAHO'OLAWE

Looking out seaward from the resorts of South Maui, it's easy to spot the small crescent island of **Molokini** ⑯, an eroded tuff cone whose submerged crater offers spectacular snorkeling. Daily diving and snorkeling boats to Molokini depart from several points along the shore, especially from Ma'alaea.

Beyond Molokini, looming low and red on the horizon, lies uninhabited **Kaho'olawe**, the smallest of Hawaii's eight major islands. The ancient Hawaiians used Kaho'olawe as a center of religious practices and a navigational school.

Sites on the island have been placed on the National Register of Historic Places.

During World War II the US Navy appropriated the island for use as a gunnery range, where the military practiced firing and detonating weapons. Native Hawaiian Rights activism from the 1970s resulted in the eventual return of the island to the state in 1994. A major rehabilitation program, removing debris and unexploded ordinance, has been underway for years, and there is now a nature reserve open only to Native Hawaiians.

LA PÉROUSE BAY

Drive another 3 miles (5km) to **La Pérouse Bay** ⑰, another good snorkeling and kayaking spot. The first Westerner to land on Maui, the French explorer Jean-François de La Pérouse (Captain Cook had sailed past without stopping), wrote in 1786 that "during our excursion we observed four small villages of about 10 or 12 houses each, built and covered with straw." Shortly after, around 1790, the area was covered by lava from Haleakala's eruption. Much of the landscape here remains a lava desert to this day.

Makena State Park, also known as Big Beach.

Windsurfing at Hoʻokipa Beach.

HALEAKALA AND UPCOUNTRY

Up on the slopes of Maui's volcano, life is a mix
of cowboy culture and geologic wonder.

Of the sunrise from atop Maui's Haleakala, Mark Twain wrote: "It was the sublimest spectacle I ever witnessed, and I think the memory of it will remain with me always." Travelers continue to be awed by dawn at the 10,023ft (3,055-meter) summit of **Haleakala**, which means "House of the Sun." But from a distance, this gently sloping shield volcano, which is dormant, not extinct, lacks pretension. The first European to sight Haleakala, Captain James Cook, who did not land on Maui, described it as simply "an elevated hill... whose summit rose above the clouds."

Indeed, as with Hawaii Island's Mauna Kea and Mauna Loa (also shield volcanoes) the Haleakala that is visible is only part of the story. It towers 2 miles (3km) above sea level, but below, it extends another 3.5 miles (6km). The exact dimensions of the part above ground weren't fully known until 1841, when an American expedition surveyed the summit basin and found it to be 3,000ft (915 meters) deep and 19 sq miles (49 sq km) in area, with a circumference of 21 miles (34km).

The island's namesake, the demigod Maui, was a magician and mythical figure in Polynesia long before the Hawaiian Islands were inhabited. According to legend, the sun was fond of sleeping

late and then racing across the sky to make up time. With the short days, Hina, Maui's mother, had trouble drying *kapa* cloth that she pounded from the bark of the mulberry. Noticing that the sun appeared each morning over Haleakala, Maui wove a rope of coconut fiber and climbed up to the summit basin's edge one night to await dawn. When the sun awoke, Maui lassoed its rays and threatened to kill it. The sun begged for mercy and promised to behave more responsibly. For most contemporary travelers watching the

⊙ **Main attractions**
Pa'ia
Triple L Ranch Maui
Makawao
Ali'i Kula Lavender Farm
Haleakala National Park

Map on page 174

*Above the clouds at Leleiwi Lookout,
Haleakala National Park.*

⊙ Tip

It can be quite cool in Upcountry – many homes have fireplaces – and it's increasingly colder as one ascends the slopes of Haleakala. In the morning and late afternoon, the winds atop Haleakala are often cold if not frigid.

sun rise or set from the summit of Haleakala, it still moves too fast. To witness the sunrise or sunset from atop Haleakala, one must first ascend the lower slopes of the volcano, an area commonly called **Upcountry**.

UPCOUNTRY

Say that you're heading Upcountry and envious listeners will know that shortly you'll be smelling eucalyptus suspended in cool air and following rolling grassy contours reminiscent of Ireland. Upcountry is the lower-slope area of Haleakala that overlooks the isthmus connecting the volcano with West Maui. Far below one can see the white ribbons of beaches, but in Upcountry, there are farms, flowers, and fireplaces. There are two routes in to Upcountry: from Kahului on the Haleakala Highway or, preferably, through Pa'ia and Makawao.

Once a sugar town, **Pa'ia** ⑱ has been changed in large part by the winds and waves at **Ho'okipa Beach** ⑲, one of the world's finest windsurfing places. Pa'ia now reflects a demographic shift from

Small surf-town life in Pa'ia.

plantation worker to windsurfer, artisan, and hipster. The town has become a haven for celebrities visiting Maui, and its main drag, Baldwin Avenue, is lined with just as many chi-chi boutiques as restaurants and tourist stores.

Just outside of Pa'ia is the **Mantokuji Mission**, a Japanese Buddhist temple with an oceanfront cemetery of more than 600 burial markers, most of them traditional Japanese. Higher up, **Pukalani** (Heavenly Gate) and **Makawao** ⑳ (Forest Beginning) lie at the geographical entrance to Upcountry. Makawao and surrounding villages were once home for both sugar plantation laborers and cattle cowboys. In recent years, Makawao has been rejuvenated by a diverse collection of newcomers ranging from upscale professionals to counterculture refugees. Even with the influx of cafés and boutiques, Makawao has retained a rough-hewn rustic feel from its days as a ranch town. On the Fourth of July, a wide variety of people turn out for the annual Makawao parade and rodeo, one of the biggest local events on Maui.

North of Makawao, on the flanks of Haleakala, stop for a picnic at **Ali'i Kula Lavender Farm** (www.aliikulala-vender.com), the biggest such farm in the islands. Beyond Makawao and Pukalani, the **Kula** area is blessed with a mild climate and rich, deep soil. As a result, its agriculture is probably the most diversified in Hawaii. During the California Gold Rush of the mid 1800s, Kula farmers grew potatoes, corn, and wheat for export to California. Nowadays, farmers harvest lettuce, cabbage, turnips, carrots, and peas. Most delectable, claim the gourmets, are the extra-sweet Kula onions, which are said to be unparalleled. Flowers of all colors and purposes are yet another Upcountry product, including many of the exquisite tropicals like heliconia, bird-of-paradise, and protea.

Highway 37 is the road that stretches from Makawao to Kula, and continuing south on this road brings visitors through the back portion of Upcountry. The road passes through **Waiakoa** and the **Church of the Holy Ghost** ㉑. This octagonal church, dating from the late 1890s, was built by Portuguese families who had settled on Maui two decades earlier.

Beyond Kula and **Keokea** (a good place to stop for coffee) on a narrow two-lane road, the 18,000-acre (7,300-hectare) **'Ulupalakua Ranch** ㉒ (www.ulupalakuaranch.com) marks a terrain shift from green and cool to brown and hot. Started as a sugar plantation in the 1850s, 'Ulupalakua is today a working cattle ranch of about 5,000 head, with additional sheep and elk. The ranch's general store offers *paniolo* gear and a deli. 'Ulupalakua Ranch is also home to Hawaii's only commercial vineyard, **Tedeschi Winery** ㉓ (tel: 878-6058; www.mauiwine.com; Tue–Sun 11am–5pm), which produces a rather diverse assortment, from pineapple wine to "champagne." The vineyard offers free tastings, tours, and a small museum.

From the winery at 'Ulupalakua Ranch, the view downslope south to the coast and **La Pérouse Bay** (see page 187) is as unobstructed as one could hope for.

Horses graze in Makawao.

ATOP HALEAKALA

Another road from Kula and Makawao climbs to the summit of Haleakala in more than 30 switchbacks, delivering exquisite views at every turn. More than half a million people visit **Haleakala National Park** ㉔ annually, many venturing into the basin either by foot or on guided horseback trips along a 30-mile (50km) system of trails. As far as visitors are concerned, the park consists of two distinct and mutually inaccessible sections, the main section at the top of the volcano, and another one extending down Haleakala's southeast flank to the Hana Coast and the 'Ohe 'o Gulch (Seven Pools; closed indefinitely for safety reasons).The National Park Service maintains two campgrounds (reservations need to be made six months ahead) in the basin for visitors, and another coastal campsite adjacent to 'Ohe 'o, which is approximately 10 miles (17km) past Hana.

Park Headquarters (tel: 572-4400; www.nps.gov/hale; daily 8am–3.45pm) offers information and a telephone, but no gas or food, and the Visitor Center (daily sunrise–3pm) at the summit has displays, restrooms, and shelter from the high-altitude cold winds. There are good overlooks of the summit basin itself at several spots along the way to the summit. At the **Kalahaku Overlook** ㉕, one may be lucky enough to see the striking Haleakala silversword, a native member of the sunflower family that flowers once a year, then dies.

Pu'u 'Ula'ula (Red Hill), the summit of Haleakala, now has a space-age tenant. Here at **Science City**, scientists track satellites across the sky and bombard the heavens with laser beams, while University of Hawaii researchers operate lunar and solar observatories. Both facilities are closed to the public.

CRATER HIKES

To drive yourself to the summit of Haleakala in time to see the dawn, you'll need to leave almost any hotel in the island by around 3am. Commercial tours pick up passengers even earlier than that; some offer the option of rolling back down the mountain on a bicycle.

Street scene in Makawao.

If you have the time and energy, it's well worth venturing down into the caldera itself, an extraordinarily desolate yet compelling wilderness of cinder cones and ash. After even the shortest of hikes, you'll have to walk steeply uphill in order to exit the crater, at an altitude of 10,000ft (3,000 meters), so prepare for a serious physical challenge. The most obvious route is to take the Sliding Sands Trail, which drops down from close to the visitor center. Distances are very deceptive once you're in the caldera, but you need to allow three or four hours for the round-trip if you want to descend at all far. A full day's hike will take you right into the heart of the caldera, and out again via the other major route, the Halemau'u Trail.

THE BACK SIDE OF HALEAKALA

There's another way to see Haleakala: from the back. Beyond 'Ulupalakua Ranch, Highway 37 becomes Highway 31, the Pi'ilani Highway, and begins a slow descent, rounding the southwest slopes of Haleakala and cutting across dry, open range where cattle roam. Pastures along this route are scarred by lava flows and abandoned stonework. Now parched and uninhabited, this vast leeward side of Haleakala once supported dryland forests and a population of Hawaiians.

In **Kaupo** ㉖, 5 miles (8km) of the road are unpaved, and most rental car contracts prohibit driving the unpaved sections due to risk of rockfalls. Check locally before you set off. Kaupo is about 1.5 miles (2.5km) past pavement's end (coming from Upcountry) just beyond **St Joseph's Church**, built in 1861. A well-defined trail winds up the southern slope and through the 8,200ft (2,500-meter) **Kaupo Gap** ㉗ into the basin atop Haleakala. Assuming it's clear, the road beyond Kaupo continues to Kipahulu and the Hana Coast, and eventually back to Pa'ia. Even if you were planning to turn around here, consider going a little farther to the eternally windswept setting of **Huialoha Church**, which was built in 1859 and is still in use.

Cinder cones seen from the Leleiwi Lookout in Haleakala National Park.

Paragliding over Kula.

Beach near the
Ke'anae Peninsula.

THE HANA COAST

On the rainy side of Haleakala, at the end of the windiest drive in Hawaii, Hana sits like an oasis, a spot almost too beautiful to be real.

Both geography and climate have conspired to keep the Hana district, the east-facing bulge of Haleakala, a separate world. Between Hana and the rest of Maui stretches the windward face of the mountain, and in Hawaii that means the rainy side of the island. Hana is so separate from Maui proper that ruling chiefs from the Big Island often claimed it as their own and defended it successfully against the challenges of Maui chiefs. Lovely, rounded Hana Bay, backed by lush grasslands and a mountainous wilderness of rain forest and waterfalls, was the site of some fierce fighting in the old days.

The road to Hana – also known as the Hana Highway – twists through jungle, over bridges, past waterfalls, and along cliff-edges for 35 miles (56km), finally straightening out in the town itself. It slices through a landscape scoured by water, cut with deep gulches, and choked with the enthusiastic flora of the rainforest. Despite infrastructure improvements over the years, the trek remains a stomach-churning drive of twists and turns, lasting a minimum of two hours, more if you divert to picnic or explore.

From the town of Hana, it's another 30 minutes along the Pi'ilani Highway to Haleakala National Park at Ohe'o Gulch, promoted, erroneously, as the "Seven Sacred Pools." At that point, one

can turn back, or else, assuming the highway is currently clear, continue on through Kaupo to completely encircle Haleakala. Either way, start early and plan to put in a long day. Remember that local people drive the road every day. They know every twist and turn, and they usually have a good reason to keep moving. It's polite to use the passing places and let *kama'aina*, or residents, go by.

THE ROAD TO HANA

Properly speaking, the **Hana Highway** begins at the one-mile marker (look

Main attractions
Hana Highway
Wai'anapanapa State Park
Pi'ilani Highway
Laulima Farmstand

Map on page 174

Surfing in Hana Bay.

◯ Tip

Souvenir T-shirts
promote the drive to
Hana as if it were a
transcontinental
expedition. It's not; it's
just a slow, winding road.
It is narrow, with several
one-lane bridges. If cars
pile up behind you, pull
over and let them past.

for the green rectangular signs on the roadside) at the bottom of Kaupakalua Road in **Haʻiku** ㉘.The gateway to the Hana Coast and the winding road is the quiet community of **Huelo** ㉙, with its small Congregational church, **Kaulanapueo** ("Owl Perch"), built in 1853. Maui's mood and ʻaina – land – begin to shift here, slipping away in the tropical wetness. From this point on, you'll be driving pretty slowly for most of the way, as pasture and open forest give way to ever-thickening jungle. Many of the bridges offer easy turnouts and places to swim. The best of these is the pool at mile 11, with the added bonus of a waterfall and covered pavilion.

Another good resting spot is at **Kaumahina State Wayside** ㉚ (www.dlnr. hawaii.gov/dsp/parks). The park's carefully tended grounds, with restrooms and picnic tables, include labeled examples of plants common to this coast. You can retrace your steps a few hundred yards/meters for a refreshing swim at **Puohokamoa Falls**. Or from the Kaumahina parking lot, hike to the upper left side of the park and experience a spectacular view of the **Keʻanae Peninsula**. The view here is due east, which may explain the name Kaumahina, or Rising Moon.

The road next drops into spectacular **Honomanu** (Bird Bay), with a rocky, black beach and canyon walls choked with flowering trees. Just after Honomanu, at about mile 16, is **Keʻanae** ㉛, a community of taro farmers who still maintain loʻi, or irrigated fields, that were first established over 500 years ago.

A narrow road leaves the highway and curves 0.5 miles (800 meters) down to a scattering of houses, a tiny cemetery, and a Congregational church built in 1860. Decades ago, when only a horse trail connected Keʻanae and Hana, there were two country grocery stores here, and the field behind the church was a baseball diamond. The school building used to face in the opposite direction, but a lethal tidal wave in 1946 spun it around on its foundations. The shoreline down here consists of jagged black lava rocks, lashed endlessly by crashing white surf.

Spectacular ocean views on the road to Hana.

Near the turn off to Ke'anae is the **Ke'anae Arboretum**, which offers a look at taro cultivation and pleasant walks among tropical and Hawaiian native plants.

CULTURAL LANDSCAPE AREA

Three miles (5km) farther is **Wailua** ㉜, another traditional taro-growing region. The state has designated this entire area as a Cultural Landscape, and life here follows patterns established long before Hawaii was discovered by Cook. Wailua's tiny **St Gabriel's Church** was one of the first to be built on this coast. The lookout on the Hana Highway above Wailua has picnic benches and a captivating view.

Continuing toward Hana, the highway offers another popular roadside stop, **Pua'a Ka'a** (Rolling Pig) **State Park**, between mile markers 22 and 23. Located here, where one least expects it, are a pay telephone, restrooms, and picnic tables, along with a natural waterfall and pool. Now you are approaching **Nahiku** ㉝, the wettest stretch of this coast. At the end of the 19th century, Nahiku was the home of America's first rubber plantation, with thousands of acres of rubber trees. The vigorous community was serviced by a small railroad and barges.

The most impressive accomplishment along this coast, however, is still active and clearly visible along the roadside as flumes, tunnels, engineered ditches, and watergates. In the late 19th century, the East Maui Irrigation Company built a water-delivery system that is arguably the boldest engineering accomplishment in post-discovery Hawaii, especially considering the awesome logistics of transporting all construction materials by horse, mule, and human power. The waterworks transformed Maui's arid central plain into verdant and extremely productive sugar cane fields.

The road begins to become easier at about mile 30. The **Hana Airport** ㉞, which has a limited commuter service to Honolulu and Kahului, is just beyond.

One mile farther, **Wai'anapanapa State Park** ㉟ offers a lava coastline ornately sculpted by nature, one of Maui's best campsites, hiking trails, and cabins set along a jet-black sand beach. Inland are a couple of caves with anchialine pools (linked to the ocean) that are great for swimming. Unfortunately, this is some of the only swimming available here; perhaps the only downside of Wai'anapanapa is that the ocean is often too rough to enjoy.

Nearby, visit the large **Pi'ilanihale Heiau** (temple). The rock platform of the *heiau* overlooks the coast and is part of an escorted or self-guided tour of **Kahanu Gardens** (tel: 248-8912; https://ntbg.org/gardens/kahanu; Mon–Fri 9am–3pm). Plant collections from Pacific islands is the focus here, including the world's largest collection of breadfruit cultivars.

HANA

Finally, the tortuous road unravels into the rolling hills and ranch pastures of **Hana** ㊱. Hawaiians say that "the sky comes close to Hana," and, indeed, moody clouds often hang low off the hills

Flags fly in the breeze at Hana Bay.

Hana Bay.

◎ Tip

If you like quiet, and you want a special place mostly for yourself, spend the night in Hana. The place is bewitching in the morning and evening hours, when the day-trip visitors are absent.

here. A local legend tells of a deity who once stood atop **Ka'uiki Hill**, the prominent cinder cone that forms the right flank of Hana Bay, and who was able to throw his spear right through the sky. Ka'uiki ("The Glimmer") served as a fortress during the wars with Kamehameha the Great. A cave here, now marked with a plaque, was the 1768 birthplace of Queen Ka'ahumanu, later the favorite of Kamehameha's many wives.

Directly above the bay and to the right, the **Hana Cultural Center & Museum** (tel: 248-8622; www.hanaculturalcenter. org; Mon–Fri 10am–4pm; $3 per person mandatory donation;) offers a brief, but thought-provoking glimpse into the area's history. Next to the museum is the small former courthouse dating to 1871, and a recently constructed *kauhale* – a compound of authentic thatch buildings constructed in the ancient style of this region. Several historic 19th-century churches add to Hana's appeal.

For a magnificent view of the Hana area, hike through the pasture above the town to the large stone cross on the hill; the cross is a memorial to Paul Fagan,

founder of the 3,000-acre (1,200-hectare) **Hana Ranch** (www.hanaranch.com), which owns much of the land in these parts. Pedestrian access to the memorial is from the parking lot across from the **Hana-Maui Resort** (www.hyatt.com/en-US/ hotel/hawaii/hana-maui-resort/oggal), a low-profile luxury retreat. A trail from the hotel's oceanfront cottages leads to the isolated red sands of Kahailulu. In addition to the hotel, camping and bed-and-breakfast accommodations are options for an overnight stay in Hana.

There are two markets in Hana. One of them is the well-known Hasegawa General Store. Rural Hawaii grew up on family-owned stores like this, established a generation or two ago by descendants of Japanese immigrants. Hasegawa Store is a general store in the fullest sense of the word, covering all the bases but with a totally eclectic inventory; prices are, given the scarcity of retail opportunities in town, usually on the high side.

BEYOND HANA

The road beyond Hana, known as the **Pi'ilani Highway**, passes through

Wailua Falls.

several miles of grassy ranchland. Watch for the next big cinder cone, Ka'uiki's twin, **Kaiwio Pele** ("Pele's Bone"), site of a legendary battle to the death between Pele, the volcano goddess, and the earth deity Kamapua'a, a pig-man. Tiny **'Alau Island**, just offshore, marks the spot where Maui, the demi-god, fished the Hawaiian Islands out of the sea with a magic hook. The spur road that curves down to the sea here passes two of Hana's most accessible beaches. **Koki Beach**, at the foot of the cinder cone, is shallow and sandy for a long way, and great for bodysurfing, but watch for riptides. As the road bends back to the main highway, it passes **Hamoa Beach** ㊲, a favorite of James Michener. The Hana-Maui Resort maintains facilities for its guests here, but the beach is open to the public.

From here to the Kipahulu district, the road encounters deep glades, sheer cliffs, and cascading waterfalls. **Wailua Falls** ㊳ is the most accessible. Then, 13 miles (21km) out of Hana, the road enters the lower portion of Haleakala National Park and crosses an arched, stone bridge that overlooks **Ohe'o Gulch** ㊴, a common turnaround spot for drivers heading back the way they came.

The parking lot here, with restrooms, is just past the bridge. A 0.6-mile (1km) trail leads down to the lower pools, which are wonderful swimming holes – though they were closed at the time of writing for safety reasons. Be aware that 250ins (6,350mm) of rain falls annually in the forests above, and the stream and pools can quickly become raging torrents. Near the bottom-most pools and along the cliffs fronting the ocean are the stone foundations of an ancient fishing village. Just south of this area is a campground, with tent sites along the foot of the dramatic basalt cliffs. Campers may stay for up to three days at a time. Fires are forbidden, but barbecue pits are provided, as well as restrooms. Bring your own water, however.

One of the most rewarding hikes on the island begins directly across the road from the parking lot: a 2-mile (3.2km)

Waves pound the rocky shore at the Hana-Maui resort.

A more gentle beach near the Hana-Maui Resort.

⊘ LAULIMA FARM STAND

There are farm stands, and then there is the farm stand at Laulima Farm (www.laulimafarm.com), just outside of Kipahulu, near Hana. In addition to selling fruits and vegetables grown on site at Laulima Farm, the farm stand serves as a gathering place for locals and visitors who wish to sample baked goods, drink estate-grown coffee, listen to music, or otherwise just relax. In this way, Laulima has become the rural Hana take on a local pub – a reliable place to strike up a conversation with just about anyone. Laulima also is renowned for its volunteer program; anyone can come and work the land in exchange for room and board. The farm stand used to sell smoothies made in a bicycle-powered blender; the smoothies are off the menu these days but photos of the blender remain.

climb inland to **Waimoku Falls**. Rangers have built two mildly spectacular bridges, and also a boardwalk to keep the ground virginal while passing through the heart of an enormous bamboo forest. Still, the trek is not easy. Waimoku Falls is high (400ft/120 meters), sheer, and powerful enough to keep observers at a distance. Afternoon showers in the hills can mean flash flooding.

KIPAHULU AND KAUPO

Beyond Ohe'o Gulch is the drier, grassy Kipahulu district and the village of **Kipahulu** . About a mile past the pools lie the ruins of the **Kipahulu Sugar Mill**, a relic of the early 20th century. Below the ruins, a narrow, paved road leads toward the ocean and to tiny **Palapala Ho'omau Church**, erected in 1857. This is the burial place of aviation pioneer Charles Lindbergh, the first person to fly solo from Paris to New York. The church is open to visitors who respect the surrounding property and homes.

The road beyond is paved except for about 5 miles (8km) of rugged, jaw-rattling dirt toward Kaupo; driving on the unpaved sections of the road is prohibited by most car rental companies. It is always liable to be blocked by rock falls; check locally before you set off. The road breezes past the soft pastures of Kipahulu, touches a cove, then climbs a spine-tingling, cliff-side grade into the sterner landscape of Kaupo. Cattle guards mark the entrance to **Kaupo Ranch**, a large cattle operation since the late 19th century. A windswept and surf-pounded peninsula juts out below the road, where **Huialoha**, a restored old Congregational circuit church is sited. Huialoha was built in 1859, when Kaupo was almost totally isolated, accessible only by sea and a primitive trail. The crumbling walls behind the church were once a school. Offshore is an ancient surfing area once known as **Mokulau** ("Many Islets"), named for the lava islets sprinkled just offshore. The winds here seem to never stop.

The small store in **Kaupo** was once the only local source of food and supplies on this part of the island, but it now caters mostly to travelers in rental cars and minivans. From here, the road continues to Upcountry.

Toward the mountain, the slopes of Haleakala rise to a deep slash at the top called the **Kaupo Gap**, 8,200ft (2,500 meters) above sea level, which opens into Haleakala basin. In ancient times, the gap was the primary route taken by Hawaiians traversing Maui on foot. It was easier to climb the mountain than to bushwhack through the coastal jungle. Horseback trips are available; hikers also make the climb, though it's nearly all up hill and can be jarring on joints.

Kipahulu Valley, on the Hana side of the gap, is a protected natural science reserve that is closed to the public. Untouched by introduced species of flora or fauna, the reserve shelters vast expanses of native trees like *koa* and *'ohi'a*, and endangered birds like the Maui parrotbill and Maui *nukupu'u*.

One of the pools at Ohe'o Gulch.

The trail to Waimoku Falls cuts through a dense bamboo forest.

📷 DISAPPEARING FLORA AND FAUNA

No doubt both the Polynesians and Europeans had good intentions, but both groups introduced plants and animals that have decimated Hawaii's own flora and fauna.

The Hawaiian Monk Seal is shy, keeping to itself in the uninhabited islands and atolls of northwestern Hawaii. You may encounter one on the less frequented beaches of the major islands; if you do, it is illegal to approach or touch it. It is one of only two indigenous mammals in Hawaii; the other is the hoary bat. The Polynesian rat, introduced by ancient Polynesians, is considered by some to have evolved enough to count as a Hawaiian species.

AVIAN DECLINE

Many species of Hawaii's native birds, evolving through the centuries with few natural predators, have all but disappeared. The mongoose, introduced to combat rats, prefers eggs and has decimated native birds. Other introduced species threaten Hawaii's birds everywhere except Kauai. The mynah, introduced by Europeans, is a pushy creature, and it has forced many other bird species from their habitat. Another serious threat to both indigenous and introduced bird species is the brown snake from Guam, a potential arrival as a stowaway on commercial and military aircraft.

FLORA

Prior to the arrival of people, the level of endemic plant species was higher in Hawaii than anywhere else on the planet. Today, the flora we associate with Hawaii – plumeria, hibiscus, pineapples, bananas, guavas – are all introduced species. Hawaii's indigenous plants are fighting for survival, and many are already extinct.

The nene is Hawaii's state bird. Males and females look identical.

The nene, or Hawaiian Goose, is found on the Big Island, Maui and Kauai, usually at higher elevations. Unlike other goose species, the nene lacks webbed feet; it has claws that are more useful on the volcanic slopes.

Pigs, introduced by Polynesians, and goats and cattle, introduced by Europeans, have destroyed Hawaii's native plant species.

Silversword plants in Haleakala National Park, Maui. The silversword is adapted to high-altitude life, but walking to close to it will crush its roots.

Hawaii's benign evolution

Statistically speaking – at least before the first humans arrived 1,500 years ago – a new species had become established on Hawaii every 15,000 years. Hawaii's extreme remoteness gave those animal and plant species that arrived a unique environment in which to grow, independent of outside influence. By the time we humans showed up, nearly 9,000 kinds of flora and fauna unique to the islands had evolved, including the silversword.

In the absence of mammals and other interlopers, plants did not develop defenses such as thorns and toxins, nor did birds develop types of behavior that protected them from predators. When people introduced numerous animal species – from birds to grazing cattle – Hawaii's indigenous species in populated areas were poorly equipped for survival.

The good news is those native plants and birds that were not in populated areas survived. Many of these specimens are found largely in inaccessible places such as the cliffs of Molokai's north shore, the boggy highlands of Kauai, and the restricted and fenced-in Kipahulu Valley of eastern Maui. Biologically, they keep the old days alive.

Today however, Hawaii's flora and fauna is challenged by a new threat – climate change. Increasing temperatures are, for instance, pushing avian malaria – an introduced disease that thrives in warm environs – further uphill, squeezing the safe zone for Hawaii's remaining native forest birds. Rising sea levels threaten to submerge low-lying islands – the habitat of nesting turtles and breeding monk seals. What's more, warmer sands could result in a loss of male turtles, for the sex is determined by temperature during incubation. Warmer waters also increase the risk of coral bleaching and disease among sea life.

Another introduced mammal, the mongoose, has decimated many of Hawaii's indigenous birds. Brought by Europeans to control rats, it preferred birds – it is a day mammal and rats prefer the night.

The reclusiveness of the Hawaiian Monk Seal (hence, the "monk") has probably assured its species' survival. Rare is the sighting of a grown Monk Seal (seen here on Poipu Beach Park on Kauai), much less a seal pup. Wisely, they prefer uninhabited islands.

The black-necked stilt is one of Hawaii's native birds, but lacks the necessary defensive behavior against introduced predators. Found only in a few inland wildlife sanctuaries, such as on Maui's central isthmus, the stilt is a delightful sighting for a birdwatcher.

Kayaking along the northern shores of Molokai.

Okala Island and cliffs viewed from Kalawao.

MOLOKAI

Quiet and underdeveloped, Molokai retains a colorful history, and a distinctive "Hawaiian" ambiance.

There's not much happening on Molokai, and that's precisely its appeal. Tourist resorts are few. Tiki bars are practically non-existent. And those big bus tours that you might spot on more populous islands such as Oahu and Maui? They are nowhere in sight.

No, life on Molokai is wonderfully slow, affording visitors the opportunity to sit down and talk with locals and learn about the island's history the old-fashioned way: through stories. Some of these stories undoubtedly will spotlight the cliffs in the north, the world's tallest ocean cliffs. Other stories will focus on the historic colony of those suffering from Hansen's Disease (formerly known as leprosy). Still others will spotlight the fish ponds, the vistas, and the untrammeled beaches. By the end of your visit, after four or five days on Molokai, you'll "get" what the place is all about.

The island is a haven for adventure-seeking travelers who want to immerse themselves in authentic Hawaii – the Hawaii they won't get anywhere else. It's for travelers who will be comfortable in hotels that are clean but not luxurious. It's also pretty much exclusively for adults; because activities are minimal, Molokai is a place where young kids would get bored and older kids might get a little stir crazy after a while.

For those who give it a chance, however, who stick around and open their

minds to the island's brilliance, the experience can be rewarding, even life-changing. Molokai is just about as Hawaiian as the Hawaiian Islands get.

VOLCANIC ORIGINS

On a map, Molokai appears to be shaped like a slender slipper, 38 miles (60km) long and 10 miles (16km) wide. The island has three geological anchors, each created by volcanic activity millions of years ago. **Mauna Loa**, a 1,380ft (420-meter) tableland at the western end of the island (not to be confused with

◉ **Main attractions**
Kaunakakai
Pepe'opae Trail
Pala'au State Park
Kalaupapa National
  Historical Park
Halawa Valley

Map on page 208

Riding mules in Kalaupapa.

⊙ Fact

Molokai's population has Hawaii's highest percentage of Native Hawaiians: it is estimated that more than 60 percent of the island's residents are of native descent. For this reason it is considered the "most Hawaiian Island."

the active volcano of the same name on Hawaii Island), was noted in ancient times for an adze quarry, *holua* slides (snowless sledding), and as a source of wood for sorcery images.

Later, the east Molokai volcano erupted, and **Mauna Kamakou** was pushed up to 4,970ft (1,515 meters) to become the island's highest point. Kalaupapa Peninsula, properly called Makanalua, was born even more recently, when 400ft (120-meter) **Kauhako**, a small shield volcano, poured forth its lava to shape a flat tongue of land in the center of the northern coast. It is separated from the rest of the island by a fortress-like barrier of *pali*, or high cliffs, perfect for isolating a colony of exiles.

AGRICULTURAL MOLOKAI

Molokai's land is primarily agricultural, and development has been limited. And, perhaps best of all for the adventurous traveler, tourists are few. Only a few paved roads transit Molokai, and some of its more spectacular sights and places of archeological interest require a 4x4 vehicle, boat, or helicopter to view.

Ho'olehua Airport ❶ is situated 7 miles (11km) away from the town of **Kaunakakai ❷**, which is on the southern coast. More than half of the island's 7,300 people live near Kaunakakai. Ala Malama, the main street, contains old buildings that have probably changed very little since the "Cockeyed Mayor of Kaunakakai," who was made famous in a *hapa-haole* (semi-Caucasian) song popular during the 1930s, strolled along its streets.

A wharf – the longest in the entire State of Hawaii – extends several hundred yards/meters out to sea at Kaunakakai; barges were loaded with pineapples here until the plantations closed down in the 1970s and 1980s. The focus is now on crops such as corn, watermelon, coffee, and onions. Before becoming king in 1863, Kamehameha V spent his summers on Molokai. The nearby **Kapuaiwa Coconut Grove** (Kapuaiwa means "Mysterious Taboo"), which originally contained 1,000 coconut trees on 10 acres (4 hectares) of land, was planted for him in the 1860s.

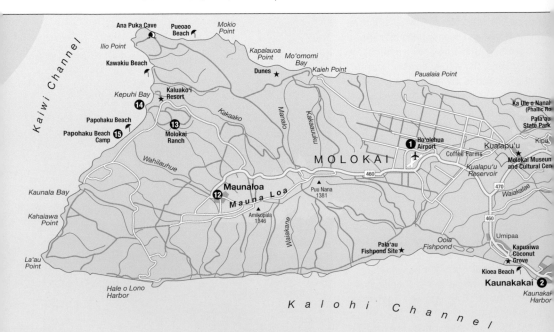

THE RAINFOREST

Shrouded as often as not by clouds, the summit of Molokai's eastern mountain, Mauna Kamakou, holds a remarkable unspoiled expanse of Hawaiian rainforest. The only route to the top is up a gravel road that branches east just south of the junction of Maunaloa Highway and the highway to Kaunakakai, and soon degenerates into muddy ruts that are only passable in a high-clearance 4x4 vehicle. Most of this area is accessible only on monthly guided tours from The Nature Conservancy, and the tours fill up months in advance. To get on the list, call the **Nature Conservancy Office** (tel: 553-5236; www.nature.org).

Nine miles (14km) up from the highway, the curious **Sandalwood Boat** ❸ is actually a hole in the ground roughly the size and shape of a 19th-century sailing ship's hold. Hawaiian laborers would fill this pit with the amount of sandalwood that such ships could carry, before selling it to Western traders. Sandalwood was once common throughout the Hawaiian Islands, but demand from China, where it was appreciated for its fragrance, encouraged the Hawaiian king to harvest it until there was no more left.

WAIKOLU LOOKOUT AND THE PEPE'OPAE TRAIL

A mile further on, the **Waikolu Lookout** offers a first glimpse of the beautiful and rugged cliffs of Molokai's northern shore, the highest sea cliffs anywhere in the world. It also marks the start of the Kamakou Preserve, which protects unique Hawaiian plants and birds. A little over 2 miles (4km) farther on, you reach the **Pepe'opae Trail**, one of Hawaii's greatest hikes, an hour-long stretch of springy boardwalk that leads through extraordinary high-altitude mountain boglands and stunted forest to reach further verdant views. The two deep valleys along this shore, Wailau and Pelekunu, cannot be reached on foot. The expensive and spectacular way to see them is by helicopter. Trips depart from Maui, or in summer you can also take a boat trip from Kaunakakai.

Boats in Kaunakakai Wharf.

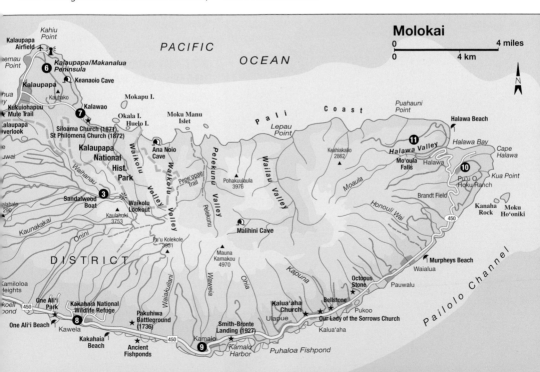

CENTRAL MOLOKAI

Branching north off Maunaloas Highway, onto Kala'e Highway, just beyond
the rainforest turn off, brings you to
Kualapu'u, an old Del Monte company
town; there are several unusual attractions en route, between Kaunakakai
and the end of the road lookouts. A bit
farther down the road is the **Molokai
Museum and Cultural Center** (tel: 567-
6436; Mon–Sat 10am–2pm). Adjacent
to the historic **R.W. Meyer Sugar Mill**,
the center provides a Molokai perspective on the Hawaiian past.

PALA'AU STATE PARK

Still heading north, you come to
Pala'au State Park ❹, where the park
road passes through an attractive for-
ested area of *koa*, paperbark, ironwood,
and cypress trees. A small arboretum
with more than 40 species of trees and
a picnic area await at the end of the
road. From the parking lot, it's a short
walk and a slight climb to **Ka Ule o
Nanahoa** ("Penis of Nanahoa"), a phallic rock 6ft (1.8 meters) high and once
visited by those who believed it was

a cure for infertility. The **Kalaupapa
Overlook ❺** offers a spectacular view
from atop the 1,600ft (485-meter) -high
cliffs above the former leprosy colony.

KALAUPAPA

In his novel *Hawaii*, published in
1959, James Michener described
the **Makanalua Peninsula ❻** (often
referred to as the **Kalaupapa Peninsula**, after the settlement) as "a
majestic spot, a poem of nature... In
the previous history of the world no
such hellish spot had ever stood in
such heavenly surroundings."

This area has had a colorful history to
say the least. In 1866, the year of Mark
Twain's visit to Molokai, the Hawaiian
government began transporting victims of Hansen's Disease, or leprosy, to
Molokai. The exiles were literally pushed
from the boat into the peninsula's rough
coastal waters, with little care whether
or not they would survive. Over the years,
more than 8,000 people were exiled to
Kalaupapa. In later years, when Father
Damien was dispatched to Molokai to
look after these patients, more than
1,000 exiles lived here. Now there are
fewer than 10 residents in Kalaupapa.
They all live there voluntarily.

KALAUPAPA NATIONAL
HISTORICAL PARK

Today, Kalaupapa is protected by the
Kalaupapa National Historical Park
(open 24 hrs; www.nps.gov/kala), which was
established in 1980 and is jointly administered by the National Park Service and
the State of Hawaii. Permission to visit
the historical park is easily obtained
through Makani Kai airlines, through
an outfitter or by contacting the Hawaii
State Department of Health in Honolulu
or Molokai. Children under the age of 16
are not permitted to visit Kalaupapa.

There are two ways to arrive: by air,
which takes you to a small airport on
the peninsula, or from the top of the
cliffs down a steep trail. The most
colorful way to manage the trail, which

*Riding mules on the
beach in Kalaupapa.*

drops 1,800ft (550 meters) to the peninsula, is on the back of a nimble-footed mule, which you can organize with the **Kalaupapa Mule Tour** (tel: 567-6088; www.muleride.com; Mon–Sat departs 8.30am, returns 3.30pm). Only 100 permits are allowed for people to enter Kalaupapa each year; visitors must go through Father Damien Tours (tel: 349-3006; www.fatherdamientours. com), and can either charter a plane, ride the mules, or hike. Tours book up in advance so call ahead. State law prohibits photographing residents without their permission. Although some residents still suffer from Hansen's Disease, they are no longer confined to the island; as previously mentioned, they live here by choice. The disease can now be cured, and, despite the fears that surrounded it for so many years, is contagious but not easily contracted.

East across the Kalaupapa Peninsula is the abandoned settlement of **Kalawao** ❼, site of the original colony. **Siloama Church**, the Church of the Healing Spring, was built here by Protestants in 1871. The Catholic church nearby, **St Philomena's**, has a monument to Father Damien, marking his original burial spot. The plan is to preserve Kalaupapa as a living community until the last resident has died or departed, then to preserve it as a historic park.

EASTERN MOLOKAI

East from Kaunakakai, the Kamehameha V Highway runs for 28 miles (61km) along the southern coast to Halawa. There is much to see along this road, the second half of which is a narrow lane twisting along the coast. It is a long drive, and a slow one. Just a few miles past Kaunakakai is **Oneali'i Park** (Royal Sands), a beach with campsites. For a small daily fee, campers may stay here for two weeks but must renew their permit every three days.

If you have the time, hiking Halawa Valley is perhaps the best way to get to know the real Molokai. The hike crosses private lands and therefore requires permission from the landowner, **Anakala Pilipo Solatorio** (tel: 542-1855; www.halawavalleymolokai.com), to proceed. Solatorio's family offers

Storefronts in Kaunakakai.

⊙ FATHER DAMIEN

Father Damien (formerly Joseph De Veuster) arrived in the islands in 1862 from Belgium. He came to Molokai in 1873 and remained until his death 16 years later. During that time, Damien organized the colony at Kalaupapa into a true community, establishing a church and small health clinic. Land was cleared, crops were grown, and a modern water system installed. By 1883 Damien had contracted Hansen's Disease and six years later he died, just 49 years old. He was buried in Kalaupapa, but his body was returned to Belgium in 1936. In 1907, the writer Jack London traced the priest's footsteps around Kalaupapa, writing a number of short stories about Hansen's Disease after his visit, including a chapter in *The Cruise of the Snark* about the Kalaupapa residents.

Tip

Molokai's biggest social event of the year takes place at Hale o Lono, a rocky harbor on the southwest coast. It is the starting point of the annual Molokai to-Oahu (www.molokaihoe.com) outrigger canoe race, held in October. The 41-mile (66km) race ends in Waikiki. A similar championship race – this time on paddle boards – is held at the end of July (www.molokai2oahu.com).

guided hikes up to a series of water-falls as well. A number of residents will claim to offer passage through this area, but Solatorio is the only rightful landowner at this time. Because the land itself is considered sacred, it is protocol to bring with you a small gift as a token of appreciation for passage.

Along the southern coastal road are numerous **ancient fishponds** dating back as far as the 15th century. These were built in order to supply food for the fami-lies of chiefs. Such ponds are found on all of the Hawaiian Islands, but the larg-est concentrations were on Oahu and the south coast of Molokai. A few of the ponds have been restored and stocked, an exercise in cultural revival with com-mercial potential, in the hope of develop-ing aquaculture. At least one or two of them welcome visitors – especially those who are willing to volunteer their time.

Above **Kawela** ❽ is a battlefield where Kamehameha the Great won an early skirmish. It's been said that his war-canoe fleet landed upon the beach here in an assault wave 4 miles (6km) long. In 1736, two decades before

Kamehameha's birth, an invading war fleet from Oahu battled combined armies from Molokai and Hawaii Island here. The Oahu chief was killed and his army defeated. Appropriately, perhaps, Kawela means "the heat."

Visitors should stop at **Kamalo** ❾, where Father Damien built the second of his two churches on this side of the island. He constructed this white, wood-frame structure in 1876 and dedicated it to St Joseph. Nearby is the spot where Ernest Smith and Emory Bronte ended the first civilian flight from the mainland by crash-ing their plane into a *kiawe* thicket in 1927. An earlier military attempt at flying to Hawaii from the mainland fell, liter-ally, 300 miles (480km) short of Hawaii. At **Kalua'aha** is the restored **Our Lady of Sorrows Church**, built by Damien in 1874. Also at Kalua'aha is the **Kalua'aha Church**, which was constructed by Con-gregationalist missionaries in 1844 but now lies in ruins.

PU'U O HOKU

Three miles (5km) beyond **Waialua**, the road twists inland and begins winding

Halawa Bay.

up to **Pu'u O Hoku Ranch** ⑩, which boasts cottages and an organic farm (www.puuohoku.com). Looking back down the mountain from a turnout before the destination (which means, "Hill of Stars"), the scenery is spectacular. Across the **Pailolo Channel** is Maui, a little more than 10 miles (16km) away, and in the distance the great dome of Haleakala. Closer is tiny 10-acre (4-hectare) **Moku Ho'oniki** (Pinch Island). It is nicknamed Elephant Rock by inter-island pilots, because it looks like a pachyderm lying at rest in the ocean, its trunk stretched out toward Maui.

Just past the ranch entrance is the sacred *kukui*-tree grove of **Kalanikaula**, or the Royal Prophet. These silvery-leafed trees once encircled the home of Lanikaula, a local *kahuna* (priest) and seer or prophet who lived here. Hawaiian laborers once refused to help Del Monte clear the area because of Lanikaula's *mana* (spirit power) and a non-Hawaiian grower who cut down some trees to plant pineapples here found that his crop wilted.

Travelers speak of seeing torch lights moving through the grove at night, said to be spirits returning to Kalanikaula.

HALAWA VALLEY

The road ends at a park and sandy shoreline on deep **Halawa Bay**, the mouth of 4-mile (6.4km) -long **Halawa Valley** ⑪. Although this is a beautiful spot, the ocean currents at the stream's mouth can be tricky, so exercise great caution. Additionally, Portuguese man-o'-war jellyfish are occasionally swept into the bay by offshore winds, and they can give the unwary a very nasty sting. Hundreds of fishing and farming families once lived here, but only a handful remain.

At the rear of the valley there are two waterfalls that feed a stream flowing into the sea. The highest is 250ft (76-meter) **Mo'oula Falls**, the legendary home of a giant lizard and there are a number of traditions and legends surrounding this lizard. The only way to see the falls these days is to go on a guided hike, so select a leader from a cadre of local guides before you arrive.

Sculpture of Father Damien in St Philomena Church in Kalawao.

⊘ THE MOLOKAI WAY

Life is different on Molokai. Legends are part of day-do-day happenings; superstition and tradition drives a large part of how locals live. These differences manifest themselves in subtle ways. On other islands, for instance, the story of a historic object might be explained with one narrative upon which everyone agrees. On Molokai, however, six different people might have six different stories about how a particular incident or event unfolded, and the only way to divine the "truth" is to listen to all of the different stories, then decide which sounds best. Oral history is an important part of understanding Molokai's history and culture; if you visit the island and haven't heard "stories" from the locals during your stay, then you aren't trying hard enough.

*A phallic stone thought
to enhance fertility in
Pala'au State Park.*

Kalaupapa coastline.

WESTERN MOLOKAI

Back through Kaunakakai and up past Ho'olehua Airport, the Maunaloa Highway runs through a dry landscape for about 10 miles (16km). **Maunaloa** ⑫, itself a former plantation town, lies at the end of the road.

Much of this dry leeward side of the island is composed of grazing land owned by the 40,000-acre (16,000-hectare) **Molokai Ranch** ⑬, the largest local landowner. When the Dole Company closed down its pineapple operations here in 1976, the firm returned almost 10,000 acres (4,000 hectares) to the ranch, much of which has been planted with hay, grown for commercial purposes. Cattle rearing continued to be the mainstay of the ranch's operation until it closed down entirely in 2008. The ranch is up on sale, allegedly for a hefty sum of $260 million.

Not far away, but hidden away from the gaze of casual visitors, is one of the most sacred spots in Hawaii. Dedicated to Laka, the goddess of hula, a difficult-to-find *heiau* (temple) is said to be the birthplace of this ancient dance form. *Halau hula* (hula school) students and

their *kupuna* (elders) gather here before sunrise to make offerings before performing at the annual Molokai Ka Hula Piko festival (www.kahulapiko.com) in the first week of June. Parts of this festival are open to the public, but if you plan to attend, it's best to go with a local guide who can explain what is happening.

KEPUHI BAY

A number of spurs branch off the main highway and wind down to the coastline. Condominiums on the west side, at **Kepuhi Bay** ⑭ near the northwestern tip, have closed in recent years, basically eliminating overnight accommodations in this area. That said, neighboring Papohaku Beach, a vast expanse of golden sand, is worth a visit, and on clear nights the lights of Oahu and Diamond Head are visible across the 26-mile (42km) -wide Kaiwi Channel. Only the strongest swimmers should venture into the ocean along the beach. The treacherous current and pounding waves, nicknamed the Oahu Express, can sweep the unwary out to sea. Camping is allowed by permit at **Papohaku Beach Camp** ⑮.

Explore Kalaupapa from the back of a mule.

Storefront and antique car near Dole Park, Lanai City.

LANAI

Privately owned but open to visitors, Lanai has changed its focus from pineapples to luxury resorts, and is primed for the big time.

Main attractions
Lanai City
Sweetheart Rock
Munro Trail
Shipwreck Beach
Garden of the Gods

Map on page 218

Lanai, Hawaii's sixth-largest island, is lots of things at once: from quintessential Hawaiian palm trees to barren red-rock landscape and whole days without sunshine up in the hills. The island's beaches are among the best in the state. With high-tech billionaire Larry Ellison now owning 98 percent of the island, Lanai has experienced significant development over the last few years. Adults-only wellness retreat Sensei Lanai, a Four Seasons Resort (formerly the Lodge at Koele) reopened in 2019 following a five-year renovation, hot on the heels of the 2016 revamp of bigger sister, the Four Seasons Resort Lanai.

THE VISITOR EXPERIENCE

Lanai offers a number of microclimates in a relatively small amount of surface area – 18 miles (29km) long and 13 miles (21km) wide, to be exact. Beaches are breathtaking; the stretch fronting the Four Seasons Resort Lanai at Manele Bay is great for sunbathing and swimming, and other beaches such as Hulopo'e offer epic snorkeling, too. Up in the mountains, in the

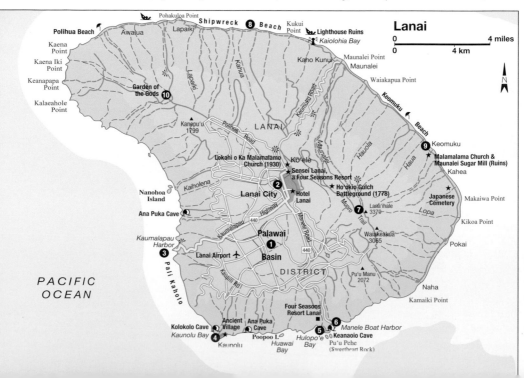

tiny town of Lanai City or at Sensei Lanai, a Four Seasons Resort, the vibe is completely different, with pine trees, putt-putt golf, and much more manic weather than down at the beach.

Outside of these tourist-centric areas, Lanai is full of adventure. Visitors rent 4x4 vehicles and go off-roading in the Martian landscape of an area known as the Garden of the Gods. On the windward side of the island, people putter from cove to cove, trying desperately to stay out of the gusts. You can drive on a dirt road to Polihua Beach in the north; you also can hike to the Kaunolu Village site and brush up on local history or go tidepooling in the surf. Perhaps the best part of these activities: you've got most of them all to yourself.

HISTORICAL OVERVIEW

The ancient Hawaiians felt Lanai was inhabited by spirits and, according to legend, people stayed away from the island until one day a hero named Kaulula'au, the son of a chief from Lahaina, crossed the channel and rid the place of danger.

The first Western residents were Mormons, who in the mid-1850s arranged generous lease terms with chief Ha'alelea of Oahu. James Dole, a persevering businessman from Boston, purchased Lanai in 1922 for $1.1 million, and planted the island with pineapple almost immediately, Dole then created a deep-water harbor at Kaumalapau and laid out a nearby town for the Japanese and Filipino immigrants who came to work on his Lanai plantation.

Dole's Hawaiian Pineapple Company prospered and was later purchased by one of Hawaii's original "Big Five" kama'aina (resident) corporations, Castle & Cooke, which kept Dole's name and operated the plantation as the Dole Pineapple Company. In 1987, California investor David Murdock bought controlling interest of Castle & Cooke. Like Dole, Murdock moved quickly, building two world-class hotels, two golf courses, new homes for the island's residents, and a recreational complex in the middle of Lanai City. Stunning the locals but acting pragmatically given the competition of cheaper Asian pineapples, he plowed up more than 13,000 acres (5,260 hectares) of what was once the world's largest pineapple plantation. Fewer than 500 acres (200 hectares) of pineapple land remain on Lanai – token fields to provide pineapples for the island's three hotels. Other fields are being replaced by experimental crops such as citrus, onions, papayas, macadamia, coffee, and grains used for cattle and other livestock feed.

Lanai hit the big time when Microsoft CEO Bill Gates got married there in 1994. Since then, celebrities and athletes have frequented the island with abandon. Finally, in 2012, Lanai became the private property of someone else: Larry Ellison, CEO of Oracle Corp. Ellison was reported to pay about $600 million for the island, and has

En route to the Garden of the Gods.

⊘ Tip

There's excellent snorkeling just outside the breakwater at Manele Boat Harbor, or you can take a snorkel cruise to the clear waters off the south coast with **Adventure Lanai Island Club** (tel: 565-7373; www. adventurelanaiislandclub. com/).

vowed to spend a reported $500 million more on infrastructure improvements. Some resorts have already been upgraded while others are in the process of being renovated.

SEEING THE SIGHTS

The heart of the island is a lone volcanic crater, **Palawai**, long extinct and weathered into a subtle depression surrounded by a great saucer of fertile but dry farmland. The **Palawai Basin** ❶ once sustained the largest pineapple plantation in the world; today, its grassy fields glimmer in the soft, muted light.

Lanai City ❷, built by Dole in the early 1920s, is home to virtually all 2,700 residents of the island. Located inland at the base of the Lana'ihale ridge, it's a classic plantation town – quiet, modest, and orderly, designed around rectangular Dole Park edged with stores, the headquarters of the Lanai Company, and the vintage 11-room **Hotel Lanai**. Nearby is Sensei Lanai, a Four Seasons Resort, one of the two award-winning Four

Seasons resorts that sustain the island's economy. Three paved roads connect Lanai City with the coast. One, heading southwest, leads to the airport and **Kaumalapau Harbor** ❸. When the pineapple was king on Lanai, more than a million pineapples a day were loaded onto barges here for shipment to the Honolulu cannery 60 miles (100km) away. Now, infrequent incoming barges are filled with supplies for the island, and a ferry from Maui deposits passengers five times daily.

A very rough road off the highway leads down to **Kaunolu Bay**, but you must hike more than 3 miles (5km) on rocky trails; it is off-limits for rental vehicles – 4x4 or otherwise. At the hike's end are the hard-to-locate ruins of **Kaunolu** ❹, an ancient fishing village, and Kamehameha's summer home. Kaonolu is rich with the *mana*, or spiritual power, of old Hawaii. Nearby is Kahekili's Leap, a scenic lookout named after the Maui chief renowned for diving into the waters below. The coastal views from here are breathtaking.

Garden of the Gods.

⊘ A REAL "SWEETHEART"

Just offshore in Hulopo'e Bay, Sweetheart Rock (Pu'u Pehe) is the centerpiece of a Hawaiian legend that revolves around two lovers: Pehe and her warrior boyfriend, Makakehau. Taken at face value, the tale bears eerie similarities to Shakespeare's "Romeo and Juliet." The climax of the story occurs during a terrible storm; when Pehe drowns in the surge, Makakehau takes her body out to the rock and buries her near the 80ft (24-meter) summit. Stricken with grief, he then jumps to his death in the churning sea below. Hawaiians believe the rock is a memorial to their love. Today the rock is only accessible (by kayak or stand-up paddleboard) when the water is flat-calm. From the Four Seasons Resort Lanai at Manele Bay there's a 3-mile (5km) round-trip hike; cross a sandy beach and climb the bluff-top for a spectacular view of the rock.

HULOPO'E MARINE LIFE

It's a much easier 20-minute drive on a paved road from Lanai City to **Hulopo'e Bay 5**. The bay, a nature conservation district that's off-limits to nearly all boats, is home to spinner dolphins, turtles, and an abundance of other marine life. Hulopo'e is the best place on the island to swim and snorkel. You can also hike along the eastern coast to reach the panoramic lookout that takes in Sweetheart Rock, with Maui rising majestically above the horizon. Conveniently, the Manele Bay resort stands in a commanding position directly over Hulopo'e Bay; a trail leads down from the hotel to the beach. Frequent shuttles carry people from Sensei Lanai, a Four Seasons Resort, a 20-minute drive away. The state even allows camping at six sites on the grass above the beach. Permits are available from Lanai Company for a maximum stay of seven days. Just around an easterly point from Hulopo'e Bay is **Manele Boat Harbor 6**.

OFF-ROAD EXCURSIONS

Lanai's most unusual touring route is surely the **Munro Trail**. This is a 4x4 dirt track that climbs along the island's eastern ridge, cresting at **Lana'ihale 7**, the high point at 3,370ft (1,030 meters). On a clear day, all the major Hawaiian islands except Kauai and Ni'ihau can be seen on the horizon. The Munro Trail continues down past **Ho'okio Gulch**, scene of a 1778 battle involving Kamehameha the Great, to Ko'ele and back to Lanai City. Start from Manele Road end, because descending is easier than ascending on the mushy, slippery Ko'ele side. The trail is impassable during rainy weather.

Another popular excursion heads out to the island's convex northeast coast. It can be reached by following Keomuku Road until it forks near the shoreline. To the left is a track to **Shipwreck Beach 8**, so named because of the rusting hulk of the *Helena Pt. Townsend*, a tanker that has sat impaled on a reef in 12ft (4 meters) of water for over 50 years. To the right is a better road to the abandoned village of **Keomuku 9**. The trip to Keomuku takes about 45 minutes; the village was abandoned after the 1901 collapse of the Maunalei Sugar Company. A short distance down the road is an oblong stone marker, a sad memorial to the Japanese immigrant workers who died of a plague during Keomoku's plantation days.

The **Garden of the Gods 10** can be reached by driving northwest along the Polihua Road, which turns into a dirt track that passes through grasslands. This is a strange playground of strewn boulders and disfigured lava formations that look spectacular at sunset, when they glow an unearthly orange. The route to the Garden of the Gods also passes one of the largest examples of a dry-land forest in Hawaii at **Kanepu'u**. Protected by high fences, it has been donated to the Nature Conservancy to preserve its vegetation. Beyond the Garden of the Gods, magnificent Polihua Beach stretches along the north coast. With its fearsome currents, it's no place for swimmers, but the views across to Molokai are stunning.

Sweetheart Rock (Pu'u Pehe) in Hulopo'e Bay.

The rusty hulk of a ship run aground at Shipwreck Beach.

Flora along the beach of Waipi'o Valley.

HAWAII: THE BIG ISLAND

The most rugged of the major Hawaiian islands and the largest, Hawaii promises real adventure, perfect beaches, and much more.

Ki'i (wooden images) surrounding the Hale o Keawe temple in Pu'uhonua 'O Honaunau National Historical Park.

The island of Hawaii, until recently was called the Big Island for a reason: it's huge. So huge, in fact, that it's almost too big to explore adequately from a single base. Instead, it's best to split a visit into two parts. And if you time your trip right, you might even get to see snow atop Mauna Kea.

Geologically the youngest of the Hawaiian islands and twice the size of all the others combined, the Big Island is a geological exhibit of considerable proportions. In Hawaii Volcanoes National Park, since 1983 the volcano goddess Pele has brought Kilauea to life, pouring ribbons of crimson lava from rifts and vents on the southeastern coast.

On the dry western side, upscale resorts stretch from Kohala in the north to Kona in the south. Save for the lushness of North Kohala, where Kamehameha the Great was born, most of the land on the western side is dry and expansive, and peppered with petroglyphs, ancient fish ponds, and other archeological treasures. It was here that Kamehameha the Great planned his conquests in the 18th century.

To the south in Kona District, Kailua is the Big Island's center of tourism and play. Once the playground of Hawaiian royalty, the sun-washed town today is crowded with boutiques, hotels, condominiums, and tourists. Down by the waterfront, delve into history at Hulihe'e Palace, 'Ahu'ena Heiau, and Moku'aikaua Church – built of black stone from an abandoned *heiau* (temple) and cemented with white coral.

Solidified lava along the Chain of Craters Road in Hawaii Volcanoes National Park.

Continuing south, the highway rounds the island at South Point, or Ka Lae, the southernmost point in both Hawaii and the United States.

On the wetter eastern coast, a half-hour's drive to the northeast of Kilauea, is rustic Hilo, the island's seat of government. Hilo is a tranquil town, with much of its charm originating in its quiet, unassuming residents. North of Hilo is the lush Hamakua Coast, where sugar plantations once reigned. One can continue beyond Hamakua and cross over through the highland town of Waimea to Kohala and the western coast. Overall, the island is perhaps best known for the volcano and coffee plantations outside of Kailua-Kona. A number of outfitters offer helicopter and boat tours of the volcano; visitors can drive to a handful of coffee plantations and tour the facilities on foot.

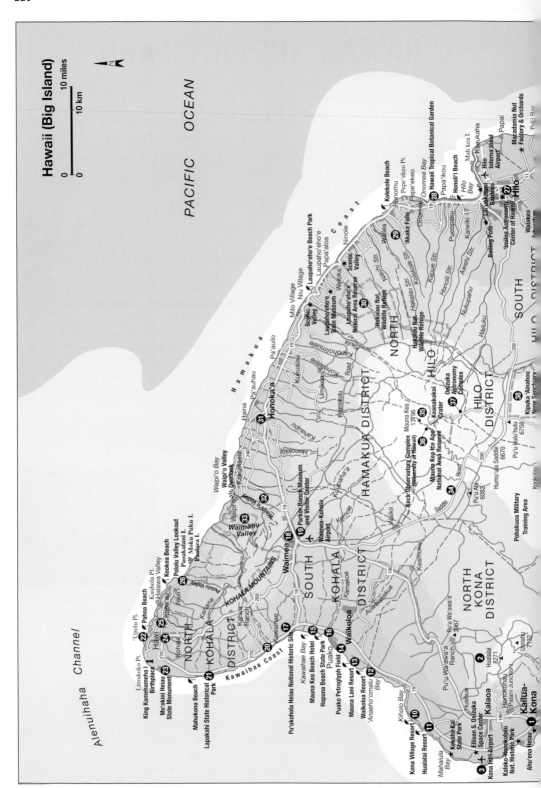

Hawaii (Big Island)

PACIFIC OCEAN

Alenuihaha Channel

0   10 miles
0   10 km

N

Limukoko Pt.
'Upolu Pt.
King Kamehameha I Birthplace
Mo'okini Heiau State Monument
Mahukona Beach
Lapakahi State Historical Park
Kauhola Pt.
Halawa Valley
Pahoa Beach
Hawi
Kapa'au
Niuli'i
Pololu Valley Lookout
Keokea Beach
Pololu Valley
Kohala
Kehena
NORTH KOHALA DISTRICT

Pu'ukohola Heiau National Historic Site
Kawaihae
Mauna Kea Beach Hotel
Hapuna Beach State Park
Puako Petroglyph Field
Puako
Mauna Lani Resort
Anaeho'omalu Bay
Waikoloa Resort
Kiholo Bay
Kona Village Resort
Hualalai Resort
Mahai'ula Bay
Kekaha Kai State Park
Ellison S. Onizuka Space Center
Kona Int'l Airport
Kaloko-Honokohau Nat. Historic Park
Kailua-Kona
Ahu'ena Heiau
Kalaoa
Honokohau (Palani Junction)
Huehue
Hualalai 8271
Pu'u Wa'awa'a 3967
Pu'u Wa'awa'a Ranch
Umiahu 4192
Pu'u Alu
NORTH KONA DISTRICT

Kawaihae Coast
KOHALA MOUNTAINS
Kohala Ranch
Kahua Ranch
Waimea
Waimea-Kohala Airport
Parker Ranch Museum and Visitor Center
SOUTH KOHALA DISTRICT
Kamuela
Kamakoa
Auwaiakekua
Keamuku
Keamoku
Puu Wa'awa'a

Waipi'o Bay
Waipi'o Valley
Waipi'o Valley Overlook
Waimanu Valley
Honoka'a
Haina
Pa'auhau
Pa'auilo
Kalopa
Honoka'a
Kukuihaele
Kaholehilonuiole
HAMAKUA DISTRICT
Hamakua Coast
Umikoa
Kanakolu
Kah
Mauna Kea 13796
Kipahulu'a
Kemole
Waikii
Kaumana
Saddle Rd
Pu'u Huluhulu 6758
Humu'ula Saddle 6670
Konikolau
Pohakuloa Military Training Area
Pu'u Oo 6082
Keck Observatory Complex (University of Hawaii)
Mauna Kea Ice Age National Area Reserve
Keanakakoi Crater
Onizuka Astronomy Complex
Kipuka 'Ainahou Nene Sanctuary
NORTH HILO DISTRICT

Milo Village
Niu Village
Scenic Valley
Laupaho'eho'e
Papa'aloa
Waleka
Laupaho'eho'e Train Museum
Laupaho'eho'e Beach Park
Laupaho'eho'e Point
Hakalau Nat. Area Reserve
Hakalau Nat. Wildlife Refuge
Ninole
Honomu
Kolekole Beach
Pepe'ekeo Pt.
Pepe'ekeo
Onomea Bay
Papa'ikou
'Akaka Falls
Hawaii Tropical Botanical Garden
Wailea
Pueogaku
Kaiwiki
Mauka
Naha'i Str.
Kolekole Str.
Kapue Str.
Honolii Str.
Awehi Str.
Nukupuahu
Kapue
Hakalau Str.
Wailoa
Mauna Kea
200
Puu Ala
Humu'ula Saddle
Mah'kea I.
Kaukaha
Pepe'ekeo
Boiling Pots
'Imiloa Astronomy Center of Hawai'i
Lili'uokalani Gardens
Macadamia Nut Factory & Orchards
Papai
Paki Bay
Honoli'i Beach
Hilo International Airport
Hilo
Hilo Bay
Wailakea
SOUTH HILO DISTRICT
19
200

Map numbered locations:
1 Kailua-Kona
2
3
10
11
12
13
14 Waikoloa
15
16 Waikoloa
17
18 Waimea
19 Parker Ranch Museum and Visitor Center
20
21
22
23
24
25
26
27 Hilo
28
29
30
31 Honoka'a
32
33 Waimanu Valley
34
35
36
37

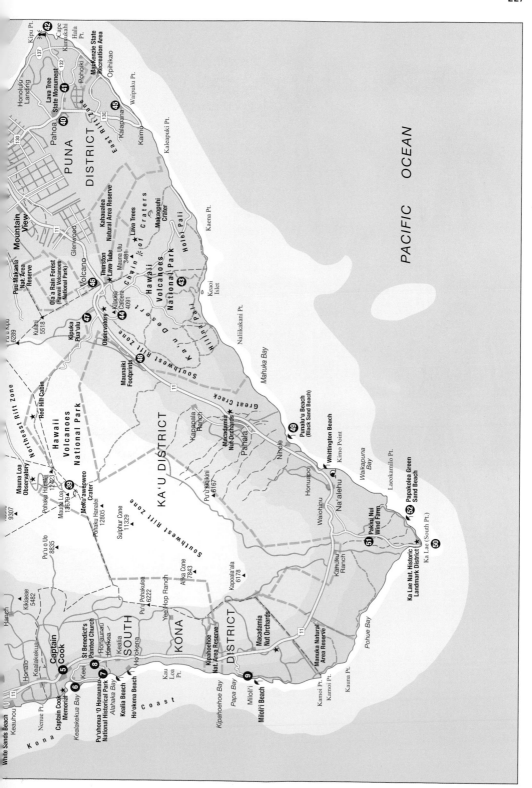

White Sands Beach

Keauhou

Nemue Pt.

Kona

Kealakekua Bay

Horiato

Kealakekua

11

Captain Cook Memorial

5 Captain Cook

6

Keei

St Benedict's Painted Church

8

7

Honaunau Keokea

Pu'uhonua 'O Honaunau National Historical Park

Alahaka Bay

Kealia Beach

Kealia

Ho'okena Beach

Ho'okena

Kau Loa Pt.

SOUTH

Kipahoehoe Nat. Area Reserve

KONA

Macadamia Nut Orchards

9

Miloli'i

Miloli'i Beach

DISTRICT

Manuka Natural Area Reserve

Kipahoehoe Bay

Papa Bay

Coast

Kamoi Pt.

Kamoi Pt.

Kauna Pt.

Pohue Bay

Hanch

Kikiaeae 5482

Pu'u o Uo 8835

YeeHop Ranch

Pu'u Pohakuloa 6222

Aiika Cone 7843

Kapaola'ala 6178

Kahuku Ranch

Ka Lae Nat. Historic Landmark District

Ka Lae (South Pt.)

50

Ka'u Kapu 6289

Kulani 5518

Kipuka Pua'ulu

47

Observatory

Kilauea 4091

44 Caldera

Ka'u Desert

Maunaiki Footprints

48

Southwest Rift Zone

Maumahu 348?

Mauna Ulu

Thurston Lava Tube

43

Chain of Craters

Makaoguhi Crater

Lava Trees

Hole Pali

Hawaii

Volcanoes

National Park

43

Keaoi Islet

Naliikakani Pt.

Mahuka Bay

Mauna Loa Observatory

Pohaku Hanalei

Mauna Loa 13679

Moku'aweoweo Crater

39

Pohaku Hanalei 12805

Sulphur Cone 11329

Southwest Rift Zone

9307

Pu'u o Uo 8835

Puu Makaala Nat. Area Reserve

Ola'a Rain Forest (Hawaii Volcanoes National Park)

46

Volcano

Glenwood

11

Mountain View

Honolulu Landing

Lava Tree State Monument

41

Pahoa

PUNA

DISTRICT

40

42

Kipu Pt.

Cape Kumukahi

Hala Pt.

137

MacKenzie State Recreation Area

Pohoiki

132

Opihikao

130

Waipuku Pt.

45

'Kalapana

Kaimu

Kaleapuki Pt.

East Rift Zone

Kaena Pt.

Hilina Pali

Great Crack

11

Kapaapala Ranch

Macadamia Nut Orchards

Pahala

Ninole

Kapu'ukiikini 6167

KA'U DISTRICT

Punalu'u Beach (Black Sand Beach)

49

Whittington Beach

Kimo Point

Honuapo

Waiohinu

Na'alehu

Waikapuna Bay

Laeokolo Pt.

Papakolea Green Sand Beach

52

Pakini Nui Wind Farm

51

PACIFIC OCEAN

Northeast Rift Zone

Hawaii

Volcanoes

National Park

Red Hill Cabin

Mauna Loa Observatory

12423

Hawaii Volcanoes National Park

Kona

KONA AND KOHALA

Hopping towns, lush farmland, posh resorts, and ancient sites are all on offer on the western coast of Hawaii Island.

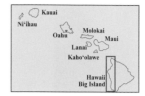

The leeward side of Hawaii Island is its dry side, meaning that the volcanoes that tower over this western coast catch the moisture-rich trade winds from the northwest and release their rain on the island's windward side. This makes the districts of Kohala and Kona prime destinations with some of the world's finest resort hotels, with beaches on this coast some of the best in Hawaii (the state) for swimming and sunbathing.

The northern part of this side of Hawaii Island is called Kohala (after the island's northernmost volcano), while the southern part is known as Kona (after the city of the same name). In the past, the only way to drive from Kohala to Kona was along a narrow road far uphill from the ocean. Today, however, a highway named for Kamehameha's wife, Ka'ahumanu, connects Kawaihae in Kohala with Kailua and Kona. The highway passes through some of the driest land in Hawaii, where beaches and archeological sites are strung along the coast. Expansive views range inland and along the coast, the landscape scarred by lava that flowed as recently as the 19th century.

The main town on this side of the island is known to locals as **Kailua**; with the district being called **Kona ❶**, it is known to the post office as **Kailua-Kona**. Generally, they're interchangeable, but Kona is commonly used for

the town, the district, and the coast. Dominating North Kona is 8,271ft (2,521-meter) **Hualalai ❷**, an awesome volcano that last erupted in 1801. The **Kona International Airport ❸** lies on one of its lava flows at Keahole. Legend has it that an 1801 eruption of Hualalai was initiated by Pele, the fire goddess, because she was jealous of the successful Kamehameha the Great. When Kamehameha followed the advice of a *kaula*, a seer, and made offerings to Pele, the eruption ceased. Today, Hualalai is home to game birds,

⊙ Main attractions
Kailua town
Captain Cook
The Fairmont Orchid
Pu'ukohola Heiau National Historic Site
Parker Ranch Museum and Visitor Center

Map on page 226

One of the pools at the Hilton Waikoloa Village.

Moku'aikaua Church on Ali'i Drive.

Sea spray crashes against Ali'i Drive's seawall by Kailua Bay.

and sheep, goats, and pigs wander over its dormant heights foraging on dry shrubs and grasses.

Pu'u Wa'awa'a, a pumice cone around 100,000 years old, rises sharply 4,000ft (1,200 meters) on the flanks of Hualalai. The typical lava flow in Hawaii is 15ft (5 meters) thick, but flows from Pu'u Wa'awa'a reached 900ft (270 meters) in thickness. Glassy black obsidian, formed by rapidly cooled lava and historically used for making sharp tools and weapons, is found here. The only other place in the Hawaiian Islands where obsidian is found is on the island of Kaho'olawe. On Hualalai's southwest flank, at about 1,500ft (460 meters), is **Holualoa ❹**, home to those seeking refuge from the hectic pace of Kailua-Kona below. It sits on the high road surrounded by coffee plants and wonderful views. A growing number of visitors are discovering the town's small galleries.

KAILUA

The town of Kailua is one of those places noted for sun and nightlife – with the sun outshining the nightlife by far. **Kailua Bay**, a harbor skirted by Ali'i Drive and a seawall, is the downtown focus. At the north end, on the grounds of King Kamehameha's Kona Beach Hotel, is an ancient temple or *heiau*, **Ahu'ena**, that was once used for human sacrifices. It was later restored by Kamehameha the Great and used as his personal *heiau*, when he settled here at the royal compound called **Kamakahonu**, or "turtle eye." This is where Kamehameha the Great retired and later died in 1819. Loyal attendants hid his bones, to prevent them being defiled by his enemies or the *mana* (spiritual essence) abused. Occasionally, someone claims to have found the burial site – caves were traditional burial locations – but it remains undiscovered. Possibly it was sealed by a lava flow, or it may even be under water, as the island's west coast has sunk an average of 9ins (23cm) every 100 years for the past eight centuries. The Ahu'ena Heiau site, which was partially demolished to build the Kona Pier, was later restored. The site provides a unique perspective for those on the nearby beach.

Ali'i Drive leads south along the harbor past the Royal Kona Resort, which is hard to miss as it juts out on a promontory through a jungle of condominiums and apartments into the ocean. The harbor area along Ali'i Drive, situated between the King Kamehameha and Royal Kona hotels, is a walking district for both shoppers and those interested in the history of the stretch.

The charming **Hulihe'e Palace** (www.daughtersofhawaii.org; Wed–Sat 11am, 12.30pm & 2.30pm guided tours by reservation), built in 1838 by the brother of Queen Ka'ahumanu, sits right on the ocean just down from Ahu'ena Heiau. Its grounds were once part of Kamakahonu. Restored in 1927, it is a wonderful museum evoking the old days when it served as a royal getaway. One Sunday a month there are free concerts held at the palace. Opposite the palace on Ali'i Drive, **Moku'aikaua Church** (http://mokuaikaua.com; closed for renovations until further notice) was built in 1837. The original church, with a *pandanus* roof and foundations of old *heiau* stones, was dedicated in 1823 but destroyed in 1835.

Sheltered from the prevailing trade winds, the waters off the Kona Coast are home to game fish considered among the best in the world. Each summer, the Hawaiian International Billfish Tournament (www.hibtfishing.com) is staged here. Blue marlin weighing 1,000lbs (450kg) have been caught within an hour's run from the pier. *Ahi* (tuna), *ono* (bonefish), *ulua* (jack crevalle), *mahi mahi* (dolphin fish), and swordfish are regularly caught.

SOUTH KONA

Up above Kailua, on the slopes of Hualalai and Mauna Loa, the climate is cooler. Moist air, bright sunshine, and porous volcanic soil produce one of the world's finest gourmet coffees: Kona coffee. Schools in this area used to close during coffee-bean harvest season so that children could help their families fill burlap sacks of the bright-red beans for delivery to the local mill. The coffee industry expanded substantially in the 1990s, riding the wave of growth in coffee drinking in the US. There are numerous boutique mills throughout the Kona

Konane, a game similar to draughts, was played by Hawaiians before Captain Cook's arrival in Hawaii.

⊘ KONA NIGHTINGALES

No, Kona Nightingales are not birds as you might quite rightly assume: they are feral donkeys, in fact. And these creatures are as much a part of the history of the western coast of Hawaii Island as volcanoes, coffee, and, more recently, the Ironman contest. Members of this breed of free-roaming animals get their names from the curious sound the donkeys make; their bray is more like a piercing bird call than a whinny. A population of hundreds of former worker donkeys once roamed the area, but the population has sadly dwindled to next to nothing in recent years. Efforts have been made to conserve the remaining herd of donkeys by enclosing a safe area away from a nearby highway to protect both the free-roaming animals and passing motorists.

⊙ Tip

Kona coffee is popular with *kama'aina* (locals) and visitors alike. A Kona blend, however, is only legally required to contain 10 percent Kona beans. One hundred percent Kona sells at premium prices, but it's well worth it.

region that welcome visitors. All along the upcountry stretch of highway south of Kailua to the town of **Captain Cook ❺** are tasting rooms where various types of Kona coffee are sold; be sure to stop and sample a cup.

The entire South Kona region has diversified, both in spirit and in economics, since the 1960s, when the area was a haven for self-exiled counterculture types, then later for artisans and craftspeople. Other newcomers settled here to become farmers by leasing land from large estates and buying up farmlands. Much of that new farmland went not into coffee production, but into vegetables, citrus fruits, and cocoa, with beans that, when processed, compare with the finest European chocolate.

Higher up Mauna Loa's slopes are forests of native trees. Around their trunks, wild *maile* wraps itself. *Maile* is prized for making *lei*, but with an increasing population, *maile* has become scarce. Sandalwood once covered many of these slopes; today, few trees remain. Whole forests of the creamy, aromatic wood were cut and sold by Kamehameha the Great and his heirs for profitable shipment to China.

THE SITE OF COOK'S DEMISE

Far below today's coffee farms, Captain Cook met his death at **Kealakekua Bay ❻**, now a state marine conservation district. Visitors arrive on day-cruises from Kailua, or drive here on a paved road descending through relatively recent lava fields. A white obelisk, on a parcel of land that is officially British territory, marks the spot where Cook and some of his crew died. It is accessible only by water, or on foot via a strenuous trail. Archeological surveys between Kealakekua Bay and Kailua have mapped at least 40 *heiaus* (temples) in the area, with one of the best preserved at Napo'opo 'o overlooking a rocky beach.

Travelers sailing south from Kealakekua Bay would be startled on reaching **Honaunau Bay** by the sight of fierce, hand-carved, wooden *ki'i* (sacred sculptures), and an immense stone platform with thick walls topped by thatched roofs. In this ancient *pu'uhonua*, or place of refuge, now known as the **Pu'uhonua 'O Honaunau National Historical Park ❼**, (tel: 328-2326; www.nps.gov/puho; daily 8.15am–sunset), Hawaiians pardoned violators of *kapu* (taboos) and war criminals who reached sanctuary here, but only if they vowed to do penance. Over the centuries, this *pu'uhonua* gained importance and accumulated *mana* (spiritual power), as more and more chiefs were buried here. Its *heiau* and Great Wall (1,000ft (300 meters) long, 10ft (3 meters) high and 17ft (5 meters) wide), have been meticulously restored to their former glory.

Near the main road and up from the historical park, **St Benedict's Painted Church ❽** is one of Hawaii's special little places. The interior of the church was painted with biblical scenes and motifs by a Belgian priest sometime around the year 1900. Outside stands a bust of Father Damien, the priest who

Kealakekua Bay State Historical Park.

worked in the Molokai leper colony (see page 211).

South along this jagged Kona shore, the people of **Miloli'i**  still fish for a living. In few places on Hawaii is there a feeling of neighborliness so strong as in this little village of hand-built stone walls topped with night-blooming cereus and no electricity or mains water supplies. Farther south along the highway, lava flows from the 1920s lift the road higher onto Mauna Loa's slopes and toward **Ka Lae**, or **South Point**, the southern-most tip of the Big Island and the United States. Too dry for farming, but with rich harvests from the sea, this was an early site of Polynesian settlement. Past South Point, the road turns northeast and ascends to Hawaii Volcanoes National Park and eventually to Hilo.

NORTH KONA

About two miles (3km) north of town is the first of three access roads that are part of the **Kaloko-Honokohau National Historical Park** (www.nps.gov/kaho; daily sunset–sunrise). This mile-long coast park has a visitor center (daily 8.30am–4pm; tel: 329-6881), which offers a self-guided tour made interesting by display boards. It's hot and dry (like the rest of this side of the island), so bring bottled water. A *heiau* (temple) platform, fish-pond walls, and an ancient *holua* (sled run) provide great insight into Hawaii's storied past.

Just north of Kaloko and south of the airport is the **Hawaii Ocean Science and Technology (HOST) Park** (tel: 327-9585; weekday guided tours can be booked online at http://nelha.hawaii.gov) where aquaculture and energy programs have been underway for more than 20 years.

North of the Kona International Airport is a controversial yet historic spot: the **Kona Village Resort** . The property was built in the 1960s as a string of luxury bungalows without TVs, phones, or anything else that disrupts the serenity of the setting. It was designed to look like the ancient village of Kalpulehu, and was

hailed for years for being a different, more traditional lodging option. Then, during a tsunami in March 2011, the property sustained significant damage and has been closed ever since. In 2023, however, Kona Village, A Rosewood Resort (www.rosewoodhotels.com) is set to open its doors on the site, with 150 standalone guest hales, a clutch of restaurants and bars (including the original Shipwreck Bar and Talk Story Bar), and a luxury spa.

Other parts of the area have recovered much more quickly from that big wave. The elegant **Hualalai Resort** , for instance, with its Four Seasons Hotel, 18-hole golf course and condominiums, is just as lovely as ever, providing visitors with plenty of options to dine and relax. There's also an impressive cultural center.

A great collection of ancient petroglyphs can be found at the Waikoloa Resort at **'Anaeho'omalu** , where they have been joined by both a golf course and relatively modern petroglyphs from the late 1800s that include English words, and figures bearing rifles. Also well preserved here are

Carved image at the ancient place of refuge, Pu'uhonua 'O Honaunau.

Keone'ele Cove in Pu'uhonua 'O Honaunau Park.

⊘ Fact

The most profitable agricultural crop on Hawaii Island is marijuana, known in Hawaii as *pakalolo* (literally "numbing tobacco"). The so-called Kona Gold is a cash crop, estimated as surpassing coffee and sugar in net revenue. It is illegal in Hawaii (except for medicinal use).

ancient fishponds on the ocean side of the Outrigger Waikoloa Resort.

The grand-scale Hilton Waikoloa Village (www.hiltonwaikoloavillage.com) has 1,113 rooms. The hotel's three towers are connected by mechanically guided boats in a canal, a sleek electric train and a mile-long walkway lined with Asian and Pacific Island art. As the oceanfront here is very rocky, the hotel is laid out around an artificial lagoon with sand to create a pretty good approximation of a beach. This is the setting for the resort's popular Dolphin Quest "swim with a dolphin" program (tel: 248-3316), under which guests can pay to share a few minutes' water time with a brace of sleek dolphins. However, the ethics of captive dolphin attractions is a contentious issue, and seeing pods of these sociable creatures in their natural habitat can be a far more rewarding experience.

SOUTH KOHALA

A few minutes further north is **Mauna Lani Resort ⓭**, with two elegant hotels, The Fairmont Orchid and Mauna Lani, Auberge Resorts Collection. In earlier days, Mauna Lani was known as Kalahuipua'a, a site of aquaculture ponds that the Mauna Lani Hotel has preserved. A walking trail leads from the hotel toward Keawanui Bay and the palm-lined ponds. Of six major ponds, the largest is 5 acres (2 hectares) in size and 18ft (6 meters) deep. A trail heads inland to a lava field, where caves have yielded an ancient canoe paddle and large fish-hooks, probably for catching sharks.

Kamehameha the Great maintained a canoe landing here, marked by a replica of an old canoe shed; inside is a full-sized replica of an outrigger canoe. Beyond is the Eva Parker Woods Cottage Museum, built in the 1920s and later moved to its current seaside location. Ancient Hawaiian artifacts are displayed inside.

A 5-minute walk up the coast, in **Pauoa Bay** fronting the Fairmont Orchid, is a submarine freshwater spring. Ancient Hawaiians would dive to the spring's opening and fill gourds with fresh drinking water.

The shoreline trail to the south follows an ancient footpath that connected fishing villages in pre-contact Hawaii. Along

Paddling an outrigger canoe at the Fairmont Orchid resort.

the path are ancient fishing platforms, a house site, and some anchialine pools – low-sited caves that were once flooded with seawater. Brackish water now fills these natural depressions in the lava.

Just north of the Mauna Lani Resort is one of Polynesia's best collections of petroglyphs, the **Puako petroglyph field** (daily 6.30am–6.30pm) ⑭. Years ago, access was through the village of Puako. Now a well-marked road at the Mauna Lani Resort ends in a parking lot, where a self-guided trail leads to a field of several thousand petroglyphs etched into the lava. The age of these petroglyphs has not been determined. Many are of uncertain meaning; others, like the circles with a dot inside, called *piko* (navel) holes, are thought to have been receptacles for the umbilical cords of newborns. Most Hawaiian petroglyphs were chiseled into smooth *paho'eho'e* lava along major trails. Long sections of this rock-lined trail are still to be found along the coast, at Koloko and at each of the Kona and Kohala resorts.

The low roads in both North and South Kohala are lined with *kiawe* trees and prickly-pear cacti. The *kiawe* tree is burned into first-rate charcoal, and the cactus blooms develop into a tasty fruit. On land found too dry for cattle, Laurance Rockefeller commissioned a luxury resort in the 1960s, the **Mauna Kea Beach Hotel** ⑮, piping in water for its grounds and golf course all the way from Waimea. For 40 years, Mauna Kea was the standard by which other Hawaii resorts were measured. Other resorts have caught up in recent years, but the Mauna Kea still is one of the island's finest.

Half a mile south lies **Hapuna Beach State Park** (daily 7am–8pm) ⑯, with the island's largest natural white-sand beach. The Hapuna Beach Prince Hotel opened in 1994 at the northern end of Hapuna Beach, and local people continue to use the popular public beach side-by-side with visitors. In summer, its warm turquoise waters offer truly superb swimming, but look for warning signs if you're here in winter, when the waves are so fierce that they scoop away enough sand to cut the beach into two separate halves.

PU'UKOHOLA HEIAU NATIONAL HISTORIC SITE

Continuing northward, hot, dusty, and dry South Kohala looks like parts of the western United States – rock-strewn grasslands but with a seacoast, and with fewer than 9ins (230mm) of rain a year. Where Highways 270 and 19 from North Kohala and Waimea meet and continue south stands the largest restored *heiau* (temple) in Hawaii: **Pu'ukohola Heiau National Historic Site** ⑰ (tel: 882-7218; www.nps.gov/puhe; daily 7.30am–5pm; free), built in 1791 by Kamehameha the Great for his war god, Kuka'ilimoku, a prelude to his military conquests. When it was finished, he invited his main Big Island rival and cousin, the high chief Keoua, to a ceremony at the *heiau*. As Keoua's canoe landed he was killed by Kahamanu's father, Ke'eaumoku. The temple was dedicated with Keoua's body on the altar. In 1991, at a re-dedication

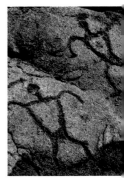

The lava flows of Kona and Kohala are rich with petroglyphs. Although carved in rock, they are fragile.

Windswept trees at Parker Ranch, Waimea.

of the site, descendants of the once-warring clans were reconciled in an impressive 'awa ceremony, complete with costumed pageantry.

Today the site comprises a number of different parts: the old temple, which visitors can only walk around; the remnants of a coastal village, which visitors can walk through; a shoreline path with interpretive signs about how the site was used; and a visitor center. Time your visit right and you might see archeological excavations in progress. Because the site has no shade, it gets very hot during summer; be sure to bring plenty of water.

WAIMEA

Waimea , sometimes called **Kamuela**, is a cool and often misty town at nearly 3,000ft (910 meters) above sea level. That mellow upland climate has made it hugely in demand as a residential community for rich local people, who, amazing as it may sound to most of us, weary of the endless sunshine on the coastal plain below. As such, this sleepy farming community is home to some of the most expensive real estate in the state.

Statue of the famous Hawaiian cowboy Ikua Purdy by Fred Fellows, at Parker Ranch.

The history of Waimea as a town dovetails with the history of a local farm, Parker Ranch. Captain George Vancouver and other early Europeans introduced goats, sheep, and cattle to the newly united island kingdom of Kamehameha the Great. The traditional low stone walls of the Hawaiians were unable to contain these domesticated stock animals, and in less than a decade, feral herds were ravaging cultivated farmlands and gnawing down young indigenous trees and plants.

In 1815, a New England farmer named John Palmer Parker offered to round up the animals in exchange for homestead land. Kamehameha gave him 2 acres (1 hectare) in the Kohala. These 2 acres grew to become what was at one time the largest privately owned ranch in America. Today, the cowboys of **Parker Ranch** run some 50,000 head of cattle over 210,000 acres (85,000 hectares) of pasture. In the 1960s, Parker's descendant, Richard Smart, sold large, unproductive coastal tracts in South Kohala to resort developers.

Although the ranch is now administered by a trust, the Parker name still crops up all over Kohala. At **Parker Ranch Museum and Visitor Center** ⑲ (tel: 885-7311; https://parkerranch.com; Mon–Fri 8am–4pm) in Waimea, visits can be arranged to the century-old family home, Mana, and a second, more modern, home, Pu'uopelu, which has an extensive art collection.

Like the 19th-century sugar barons, Parker had to import workers for his ranch, primarily Spanish-speaking cowboys from Mexico who were called *paniolos* (derived from the Spanish word, *español*) by Native Hawaiians. Today, all cowboys in Hawaii are called *paniolos*, and ranchlands are known as *paniolo*-country.

In later years, Portuguese joined them, and local men were trained as ranch hands, too, as were Asian immigrants. Today, *paniolos* have no racial or ethnic identity.

For years, Parker Ranch supplied most of the locally produced beef in Hawaii, butchering it at a company-owned slaughterhouse in Honolulu. Until a port was built, cattle were herded to the surf at **Kawaihae ⑳** and forced to swim through the ocean to waiting ships, which hauled them aboard in slings. Nowadays, they are driven through gates onto enclosed barges.

NORTH KOHALA

In 1968, archeologists excavated a 600-year-old Hawaiian fishing village, Lapakahi, near Highway 270 that skirts North Kohala's coastline. The area is protected as **Lapakahi State Historical Park ㉑** (www.hawaiistateparks.org; daily 8am–4pm; free). The park, which offers self-guided tours, preserves the restored foundations and stone enclosures of this commoners' fishing village. It is also the entry point to the part of the island known as North Kohala. Essentially, the region encompasses the entire northern tip of Hawaii Island, and is one of those windswept, wide-open places enveloped in mysticism.

Literally at the end of the road is the Big Island's northernmost point, **'Upolu Point ㉒** (named for an island in Samoa). Past a small airfield along the coast, is the well-preserved and partially restored **Mo'okini Heiau ㉓**, built around AD 800, it's said, by a *kahuna* (priest) from Tahiti. Today, a *kahuna* from the Mo'okini family of North Kohala still maintains the *heiau*. Within sight of the *heiau* is the **birthplace of Kamehameha the Great**, *c.*1752. Signs mark both Mo'okini Heiau and Kamehameha's birthplace, and the *heiau* in particular is well worth the short side trip on an unpaved road that's frequently rendered impassable by rain.

THE BACKBONE OF NORTH KOHALA

Defining North Kohala are the **Kohala Mountains**, the remains of an extinct 700,000-year-old volcano. In addition to the coastal road on the west side, Highway 250 ascends from Waimea to the ridge line and then through ranchland and groves of trees planted decades ago as windbreaks. The winds, called

Trees and dry scrubland along the Kohala Coast.

'apa'apa'a, that whip across the Kohala ridge are powerful and persistent.

At the north end of the peninsula is **Hawi** , an old sugar town that has sprouted a surprising amount of character and many good restaurants in the last few years. In adjacent **Kapa'au** ㉕, in front of the town's historic civic center, is the original **Kamehameha the Great statue**. It was lost at sea off the Falkland Islands and later recovered and taken to the Big Island town of Kapa'au. Its replacement stands opposite 'Iolani Palace in Honolulu.

In the 1880s, Kohala led the island in sugar production. Chinese laborers were hired by a businessman to construct a narrow-gauge railway from **Niuli'i**, beyond Kapa'au, to the port of Mahukona, on North Kohala's western coast. Formally opened by King Kalakaua, the railroad was abandoned half a century later when trucks replaced trains.

From Kapa'au, the road continues until the **Pololu Valley Lookout** ㉖ with its expansive coastal views, alternating seacliffs and valleys leading to the **Hamakua Coast**. A steep, quadriceps-burning trail leads down to Pololu Valley's rocky

Ensconced in a hammock in Hawi.

beach, which is partially visible from the lookout. You can hike the trail independently, or join Hawaii Forest and Trail (tel: 800-464-1993; www.hawaii-forest.com) on a memorable horseback and hiking excursion to waterfalls deep into the valley. Whichever approach you take, note that the trail can be slippery after a rainstorm.

Dense forests cover the round, eroded highlands of Kohala, scarred by deep-cleft valleys and ravines. Along their eastern ocean faces, water seeps out of cracks in the cliffs and plunges 1,000ft (300 meters) to the sea. At the turn of the 20th century, a technique for tapping this mountain water was established. Christened in 1906, the **Kohala Ditch** was a watercourse 18 miles (29km) long that funneled the headwaters of Waimanu Valley to Honokane, terminating in an 850ft (260-meter) artificial waterfall. Immigrant Japanese laborers bored and blasted 44 tunnels 8ft (2.4 meters) wide and 7ft (2 meters) high; the longest tunnel was nearly 0.5 miles (1km) long. At least six men died and countless others suffered from exposure and chills while working in the icy darkness of the flooded tunnels.

HILO AND THE WINDWARD SIDE

While the windward side of Hawaii Island is one of the wettest regions in the US, don't let the weather put you off from discovering all it has to offer.

Wet, warm, and sensuous in its appeal, the windward side of Hawaii Island is a tropical paradise unlike any other. Terrain is lush and verdant. Rivers and streams are almost permanently swollen. Waves and sea conditions are nightly news. And the seafood is second to none. Beaches and waterfalls grab most of the attention, but the big mountain of Mauna Kea towers over everything, serving as the only place in the islands you can build a snowman with natural snow. It is a place where Mother Nature rarely lets humans forget who is in charge.

HILO

Hilo ㉗ is undeniably a tropical city. Unpretentious and subtle, it can yield its charm quickly or take forever, depending upon a traveler's receptiveness. Named for the first night of a new moon, or possibly for an ancient Polynesian navigator, Hilo has been a center of trade since ancient Hawaiian times. At the **Wailuku River**, which spills into **Hilo Bay** at the northwest end of today's Hilo, ancient Hawaiians shouted their bargains across the rapids and gingerly made their exchanges. Later, foreign ships found deep anchorage between the coral heads of its wide bay, and eventually a channel was dredged so that larger steamships could anchor.

Outrigger canoe on the beach of Waipi'o Valley.

Blacksmiths, missionaries, farmers, jewelers, tailors, teachers, and dentists dropped anchor in Hilo, opening shops, churches, offices, and schools.

Nearby, visitors marvel at plant life inside the Hawaii Tropical Botanical Garden, wonder at the volume of water while watching 'Akaka Falls, and embrace authentic local culture at places such as Honoka'a and in the Waipi'o Valley below. While a drive up Mauna Kea is great for perspective (especially on clear days), the region's big volcano pales in comparison to the

Main attractions

Pacific Tsunami Museum, Hilo
'Imiloa Astronomy Center
Wailuku River State Park
Akaka Falls
Waipi'o Valley
Keck Observatory

Maps on pages 226, 242

lava light show available daily down near Kilauea in the national park. The best place to see the active volcano is in Puna, a city that is still very much part of the windward vibe.

HILO'S HISTORY

The Japanese especially embody Hilo's growth. The first generation that came as sugar cane laborers raised English-speaking children, the *nisei,* or second generation, who flocked not to the plantations for work but to government service and free enterprise. Respectful of their parents, the *nisei* and later *sansei* – third generation – descendants have run the island with particular sensitivity to the needs of older people.

Hilo's importance once revolved around its sheltered harbor. While cruise ships, freighters, and kayaks still ply its waters, the heart of town has moved inland, along Kanoelehua Avenue. Hilo's downtown buildings are dilapidated, although several have been artfully restored, with wooden awnings overhanging the sidewalks. Along **Waianuenue Avenue**, iron rings

to which horses were once tethered are still embedded in the curb.

Downtown Hilo once stretched along the black-sand harbor, so the town was nicknamed the Crescent City. But in 1946, a *tsunami* swept half the town inland, then dragged the debris seaward. Hilo was rebuilt, and a stone breakwater was constructed across the bay to shield the harbor. Then in 1960 another *tsunami* broke through and blasted the shore. This time there was no rebuilding. Lowland waters were drained and a hill of 26ft (8 meters) was raised above sea level, where city planners built a new government and commercial center, calling it **Kaiko'o**, or the strong seas. The old buildings that survived form a historical downtown district with a time-worn veneer that makes Hilo unique; the so-called Renaissance-Revival style was obviously popular for buildings from the early 1900s.

Downtown Hilo has undergone a partial restoration, and a fine walk that mixes old plantation ambiance with trendy hipness takes in the central area, bordered by Kino'ole Street,

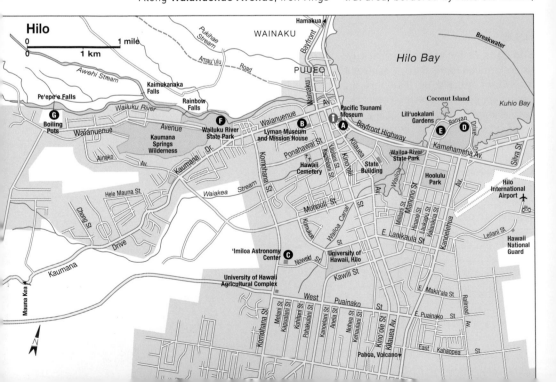

Furneaux Lane, Kamehameha Avenue, and Waianuenue Avenue.

The **Pacific Tsunami Museum**  Ⓐ (tel: 935-0926; www.tsunami.org; Tue–Sat 10am–4pm) in the heart of old Hilo tells the dramatic story of the *tsunamis* that have hit the islands.

A few blocks inland is the **Lyman Museum and Mission House** Ⓑ (276 Haili Street; tel: 935-5021; www.lymanmuseum.org; Mon–Fri 10am–4.30pm), a reminder of the island's early missionary days. Built in 1839, the restored house is the oldest frame building in Hilo. Next door, a newer museum complex features Hawaiian and other ethnic history exhibits; upstairs is a world-class shell and mineral collection. Contemporary arts are on view at the East Hawaii Cultural Center Gallery (tel: 961-5711; www.ehcc.org) on Kalakaua Street.

A couple of miles farther inland stands the innovative **'Imiloa Astronomy Center** Ⓒ (600 'Imiloa Place; tel: 969-9703; www.imiloahawaii.org; Sat–Sun 9am–4pm). This sets out to explain the work and discoveries of the various observatories atop the Big Island's highest mountain, Mauna Kea, and also to acknowledge Hawaiian religious beliefs about the entire cosmos, as well as the sacred mountain.

At the other end of the harbor to the east is the venerable **Banyan Drive** Ⓓ, a crescent road lined with voluptuous banyan trees shading most of Hilo's finer hotels. Japanese-style **Lili'uokalani Gardens** Ⓔ, nearby and off Banyan Drive, have stone bridges, lanterns, and a tea ceremony pavilion. The garden is open 24h and it's free.

From the Naniloa Volcanoes Resort, one of several Hilo hotels with superb harbor views, 13,800ft (4,200-meter) **Mauna Kea** dominates the western horizon. Dark forests circle the mountain above bright-green sugar cane, thinning out as the altitude rises, and finally vanishing – along with shrubs, grasses, and bird life – at the alpine heights where snow in winter gives the mountain its Hawaiian name, White Mountain. A long and broad saddle separates Mauna Kea, the island's older main volcano, from Mauna Loa, or Long Mountain. The road that traverses this saddle – appropriately

⊘ Tip

A note of caution if you are traveling to Hawaii Island in April, around Easter. Hilo is the site of the state's most popular hula competition and performance, the annual Merrie Monarch Festival (www.merriemonarch.com). Hotel rooms for this week are reserved a year in advance. Book as far ahead as you can (see page 87).

Stallholder at Hilo Farmers' Market.

⊘ NUTS ABOUT NUTS

While not an indigenous species, no nuts are as "Hawaiian" as macadamia nuts which explains the draw of the Mauna Loa Macadamia Nut Factory and Visitor Center (tel: 966-8618; www.maunaloa.com; Mon–Fri 8.30am–5pm). The factory is located 5 miles (8km) from downtown Hilo and set at the end of a wending road that takes you through sun-baked macadamia tree orchards. On the self-guided tour, visitors can view the nut processing plant, and see workers husk, dry, and bag nuts for sale. You may also be able to watch as they hand-dip mac-nut shortbread cookies in chocolate. Free samples are offered in the tempting on-site gift shop and there is also macadamia ice cream that is made in-house and sold from a window on the side of the building.

⊙ **Fact**

Honoli'i is said to be where the demigod Maui came to his end while chasing a young maiden up a tree. He had turned himself into an eel during the pursuit, but a passing *kahuna* (priest) killed him.

it's named Saddle Road – provides the only access to the mountain.

Perhaps once in a generation Mauna Loa erupts. In 1975, lava flowed to within a short distance of Hilo. It wasn't the first time lava had put Hilo at risk. In the late 1880s, a perilous flow from Mauna Loa headed toward Hilo, stopped only, it is said, when the volcano goddess, Pele, heeded pleas from a high princess. In 1942, American military aircraft dropped water and explosives on the leading edge of a similar flow to halt the lava. The danger remains very real; volcanic activity remains a constant threat to Hilo.

Like the town itself, nearby scenic sites are quiet and contemplative places. **Rainbow Falls** in the **Wailuku River State Park** ⑤ sport a prismatic halo in mid-mornings (around 10am) and late afternoons, when the sun is oblique to its cascade. Further upstream are the odd **Boiling Pots** ⑥, a section of bubbling water at the base of Pe'epe'e Falls.

NORTH OF HILO

The path to Rainbow Falls.

When sugar was king along the **Hamakua Coast** north of Hilo, a railway carried cane, freight, and commuters between the sugar mills of Hamakua and Hilo. A simple, winding road between the workers' camps carried cars and horse-drawn carts, with palm trees for fence posts along the sea cliffs. After the 1946 *tsunami* undercut most of the railway bridges, the tracks were torn up. Trucks took over, clogging the old road until a new highway was built.

You can return to plantation times and enjoy a glimpse of an old-fashioned part of Hawaii by driving along the deserted road, using the main highway to bridge its gaps. A turn-off leads to **Honoli'i**, a river estuary and beach park with the only reliable, year-round surfing waves in the Hilo vicinity.

After picking up the highway, a right turn past **Papa'ikou** marked "Scenic Drive" follows a beautiful 4-mile (6km) stretch along the coast past **Onomea Bay**, once a major sugar port. **Hawaii Tropical Botanical Garden** ㉘ (tel: 964-5233; www.htbg.com; daily 9am–5pm) is a 17-acre (7-hectare) privately owned preserve with 2,000 species of plants and flowers, including palms, bromeliads, ginger, heliconia, and orchids. Take a self-guided walk through the property along a trail that turns from raised boardwalk to packed dirt and back to boardwalk again, and meanders through fern and palm groves.

The old road rumbles over single-lane wooden bridges covered with bright-red African tulip flowers in spring and squashed guavas in autumn. Plantation workers have, by and large, left the camps to buy homes on company land. Near **Pepe'ekeo**, their fine gardens and flower beds are turning old cane fields into lush, warm neighborhoods. At the town of **Honomu**, a spur road leads to the 400ft (120-meter) **'Akaka Falls** ㉙, and their neighbor, **Kahuna Falls**, both of which can be seen on an undulating mile-long hiking trail that appears seemingly out of nowhere. Somewhere in the area is a special rock, a stone of the

fire goddess Pele, which causes the sky to cloud over and rain whenever struck by a branch of the *lehua ʻapane*.

THE HAMAKUA COAST

Change comes so slowly to Hamakua that few people notice it. A new house, a new car, a new storefront appear, but never anything startling. Places like **Papaʻaloa**, **Laupahoʻehoʻe**, **Paʻauilo**, and **Paʻauhau** look and feel much as they have for generations. On weekends, families secretly wager on the cockfights brought from their home islands in the Philippines. Fathers and sons take their dogs into the muddy forests on pig-hunting expeditions. Children and old men play softball in the parks. The paternal mills and the fraternal labor unions made Hamakua's plantation workers the highest-paid agricultural workers in the world. But as elsewhere in Hawaii, sugar died here. The largest mill and employer closed in 1996, and the fields of untended cane have rapidly vanished. What will replace the fields and the jobs still remains to be seen. Some agri-businessmen have hedged their bets by planting macadamia trees, which take a long time to mature but then bear nuts for decades. It is a lucrative market, but the competition from foreign producers is fierce. Another alternative to sugar cane is a fast-growing eucalyptus tree, which is harvested for paper, pulp, and as a source of fuel.

Slicing through the Hamakua coast are three great gulches: Maulua, Laupahoʻehoʻe, and Kaʻawaliʻi. The streams that cut through these volcanic channels have their sources far uphill where few people venture. With permission from neighboring ranchers to unlock their gates, the occasional hunter or forester rides up into the high terrain of the **Laupahoʻehoʻe Natural Area Reserve** ㉚ (www.dlnr.hawaii. gov/ecosystems/nars/hawaii-island/laupa-hoehoe-2), which protects the watershed of the island's windward side, a landscape misty in summer and frosty in winter. Here, the tall indigenous *koa* and *ʻohiʻa* trees stand. Hidden in the reserve are some cold-weather trees

View over Waipiʻo Valley from Waipiʻo Lookout.

◎ WONDER WAIPʻO

You don't have to descend from the end of Route 240 into the Waipiʻo Valley to experience the valley's natural beauty. That said, getting from the road to the bottom of the valley will enable you to fully appreciate some of what makes the valley so unique. For starters, consider the one-mile road itself: one of the steepest roads in the world with an average 25 percent grade for the entirety of its 900ft (270-meter) descent. Then at the bottom, there's the black-sand beach and, in addition to about 50 full-time human residents, the valley is home to nearly a dozen wild horses, and countless wild boar. Finally, of course, is the history: the valley once was a choice gathering spot for island royalty, and was home to Kamehameha I when he was a child.

⊘ Tip

You can get a tour to Waipi'o valley with Waipi'o Na'alapa Trail Rides (tel: 775-0419; www.naalapastables.com) or Valley Wagon Tours (tel: 775-9518; www.waipiovalleywagontours.com).

that were planted in the 1920s by foresters: spruce, cypress, maple, Dutch elm, and redwood.

The **Laupaho'eho'e Train Museum** (tel: 962-6300; Mon, Wed & Fri 10am–2pm, rest of week appointment only; www.thetrainmuseum.com) is worth a quick stop, containing historic images of what is impressive early 20th-century engineering.

WAIPI'O VALLEY

Nine miles (14km) beyond **Honoka'a** ㉛, a rustic former sugar town, lies the broad and deep **Waipi'o Valley** ㉜, the first of several windward valleys along North Kohala's wilderness coastline. Waipi'o was a population center before European contact, home to thousands, including fishermen and farmers who built irrigated terraces to grow taro in the rich earth, which was said to have become red when Kanaloa, one of the four primary gods, beat Maui against the rocks.

Waipi'o's **Hi'ilawe Falls** fed a river stocked with fish that skilled men and women would catch with their bare hands. The black-sand beach knew the keels of dozens of canoes that crossed treacherous currents to trade with neighboring valleys, but by the early 20th century, young people had moved away to work on the plantations or to live in more accessible towns. In the valleys, rice replaced taro grown by Japanese and Chinese settlers. After World War II, two *tsunamis* flooded the valley floor and it was largely abandoned. Today, a few families call Waipi'o home. Most visitors take in Waipi'o from the clifftop lookout. The valley is accessed via a steep dirt road, technically off-limits by rental car companies (though 4x4s manage the road in good conditions) but open to hikers or on organized tours.

In the 1960s, the Peace Corps, newly initiated by President Kennedy, trained volunteers here to prepare them for life in rural Asia. Today, the Peace Corps

village is gone, but visitors may pitch a tent a short hike away from a natural swimming hole below 300ft (90-meter) Hi'ilawe Falls. Dedicated hikers can cross the beach and scale the trail on the far side toward **Waimanu Valley** ㉝, 7 miles (11km) north over mostly irregular terrain.

THE HIGHEST POINT IN HAWAII

The Hilo and Kona sides of Hawaii have never been directly linked. The only overland road through the center of the Big Island, winding between Mauna Kea and Mauna Loa, is **Saddle Road** ㉞, which connects Hilo with Waimea.

Most rental car companies used to prohibit travel on the Saddle Road, but over recent years vast improvements have been made, so it is now possible to head skyward towards the summit of **Mauna Kea** ㉟, which towers over the Pacific at 13,796ft (4,185 meters) – though note that you can only reach the halfway point in a normal car (not 4x4). It is the highest point in Hawaii and the Pacific Basin. Measured from its base below the ocean's surface, it is the tallest mountain on earth at more than 30,000ft (9,100 meters). Now dormant, Mauna Kea last erupted 3,500 years ago. More than 15,000 years ago, a glacier chilled the slopes of Mauna Kea. Today, a continual layer of permafrost sustains **Lake Wai'au**, close to the summit. Poli'ahu, the snow goddess and enemy of the fire goddess Pele, is said to live atop the volcano. It is said that when the gods disapproved of someone's presence on the mountain, they would turn him or her into stone; there are a lot of stones on the mountain.

Supplies of a dense and steel-hard basalt for use in adzes attracted ancient Hawaiians to the area. The Mauna Kea adze quarry, 11,000ft (3,350 meters) above sea level, is a National Historic Landmark. It covers nearly 8 sq miles (21 sq km). The site contains 40 *heiaus* (temples) and other shrines, and a trail leads to Lake Wai'au.

No site in the Northern Hemisphere is so high, so clear, so free from light and heat, and so easily accessible as Mauna Kea's summit. To take advantage of this unobstructed view of the heavens, the University of Hawaii and the governments of the US, Canada, Japan, and the UK have built 13 giant telescopes on summit cinder cones. The **Keck Observatory ㊱** (tel: 885-7887 (for information on weather and road conditions); www.keckobservatory. org; Visitors' Gallery Mon–Fri 10am–4pm) is the most powerful optical telescope in the world, with mirrored segments aligned by computer to create a light-gathering surface of 33ft (10 meters). The observatory at the summit of Mauna Kea provides a visitors' gallery with exhibits describing the site's research and operations. You need a 4x4 vehicle for the trek up a road that angles off Highway 20 toward the peak of Mauna Kea (off-limits to most rental cars). Hawaiian Forest & Trail offers summit tours (tel: 331-8505; www.hawaii-forest.com). For details, call Mauna Kea Support Services (tel: 961-2180) at the Mauna Kea Visitor Information Station. Plans for building a huge Thirty Meter Telescope at the observatory have been staunchly opposed by environmentalists, and those who consider the summit a sacred site. However, in late 2017, a permit was granted to start construction and work is (slowly) underway. At a lower elevation is the **Onizuka Astronomy Complex ㊲** (tel: 961-2180; www.ifa. hawaii.edu/info/vis; daily 11.30am–7pm), with evening star-gazing and displays in honor of Hawaii's first astronaut, who was killed in the 1986 *Challenger* space shuttle disaster.

SADDLE ROAD HISTORY

A direct Kona–Hilo road has long been in the pipeline. In 1849, Kamehameha III approved a plan to survey and build a road over Crown lands from Kona, the seat of government, to Hilo, the only deep-water port. Convict laborers began at the edge of the forest and followed a nearly straight line. After 10 years they had reached halfway to Hilo when Mauna Loa erupted. A broad river of lava poured down the mountain and covered part of the road; the project was not completed until the 1940s, when the US military built an access road that was poorly maintained for decades.

In the last decade, however, county, state, and federal governments have teamed together to resurface portions of the old road and build new sections, as well. The last of the new sections opened in 2013; it has breathtaking views of the coastline and the Hualalai and Kohala volcanoes. In the future, plans are to complete a section of Saddle Road to intersect with State Route 19.

A scant 400 yards/meters from the edge of the 1859 flow, high up in what is called the **Saddle**, stand the stone remains of a monument to a 16th-century king, 'Umi, the first known king of the Big Island. He completed his military unification of Hawaii here on a desolate plateau inland behind dormant Hualalai,

Steep gradient warning on Mauna Kea; holes in the sign prevent it being blown down by the wind.

which, at 8,271ft (2,521 meters), is the island's third-largest volcano. At this location, Mauna Kea, Mauna Loa, and Hualalai appear nearly the same size. 'Umi, according to some stories, ordered a census. Stones were used to represent people, animals, and units of land. These heaps of stones were fashioned into a place of worship, Ahua 'Umi Heiau, and probably decorated with offerings.

It has been 500 years since armies bivouacked on the plain in this geographical center of the island, but only a few miles away in the Saddle at **Pohaku-loa**, the American military practices war games. Near the Saddle's high point is the **Kipuka 'Ainahou Nene Sanctuary** ㊳, one of the preserves of Hawaii's indigenous goose, or *nene*. The bird can also be found in Haleakala National Park on Maui and Koke'e on Kauai.

MAUNA LOA

Unlike Mauna Kea, Hawaii's southern volcano, **Mauna Loa** ㊴, is not yet dormant. Indeed, the Big Island districts of Kona, Ka'u, Hilo, and Puna remain vulnerable to a possible major eruption. Mauna Loa's last eruption was a 1984 fountain inside the summit caldera of **Moku'aweoweo**, a name that refers to the 'aweoweo fish whose red color has obvious volcanic parallels. Mauna Loa has erupted 36 times since European contact. Several times, it has threatened Hilo, situated on its northeast flank; in 1984, flows stopped just 5 miles (8km) away.

Mauna Loa is a shield volcano, growing through the accumulative stacking of thin lava flows 10–15ft (3–4.5 meters) thick. This process gives the shield volcano its gentle convex shape, in contrast to dramatically explosive volcanoes such as Mt Fuji and Mt St Helens. Lower than Mauna Kea, at 13,679ft (4,169 meters), Mauna Loa ("Long Mountain") has more mass than any other mountain on the planet, with more volume (almost 10,000 cubic miles/40,000 cubic km) than the entire Sierra Nevada range in California. For most hikers, the trail to the summit is a two-day climb, with a cabin at Red Hill providing overnight shelter. With fog and sudden storms a possibility, the summit hike can be risky.

Subaru and Keck telescopes on the summit of Mauna Kea at sunset.

From the summit caldera, two prominent rift zones, which are fractured areas of weakness, extend deep into the ocean. The first rift zone passes through South Point at the bottom of the island, and the second, the northeast rift zone, extends toward Hilo.

SOUTH OF HILO

Travelers often bypass the **Puna** area south of Hilo off Highway 130. The road that once linked Puna to Hawaii Volcanoes National Park (see page 251) was closed in 1984 after lava covered it in several places. Scores of homes, the village of Kalapana, and several historic sites have been destroyed by the slow flows of Kilauea, whose most recent period of activity began in 1983. All of this history confirms that Puna is the best place outside the Hawaii Volcanoes National Park to see the active volcano of Kilauea today.

The gateway to the Puna area is the town of **Pahoa** ⓰, once a major supplier of *'ohi'a* wood to the railroads, which used the wood for ties. Its small downtown area is interesting, with raised wooden sidewalks and old buildings along its main street. The historic Star of the Sea painted church was moved here after lava covered its original site near the coast. The area surrounding Puna is known for producing tropical flowers, papaya, and illegal *pakalolo* (marijuana).

In 1790, lava flows flooded then drained a rainforest, leaving shells of solidified lava around now-vaporized trees. The lava-tree mold forests of **Lava Tree State Monument** ⓵ (www.dlnr. hawaii.gov/dsp/parks/hawaii/lava-tree-state-monument) are eerie, especially in early mornings before the mists have lifted.

Costal Route 137 leads to volcanically heated thermal springs at Ahalanui Beach Park, and naturist sunbathing at Kehena. To the North lies the island's westernmost point, **Cape Kumukahi** ⓶, which grew dramatically after eruptions in 1955 and 1960. The Cape's namesake may have been one of two men: a chief who mocked Pele or a migratory traveler from Tahiti. Either way, Kumukahi means "first beginning." Partially covered by the recent flows is a cemetery for Japanese immigrants. The coastline of Puna is volcanic and rough, with few satisfactory beaches.

Lava flow from Kilauea.

HAWAII VOLCANOES NATIONAL PARK AND KA'U

There's more to Hawaii Volcanoes National Park than watching an active volcano do its thing; there also are great hikes and a crash-course in Earth Science.

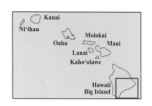

The best sights to see on the Big Island are nature at its most awesome, a spectacle that unfolds daily inside **Hawaii Volcanoes National Park** ⑭ (tel: 985-6000; www.nps.gov/havo; daily). The main attraction is Kilauea, an active volcano that has erupted consistently since 1983. Getting to the part of the park where you can see molten lava takes time; most visitors spend a full day. Other parts of the park to explore are canopied, misty rainforests filled with giant tree ferns; dried lava flows from yesteryear; the windswept deserts of Ka'u; and interpretive exhibits at park visitor centers. There also are great hikes up to the top of **Mauna Loa**. The park is so big, you could visit every day for a week and still miss more than half the park.

AN ACTIVE VOLCANO

On Mauna Loa's slopes is a rift zone, where lava that sometimes feeds the summit crater oozes from cracks lower on the mountain. This is the Big Island's biggest draw, along with the beaches of Kohala and Kona. All of the current activity is from **Kilauea** ⑭, the youngest of Hawaii's volcanic mountains, which has erupted steadily since 1983, the longest continuously erupting volcano in the world. The most dramatic eruption was in 2018, when lava flows destroyed around 700 homes and

forced thousands of islanders to flee. At the time of writing, in December 2021, the volcano was erupting again, though all activity was confined to the summit. Like all Hawaiian volcanoes, Kilauea is a dome-like shield volcano with deceptively gentle slopes. It rises southeast of Mauna Loa, more than 20,000ft (6,000 meters) above its base on the ocean floor.

At the **Kilauea Visitor Center** Ⓐ (daily 9am–5pm), the latest information about eruptions, road closures, and flow activity is displayed on maps, information

◎ Main attractions
Kilauea Visitor Center
Thomas A. Jaggar
  Museum
Halema'uma'u Crater
Thurston Lava Tube
Chain of Craters Road
Papakolea Green
  Sand Beach

**Maps on pages
226, 252**

A tenacious plant takes root in solidified lava.

Heed the warning signs in the Volcanoes National Park.

boards, and on film. Geologists and other experts also are on hand to provide lectures and answer questions about what's happening in the right outside, and down where the lava hits the sea.

From the visitor center, the 11-mile (17km) **Crater Rim Drive** passes over some of the Pacific's most bizarre scenery as it skirts past wheezing steam vents at **Steaming Bluff** (Sulfur Banks) **B**, where seeping ground water hits hot rock; there are several breathtaking views of the caldera. Lava flows in the caldera just below the first stretch of road and the Volcano House hotel date from 1919.

The Hawaiian Volcano Observatory , operated by the US Geological Survey, is one of the world's premier volcanology and geophysical research centers. However, the observatory was severely damaged in the 2018 Kilauea eruption and is looking for a new permanent site.

THE PRIMARY VENT OF KILAUEA

The road slips into the Southwest Rift zone, crossing lava flows from 1971, 1974, and 1921 to an overlook of **Halema'uma'u Crater C**, the collapsed depression within Kilauea Caldera. From the parking lot near the crater, whiffs of sulfuric gases escaping the earth along the short trail are reminders that there is still plenty going on down below. Halema'uma'u is the primary vent of Kilauea. The crater of Kilauea is 2.5 miles (4km) by 2 miles (3km) in size, its walls a set of step-like fault blocks that form cliffs as high as 400ft (120 meters). From the early 1820s until 1924, Halema'uma'u was a lake of active lava, then it went into a period characterized more by steam. In 2008, lava eruptions returned to the crater and have been going off pretty much daily ever since. Halema'uma'u is said to be the fire goddess Pele's current home. At the crater's rim, offerings of *lei*, *ti*-wrapped stones, and money are left for Pele's appeasement.

Compared to explosive volcanoes in the Mediterranean or around the Pacific Rim, Hawaii's volcanoes are relatively benign, allowing visitors

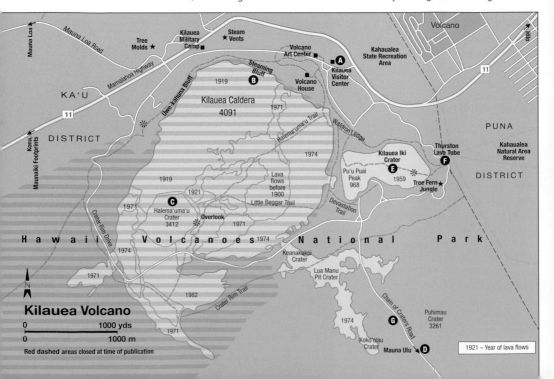

Kilauea Volcano

0 ___ 1000 yds
0 ___ 1000 m

Red dashed areas closed at time of publication

1921 – Year of lava flows

"drive-through" access to eruptions and lava flows. Only twice in recorded history have dangerously explosive eruptions occurred in Hawaii. The most recent was in 1924, when steam pressure expelled Kilauea volcano's plug and enlarged Halema'uma'u's diameter from 1,200ft (360 meters) to 3,000ft (900 meters), and left a hole 1,300ft (400 meters) deep. An eight-ton block of basalt was tossed 3,000ft (900 meters) from Halema'uma'u's center. Dust clouds rose to 20,000ft (6,000 meters).

HISTORIC HOT SPOTS

In recent decades, Kilauea's eruptions have been primarily along the Southwest Rift and the East Rift zones, areas of structural weaknesses in the shield volcano. The Southwest Rift extends through Ka'u, and the East Rift to Puna. The most accessible of these sites since 2008 has been in the heart of the Halema'uma'u crater. During daylight, the robust plume of volcanic gas is a constant and dramatic reminder of the molten rock churning

in a lava lake beneath the crater floor. After sunset, the crater continues to thrill with a vivid glow that illuminates the clouds and the plume as it billows into the night sky.

Earlier this millennium, a vent on the East Rift, **Mauna Ulu D**, was the biggest attraction. Over the years that vent has buried almost 13 miles (19km) of park road, some of it under 300ft (100 meters) of lava, and added more than 600 acres (243 hectares) of land to Hawaii Island.

Kilauea Iki Crater E was where a 2,000ft (600-meter) volcanic geyser erupted in 1959, possibly the highest volcanic fountain ever recorded. Another popular stop is the **Thurston Lava Tube** F, where a short trail weaves through primal groves of fern to a short lava tube.

It is very likely that by the time of publication, another eruption zone will have appeared inside Hawaii Volcanoes National Park. For all of the latest updates on eruptions, where to see them and when are the best times to go, visit the park website or – on the

Halema'uma'u Crater, the primary vent on Kilauea.

Ø ALL ABOUT LAVA TUBES

Lava tubes are naturally occurring conduits that are formed by flowing lava that hardens on the outer edges as this outside layer starts to cool. Tubes can be actively draining lava from a volcano during an eruption, or can be extinct, meaning the lava flow has ceased and the rock has cooled and left a long, cave-like channel. Inside Hawai'i Volcanoes National Park, there are a number of these tubes, many of which are big enough to walk through. Perhaps the most famous of these lava tubes is Kazumura Cave, which has been surveyed at almost 41 miles (66km) long and 3,614ft (1.1km) deep, making it one of the longest and deepest lava tubes in the world. A number of private tour outfitters lead guided excursions through Kazumura Cave.

island itself – ask a hotel concierge. Just about all of the modern-day eruption sites are accessible via the **Chain of Craters Road** N, which cuts off the Rim Road and descends along the East Rift, passing prehistoric pit craters and heading toward the ocean toward a fault scarp covered with lava flows that look like black molasses. Because lava flows change all the time, the National Park Service maintains facilities at roadblocks on this road. From those roadblocks, there are usually marked walks to safe viewpoints. Caution is required when hiking off the marked trail, as the lava cover can be unstable, and deaths have occurred here. It was once possible to continue along this road to Hilo. In the 1980s and 1990s, lava flows obliterated scores of homes, the village of **Kalapana** N, archeological sites, the road itself, and the national park's Waha'ula Visitor Center. In 1997, the **Waha'ula** *luakini heiau*, once used for human sacrifices, was finally swallowed up, too. Waha'ula was first established by a Tahitian priest in the 13th century, and

Entering a lava tube.

later used by Kamehameha the Great. According to legend, when a young chief passed through smoke coming from the *heiau* – a taboo, as the smoke was considered a shadow of the *heiau's* god – he was killed and his bones were thrown in a pit.

About 25 miles (40km) out at sea, 3,000ft (900 meters) below sea level, a new island-to-be, **Lo'ihi**, is developing on the East Rift. Thousands of years from now, it will surface as either a new island or an extension of the Big Island itself.

VOLCANO

Just outside of the national park boundary, on the road to Hilo and not far from the Kilauea Visitor Center, **Volcano** N is a small town set amid forests and mists situated 3,700ft (1,100 meters) above sea level. There are several bed-and-breakfast guesthouses in the town for those wanting to stay up here, rather than returning the same day to Hilo or Kona. The well-appointed Kilauea Lodge (tel: 967-7366; www.kilauealodge.com), with

its popular restaurant, is well worth an overnight stay, as are the many village bed-and-breakfasts. Country Goose Lodge (tel: 808-967-7759; www.country-goose.com), Volcano Rainforest Retreat (tel: 800-550-8696; www.volcanoretreat.com), and Volcano Village Estates (tel: 967-7986; www.volcanovillageestates.com) are all reliable choices. Volcano Places (tel: 808-967-7990; www.volcanoplaces.com) coordinates the rental of a number of vacation homes, as well.

The Volcano area attracts artisans, writers, and craftspeople. Many of their works are offered for sale at the **Volcano Art Center** (tel: 967-8222; www.volcanoartcenter.org; daily 9am–5pm) next to the Hawaii National Park headquarters and housed in the *c.*1877 **Volcano House** (tel: 866-536-7972; www.hawaiivolcanohouse.com), once perched on the caldera's edge, but moved back in subsequent years to avoid lava flows. The original Volcano House holds the distinction of being the oldest hotel on Hawaii Island. The current incarnation, a 33-room hotel that overlooks Halema'uma'u is comfortable but rustic. Volcano House is the only hotel inside the national park and is a short walk from the visitor and art centers. During the day, it's crowded with visitors, but in the evenings it's quiet and pleasant.

From the main highway and still inside the national park, a side road leads to **Kipuka Pua'ulu** ㊼ (Bird Park; www.nps.gov/havo/planyourvisit/hike_day_kipukapuaulu.htm), an idyllic hideaway with a nature trail through meadows and one of the thickest concentrations of native plants in Hawaii.

A *kipuka* is an isolated ecosystem created when a lava flow shunts around an "island" of older growth or a habitat, isolating it. These *kipuka* are important biological research areas where native species continue to flourish independent of outside influences. Biologists often create artificial *kipuka* for research. In 1968, the

National Park Service isolated an area near the coast with fences, protecting it from the wild pigs and goats that roam the Big Island. Something grew within the fenced *kipuka* that had never been seen before by modern scientists: a large bean plant with purple flowers. Until the fence was put up, island goats had eaten the bean plants before they could mature.

KA'U

To the southwest of Kilauea and Volcano is **Ka'u Desert**, downwind from the summit and where noxious gases and dehydrated breezes inhibit vegetation. In 1790, an eruption of gas and dust suffocated a phalanx of warriors headed to battle Kamehameha the Great. Their footprints pressed into the hardening cinder, as they unsuccessfully sought to escape, can still be seen at **Maunaiki** ㊽, preserved under glass at the end of a mile-long trail, and accessed from the main highway coming from South Point.

From the national park, the road descends along the Southwest Rift

Old lava flows surround the Chain of Craters road in Hawaii Volcanoes National Park.

of Kilauea. **Punalu'u Beach** ⓭ is a black-sand beach near the small Sea Mountain Resort, and it's worth a stop. If the tiny black sand crystals made of eroded lava rock don't impress, the wildlife will: the beach is frequented by endangered hawksbill and green turtles, which can often be seen basking on the black sand. There also are at least three *heiaus* here.

Beyond Punalu'u is Na'alehu, a traditional Hawaiian town billed as the southernmost in the US, with a bakery renowned for its sweet bread. Turning off the main highway, a dead-end road traverses 12 miles (19km) of cattle range southward to **Ka Lae** ⓮ (The Point), or **South Point**. Along the way, the road passes immense wind turbines, spinning in the unceasing winds that whip this cape; privately owned **Pakini Nui Wind Farm** ⓯ feeds electricity into the island's main power grid.

Somewhere along South Point, some of the first Polynesians landed in Hawaii, calling it Ka Lae. Modern-day visitors sense somehow that this is a special place. Clear, blue waters smash against the 50ft (15-meter) -high basalt cliffs. Small fishing boats are often tied up below. The ocean is tempestuous, the wind forceful, and the isolation nearly complete. The ancient Hawaiians built the **Kalalea Heiau**, a temple dedicated to fishing, right on the cliff's edge. Today, this is the southernmost place in the United States. Due south is Tahiti.

A 3-mile (5km) hike east from South Point through a grassy plain leads to the unique **Papakolea Green Sand Beach** ⓰. Here, an entire cinder cone of olivine has collapsed into a little bay and been reduced into polished sand by the surf. The beach is one of only four green-sand beaches in the world (the others being Talofofo Beach in Guam; Punta Cormorant in the Galápagos Islands; and Hornindalsvatnet, in Norway). Signs at the trailhead indicate it is possible to drive a vehicle down to the beach, but don't be fooled; the road is extremely rough and you might not make the distance. If you'd rather not hike to the beach, some locals have been known to drive out tourists for $10 apiece. Be sure to negotiate a price before setting off.

Moving north through **Ka'u District**, one finds an increase in gray and black lava – the result of the Mauna Loa flows of 1907, 1919, 1926, and 1950. Where the local microclimate has permitted, lichens, grass and *'ohi'a* – usually the first tree to appear in lava flows – sprout from the new earth. This is one of the least-populated places in Hawaii. During the 1950s and 1960s, however, unscrupulous real estate salesmen trafficked in these barren lava acres, hawking them sight-unseen to Americans as properties in paradise. Nevertheless, some of those living here came knowing full well how barren the land was going to be and they've come to like the ravaged landscape, even if swaying palm trees and white-sand beaches are distinctly lacking on the ground.

Horses graze along South Point Road in the Ka'u district.

Papakolea Green Sand Beach.

📷 A STATE OF FIRE IN THE PACIFIC OCEAN

Hawaii Island is one of the few places in the world to witness a volcanic eruption in relative safety, due to the type of volcanic craters that characterize the Hawaiian archipelago.

The islands of Hawaii sit almost in the middle of the Pacific Plate, a piece in the giant jigsaw puzzle that is the Earth's crust. This Pacific Plate is moving slowly to the northwest. Each of the islands in the Hawaiian chain, from the smallest atoll in the northeast to Hawaii Island, was formed as the plate moved over a "hot spot" 50 miles (80km) deep in the Earth's mantle.

The oldest Hawaiian Islands are in the northeast near Midway Islands. The process of island growth continues. Kilauea Volcano, on Hawaii Island, offers the world's most active continuing eruption. Since 1983 it has been erupting in one way or another, most explosively in 2018. It has continued bubbling away and spitting out lava sporadically in the following years.

A ranger from Hawaii Volcanoes National Park about to measure the levels of hazardous gases being emitted from the opening of a lava tube near Kalapana, on the Big Island.

VOLCANO CREATION

Two Hawaii volcanoes, Mauna Loa and Kilauea, have summit calderas, created when lava drains from an underground magma chamber, causing the volcano summit to sink. In contrast, Maui's Haleakala has neither crater nor caldera, but rather a summit basin created by erosion.

Mauna Kea is the world's tallest volcano, measured from its base 18,000ft (5,500 meters). Mauna Loa, also on the Big Island, is the planet's most massive mountain, at 10,000 cubic miles (16,000 cubic km) in volume.

Established in 1916, Hawaii Volcanoes National Park on the Big Island displays the results of hundreds of thousands of years of volcanic activity, migration, and evolution – processes that thrust a bare land from the sea and clothed it with complex and unique ecosystems.

Pu'u 'O'o vent, Kilauea Volcano. Most spectacular at the Kilauea Volcano, in Hawaii Volcanoes National Park, is when a rift opens and lava spurts into the air in a fountain. This happens sporadically and often doesn't last long, but if you are anywhere nearby when it does occur, rush to the national park.

An offering to Pele, the goddess of fire, left on the rim of the Kilauea caldera.

Pele: goddess of Hawaii's fire

Stay in Hawaii long enough and you'll encounter the name of Hawaii's goddess of fire, Pele.

Traditional beliefs attribute the current eruptions of Kilauea to Pele. Nomadic by disposition, she arrived in Hawaii from Tahiti in a canoe provided by the god of sharks. After arriving in Ni'ihau, a small island to the east of Kauai, she traveled along the islands looking for a volcano to call home.

The only suitable location was Hawaii Island. Arriving there, she went after the reigning fire god, Aila'au, hoping to move in with him. Her reputation had preceded her, especially the stories about her awesome power and rather tempestuous personality. By the time Pele reached Kilauea, Aila'au had already fled.

A visit to Hawaii Volcanoes National Park will reveal the reverence that many contemporary Hawaiians have for Pele. Offerings pepper the caldera rim of Halema'uma'u. Even outsiders learn of her power. Tourists who've taken lava souvenirs home often later return them to national park authorities, hoping to rid themselves of the bad luck that suddenly befalls them.

A house sits atop a lava flow that engulfed Kalapana in September 2013.

Freshly cooled lava on Kilauea Volcano. The ropy, smooth character of paho'eho'e lava, seen along the Chain of Craters Road near Kilauea, is easily distinguished from the jagged and rough texture of 'a'a lava. Lava flows create new land but also destroy nearly everything in their path.

Kilauea's usually passive flows can take on explosive force when reaching the cooler ocean or during the more spectacular fountaining.

Crossing the Hanakapi'ai Stream on the Hanakapi'ai Falls Trail, Hanakapi'ai Valley.

KAUAI

Long the most reclusive and independent of Hawaii's islands, Kauai attracts hikers, kayakers, and others with its laidback lifestyle and dramatic landscape.

Waves break upon the black rocks at Po'ipu Beach Park, Koloa.

The historian Edward Josting called Kauai a "separate kingdom" when he detailed the history of this idyllic island, for it remained stubbornly independent after all the other Hawaiian islands had succumbed to Kamehameha the Great's conquest in the 1790s.

That moniker still is true today. Kauai moves at its own pace, has its own style of beach living, and harbors miles upon miles of challenging but breathtaking hiking trails. There's also lots of forest – they don't call it the "Garden Isle" for nothing.

Anchoring this nearly circular island, reportedly the wettest place on earth, is the summit of Wai'ale'ale. Down by the coast, the island is ringed by perfect, white-sand beaches that stretch from Ha'ena Point on its northern coast to the Po'ipu Resort on its southern shore. The beaches continue to broad and beautiful Polihale Beach in the west.

On the southeastern coast is Lihu'e, Kauai's largest urban center and main airport. Northward from Lihu'e, the road passes through the green and wet Windward Coast to the spectacular North Shore, Hanalei Bay and Lumahai Beach. The road stops here. Beyond is the 14-mile (22km) long Na Pali coast, accessible only by foot or boat. Westward from Lihu'e is the dry side of the island, along with some of Kauai's most important historical sites. At Waimea, Captain

Hanakapi'ai Falls, Na Pali Coast State Wilderness Park.

Cook first set foot in the Hawaiian Islands. Nearby, an ascending road leads inland along spectacular Waimea Canyon to Koke'e, where mists compete with the sun, providing stunning views from 4,000ft (122-meter) lookouts.

More than half of this 550-sq mile (1,430-sq km) island is reserved for conservation and preservation. Alaka'i Swamp, a boggy dwarf forest high in the verdant interior, provides safe harbor for a number of endangered plants and birds. Elsewhere are many nature preserves and botanical gardens. Retreat to the seemingly silent places of Kauai, and sometimes you'll hear the song or catch a flash of the red or yellow feathers of a rarely seen 'apapane or 'akialoa, two types of Hawaiian honeycreepers.

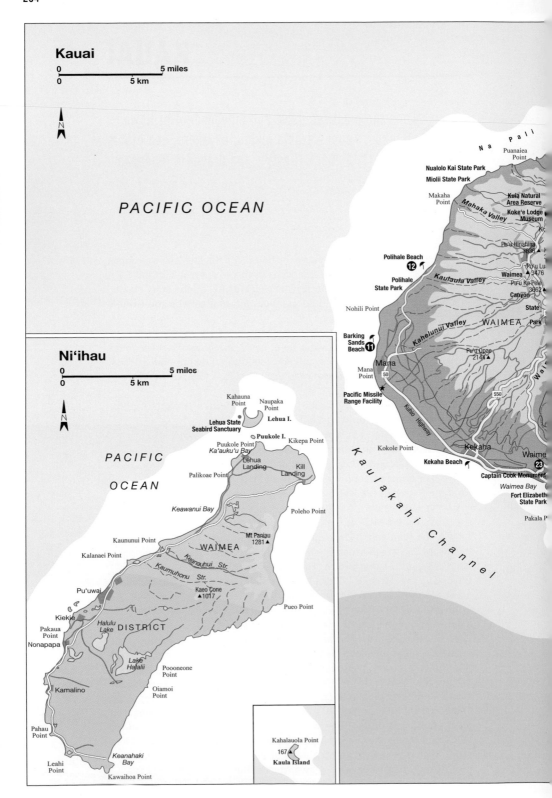

Kauai

0 _____ 5 miles
0 _____ 5 km

N

PACIFIC OCEAN

Na Pali

Puanaiea
Point

Nualolo Kai State Park
Miolii State Park

Makaha
Point

Mahaka Valley

**Kuia Natural
Area Reserve**
**Koke'e Lodge
Museum**

Pu'u Hinahina
3636 ▲

Polihale Beach ⑫

Pu'u Lu
3476 ▲ **Waimea**

**Polihale
State Park**

Kaulaula Valley

Pu'u Ka Pele
3662 ▲
Canyon

Nohili Point

Kahelunui Valley

WAIMEA

State

Park

Pu'u Opae
2144 ▲

**Barking
Sands
Beach** ⑪

Mana

Wai

Mana
Point

50

**Pacific Missile
Range Facility**

Kuhio Highway

550

Kokole Point

Kekaha

Waime

Kaulakahi Channel

Kekaha Beach

Captain Cook Monument ㉓

Waimea Bay
**Fort Elizabeth
State Park**

Pakala P

Ni'ihau

0 _____ 5 miles
0 _____ 5 km

N

PACIFIC

OCEAN

Kahauna
Point

Naupaka
Point

**Lehua State
Seabird Sanctuary**

Lehua I.

Puukole I.

Puukole Point
Ka'auku'u Bay

Lehua
Landing

Kikepa Point

Palikoae Point

Kill
Landing

Keawanui Bay

Poleho Point

Kaununui Point

▲Mt Paniau
1281 ▲

Kalanaei Point

WAIMEA

Keanauhui Str.

Kaumuhonu Str.

Pu'uwai

Kaeo Cone
▲1017

Pueo Point

Kiekie

*Halulu
Lake*

DISTRICT

Pakaua
Point

Nonapapa

*Lake
Halalii*

Poooneone
Point

Kamalino

Oiamoi
Point

Pahau
Point

*Keanahaki
Bay*

Leahi
Point

Kawaihoa Point

Kahalauola Point

167 ▲
Kaula Island

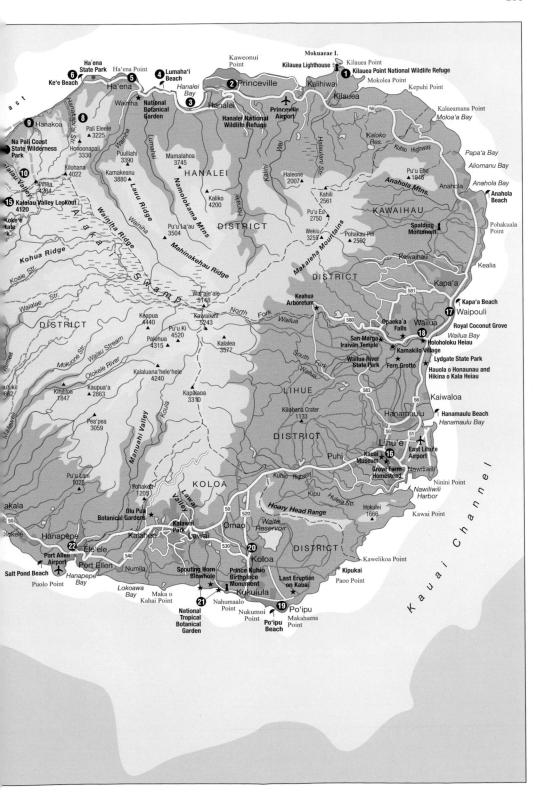

NORTH AND WEST KAUAI

Kauai is considered the "Garden Isle," and the
lush landscape of the north and west of the island
are a big part of how it earned this moniker.

Tropical paradise is different for every one of us, but in the original show, *South Pacific*, the notion takes the form of a place called Bali Hai. When the show was made into a movie, this mystical and magical spot was filmed in a mystical and magical part of Hawaii where a lush ridge of green traces a line high on the horizon, then drops all the way to meet the sea. Not surprisingly, it was filmed in Hanalei Bay, on the windward North Shore of Kauai.

All of the "Garden Isle" is green, but perhaps nowhere is the island greener than it is here. Taro fields; palm trees; you name the tropical flora, and it more than likely grows in this lush pocket of Kauai. The north is home to the Na Pali Coast, some of the most stunning coastline anywhere in the world; the Kalalau Trail (www.kalalautrail.com), one of the most iconic hikes on American soil; Tunnels, one of the most fabled surfing spots; and the Princeville, one of the most luxurious resorts in the world. The forests surrounding these spots have proven to be an uncrowded refuge for endemic plants and native birds; of all the Hawaiian Islands, Kauai has lost the fewest of its native feathered friends.

This eco-conscious vibe continues in the western quadrant of the island, where nature's beauty takes a very different form in Waimea Canyon. Known

as the "Grand Canyon of the Pacific," this site – and the area that surrounds it – is remarkable for what it represents; just as geologic forces built Kauai, so too are geologic forces (in the form of erosion) slicing it in two. Put simply, in a state with a multitude of incredible natural features, there simply is nothing like this.

KILAUEA AND HANALEI BAY

Technically speaking, north Kauai begins at the small town of **Kilauea**. A tiny downtown stretch is notable for

⊘ **Main attractions**
Hanalei Bay
Na Pali Coast
Kalalau Trail
Waimea Canyon
Koke'e

Map on page 264

Hanalei.

Admiring the view towards Hanalei Bay.

Limahuli Garden and Preserve.

its coffee shops, but the main attraction here is the **Kilauea Point National Wildlife Refuge ❶** (tel: 828-1413; https://fws.gov/refuge/kilauea_point; Tue–Sat 10am–4pm), where visitors can follow trails and look for sea birds that roost here year-round. If you have the time, follow the trails to the Kilauea Point Lighthouse on the point and take a tour. The structure was built in 1913, is a National Historic Landmark, and was renovated to commemorate its 100th anniversary.

A few miles beyond Kilauea Point is **Princeville ❷**, a 2,000-acre (800-hectare) resort area (www.princeville.com) containing several golf courses and a large clubhouse, airport, shopping center, private houses, several luxurious condominium projects, and the elegant St. Regis Princeville Hotel. Princeville offers striking views of Hanalei Bay and the sheer mountains at Hanalei, which is one of the wettest and greenest parts of the island. When rain mists the mountains, countless waterfalls hang like strands of silk thread from the dark green cliffs. It was in these lush

mountains that films such as *Jurassic Park* and *Raiders of the Lost Ark* were filmed. In the distance, near where the sun sets, is the stretch that served as *South Pacific's* Bali Hai; a small peak that rises where the mountains enter the ocean. Beginning at Princeville and continuing to the end of the road at Ha'ena are several valleys, each fronted by a curved, white, and sandy beach.

Hanalei Bay ❸, the largest bay on Kauai, is a favorite spot for yachts in summer. In winter, when big surf from the north makes anchorage riskier, the bay's outer reef provides a challenge for the island's surfers. Sheltered from the open sea, Hanalei is spared the largest surf that crashes against Kauai's North Shore. Waves generated by storms in the north Pacific can reach 30ft (9 meters), although surf of 10–20ft (3–6 meters) is more common. From fall to spring, the huge waves create clouds of floating sea mist known as 'ehukai all along the North Shore. In late afternoon, the descending sun gives the mist a golden cast. At **Tunnels Beach**, just outside of Hanalei

⊘ MARKET OF MARKETS

On an island like Kauai, where plants and fruits and vegetables reign supreme, pretty much every farmers' market is a good one. One market, however, rises above the rest: the weekly event on Saturdays on the main park in downtown Hanalei. To say the produce is spectacular would be an understatement; in addition to selling traditional Hawaiian items such as taro and poi, vendors peddle beautiful tomatoes, lettuce, and other fruits and veggies they have grown organically. The market also always features a kaleidoscope of tropical flowers – everything from orchids to bird of paradise flowers. In addition, the market has a slew of craft vendors. Perhaps the only downside is demand; produce tends to sell out quickly so get there early to secure the goods.

Bay, these waves can be epic – both for humans and sharks alike.

LUMAHA'I AND LIMAHULI

Beyond Hanalei is an 8-mile (13km) stretch of scenic coast, a glorious mix of mountains, beaches, and sea, known as the North Shore. Highlights include the photogenic series of beaches called **Lumaha'i ❹**, where brilliant white sands are interspersed with black lava-rock promontories. The blue of the sea shimmers beyond the sand, and the green of *hala* trees (also known as *pandanus*) glows behind it. Access to the beach is down a short dirt trail overhung with exotic *hala* trees. This is the beach where Mitzi Gaynor sang to the world in the movie *South Pacific* that she'd "wash that man right out of my hair." And there's the long stretch of reef-sheltered beach up against that other stand-in for *South Pacific*: the beach at Princeville in Hanalei Bay, which boasts good snorkeling as an additional reward.

Past these beaches, at least botanically speaking, the North Shore becomes Kauai at its most tropical, with waving palms, hibiscus, plumeria, ginger, and a host of other flowers. The **Limahuli** section of the National Tropical Botanical Garden (tel: 826-1053; www.ntbg.org; Tue–Sat 8.30am–4.30pm), 5 miles (8km) on from Lumaha'i Beach, is dedicated almost entirely to native plants such as these and includes a 900-acre (360-hectare) natural preserve that encompasses much of this striking valley. Walking the grounds and experiencing some of the terraced hillsides is an education in island farming techniques that have survived for centuries.

Wai'oli Hui'ia Church, Hanalei.

THE NA PALI COAST

The volcano goddess, Pele, was associated with Kauai long before she established her current home at Kilauea on the Big Island. One story about Pele places her at beautiful **Ha'ena ❺**, beyond Hanalei Bay and at the end of the road before Na Pali, during a big hula festival. In order to join the dancing, Pele took the form of a beautiful young woman, then fell in love with a

Hanalei.

⊘ NA PALI'S PAST

Today there is little to indicate the large numbers of people who once inhabited Na Pali's valleys. Extensive stonework that formed the taro paddies of Nu'alolo-aina (*'aina* means sea), a hanging valley, and the remains of a fishing village at Nu'alolo-kai (*kai* means fertile land) survive. The people of Nu'alolo-aina had access to the sea, while the people of Nu'alolo-kai had little land or fresh water, so each group worked with what it had. They formed a trading relationship, a single community built, of necessity, in two valleys.

In centuries past, the residents maintained the trails, but they are now impassable. A tree trunk that spanned a section of cliff between Honopu and Awa'awapuhi has rotted away, and a ladder that connected the upper and lower sections of the Nu'aloloaina and Nu'alolo-kai trail is long gone.

handsome Kauai chief, Lohi'au. The remnants of the hula platform can still be found on the hillside, to the west of **Ke'e Beach** , where the road ends. This is a popular spot that marks the start of the **Na Pali Coast State Wilderness Park** (www.dlnr.hawaii.gov/dsp/parks/kauai/napali-coast-state-wilderness-park), perhaps one of the world's most exquisite places. Though inaccessible to vehicles, this coastline can be enjoyed in a number of ways: by helicopter, kayak, paddleboard, or boat. Most people go by boat, preferring to experience the 4,000ft (1,220-meter) cliffs that drop into the ocean from the comfort of a floating vessel with a full bar. Charter tours are available in rigid-hulled inflatable boats or in catamarans. Almost all of these trips leave from Hanalei Bay.

Geologically speaking, the Na Pali Coast is a wonder. After the island was created hundreds of thousands of years ago, two forms of erosion have been working to create the natural rock spires we see today. From the bottom, wind and surf have chipped away at the rock to create caves and sea stacks. From the top, rain in the form of waterfalls has worn away saddles that, eventually, have become chasms. Over time, the cliffs have developed their unique appearance.

THE KALALAU TRAIL

There is another way to traverse the Na Pali Coast: by foot. From Ha'ena, a short oceanside trail leads to an ancient *hula heiau* (temple) plus spectacular scenic views. A far longer, 11-mile (18km) trail has become established as one of the most iconic hikes in all of America: the Kalalau Trail. The trail begins gradually, rising on a ridge and dropping into lush **Hanakapi'ai** . This area boasts a valley with a lovely pool and waterfall toward the cliffs, and a crescent of white sand on the ocean side. The ocean here becomes extremely dangerous in winter, and numerous unwary visitors have drowned. Hiking to and from Hanakapi'ai usually takes at least three hours.

From Hanakapi'ai, the Kalalau gets serious, zigzagging a heart-thumping course upward, scurrying in and out of valleys and across a sheer cliff face to **Hanakoa** , a hanging valley. Like several others here, Hanakoa sweeps from the heights in a flourish of vegetation and ends abruptly, hanging over the ocean, its stream turning into a misty waterfall that falls on the rocks and sea below. After passing a rough trail shelter, more jungle and an infinite number of shallow valleys and cliffs, the trail drops and then ends in **Kalalau Valley** , the largest of Na Pali's valleys. The section of the trail from Hanakoa valley can only be tackled by those who have a permit to camp overnight at Kalalau or at Hanakoa. Permits are available from the state parks office in Lihu'e but are limited and often sell out up to a year in advance especially in summer. (See www.hawaiistateparks.org/parks/kauai/napali.cfm for

A traditional grass hut in Limahuli Garden and Preserve.

more information). Conditions at these campsites are rustic at best.

THE WONDERFUL WEST

Kauai provides its residents with many avenues to the sea, as the island is ringed with sandy beaches. The largest is the stretch of nearly unbroken sand along the western coast, from Waimea stretching northward more than 15 miles (24km) along Highway 50 through sugar plantations and shorefront property. Along the beach north of Waimea is the Pacific Missile Range Facility at **Barking Sands** ⑪, which remains the site of controversial military testing. At the end of the highway – and the end of this long stretch of sand and former cane fields – is **Polihale** ⑫ (www.hawaiistateparks.org/parks/kauai/polihale-state-park). A state park, this beach is Hawaii's longest at over 15 miles (24km); it is usually empty due in part to the rough access road, and often dramatically draped with mist. Polihale offers campsites and showers; permits are available from the park's office in the state office building in downtown Lihu'e. Hidden in the cliffs at the Na Pali coast end are a couple of *heiaus*, or temples. Unless you know exactly what you're looking for, however, you'll not find them. There is no public access trail from here to the looming cliffs of the Na Pali coast.

All along this western coast, the modest rise of **Ni'ihau** breaks the horizon less than 20 miles (32km) offshore.

WAIMEA CANYON

Perhaps the region's most notable feature is a giant gash in the landscape on the back side of the Na Pali Coast: a geologic phenomenon known as **Waimea Canyon** ⑬. The chasm often is referred to as "The Grand Canyon of the Pacific," and the nickname is apt. Over the course of tens of thousands of years, the Waimea River has helped cut this canyon into the hillside. Today, the waters that continue to do the cutting start high in the bogs of the Alaka'i Swamp. After every major storm, waterfalls tumble from the swamp, through the canyon and into deep valleys carpeted in green. As the plum- and guava-dotted valleys converge into gorges, a change in flora occurs. The wetness of the swamp is left behind as the vegetation becomes sparse.

Downstream, the *ohi'a* gives way to *kukui*, the candlenut tree. The gorges meet with the main canyon, and the *kukui* gives way to dry country trees: the native *wiliwili* and introduced *kiawe* (mesquite) and *lantana*. The weather lower down is hot and dry, and the streambed holds the only moisture. Red dust blows from barren hillsides; by the time the **Waimea River** meets the sea at Waimea town, its currents carry a heavy suspension of red earth.

The scenery is still elegant and primal, but visitors should arrive early before the mists have cleared, before the rainbows have had time to form, and before the caravans of other

⊙ Fact

Barking Sands got its name from the sound made – something like a tired barking dog – when walked upon. The unusual structure of the grains of sand generates the sound.

Hiking the Hanakapi'ai Falls Trail, Na Pali Coast State Wilderness Park.

tourists in rental cars and tour buses gather. For the more experienced hiker, there is the **Kukui Trail**, which drops in a steep, zigzagging course down the side of the remarkable Waimea Canyon. If you hike here, be on the lookout for others who might be sharing the path – a herd of local mountain goats has been known to use the trail more frequently than humans.

KOKE'E

Just after the second canyon lookout, **Koke'e**  is the only inhabited place in Kauai's higher elevations. There are a dozen state-owned cabins here that anyone can rent as long as reservations are made well in advance. The cabins, which are basic and rustic, are managed from **Koke'e Lodge** (www.kokeelodge.com), which offers facilities including a restaurant, bar, store, and information center. Educational activities are also run from here.

Next to the lodge is the **Koke'e Museum** (tel: 335-9975; www.kokee.org; daily 9am–4.30pm; donation requested) with displays on the natural history of

Kauai and the other islands. Prints and living examples of important plants are exhibited. A selection of maps and travel guidebooks are also sold here. Located in the state park, the lodge and museum are fronted by a spreading lawn where protected *moa,* or wild Hawaiian chickens, strut.

Activities in the Koke'e area include a casual stroll around the **Iliau Nature Loop**, or, if you're in the mood for less strenuous activity, a drive to **Kalalau Valley Lookout**  at the end of the road reveals one of the world's finest views on a clear day: the panorama of Kalalau Valley, the largest valley along the Na Pali Coast.

The view from that 4,000ft (1,200-meter) -high lookout will more than reward the trials of the twisting drive to Koke'e. Low clouds sometimes obscure the view of the valley, but the lookout point offers a fine opportunity to see some of Kauai's native birds, such as the red-and-black *'apapane* and vermilion-colored *'i'iwi*, which frequents the *ohi'a* tree, common throughout the valley.

Hanakapi'ai Falls.

Waimea Canyon State Park.

Rock pooling at Poʻipu Beach Park, Koloa.

SOUTH AND EAST KAUAI

There are beaches, and then there are the beaches of Po'ipu and Kapa'a – some of the most intimate strips of sand in all of Hawaii. No wonder so many visitors flock to south and east Kauai.

Not much happens on Kauai, but when it does, it happens in the south and east. Here, on white-sand beaches such as Po'ipu, Kalapaki, Hanama'ulu, Waipouli, and Kapa'a, visitors come in droves to kick back, sip Mai Tais and escape the madness of other-island resorts. The eastern part of the island always has had a bit of a buzz about it; as recently as a few decades ago, this was sugar cane country and the site of Kauai's first processing plants and first railroad. Today, these historic sites provide an informative overview as to how the most remote major island managed to survive. In the south, the name of the game is innovation. Hanapepe Town comes to life every Friday night when visitors descend for an up-close look at the local art scene. Waimea Town, technically the first place Captain Cook made landfall in the Hawaii (before he moved along to Hawaii Island), has become a hub for technological innovation. Along with its lush jungles and glorious beaches, Kauai certainly has its share of secrets to discover.

LIHU'E

On the island's southeast coast, **Lihu'e** ⑯ is the seat of county government, the island's major business district and shopping area, and the site of Kauai's

airport. Nearby, **Nawiliwili Harbor**, the island's major port, plays host to a growing number of cruise ships on inter-island and trans-Pacific itineraries. It's also home port to a number of deep-sea fishing charters. Also nearby: **Kalapaki Beach**, a quiet white-sand beach that fronts the beautiful Haupu mountains and looks out onto Nawiliwili Harbor. Nearby Hōkūala ("Rising star"; www.hokualakauai.com) is the island's newest resort, offering luxurious oceanfront accommodations, a farm-to-fork restaurant, and spa.

Main attractions

Kalapaki Beach
Kauai Museum
Po'ipu
Koloa Rum Company
National Tropical
  Botanical Garden
Hanapepe

Map on page 264

Cycling on a trail beside the Kuhio Highway, outside Kapa'a.

Kauai has several top-class golf courses; some are part of resorts, others are independent.

Kayaking on the Wailua River.

Since the 1850s Kauai has been a sugar-producing island, and the history of sugar's heyday can be studied at two highly recommended museums in Lihu'e. In the center of town, on Rice Street, **Kauai Museum** (tel: 245-6931; www.kauaimuseum.org; Mon–Thu 9am–2pm) is, without question, the best museum on the island. In addition to collections that tell the story of life on Kauai in the past, the museum frequently displays the work of local artists. It also occasionally offers courses in such activities as *lau hala* weaving and *lei*-making. Located off Nawiliwili Road (Highway 58), also in Lihu'e, is the **Grove Farm Homestead & Sugar Plantation Museum** (tel: 245-3202; www.grovefarm.org; Mon, Wed & Thu: tours 10am and 1pm, reservations required). For close to a century this was a plantation-owner's home; today it provides insights into the era of plantation agriculture in Hawaii.

Both museums offer a good introduction to the contributions made by Kauai's elite *kama'aina* (long-time resident) families, with names that become more familiar during one's stay on the island: Rice, Wilcox, Sinclair, Gay, and Robinson. Many had missionary roots but later made their fortunes in sugar and ranching. Some of these *kama'aina*, such as William Harrison Rice and his son, William Hyde Rice, had a strong affinity for Native Hawaiian people and their culture, and did a great deal to keep the language and legends alive. Kauai Museum was founded by Rice's progeny, while Grove Farm Homestead was established by George N. Wilcox, whose parents were among the earliest American Protestant missionaries to Hawaii; they left a legacy of land and sugar.

The Wilcox holdings comprise some of the largest privately owned land on Kauai, including one of the few remaining plantations in the islands. With the decline of the sugar industry, Grove Farm has branched into land development, including Kukui Grove, Kauai's largest shopping mall. The Wilcox family also retains extensive holdings on the North Shore and developed a shopping center in Hanalei. The

Sinclair-Robinson-Gay clan, which purchased the tiny island of Ni'ihau in 1864, continues to be active in cattle ranching and sugar cultivation. The Robinsons, who manage Ni'ihau, are perhaps the most secretive of the *kama'aina* families.

WAIPOULI AND KAPA'A

The stretch of coastline east from Lihu'e is sometimes called the Coconut Coast because of its preponderance of palm trees, bays, and beautiful beaches. This stretch runs from **Waipouli** to **Kapa'a**, and since 1990 this area has become one of the island's biggest resort areas, complete with condominiums, supermarkets, gas stations, and all of the other amenities to serve visitors. (It's also one of the best places on the island to buy shave ice.)

Up Kuamo'o Road toward the mountains and the spectacular beach at Opaeka'a Falls, just outside **Wailua** is a large gathering of rocks that includes a birthstone and a *piko* (navel) stone. Modern-day attractions in the area include the Wailua Golf Course, a municipal 18-hole facility; Wailua Beach; the Wailua River, which carries tour boats to the **Fern Grotto**, a natural though commercialized wedding site; and the modern Coconut Plantation Marketplace.

Heading inland on Route 53, there's a turnoff for **Kamakilo Village**, where you can visit a reconstructed *hale*, a type of a traditional Hawaiian village house (tel: 823-0559; daily 9am–5pm, summer 8am–7pm). Farther along, off Kaholalele Road, look out for the spires of **Kauai's Hindu Monastery**, a religious retreat built on acres of lush, rainforested valley. The San Marga Iraivan Temple has existed here for years, while the Kadavul Temple is a more recent addition. Guided tours are offered by warm and welcoming devotee-guides (tel: 822-3012; www. himalayanacademy.com).

PO'IPU AND BEYOND

On Kauai's southernmost point, **Po'ipu** is the sunniest of the island's districts. It has several large hotels, plus

Koloa Rum Company's tasting room and store on the Kilohana Plantation.

Outside the Kauai Museum, Lihu'e.

⊘ OPAEKA'A FALLS

It's not as tall as some of the waterfalls outside Hanalei, but this 151ft (46-meter) cascade, along the Wailua River on the east side of Kauai, has become one of the island's most popular waterfalls. The popularity stems from accessibility; the attraction is just 2 miles (3km) up Kuamo'o Road from Highway 56, and there's a convenient roadside lookout. The name of the waterfall tells a bit of history; opaeka'a means "rolling shrimp," and when freshwater shrimp were abundant in the stream, they would roll in the water from the force of the falls. On the opposite side of the road near the falls is the relatively well-preserved ancient temple of Poli'ahu Heiau. It is named after the snow goddess, Poli'ahu, sister of Pele, and is worth a quick look.

NI'IHAU

Across the Kaulakahi Channel from Kauai's west side, Ni'ihau rises dimly through sea mists like some slumbering prehistoric creature 17 miles (27km) away.

It sees little rain because it falls in the lee of Kauai, whose mountains collect most of the moisture. The mystique of this windswept, privately owned island, whose estimated 250 residents are seemingly caught in a 19th-century time warp, has been perpetuated by the owner's patriarchal restriction on visitors.

Owned by the Robinson family since 1864, Ni'ihau has been cloaked in myth from the time the first Polynesian explorers came upon the 6- by 18-mile (10 by 29km) sliver of arid land. Early chants relay that Ni'ihau and its tiny islet neighbors, **Lehua** and **Ka'ula**, were triplet siblings born to the ancestral gods Papa and Wakea.

Another chant postulates that Pele chose Ni'ihau as her first home. Interestingly, many volcanologists now theorize that Ni'ihau was the first of the current Hawaiian islands to break the surface of the ocean. Seventh largest in the chain, its highest point is 1,281ft (390 meters) above sea level.

Making a Ni'ihau shell necklace.

Ni'ihau was Captain James Cook's second stop (following Kauai) in the islands during his voyage of exploration in 1778. In 1864, King Kamehameha V sold it to Elizabeth (McHutcheson) Sinclair, widow of a Navy officer who had perished, along with their eldest son, in a shipwreck. Mrs Sinclair saw Ni'ihau lush after two years of abundant rainfall and believed it would make a good ranch home for her remaining five children. For her $10,000, she acquired not only an island, but also the 300 Hawaiians living on it.

MODERN ISLAND LIFE

Today, family heirs Keith and Bruce Robinson manage the ranch and island. They continue to guard the privacy of Ni'ihau's Hawaiian populace to the extent that the island is one of the last true enclaves of a lifestyle that has long since disappeared elsewhere. Life on the island, however, is quite unembellished and without frills.

Ni'ihau is the only island in Hawaii where Hawaiian is the primary language. Today, children attend a grammar school with three classrooms in **Pu'uwai**, the island's only village. Though many homes do not have electricity and most do not have indoor plumbing or telephones, the school has solar-powered computers. Other schools for Ni'ihau's children are on Kauai, where kids go to live with relatives. They must go to Kauai or Oahu to attend high school.

State education officials and tax officers visit the island, and a couple of doctors make infrequent checks on the populace. Otherwise, access is limited to visitors who pay for an expensive helicopter tour (tel: 441-3500; www.niihau.us/heli.html) or less costly day-long snorkeling tours to remote ends of the island, which do not allow passengers to set foot on the soil (tel: 335-0815; www.holoholokauaiboattours.com). There are virtually no county services, no county roads, and no sewers. Few people use cars; horses and bicycles are more common.

Nearly all residents still work for the Robinsons, rearing cattle and sheep, making charcoal from *kiawe* trees and gathering honey. Twice a week a barge arrives at Ka'auku'u Bay to carry goods across the sea to market and to deliver mail and other necessities.

many smaller hotels and condominiums, and has evolved as an enclave around this stretch of overnight accommodations. Most of the hotels face the ocean; on the other side of the main road through the area, you'll find restaurants, supermarkets, and shopping centers designed to serve the tourists who come and stay a while. In addition to the white-sand beaches (with water that generally is calm), there are several scenic spots in the area, such as **Spouting Horn**, a natural water spout in the shoreline rocks of an old lava flow, and **Brennecke's Beach**, renowned for its great bodysurfing waves. This portion of the island suffered most from the wrath of 1992's Hurricane 'Iniki. Although many homes, especially those along the coastline leading to Spouting Horn, were destroyed, they have all been rebuilt.

The coast westward from Lihu'e, the dry leeward side, might as well be a different island from the opposite side. Little rain falls past Kalaheo a town in the heart of the Anahola Mountains in the center of the island.

Kauai's "Hawaiianness" is obvious, but since 1835, when Hawaii's first commercial sugar plantation was started at **Koloa 20**, the island's ethnic character has gone through radical changes. As in other parts of Hawaii, sugar attracted a diverse set of people willing to work in its dusty, itchy fields and pungent mills. First came the Chinese, then the Japanese, Portuguese, Puerto Ricans, and lastly the Filipinos. Thus many of Kauai's communities developed as plantation towns, with the different races separated into camps. You can learn more about town's complex history and its sugar industry at the **Koloa History Center** (9am–9pm).

Koloa is one of these towns, welcoming visitors with rustic charm and a cluster of shops and restaurants. One of its attractions, the **Koloa Rum Company** (3-2087 Kaumuali'i Highway; tel; 246-8900; www.koloarum.com; opening hours vary, check the website), offers tours of the on-site spirits production facility and tastings in a bar. The town also has a monument to its plantation

Salt Pond Beach Park, in Hanapepe, has the only natural salt pond in Hawaii that is still used to make salt during the summer.

Opaeka'a Falls, Wailua River State Park.

☉ THE LITTLE PEOPLE

It's difficult to visit Kauai without hearing at least a handful of references to the *menehune*, little people who are reputed to have inhabited the island in the distant past. As the legend goes, these pint-sized humans were believed to farm remote valleys on the island's North Shore, and were reportedly responsible for several stone constructions across the island. Menehune were seldom seen, working only after dark, and it was said that they accepted as payment only a single shrimp per worker. Among the construction projects associated with them are the Menehune Ditch near Waimea on the leeward coast, which exhibits a knowledge of stonework not seen elsewhere in Hawaii, and the 'Alekoko Fishpond, also called the Menehune Fishpond, near Lihu'e's Nawiliwili Harbor.

Trees create a tunnel over the road linking the east side of Kauai to Koloa and Po'ipu.

Po'ipu Beach Park, Koloa.

past, a Buddhist temple, and several historic churches to add flavor and interest to a visit.

Today, many of the sugar firms that started the towns are gone or have merged with other companies, but the communities themselves persist. Waimea, Numila (the Hawaiian pronunciation of New Mill), Puhi, Kealia, and Kilauea are a few of the towns that have lost the plantations that helped build them. In 2009, Gay & Robinson, Kauai's last big sugar company, closed its mill at Makaweli and got out of the business altogether.

NATIONAL TROPICAL BOTANICAL GARDEN

The prestigious **National Tropical Botanical Garden ㉑** (tel: 332-7324; www.ntbg.org; tours daily, check hours online; reservations essential) in Lawa'i Valley is a facility that saves endangered tropical plants, and locates and grows flora of medicinal and economic importance. In recent years, the garden has begun collecting and propagating Hawaii's unique

endemic plants. The gardens also include **Lawa'i Kai**, the verdant estate of John Gregg Allerton, who willed his estate to the nation upon his death.

Lawa'i Kai is a wild wonderland of vegetation and statuary at the base of Lawa'i, where it meets the sea in a clean, white-sand beach. The estate's lovely gardens and buildings, including Queen Emma's summer home are open to the public (tour times vary, check the website for further details) see page 269).

HANAPEPE AND WAIMEA

West of Koloa on the south shore sits **Hanapepe ㉒**, known lovingly as "The Biggest Little Town" on Kauai. This is a place built on salt; a group of pre-contact salt ponds that have been worked by local Hawaiian salt gatherers for generations lie just beyond the main drag.

In recent years, the town's historic buildings have become chock-full of independent art galleries and tiny cafés. Hanapepe Town celebrates its local artists every Friday, from 5–9pm,

as painters, sculptors, and craftsmen open the doors of their art galleries and home studios to introduce new-comers to their respective work. For an island that never has too much happening, Friday nights in Hanapepe are about as hopping as things get. Meanwhile on Thursdays from 3pm, visitors and locals alike head to the farmers' market offering fresh, locally grown, seasonal produce. Pick up supplies for lunch to go, or for rustling up dinner on self-catering stays.

Waimea ㉓, a historic seaport, is not far from where British discoverer Captain James Cook first landed in Hawaii in 1778. When Cook arrived, the local chiefs had moved their courts from the warmth of the island's leeward side to cooler Wailua on the east side of the island, and were nowhere to be found. Cook left Waimea before these chiefs could return to greet him. He eventually found his welcome, and end, on Hawaii Island, but it's hard to visit Waimea and not contemplate how different Hawaiian history would be if the *ali'i* had been home.

Today, Waimea is an off-the-radar spot that is worth exploring. On the south bank of the Waimea River is the old Russian **Fort Elizabeth** ㉔, now protected as a state park. In 1816, an agent of the Imperial Russian government came to Kauai to recover the cargo of a ship that had broken up on the island's shore.

The agent, Dr Anton Sheffer, convinced Kauai's King Kaumuali'i that together they could conquer the rest of the islands. Sheffer's Machiavellian bid for Hawaiian power failed miserably, but crumbling ruins of the old fort, named after Czar Alexander I's queen, remain as a testimonial to Sheffer's adventurism and folly.

For a more modern monument, be sure to check out the **West Kauai Technology & Visitor Center** (www.westkauaivisitorcenter.org), a great place to learn more about Kauai's rich history and heritage. The center features interesting exhibits, educational programs and weekly activities that reflect the diversity of Kauai's agricultural community.

⊘ Fact

John Gregg and his adoptive father, Robert, spent many years traveling all over the world, collecting art and botanical species. Robert died in 1964 and John Gregg in 1986.

Wailua River in Kapa'a.

Ziplining at World Botanical
Gardens, Hakalau, Big Island.

HAWAII

TRAVEL TIPS

TRANSPORTATION

Getting there **284**
   By air................................... **284**
   By sea.................................. **285**
Getting around **285**
   By air................................... **285**
   By bicycle **285**
   On foot................................. **285**
   By bus **286**
   By car.................................. **286**
   By sea.................................. **287**
   By taxi **287**

A – Z

Accommodations **288**
Admission charges **288**
Animals **288**
Budgeting for your trip **288**
Children................................... **288**
Climate and weather **289**
Crime and safety...................... **289**
Customs regulations................. **289**
Disabled travelers.................... **289**
Eating out **290**
Emergencies **290**
Embassies and consulates....... **290**
Electricity **290**
Festivals **290**
Health and medical care.......... **292**

Internet **292**
LGBTQ travelers........................ **293**
Maps.. **293**
Media....................................... **293**
Money...................................... **293**
Opening hours.......................... **293**
Postal services......................... **294**
Public holidays......................... **294**
Religion **294**
Shopping **294**
Tax **296**
Telephones............................... **296**
Time zone................................. **297**
Tipping..................................... **297**
Tourist information **297**
Tour operators **297**
Visas and passports.................. **297**
Weights and measures **297**
What to bring **297**
What to wear **297**

LANGUAGE

Background............................... **298**
A language of the Pacific **298**
Pronunciation guidelines.......... **299**

FURTHER READING

Non-fiction **300**
Fiction **300**

TRANSPORTATION

GETTING THERE

Because Hawaii is an archipelago, and because those islands sit right in the middle of the Pacific Ocean, getting to them often presents visitors with one of the biggest challenges of their respective trips. In reality, there are only two options – you either fly in or come by sea.

By air

Hawaii is regularly serviced from the US mainland, Canada, Europe, the South Pacific, and Asia. Flying time is about 10 hours from New York, eight hours from Chicago, and five hours from Los Angeles. The Hawaiian Islands also are a major stopover point for flights traveling between the US mainland and Asia, Australia, and New Zealand.

Oahu

It might be Hawaii's most populous island but Oahu only has one commercial airport, **Daniel K. Inouye International Airport**, also known as **Honolulu Airport** (tel: 808-836-6411; http://airports.hawaii.gov/hnl). However, over the years this has become one of the busiest airports in the entire US: in 2020, the airport

recorded over 6.6 million passengers. Most planes touch down on a series of reef runways, completed in 1977 on a shallow reef-lagoon between Honolulu Harbor and Pearl Harbor. The interior of the airport's main terminal is adorned with Hawaiian arts and crafts created by top local artists. (In 1967, a Hawaii legislative act designated one percent of all appropriated public works funds for the purchase of artwork for state buildings, including the airport.) Japanese, Hawaiian, and Chinese gardens also enhance the terminal's promenade areas.

In addition to the main terminal building, the airport operates two other terminals: the inter-island terminal and the small domestic flights terminal used by Mokulele Airlines only. The airport operates a free shuttle system between these buildings from 6am to 10pm.

Maui

Maui has three airports. The main one, **Kahului Airport** (tel: 808-872-3830, http://airports.hawaii.gov/ogg), handles a growing number of direct flights from the US mainland and many inter-island hops. The airport boasts a Visitor Information Center,

major rental car counters, and taxi and shuttle stands.

The two other airports, the **Kapalua-West Maui Airport** (tel: 808-665-6108; http://airports.hawaii.gov/jhm) and **Hana Airport** (tel: 808-248-4861; http://airports.hawaii.gov/hnm), are significantly smaller; both are served by inter-island airlines (see page 285). Flying to Hana from one of the other Maui airports is a fast and efficient option if you don't want to drive the Hana Highway. Be warned: these flights can be expensive.

Hawaii Island

Hawaii Island has two main airports, the **Ellison Onizuka Kona International Airport** at Keahole (tel: 808-327-9520; http://airports.hawaii.gov/koa) on the popular west side, and **Hilo International Airport** (tel: 808-961-9300; http://airports.hawaii.gov/ito) on the outskirts of Hilo. A third airport, dubbed Waimea-Kohala Airport (tel: 808-887-8126; http://airports.hawaii.gov/mue) is used for inter-island commutes. It is called Kamuela Airport by locals.

Kauai

On Kauai, **Lihu'e Airport** (tel: 808-274-3800; http://airports.hawaii.gov/lih) has direct flights daily from San Francisco and Los Angeles on the US mainland, as well as numerous inter-island flights from Honolulu and other neighboring island airports. Lihu'e Airport is the smallest of all the airports on the four major Hawaiian Islands.

Molokai and Lanai

Molokai's Ho'olehua Airport (tel: 808-567-9660; http://airports.hawaii.gov/mkk) in south-central Molokai, handles inter-island flights only. The same is true at Lanai Airport (tel: 808-565-7942; http://airports.hawaii.gov/lny), 10 miles from Lanai City.

⊙ Distances from Honolulu

Anchorage 2,781 miles/4,475km
Auckland 4,393 miles/7,068km
Equator 1,470 miles/2,352km
Hilo, Hawaii Island 214 miles/344km
Hong Kong 5,541 miles/8,915km
Kailua-Kona, Hawaii Island 168 miles/270km
Kahului, Maui 98 miles/158km
Kure Atoll 1,367 miles/2,200km
Lanai 72 miles/116 km
Lihu'e, Kauai 103 miles/166km
London 7,226 miles/11,627km

Los Angeles 2,557 miles/4,114km
Manila 5,293 miles/8,516km
Midway Is. 1,309 miles/2,106km
Molokai 54 miles/87km
New York 4,959 miles/7,979km
North Pole 4,740 miles/7,631km
Papeete, Tahiti 2,741 miles/4,410km
San Francisco 2,397 miles/3,857km
Tokyo 3,847 miles/6,190km
Vancouver 2,709 miles/4,359km

Hire a Jeep and hit the Hana Highway on Maui.

Trans-Pacific Airlines

Air Canada
Tel: 888-247-2262
www.aircanada.com
Air China
Tel: 800-882-8122
www.airchina.com
Alaska Airlines
Tel: 800-252-7522
www.alaskaair.com
American Airlines
Tel: 800-433-7300
www.aa.com
Delta Airlines
Tel: 800-221-1212
www.delta.com
Hawaiian Airlines
Tel: 800-367-5320
www.hawaiianairlines.com
Air New Zealand
Tel: 800-262-1234
www.airnewzealand.com
United Airlines
Tel: 800-864-8331
www.united.com
WestJet
Tel: 888-937-8538
www.westjet.com

By sea

Numerous cruise ships including **Crystal Cruises** (www.crystalcruises.com), **Princess Cruises** (www.princess.com), and **Royal Caribbean** (www.royalcaribbean.com) now make Hawaii a port-of-call, stopping in Honolulu as well as the neighbor islands as part of their itinerary. A few lucky souls, of course, arrive by private yacht.

GETTING AROUND

Once you're in Hawaii, getting around can be easy or difficult, depending on where you're headed and how much you're willing to spend to get there. If you're staying on one island, the best option is to rent a car; it's cheaper than taking taxis everywhere and more reliable (and efficient) than public transportation. If you're island hopping, you'll either have to fly or take a ferry, though ferries only run between Maui and Lanai.

By air

Flights between islands are frequent, every half hour or hour. There is one primary carrier, **Hawaiian Airlines**, which use jets between all major airports.

Mokulele Airlines (www.mokuleleairlines.com) is another airline that offers small-plane flights from many of the major airports to smaller airports (such as Hana and Lanai).

With the exception of morning and late afternoon commuter times, when local workers and businesspeople are returning to their home islands, you can usually get a seat on one of these inter-island flights at short notice. If one flight is full, there is another flight in about 30 minutes to an hour. However, weekends and holidays are busy times; reserve ahead if possible. Inter-island flights are short, from 20 to 45 minutes, depending on the route.

Hawaiian Airlines often offers hotel and rental car deals with its flights, again often on very short notice. The first couple of early-morning flights and the last couple of flights at night are sometimes also discounted.

Inter-island flights

Hawaiian Airlines
Tel: 800-367-5320
www.hawaiianairlines.com
Mokulele Airlines
Tel: 808-495-4188
www.mokuleleairlines.com

By bicycle

Cycling aficionados love riding around Hawaii – many say the Aloha State offers some of the most challenging and rewarding road system in the US. The same rules of the road apply to bicycles and cars; bicyclists are expected to ride with traffic and obey all traffic signals. If you're cycling, be aware that some drivers may have trouble spotting you. It's also a good idea to bring raingear; though the weather on the islands is usually sunny especially in winter it can rain at any time.

On foot

When all else fails, when you have no other method of getting around the Hawaiian Islands, you always can walk. Pedestrians are permitted on all local roadways, provided they are in the shoulder. Hitchhiking also is quite common, especially in surfing areas. If you are walking at night, use caution and wear reflective clothing so drivers can see you. And if you do choose to hitch, be careful which vehicles you enter; if you feel the slightest bit unsafe, keep walking or dial 911.

By bus

All four of the major Hawaiian Islands have some form of mass transport. Depending on where you want to get to and how long you're willing to wait to get there, utilizing these systems may make sense during your visit.

Oahu

Without question, the bus system on Oahu, dubbed **TheBus** (www.thebus.org), is the best in the state. This bus system covers the entire island, and the fare is the same regardless of whether you travel six blocks or all the way around. TheBus is especially efficient in downtown Honolulu, with buses stopping every 15 minutes around Waikiki and the Ala Moana Shopping Center.

As of late 2021, fares for TheBus were $2.75 per ride ($5.50 for a one-day pass). Exact change is required and dollar bills are accepted. A one-day pass is available at 7-Eleven stores and the Buss Pass office. For details, check the company's website. Important route numbers for Waikiki are 2, 4, 8, 19, 20, 57, and the City Express Route A. Route booklets listing other routes are available all over town.

The open-air **Waikiki Trolley** (tel: 593-2822, www.waikikitrolley.com) is another reliable option for

getting around town. This system has three lines and makes dozens of stops. The City Arts District Line (Red Line) travels between the Waikiki Shopping Plaza and Diamond Head with stops including the State Capitol, King Kamehameha Statue and Chinatown. The Ocean/Diamond Head Line (Blue Line), hugs Honolulu's Hanauma Bay, linking the Waikiki Shopping Plaza with Kahala Mall with stops including Sea Life Park and Diamond Head State Monument. The Ala Moana Shopping Line (Pink Line) stretches from Waikiki to the Ala Moana Shopping Center with stops at selected hotels. A one-day, all-line ticket costs $45; four-day tickets (also good for all four lines) cost $65 and seven-day tickets – $75. There are discounts for children and seniors and when ordering online.

Maui

There has been talk of implementing an island-wide public transportation system on Maui for years. Until it happens, the best option for this island is **Maui Bus** (tel: 871-4838; www.mauicounty.gov/605/Bus-Service-Schedule-Information). Operated by Roberts Hawaii, this system offers 11 routes between various communities. Two routes – the Upcountry and Haiku Islander routes – include a stop at Kahului Airport. Buses cover all of the island's major destinations, and fares are $2 per person.

Hawaii Island

The best bus option on Hawaii Island is the **Hele-On Bus** (tel: 961-8744; www.heleonbus.org), which covers all major towns and runs the four-hour trip from Kona to Hilo several times

each day. Fares for this system are $2 per ride.

Kauai

On the Garden Isle, The Kauai Bus (tel: 246-8110, www.kauai.gov/transportation) runs from Hanalei to Kakaha every day. The bus network also provides transportation to Lihu'e. Fares are $2 per ride.

By car

Most visitors to Hawaii prefer to rent cars. This option provides travelers with the flexibility to go where they want, when they want. (On Molokai, renting a car is the only way to explore without the help of a tour outfitter.) It also is more affordable than taking taxis (see page 287); most rates start from $65 per day for economy cars, and child car seats are an additional charge of $14 per day. Note, however, that prices are based on demand rather than size of the vehicle.

All major car rental companies operate in Hawaii and many have 24-hour counters at most airports. Book in advance – or through online travel agents – for the best deals. Drivers generally are required to be 21–25 years or older, have a valid driver's license (non-US license holders should check if their car rental company requires an international license), and a major credit card. It's also a good idea to fork

Watch out for donkeys crossing in Waimea, Big Island.

A tram in Honolulu, Oahu.

over the extra cash for the loss/damage waiver; rental agencies in Hawaii are notoriously nitpicky about dings and scratches on their cars, and this surcharge covers you against any faults they may find. Car rental agencies in Hawaii include (all telephone numbers are for the car-hire offices located at Honolulu's International Airport):

Alamo tel: 808-833-4585; www.alamo.com

Avis tel: 808-834-5536; www.avis.com

Budget tel: 808-836-1700; www.budget.com

Dollar tel: 866-434-2226; www.dollar.com

Enterprise Rent-a-Car tel: 808-836-2213; www.enterprise.com

Hertz tel: 808-837-7100; www.hertz.com

National tel: 808-834-6350; www.nationalcar.com

Thrifty tel: 877-283-0898; www.thrifty.com

Driving

It is worth noting that driving in Hawaii is much like driving on the US mainland. Traffic advances on the right side of the road, and it is legal to make right turns on red lights unless posted otherwise. All passengers must wear seatbelts and infants and young children must be strapped into car seats or booster seats as appropriate. Pedestrians, whether in a crosswalk or not, always have the right of way. Most roads are paved; highways are well maintained; signs are in English and/or international symbols; speed

limits and distance are indicated almost exclusively in miles and miles-per-hour.

All car rental companies offer emergency roadside assistance; don't hesitate to dial the numbers on your contract for any reason during your trip (including flat tires). Another option in the event of a breakdown is to contact **AAA Help** (tel: 800-222-4357). If you or one of your passengers appears injured, dial 911.

Though the islands are not nearly as populated as urban centers on the mainland, some of the busiest roadways still experience traffic during rush hour (7–9am and again from 4–6pm). Traffic is the worst on Oahu in and around Honolulu, where drivers have been known to inch forward on freeways for miles. In recent years, Maui has started to see rush hour traffic, as well – especially between Lahaina and the Kahalui area. Thankfully, traffic on Hawaii Island and Kauai generally only is a result of construction or unexpected lane closures on major roads.

Gasoline prices are higher on the islands than they are on the mainland, but usually can be obtained for $3.2–4 per gallon.

By sea

For seafaring types, **Norwegian Cruise Line** (tel: 866-234-0392; www.ncl.com) offers weekly seven-day cruises that depart Honolulu for Kauai, Maui, and the Big Island. Tours, in-port activities and rental cars are all optional.

There are daily ferry services between Lahaina, Maui and Manele Bay, Lanai, with **Expeditions Lanai Ferry** (tel: 800-695-2624, www.go-lanai.com). The 9-mile (14km) crossing takes 45 minutes, depending on ocean conditions (which, especially in the afternoon, when the winds pick up, can almost guarantee seasickness). Reservations are recommended.

By taxi

Taxi service is available on all islands, including Lanai and Molokai. Rates vary from island to island (but are generally expensive – around $3-4 per mile); all taxis are metered, and most are available for sightseeing at a fixed rate. Honolulu, of course, has the most taxis, but don't expect to flag one down on the street. If a taxi is required, go to a nearby hotel. On other islands, it may be necessary to call a taxicab company and pre-arrange a ride.

There are dozens of cab companies on every Hawaiian island. On Oahu, try The CAB (tel: 422-2222, www.thecabhawaii.com). On Maui, use CB Taxi (tel: 243-8294, www.cbtaxi-maui.com). On Hawaii Island, book with Jun's Taxi (tel: 808-756-3191, www.junstaxi.com). And on Kauai, try Kauai Taxi Company (tel: 808-246-9554, www.kauaitaxico.com). For additional listings, look to the Hawaii Tourism Authority (www.gohawaii.com) or check the yellow pages under the heading "Taxicabs."

A - Z

A

Accommodations

Considering that Hawaii attracts travelers of every kind, the islands abound in accommodations of every persuasion. Resorts, hotels, inns, rental condominiums, bed-and-breakfasts, hostels, and campsites – the islands have them all. Because there are so many different classifications of accommodations in Hawaii, the quality of these accommodations varies widely. Many of the international luxury hotel chains have built brands around a certain standard of excellence; if you can afford these properties (often at upward of $500 per night), you probably know what you're looking for. On the flipside, the quality of rooms at properties on the lower end of the scale can vary widely. Definitely do your research (both here and online, at property websites) before you book. Prices fluctuate considerably in Hawaii; they are most commonly dictated by season and location. During rainy season, for instance, especially in resort areas such as Wailea on Maui, some of the highest-end rooms might be $200–$300 less than they are during high season (which is summer). Location also determines price; the closer you are to a "beachfront" location, the more expensive your nightly rate likely will be.

Admission charges

Admission fees to museums or other public buildings in Hawaii, and also to state or county parks, range between $6 and $23 per adult, with reduced fees available for children. The two national parks, Haleakala on Maui and Hawaii Volcanoes on Hawaii Island, charge $15 each per person, while the cost for a single private vehicle (carrying up to 14 people) is $30. The charges that will make a serious impact on your budget are likely to be those for commercial tourist attractions, and especially so on Oahu, where the very cheapest adult admission to the Polynesian Cultural Center costs $69.95, and an adult entrance to Sea Life Park is $39.99.

Animals

Hawaii is free of rabies, snakes, and poison ivy, and state officials work hard to keep it that way. Incoming animals are placed in quarantine for 120 days at the owner's expense, although recent legislation now permits dogs and cats that meet certain pre- and post-arrival requirements to be quarantined for only 30 days.

B

Budgeting for your trip

Broadly speaking, Hawaii ranks at the expensive end of American vacation destinations. Prices are generally high, as so much of what is consumed in the islands has to be shipped there from across the Pacific or beyond. In addition, many tourists are happy to pay premium rates for a once-in-a-lifetime holiday in paradise. However, it is possible to keep costs down. The finest hotels tend to charge at least $270 per room per night, and often double that. For pretty good accommodations close to the sea, it's perfectly possible to pay $125–150 in a hotel, or perhaps $100 for a rented condo. All the islands hold significantly cheaper options too, well worth considering if you expect to spend most of your time exploring.

Only on Oahu is it realistic to think you won't need a car; typical rental rates would be $300–400 per week for a compact vehicle. Gas isn't cheap, but you won't use all that much, because you can't drive very far on such small islands. Taxi fares vary greatly from island to island, but because most of the major airports are at least 10–15 miles from major tourist destinations, plan on spending $30–50 to travel to your destination by taxi. Finally, ticket prices for bus travel vary from island to island but no transit fees exceed $3 per ride.

The average visitor spends about $30 per day on food and drink; even if you buy and prepare your own meals, it's hard to go much lower than say $20 per day, while at the other end of the spectrum there are plenty of fine-dining restaurants charging $50 or more for a single meal. Average beers cost anywhere from $3 to $7 per pint; the average glass of house wine ranges from $6 to $12 (or $15 at posh restaurants).

You'll never have to pay to go on the beach and will rarely have to pay to access the islands' best hiking trails. Still, prices for most kinds of commercial activity – a snorkel- or whale-watching cruise, a bus tour, a submarine ride, a guided hike, or bike ride – also tend to be high.

C

Children

Unless otherwise specified (or unless you're heading to a bar), most places in the Hawaiian Islands are child-friendly and actually encourage families to visit together. Many restaurants have children's menus and offer young kids crayons when they sit down. Many attractions charge reduced-price admission fees for children. Also, most luxury hotels will recommend babysitting services for a (steep) fee.

Private and independent babysitting services exist on every island and many travelers use them without incident. If you opt to reserve a childminder through this type of service, be aware of minimum fees; most will not book unless you can guarantee at least four hours of work.

Climate and weather

There are seasons in sub-tropic Hawaii, it just takes time to recognize them. Rarely does the mercury drop below 60°F (15°C), nor go higher than about 90°F (32°C). The surrounding sea and northeasterly trade winds are a natural air-conditioning system. However, when the trade winds stop, and less frequent southerly winds take over, the result is often sticky and humid.

Certain areas on each island – usually on the windward side of mountains – receive more rainfall than others. One of the wettest spots on Earth is Mount Wai'ale'ale on Kauai, which has been drenched by as much as 486ins (12,340mm) of rain in a year.

Sometimes during volcanic eruptions on the Big Island, a smoky pall lingers over the islands for several days, especially in the Kona area. Islanders call this volcanic haze "vog," or volcanic smog. People suffering from asthma or other respiratory conditions may wish to take extra precautions during "voggy" weather.

Seasons

During the dry season (April to October) most of Hawaii experiences balmy 73–88°F (23–31°C) weather and only intermittent rain. In higher places such as Upcountry and Haleakala on Maui, and Koke'e on Kauai, temperatures range from 48°F to 72°F (9–22°C). In the wet season (November to March), temperatures are cooler, ranging from 65°F to 83°F (18–28°C.) It also rains more consistently during this time of year (though few rainstorms in the islands ever last for more than an hour or two). In wet season, it's a good idea to bring a jacket for cold and rainy nights. In mountainous parts of the Big Island the average temperature drops to 31°F–58°F (-1–14°C) during the winter and at night. Snow falls on Mauna Kea (and sometimes Haleakala on Maui) in the winter, so bring warm clothing if you intend to tour these areas.

While sunbathing is a common activity here, don't overdo it. Slowly create a tolerance for Hawaii's strong sunlight by taking no more than 30 minutes of direct sun exposure the first day, 40 minutes the second day, 50 minutes the third day and so on. To prevent sunburn, be sure to wear sunscreen and keep applying it – you will find instructions on use on the container.

Flash floods

In the mountain areas, intense rain can cause flash floods. If you are hiking, take care during heavy rains as flash floods can occur without warning. If a flash flood watch has been issued by the National Weather Service, be alert: flooding is possible. A warning means that flooding is imminent or already occurring. If you are in a flood-prone area, get to higher ground immediately.

Hurricanes

Hurricanes are infrequent in Hawaii, but when they do touch the islands, they generally hit hard. Take all warnings seriously. The hurricane season is from June through November. When the civil defense sirens sound, tune to local radio or television stations for emergency disaster instructions. Stay indoors during high winds, and evacuate areas that may flood. Evacuation orders by authorities must be followed at all times.

Tsunamis (tidal waves)

Earthquakes, particularly on Hawaii Island, sometimes forebode a *tsunami*, the correct term for a seismic or tidal wave. Earthquakes elsewhere, including Alaska, can send a *tsunami* to Hawaii. They can occur with little warning or time for preparation. When a *tsunami* warning is issued, leave coastal low-lying areas immediately.

Crime and safety

Hawaii has earned a reputation for hospitality and all the good cheer that the word *aloha* implies. However, travelers should be warned that all types of crime – including burglaries, robberies, assaults, and rapes – do occur on the islands. To avoid them, follow the usual precautions as when traveling anywhere else. Use common sense. Don't carry jewelry, large amounts of cash, or other valuables. In areas far from population centers, car break-ins and beach thefts of unattended personal property are becoming common, even at popular tourist sites.

If your hotel has a safe in the room, it is advisable to use it.

Customs regulations

Travelers from the mainland United States to Hawaii are not eligible for duty-free shopping, but travelers from other nations are. There is no limit to the amount of money travelers are allowed to bring into Hawaii – or any part of the United States, for that matter – but any amount exceeding $10,000 requires a formal report with US Customs.

In order to prevent the spread of fruit flies and other hazardous plant insects and disease, no fruit, plants, or live snails from the mainland are allowed to be brought into Hawaii, and no fruit, plants, or live snails from Hawaii are allowed to be brought back to the mainland. Airline passengers must pass through inspection stations to make sure they comply with these rules.

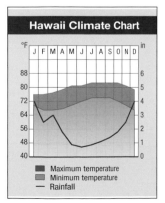

Hawaii Climate Chart

D

Disabled travelers

Hawaii is very well geared towards meeting the needs of disabled travelers. Download detailed reports on facilities from the website of the State of Hawaii Disability and Communication Access Board (tel: 586-8121; health.hawaii.gov/dcab). Specific information on Hawaiian hotels is also available from

Access–Able. Many vehicles on public transportation networks on Oahu and Maui are adapted for travelers with disabilities.

Eating out

It's easy to eat well on the Hawaiian Islands. With a multitude of good restaurants serving up a bevy of different cuisines, there are options at every price point. The chefs here enjoy experimenting, adding a little Asian to Continental, or Italian to Pacific. The results are excellent, including the popular "Pacific Rim" cuisine that has gained international respect. In addition, there are numerous ethnic cuisines to be enjoyed: Thai, Vietnamese, Korean, Chinese, and Japanese are only a few of the ones you see every day.

If you're eating breakfast or lunch, reservations aren't necessary. For dinner, however, especially in some of the busier tourist spots such as Honolulu on Oahu and Lahaina or Paia on Maui, it's always a good idea to book a table in advance by phone or on line.

Hawaii restaurants span the gamut from roadside shack to swanky and formal. In between is everything from casual beachfront tiki bars to family-friendly diners and bistros. Most of the time, the best restaurants are located in central commercial areas: on rare occasions, good restaurants will stand alone. It's common to find multiple cuisines clustered in one area. The exception is Honolulu's Chinatown, which boasts a preponderance of restaurants serving Asian food.

Etiquette in Hawaiian restaurants is the same as it is in restaurants on the US mainland. Beach attire is generally acceptable for breakfast and lunch, but for dinner guests should spruce up a bit (read: no ballcaps or tank tops). Tipping servers also is customary; 15 percent is standard for average service; good service deserves 20 percent.

Emergencies

Hawaii has its own response units, and outposts of major national responders as well. In the event of emergencies, there are a number of options to call for help:

American Red Cross, tel: 1-800-733-2767
Coast Guard Search and Rescue, tel: 800-552-6458
Dental emergency service, tel: 944-8863
Fire, Police, Ambulance, tel: 911
Lifeguard Service, tel: 723-7861
Poison Center, tel: 941-4411
Sex Abuse Treatment Center, tel: 524-7273
Suicide and Crisis Center, tel: 832-3100

Embassies and consulates

There aren't many embassies in Hawaii – most of the formal diplomatic outposts are on the mainland, in Los Angeles, or in San Francisco. Still, the islands are home to a number of consulates:
Australia, tel: 524-5050
Japan, tel: 543-3111
Korea, tel: 595-6109
Philippines, tel: 595-6316
Taiwan, tel: 595-6347

Electricity

Standard US 110-120 volts, 60 cycles AC. Large hotels usually are able to provide voltage and plug converters.

Festivals

For such a relatively small state, Hawaii has a host of festivals throughout the year. Some are more tourist-friendly than others; those are listed here. An up-to-date calendar of events can be accessed at www.gohawaii.com.

January
Hula Bowl
The Pacific Islands Arts Festival, Kapiolani Park, Waikiki, Oahu;
Second or third weekend.
An annual gathering of artists and artisans from the islands who create and display their own work for sale in the popular Kapiolani Park. There is jewelry, fabric art, woodwork, ceramics, photography and fine art to choose from.
Lunar New Year
Chinatown, Honolulu;
Mid- to late January.
A 15-day celebration starting on the day of the second new moon after

Etiquette

All etiquette rules for the mainland United States apply to the Hawaiian Islands as well. In addition, it is custom in Hawaii to remove shoes before entering someone's private home. Furthermore, when addressing elderly women, it is customary to say, "Mama." Finally, it's worth noting that islanders can be lax about time, especially when going on dates and to meetings outside of strictly commercial business circles. This habit of being "fashionably late" by around 10 minutes is generally known as being on "Hawaiian time."

the winter solstice. Drums, firecrackers, and traditional lion dances chase bad spirits out of homes and shops, clearing the way for a *kung hee fat choi* (Prosperous New Year).
Winter Footholds Dance Concert
Kennedy Theatre, Honolulu;
Second half of January .
Biannual dance concerts featuring undergraduates and graduates of the Department of Theatre + Dance held at the impressive Theatre Kennedy. http://manoa.hawaii.edu/liveonstage/kennedy-theatre.

February
Punahou Carnival
Manoa Valley, Honolulu;
Early February.
Largest and most popular school carnival in the state. Attractions include fruit jams, jellies, and other homemade local foods on sale; white elephant tent; art sale; games; rides; attractions.
Great Aloha Run
Honolulu area;
President's Day (3rd Monday in February).
Annual 8.2-mile (13.2km) fun run to benefit Oahu charities. Begins at Aloha Tower and finishes at Aloha Stadium. www.greataloharun.com

March
Honolulu Festival
Waikiki;
Mid-March.
A Waikiki parade is the highlight of this series of events that highlight links between Hawaii and Japan. www.honolulufestival.com

Prince Kuhio Festival
Kauai (various locations);
Late March.
The birthday of Prince Jonah Kuhio Kalaniana'ole is a state holiday. On Kauai, where he was born, the celebration spans two weeks with parties and events in multiple locations.

April
Celebration of the Arts
The Ritz-Carlton, Kapalua, Maui;
Early April.
Annual arts festival featuring hula and chant performances, art workshops, and creative demonstrations.
www.kapaluacelebrationofthearts.com
Merrie Monarch Festival
Hilo, Hawaii Island;
Mid-April.
A *ho'olaule'a*, arts and crafts fair, and a parade highlight the week-long hula festival, which honors King David Kalakaua. The Merrie Monarch hula competition is considered Hawaii's finest and most prestigious. www.merriemonarch.com

May
Lei Day
Statewide;
May 1.
Hawaiians celebrate May Day island-style – dressed in cheerful, printed *mu'umu'u* and *aloha* shirts, lots of *leis* (garlands) and smiles. Students throughout the islands – notably at elementary school level – perform multi-ethnic dances and songs in full costume.
Parade of Farms
Oahu;
Early May.
Local tours allowing to experience farm life and experience homegrown food. www.parade-of-farms.org
Maui Onion Festival
Ka'anapali, Maui;
Early May.
Food demonstrations (featuring the famous Maui onion), entertainment, and a Maui onion cook-off highlight this festival at Whaler's Village in Ka'anapali, Maui. www.paradise-found-in-maui.com/maui-onion-festival.html
World Fireknife Dancing Championships
La'ie, Oahu;
Mid-May.
Hosted by the Polynesian Cultural Center, this annual competition features top fireknife dancers from around the world performing amazing feats with the traditional Samoan fireknife.
Tel: 293-3333; www.worldfireknife.com

Molokai Ka Hula Piko
Papohaku Beach Park, Molokai;
3rd Saturday of May.
Annual festival celebrating the birth of the hula on Molokai; the event includes a sunrise ceremonial, hula and music performances, arts and crafts, and food booths.
www.kahulapiko.com
Honoka'a Western Weekend and Rodeo
Honoka'a, Hawaii Island;
Late May.
Annual Memorial Day festival with a rodeo, parade, ethnic foods, arts and crafts, entertainment, and country dance. www.honokaawesternweek.org

June
Aloha Freedom Festival (50th State Fair)
Aloha Stadium, Honolulu;
Early June.
The fair for the 50th state usually boasts Hawaiian quilt-making contests, local musicians and a rainbow of ethnic dances, produce and live-stock shows, food booths, carnival rides and commercial booth displays, and specially scheduled entertainment. www.ekfernandezshows.com
Pan-Pacific Festival
Honolulu;
Early June.
Also known as the "Matsuri in Hawaii Festival," this event celebrates the cultures of Hawaii, Japan, and the Pacific. Cultural demonstrations and entertainment take place at various sites. www.pan-pacific-festival.com
King Kamehameha Celebration
Statewide;
June 11.
King Kamehameha Day honors Hawaii's great king who united all the Hawaiian Islands under single rule. On Oahu events include a *lei*-draping ceremony at the King Kamehameha Statue in downtown Honolulu. A similar ceremony is held at the "other" Kamehameha statue in Kapa'au, on Hawaii Island.
www.kamehamehafestival.org
Kapalua Wine & Food Festival
Kapalua, Maui;
Mid-June.
This three-day affair gathers winemakers and chefs from around the globe and includes seminars, demonstrations, tastings, and spectacular evening galas.
www.kapaluawineandfoodfestival.com
Pu'uhonua 'O Honaunau Festival
Pu'uhonua 'O Honaunau,
Hawaii Island;

Late June.
This week-long celebration at one of Hawaii Island's most important monuments features traditional Hawaiian games, entertainment, food, and cultural demonstrations.
www.nps.gov/puho

July
Hawaii State Farm Fair
Kualoa Ranch, Oahu;
Mid-June.
Midway rides, carnival games, food booths, agricultural exhibits, and entertainment are featured at this annual fair.
http://hawaiistatefarmfair.org
Makawao Stampede
Makawao, Maui;
July 4.
For more than 50 years, this cowboy town in Upcountry Maui has celebrated America's Independence Day with an old-school rodeo. Traditional rodeo events are complemented by traditional Hawaiian dance.
Koloa Plantation Days
Koloa, Kauai;
Mid-July.
This week-long festival pays tribute to Hawaii's once-thriving sugar plantations. Entertainment includes sporting events, rodeo, cooking demonstrations, and a parade.
www.koloaplantationdays.com
Queen Lili'uokalani Keiki Hula Competition
Neal Blaisdell Center, Honolulu;
Mid-July.
This annual statewide hula competition features Hawaii's top young hula students and crowns a hula champion. www.keikihula.org
Hawaii All-Collectors Show
Honolulu;
Late July.
Collectors of things Hawaiian (and even non-Hawaiian) should not miss this annual end-of-July production at the Neal Blaisdell Exhibition Hall. Antique coins, postcards, dolls, toys, records, *aloha* shirts, and more are available for sale. www.ukulele.com
Bon Odori Dance Festival
Statewide;
Late July and early August.
Japanese Buddhists honor deceased ancestors during this festival of lively dance. Temples throughout the islands hold these dances (around 7.30pm to midnight), and visitors are invited to join. The season ends with the Floating Lanterns Festival at the Jodo Mission in Hale'iwa, on Oahu.

August

Hawaiian International Billfish Tournament
Kailua, Hawaii Island;
Early August.
Giant marlin are caught during this popular annual fishing tournament. www.hibtfishing.com

Pu'ukohola Heiau Cultural Festival
South Kohola, Hawaii Island;
Mid-August.
This annual cultural festival features demonstrations, food tastings, arts and crafts workshops, and hula performances. www.nps.gov/puhe

Duke's Oceanfest
Waikiki Beach, Oahu;
August.
Ocean sports festival held annually in honour of Native Hawaiian surf legend and Olympic champion swimmer Duke Kahanamoku.
www.dukesoceanfest.com

September

Aloha Festivals
Statewide;
Throughout September.
Hawaii's biggest festival, with statewide, month-long celebrations encompassing beautiful floral parades, street parties, special ceremonies, and community events to celebrate the spirit of *aloha*.
www.alohafestivals.com

Maui Marathon
Maui;
Mid-September.
Popular with runners from around the world, the 26-mile (42km) run starts at Kahului and ends at Ka'anapali. www.mauimarathon.com

A Day at Queen Emma's Summer Palace
Honolulu;
September 23.
Hawaiian arts and crafts, entertainment plus food highlight this annual tribute to Hawaii's Queen Emma, held at the home she once kept outside Honolulu. www.daughtersofhawaii.org

October

Ironman World Triathlon
Kailua-Kona, Hawaii Island;
Early October.
Hard-core athletes come from all over the world to compete in a 2.4-mile (4km) open-ocean swim, followed by a 112-mile (180km) bike ride, and a full 26-mile (42km) marathon. The event is held annually on Hawaii Island. www.ironman.com

Molokai Hoe
Molokai and Oahu;
Mid-October.
This open-ocean, outrigger canoe race starts at Hale o Lono Harbor on Molokai and ends at Fort DeRussy Beach in Waikiki. The first finishers are expected in Waikiki at around noon–12.30pm and it's great fun to watch and be a part of the crowd.
www.molokaihoe.com

Hawaii International Film Festival
Oahu;
Mid-November.
Acclaimed two-week festival features international films and celebrates an "East meets West" theme. Generally held on Oahu during the second week of November, followed by a week-long stint on the neighboring islands. www.hiff.org

Lahaina Halloween
Lahaina, Maui;
October 31.
Hawaii's biggest Halloween party takes place on Halloween night in Lahaina, Maui, with costumed parades and plenty of raucous entertainment. www.lahainahalloween.com

November

Kona Coffee Cultural Festival
Kailua, Hawaii Island;
Early November.
Week-long festivities include judging of coffee recipes, Kona coffee-farm tours, and local parade and pageantry. http://konacoffeefest.com

Hickam Fall Craft Fair
Honolulu;
Early November.
Annual handcrafters' fair features more than 130 booths offering handmade arts and crafts. There are also pony rides and make-n-takes for the keiki.

Made in Hawaii Festival
Honolulu;
Mid-November.
The state's largest crafts event showcasing Hawaiian artisan-made products. www.madeinhawaii festival.com

Surfing Contests
North Shore, Oahu;
November through February.
Winter means big waves on Oahu's North Shore, luring pro-surfers to its shores. World championship contests are scheduled each year, dates determined by the condition of the surf. Check local newspapers for day-by-day announcements.

December

Honolulu Marathon
Honolulu;
Early December.
Every year, thousands of dedicated runners set off from the Aloha Tower on a marathon course along Oahu's south shore. The Honolulu marathon ends at Kapi'olani Park Bandstand.
www.honolulumarathon.org

Pearl Harbor Day
Oahu;
December 7.
In memory of those who were killed during the Japanese bombing of Oahu on December 7, 1941, a memorial service is held every year at the USS *Arizona* Memorial.

H

Health and medical care

The Covid-19 virus rapidly spread across the world in 2020, causing the shuttering of tourist attractions, restaurants, and bars, and the cancellation of various festivals and events. At the time of writing in December 2021, all travelers to Hawaii are required to show evidence of a negative Covid-19 test result, taken no more than 24 hours before flying. In addition, all non-US citizens must be fully vaccinated and upload vaccination records to Hawaii's Safe Travels website (https://travel.hawaii.gov/#/). However, policies change frequently so be sure to check the most up-to-date state guidance prior to travel at www.hawaiicovid19.com/travel.

Most of the larger hotels have a physician on call. Other medical services can be obtained at hospitals and/or clinics, which are prevalent on every island except Lanai and Molokai. At bigger hospitals, the quality of care is superb. At some of the smaller clinics, care may be less so. It is always prudent to take out travel insurance that covers medical issues; there is no free health care in the United States.

For prescription medicine, there are pharmacies located in most towns around the islands. In larger towns, at least one pharmacy usually is open 24 hours. Pharmacies only are necessary to fill prescriptions; all supermarkets (and many corner markets) in the United States sell a sampling of over-the-counter medications for minor ailments.

I

Internet

Internet access is widely available throughout Hawaii. Upscale hotels invariably offer high-speed access from guest rooms, while most resorts offer free Wi-fi in their respective lobbies. Free Wi-fi also is available at most coffee shops. All state libraries and most university libraries provide free access and these days, a number of other types of commercial enterprises – from restaurants to boutiques – also offer free Wi-fi.

L

LGBTQ travelers

Hawaii always has been a popular spot among LGBTQ travelers, and the destination became even more gay-friendly when the state legislature legalized same-sex marriage in 2013. Since this historic change, many accommodations have added gay-friendly packages and special deals for same-sex couples seeking to plan destination weddings. Some of the properties that are gay friendly include Hotel Renew (www.hotelrenew.com) at Waikiki on Oahu and Sugar Beach Resort (www.sugarbeachresort.net) on Maui.

M

Maps

If you are doing any serious exploring or adventuring, don't rely on the free maps distributed by hotels or rental-car agencies. By far the best maps of the Hawaiian Islands are published by the University of Hawaii, and are available at most island bookstores. If you need detailed hiking maps, then make a visit to the state parks office in Honolulu, or inquire at ranger stations at Haleakala or Hawaii Volcanoes national parks.

Media

Newspapers

Hawaii has a handful of island daily and weekly newspapers. On Oahu, the main dailies are *Midweek Oahu*

(www.midweek.com) and the *Honolulu Star-Advertiser* (www.staradvertiser.com); this is the de facto daily for other islands as well. Neighbor islands also have their own daily newspapers, with circulation restricted to that specific island. These papers publish wire copy about state and national stories, but have the feeling of community newspapers (because their respective readerships are so small). A variety of other newspapers are published by ethnic groups, the military, religious organizations, and by the tourism and business industries. On Maui, *The Maui News* (www.mauinews.com) is the main source of information on the island. The Associated Press maintains a bureau in Honolulu to cover both Hawaii and the areas around the Pacific.

Radio

Honolulu's listeners have some 30 radio stations to listen to; there are fewer stations elsewhere on Oahu and on other islands. Hawaii Public Radio news and fine arts can be found on KHPR 88.1 in Honolulu; KKUA 90.7 on Maui, Molokai, and Lanai; and KANO 89.1 in Hilo. Hawaii Public Radio talk and music can be found on KIPO 89.3 in Honolulu; KIPM 89.7 on Maui, Molokai and Lanai; and KIPL 89.9 on Kauai. ESPN sports radio is KKEA 1420 AM. KHUI (99.5 FM) and KINE (105.1 FM), both in Honolulu, broadcast both contemporary and traditional Hawaiian music. Listings in the local newspapers give relevant frequencies.

Television

There are more than 10 broadcast television channels that originate in the state of Hawaii. These include channels 2 (KHON-FOX); 4 (KITV-ABC); 5 (KFVE); 9 (KGMB-CBS); 11

(KHET-PBS); and 13 (KHVO-ABC). For broadcasts originating on Oahu (in Honolulu), relay transmitters serve the neighbor islands, while private companies provide cable TV programming by subscription only. Most of the other islands have their own local access channels. The majority of moderate-to-good hotels offer cable viewing to guests, showing a vast array of channels and, in a separate facility, first-run movies.

Money

Hawaii uses standard US currency and coins in all denominations. $1 = 100 cents. All major credit cards are accepted, including American Express, Visa, MasterCard, and Discover. Most car rental companies require a credit card. Cash machines (ATMs) are everywhere, especially at banks and shopping centers; ATMs accept bank cards from the mainland (and abroad) and are accessible 24 hours a day.

Currency exchange

Currency conversion is readily available at all of the state's international airports, and at most major banks. Currency exchange is also available at most hotels, although the rate tends to be a little less favorable than at a bank. There are no street money changers in Hawaii.

O

Opening hours

Normal banking hours are Monday to Friday 8am–4pm. Some banks are open on Saturday until noon. Typical opening hours for offices and small businesses in Hawaii are 9am or 10am until 5pm or 6pm.

General store on Maui.

The majority of shops, especially in larger malls and popular tourist areas, usually stay open later, until 10pm. One word of warning: most Hawaiians take "lunch" break around noon or 1pm. Often, instead of actually eating lunch, they are swimming or surfing at the nearest beach. Some shops and businesses are also open on Sundays.

P

Postal services

Believe it or not, normal American postal rates apply across Hawaii. From Honolulu, it costs the same price to mail a letter to New York City as it does to Maui. Stamps are sold at all post offices; most supermarkets, corner stores, and some ATMs sell them. Post boxes in Hawaii look the same as they do across the mainland US – blue boxes with an arched top.

Many resort hotels will mail postcards free of charge.

Public holidays

Hawaii observes all the US national holidays, plus three state holidays – Prince Kuhio Day, Kamehameha Day, and Admission Day. On national holidays, all government offices, banks, post offices, and most businesses – except shops – close. On state holidays, local government offices and banks close, but federal offices and post offices remain open. Here are the important holidays to note:
New Year's Day: January 1
Martin Luther King Day: third Monday in January
Presidents' Day: third Monday in February
Prince Kuhio Day: March 26
Good Friday: Friday preceding Easter Sunday
Memorial Day: last Monday in May
Kamehameha Day: June 11
Independence Day: July 4
Admission Day: third Friday in August
Labor Day: first Monday in September
Columbus Day: October 12
Veterans Day: November 11
Thanksgiving Day: fourth Thursday in November
Christmas Day: December 25

R

Religion

Hawaii's most common religion is Christianity, however, there are a great deal of other religions alive and actively practiced in Hawaii. Tolerance is very high for all religions – Hawaii is a melting pot, after all. Religion is rarely talked about and is considered very personal, so if speaking to the locals, wait for them to bring it up, if at all.

Traditional Hawaiian cultural practices are on the rise with the rebirth of the culture, although there are not many who identify solely with this as their religion.

S

Shopping

Shopping in the Hawaiian Islands can be an all-consuming experience; with so many malls and so many boutiques, it will be hard to see everything that is on offer. Here's an inside look at what to buy, what *not* to buy and where to shop when you're out and about on the various islands.

What not to buy

As with any major tourist destination, Hawaii has shops and vendors that sell items they should not be selling. One of the offending items: black coral, which is harvested from the waters between Maui and Lanai and is believed to be rare. It also pays to inquire about the origin of many items advertised as "authentic" Hawaiian; upon investigation many of these items turn out to be manufactured in China or Indonesia.

What to buy

Typically Hawaiian goods range from Polynesian kitsch *tiki* gods with olivine stone eyes to fine Ni'ihau shell *leis* that may cost as much as $2,500 for four strands.

Aloha wear

Hawaii has its own fashions, the *mu'umu'u* and *aloha* shirt. The first *mu'umu'u*, designed and introduced by the early missionaries, was a loose, lengthy, high-necked, long-sleeved shroud. Because of variations in its style, *mu'umu'u* has come to refer to

just about any casual smock, long or short, made of Hawaiian print fabric. The *aloha* shirt was first marketed in the 1930s by a Chinese tailor in Honolulu. *Mu'umu'u* and *aloha* shirts are sold and worn everywhere. Some island occasions, such as wedding receptions and dinner parties, specify "*aloha* attire" as the preferred mode of dress.

Antiques

The notion of "antiques" means something different in Hawaii, which has only been a state for the better part of 60 years. Most "period" pieces date back to the time of monarchy, which lasted until 1893; these pieces include jewelry, furniture, and clothes. More modern "antiques" include Hawaiiana such as Pan-Am posters, 1950s-era suitcases, and hula girl paraphernalia.

Arts and crafts

Perhaps the most famous byproduct of Hawaii's burgeoning artisan scene is the appliqué quilt. This handiwork is available in countless artisan shops across the islands. Other arts and crafts products span the gamut from hand-woven baskets to hand-sewn garments, hand-carved bowls to hand-hewn fish spears.

Books

Every island has great bookstores, though independent stores are not too many. On Oahu, check out **BookEnds** (600 Kailua Road, Kailua; tel: 261-1996), an independent shop that specializes in children's books. On Maui, visit the **Maui Friends of the Library Used Book Store** (658 Front Street, Lahaina; tel: 667-2696; www.mfol.org), with a huge section reserved for new Hawaiiana books. On Hawaii Island, check out **Kona Bay Books** (74-5487 Kaiwi Street, Kona; tel: 326-7790; www.konabaybooks.com). Finally, on Kauai, try **Talk Story Bookstore** (3785 Hanapepe Road, Hanapepe; tel: 335-6469; www.talkstorybookstore.com).

Hawaiian instruments

Popular Hawaiian hula instruments include the *ipu*, *pu'ili* (slashed percussive bamboo sticks), *'uli'uli* (a feather-topped gourd rattle filled with seeds) and *'ili'ili* (small smooth stones used like castanets in a set of four). There are also the *hano* (nose flute) and *'ukulele*. All are available at island hula supply shops and some music stores. *Ipu* are tan-colored bottle gourds that are hollowed-out and dried and used as a drum, a hula instrument, or a food and water receptacle.

Leis

There are many variations on the traditional Hawaiian *lei* (garland). The tradition of stringing and wearing the brown and black-and-white *kukui* nuts, commonly called candlenuts, is still very popular. *Koa*-seed *leis* are also appealing, but most of these are strung in the Philippines.

Small, rare shells are washed up onto the beaches of the privately owned island of Ni'ihau, where some of the 200-plus residents will gather and string them into *leis* or necklaces. There is a beautiful range of delicate, subtle colors. The *leis* are very expensive, and found only in upscale shops, especially on Kauai.

Feathers of birds such as the pheasant and peacock are made into attractive *leis* and hat bands. In ancient Hawaii, items made of feathers were reserved for royalty and high-ranking *ali'i*.

Local produce

Plums, cherries, mangos, guavas, apricots, lemons, and limes are salted and preserved in the form of sweet-sour pickles known as "crack seed." Introduced by the Chinese, these preserves have become a favorite snack treat in Hawaii. Shops specializing in these pickled seeds can be found downtown and in major suburban shopping areas.

For a sweeter tooth, tropical fruits such as guava, *poha*, mango, passion fruit, papaya, and coconut are made into unique, luscious spreads. Macadamia nuts are delicious roasted and eaten plain or chocolate-covered, this rich nut, grown and packaged in Hawaii, is true gourmet fare.

Photographs of old Hawaii

Peer into Hawaii's past. Leaf through the photo albums at the Hawaii State Archives (364 S. King Street, Honolulu. tel: 586-0329; www.ags. hawaii.gov/archives), in the 'Iolani Palace grounds. The archives are open Mon–Fri 9am–4pm. Copies are available but generally take up to two weeks for delivery (by mail). Or visit the archives at the Bishop Museum (tel: 847-3511; www.bishopmuseum.org), by far the largest in the state with more than 500,000 images. Here, copies are more expensive, but the choice is greater.

Plant-based products, wood, and textiles

Tapa (bark cloth), properly called *kapa*, is made into popular items – place mats, wall-hangings, bags, and hats. However, the *tapa* for sale may not be Hawaiian *kapa*, but a related fabric made in Samoa and Tonga. The art of making real Hawaiian *kapa* was lost during the 19th century, but is now enjoying a revival with a new generation of artisans. *Lauhala* (pandanus), coconut fronds, makaloa sedge, and the rootlets of the *ieie* forest vine are used to weave mats, baskets, bowls, hats, and more.

Monkeypod, *koa*, and *milo* are three popular island woods used in the making of furniture, *calabashes* (large ceremonial bowls), and other fine wood creations. *Koa* and rosewood are also used to make quality guitars and *'ukuleles*.

Scrimshaw

This Pacific art came into its own in the 1800s when bored sailors on whaling vessels scratched pictures on whale teeth. Nowadays, a number of non-endangered materials are used, such as fossilized walrus tusk. Maui is a good place to look at and purchase scrimshaw; it also has the richest whaling history anywhere in Hawaii.

Sea shells

Arguably one of the best souvenirs from a beach-oriented place like Hawaii, these are free and come in a seemingly infinite number of shapes and sizes. Just don't take home too many; sea life need them too.

Surfboards

Custom-made fiberglass surfboards can be adapted to your height, weight, and personal taste in design by some of the finest board shapers in the world.

Where to shop

All the Hawaiian Islands, with the exception of less-developed Molokai and Lanai, offer endless retail possibilities, from shopping centers to surf shops to small-town treasures or chic resort boutiques. Here's a look at some of the larger shopping destinations on each of the major islands. Check out local markets too.

Oahu

Ala Moana Center, one of the largest open-air malls in the world, housing about 200 stores (including more than two dozen eateries) and covering 50 acres (20 hectares) across from Ala Moana Park in Honolulu. Free island entertainment regularly takes place on the mall's centerstage (tel: 955-9517; www.alamoanacenter. com; Mon–Thu 11am–7pm, Fri–Sat 10am–8pm, Sun 11am–6pm).

Aloha Tower Marketplace, located at Pier 9 near the downtown Honolulu business district. This harborside complex features an interesting array of shops and restaurants (tel: 544-1432; www.alohatower.com; daily 8am–10pm, restaurants and bars close later).

Chinatown, an integral part of downtown Honolulu and by far the most interesting shopping area in the islands. Watch noodles being made, take your ailments to an acupuncturist's or herbal medicine shop, choose from more than 30 restaurants, or visit the shops and galleries on side streets from Hotel Street. At night, a section of Hotel Street retains its sailors-on-liberty flavor, with strip joints and bars that should not be entered alone.

Downtown Honolulu, on Bishop Street, which was named after the islands' first banker and is today the financial center of Hawaii. All the major banks are here, along with airlines, restaurants, and shops. Every Friday there are entertaining free concerts at Tamarind Park, which spotlight the best Hawaiian, contemporary and jazz musicians. Business hours are 8am–5pm.

Kahala Mall, in the Kahala residential district just east of Diamond Head and Waikiki, home of the designer pizza and a movie complex (tel: 732-7736; www.kahalamall-center.com; Mon–Sat 10am–9pm, Sun 10am–6pm, although the supermarkets are open 24 hours).

Kapahulu Avenue, which ends in Waikiki, offers an interesting selection of shops that feature collectible Hawaiiana approximately 1 mile (1.5km) from the beach.

Pearlridge Center, 1005 Moanalua Road, in 'Aiea. The largest enclosed shopping space in the state (tel: 488-0981; www.pearlridgeonline.com; Mon–Sat 10am–8pm, Sun 10am–6pm).

Royal Hawaiian Shopping Center, along Kalakaua Avenue in Waikiki, offering a wide variety of shops and cafés on three levels and daily entertainment at its central courtyard (tel: 922-2299; www.royalhawaiicenter. com; daily 11am–8pm).

T Galleria by DFS, 330 Royal Hawaiian Avenue, in Waikiki. A nautically themed complex, complete with multi-level aquarium, packed with designer stores including Hermès, Cartier, Michael Kors, and Marc Jacobs. Best of all: it's duty-free. (tel 931-2700; www.dfs.com).

Waikele Center, 94–790 Lumiaina Street, Exit 7 off H-1, about 15 minutes west of Honolulu. Home to 50 outlets including Calvin Klein, Ralph Lauren, and the like – discounts abound at the factory outlet shops (tel: 671-6977; www.waikelecenter.com; Mon–Fri 10am–9pm, Sat 10am–7pm, Sun 11am–7pm).

Waikiki Shopping Plaza, on 2250 Kalakaua Avenue in Waikiki, offering popular international brands, exclusive boutiques, and plenty of dining opportunities (tel: 923-1191; www.waikikishoppingplaza.com; hours vary, check online).

Ward Village, on Auahi Street in Kakaako, near Waikiki. With Hawaii's largest multiplex (16 screens) and trendy shops and restaurants like Dave & Buster's (games and dining), the complex is a popular destination in and of itself. 135 stores, 40 restaurants (tel: 591-8411; www.wardvillage.com; Sun–Thu 11am–6pm, Fri–Sat 11am–7pm).

Maui

Kahului is the focus of Maui's urban commerce, but don't overlook the street shopping of historic Wailuku, just above Kahului, and of Makawao and Pa'ia, toward Upcountry. As nearly everybody visiting Maui stays in either the Wailea or Ka'anapali resorts, those are rich with shopping opportunities, mostly within the resorts. Lahaina lives off both shopping and eating; wander its streets to find an abundance of temptations.

Lahaina Cannery Mall, 1221 Honoapiilani Highway. West Maui's most comprehensive indoor shopping mall, north end of Lahaina (tel: 661-5304; www.lahainacannerymall.com; daily 11am–6pm).

Queen Ka'ahumanu Center, 275 Ka'ahumanu Avenue, Kahului. Maui's largest mall with over 75 shops and eateries (tel: 877-4325; www.queenkaahumanucenter.com; Mon–Thu 10am–8pm, Fri–Sat 10am–9pm, Sun 10am–5pm).

The Shops at Wailea, 3750 Wailea Alanui. An elegant upgrade of the old shopping village, with dozens of shops and restaurants in a multi-level mall (tel: 891-6770;

⊙ Kona Coffee

Hawaii's own homegrown and roasted coffee beans are produced in the Kona region of Hawaii Island, on the only commercial coffee plantations in the United States. The resulting product has been accorded a gourmet status in international coffee-drinking circles. If you're a purist, stay away from the blends, which require only 10 percent Kona beans.

www.theshopsatwailea.com; daily 10am–8pm).

Whaler's Village, Ka'anapali Resort, West Maui. This outdoor venue includes more than 50 shops, several popular restaurants on the beach, and a 40ft (12-meter) sperm whale skeleton (tel: 661-4567; daily 9am–9pm; www.whalersvillage.com).

Hawaii Island

The commercial centers of Hilo and Kailua are the obvious choices here. Historic downtown Hilo is small, compact and undergoing a revival, and is good for quiet walking and browsing. Kona's waterfront thrives on tourism, and the offerings range – with the emphasis on low-end souvenirs – from T-shirts and postcards to at times dubious art. The resort hotels of Kohala – Mauna Lani, Waikoloa, Mauna Kea – have what those with gold cards are looking for. Smaller towns such as Holualoa, Honoka'a, Volcano, and Waimea are great places to find artisans who exhibit work in shops and galleries. Hanapepe is the island's best destination for art.

Kings' Shops, Waikoloa Beach Resort, South Kohala. Hawaiiana exhibits throughout this shopping complex complement the nearly 40 shops and restaurants (tel: 885-8811; www.kingsshops.com; daily 10am–8pm).

Prince Kuhio Plaza, 111 East Puainako Street, Hilo. Largest enclosed mall on the Big Island (tel: 959-3555; www.princekuhioplaza.com; Mon–Sat 11am–7pm, Sun until 6pm).

Kauai

In keeping with its personality, Kauai's shopping is lower-key than other islands', but pleasurable and often unique. Shopping centers are found in Lihu'e, Po'ipu, Koloa, Kapa'a, Princeville, and Hanalei on the North Shore. Shopping tends to

be decentralized, with small, quality pockets of stores.

Coconut Marketplace, on the main highway, near Kapa'a. Open-air shopping mall with 70 assorted shops, a good selection of casual restaurants and a movie theater (tel: 822-3641; www.coconutmarketplace.com; Mon–Sat 9am–8pm, Sun 10am–6pm). There's also a farmers' market on Tuesday mornings.

Kilohana, Route 50, 1.5 mile (2km) north of Lihu'e. Plantation estate with high-quality retail shops, galleries, and an old sugar cane train (tel: 245-5608; www.kilohanakauai.com; daily 9.30am–9.30pm).

Kukui Grove, Highway 50, near Lihu'e. Kauai's largest mall (tel: 245-7784; www.kukuigrovecenter.com; Mon–Fri 9.30am–7pm, Sat 9.30am–6pm, Sun 10am–6pm).

Po'ipu Shopping Village, 2360 Kiahuna Plantation Drive. Pleasant outdoor mall with shops and restaurants. On weekends the mall also brings in live entertainment (tel: 742-2831; www.poipushoppingvillage.com; Mon–Sat 9.30am–9pm, Sun 10am–7pm).

T

Tax

Hawaii does not have a state sales tax, but instead has something called a General Excise Tax, which means that just about every kind of transaction is assessed with an average 4 percent surcharge statewide.

Telephones

From the middle of the Pacific, you can dial directly to almost anywhere in the world. Because of underwater fiber-optic cables, the quality of phone calls to both Asia and North America is excellent. Cellular service is reliable as well; major carriers servicing the Hawaiian Islands include AT&T, Verizon, Sprint, and T-Mobile, and all of them sell pay-as-you-go plans for international travelers. If you prefer dialing out from a hotel, note that most hotels charge $0.75–$1 for local calls, and up to $1 per minute for long distance. If you can find public telephones (most of them have been phased out), they cost $0.35 per minute for local calls.

Area and dialing codes

The telephone area code for all the Hawaiian Islands is **808**.

Same-island calls:

dial number.

NB 800 numbers need to be preceded by a 1 ie 1 + 800 + number.

Inter-island (direct):

1 + 808 + number.

Mainland (direct dial):

1 + area code + number.

International (direct dial):

011 + country + city + number.

Home-country direct:

Operators in some countries can be called directly from Hawaii by special toll-free 800 numbers. Call 643-1000 for a list of numbers and foreign countries where this particular service is available.

Directory assistance

Operator assistance: dial 0.

Same-island: 1 + 411.

Inter-island: 1 + 808 + 555-1212.

Mainland: 1 + area code + 555-1212.

Time zone

Hawaii is GMT-**10 hours**, which means it is 10 hours behind Greenwich Mean Time, two hours behind Pacific Standard Time, three hours behind Mountain Standard Time, four hours behind Central Standard Time and five hours behind Eastern Standard Time. As Hawaii does not adjust to Daylight Saving Time, these time differences grow by one hour between April and October (or, some years, November).

Tipping

Tipping for service is expected in Hawaii, as tips are considered part of a service worker's overall salary. In general, airport porters' baggage-handling fees run at roughly $1 per bag, and taxi drivers are usually tipped 15 percent in addition to about 25¢ per bag. A 15–20 percent tip at a fine restaurant is the norm, and at other eating establishments you should tip whatever you feel is fair, typically 15 percent.

Tourist information

The Hawaii Visitors and Conventions Bureau is in charge of promoting Hawaii to the general public. While the majority of the organization's efforts focus on media and corporate tourism, the outfit does have a public-facing arm and provides visitor guides upon request (tel: 800-4-2924). It also maintains an informative website, gohawaii.com. Under the auspices of this office, each of the four largest islands has its own visitors' bureau:

Kauai, tel: 800-262-1400

Oahu, tel: 877-525-6248

Maui, tel: 800-525-6284

Hawaii Island, tel: 800-648-2441

Tour operators

Many US-based tour operators offer tours in Hawaii that are available to customers from anywhere in the world; the most useful include **Backroads** (tel: 800-462-2848; www.backroads.com), **Roberts Hawaii** (tel: 808-539-9400; www.robertshawaii.com), **Pleasant Holidays** (tel: 800-742-9244; www.pleasantholidays.com), the **Sierra Club** (tel: 415-977-5500; www.sierraclub.org), and **Tauck** (tel: 800-810-8020; www.tauck.co.uk).

V

Visas and passports

For the latest travel restrictions related to the Covid-19 pandemic, please check online at https://travel.state.gov. Details of the visa waiver scheme, under which travelers carrying passports issued by Britain, Ireland, and most European countries, as well as Australia and New Zealand, do not need visas for trips to the United States lasting less than 90 days, can be obtained from your travel agent or via www.travel.state.gov.

W

Weights and measures

Hawaii uses the imperial system of weights and measures. Metric weights and measures are rarely used.

What to bring

Hawaii is very much part of the modern US, so if you forget to bring something, you'll most likely be able to buy it there. Camera equipment and accessories are widely available in tourist areas, but there are surprisingly few bookstores or map outlets in the resorts. If you take prescription drugs, make sure you bring sufficient for your visit and if travelling with infants, it is safest to bring the formula or baby food they arc familiar with as you might not be able to find it in Hawaii.

What to wear

Although Hawaii is a sub-tropical destination, characterized at sea level by consistently comfortable temperatures, you're likely to encounter rain at some point during your stay, so you'll be glad of light, waterproof clothing or perhaps an umbrella. If you plan to venture at all higher, to areas like Maui's Upcountry, Waimea on the Big Island, or Koke'e on Kauai, you'll need something warmer too. And if you head towards the summits of the volcanoes, most notably for the dawn at Haleakala on Maui, you should be prepared for literally freezing temperatures.

All the islands hold rough volcanic terrain, so good walking shoes or hiking boots are very useful, and in many places the ocean floor can be rocky and abrasive, so reef shoes are a good idea too.

Dress is cool and casual in Honolulu. Light, loose garments are suitable for the summer months. Hawaiian-print *mu'umu'u* and *aloha* shirts are practical all-round garments. Thongs, flip-flops, slippers, *zoris* – all different names for the same thing – are ideal for the beach.

A few exclusive restaurants and nightclubs require a coat, maybe a tie, and definitely shoes, but they are the exceptions. Leather sandals and shoes are appropriate for nightlife. In most island homes, shoes are removed at the entrance.

Aloha Friday

Friday is usually greeted in the islands with *aloha* wear, where even businessmen don *aloha* shirts of bright and cheerful Hawaiian prints instead of formal suits and ties. Ladies often tuck a plumeria behind their ear, or drape a *kukui* nut or flower *lei* on their shoulders for their *mu'umu'u*. This is a Friday custom that has become *de rigueur* here, even in state, federal and business offices, and at public schools. And in most businesses, it is no longer limited to Friday only.

LANGUAGE

BACKGROUND

Until the 1970s, most linguists agreed that the Hawaiian language stood little chance of survival. In the background, however, local people of all persuasions could be heard chattering in pidgin English, a hybrid island language that flits in and out of conversations like a sassy mynah bird. A typical after-work conversation between people of Hawaiian, Chinese, Japanese, Korean, Filipino, or Samoan backgrounds might include an invitation like this: "Hey, pau hana like go my hale for grind? Get plenty 'ono pupu – even pipikaula and poke in da fridge." Translation: "Hey, after work would you like to go to my house to eat? We've got plenty of tasty appetizers, even some beef jerky and raw fish marinated with seaweed in the refrigerator."

Today, pidgin continues to predominate among locals, but increasingly, true, grammatically correct Hawaiian is heard among part-Hawaiian members of many families and other individuals at social get-togethers. The startling change can be credited to a renaissance of pride in being Hawaiian and the establishment of language immersion schools (funded by the Hawaii Department of Education with assistance from the Office of Hawaiian Affairs), where all classes are taught in the native language. Today, not only children take classes to 'olelo (speak) Hawaiian, their parents do so too, in order to keep up with their multilingual kids.

Even a straightforward conversation in English will be peppered with Hawaiian words that are known to all residents of the islands, and that sometimes better describe something than an equivalent word in English. Pau hana, used in the example above, could superficially be translated as "after work." Yet, in Hawaiian it has a richer meaning and texture that,

nonetheless, defies description. You have to be in the islands for a while for the subtleties to take effect.

To describe the Hawaiian language in English is problematical because it is a language of emotion, poetry, and nature-related sound and nuance. It is an ancient language that was not transliterated until after 1820, when American missionaries arbitrarily chose 12 English letters to represent the Hawaiian sounds they thought they heard. While any transliteration of one language into the letters and sounds of another isn't perfect, the Romanization of Hawaiian works well, mostly.

A language of the Pacific

For hundreds of years, the language had thrived expressively and melodically as the exclusively spoken tongue of a Polynesian people who were rich in an unwritten literature; this included complicated poetic chants detailing history, genealogies, and mythologies set to memory and passed orally from generation to generation.

Historians have not determined all of the intricacies of the development of the Hawaiian language, but a fairly clear picture has emerged regarding its relationship to other languages. Hawaiian belongs to the Austronesian (formerly called Malayo-Polynesian) language family. These were the languages spoken by seafaring peoples who settled over a broader area of the globe than was covered by any other group until the 18th and 19th centuries, when Europeans began extensively exploring beyond their known world.

Hawaii is the furthest point of Austronesian expansion to the north, with Easter Island the eastern extent and New Zealand the most southern. From these points westward, Austronesian tongues are spoken through the Pacific to Indonesia,

Malaysia, the Philippines, and parts of Taiwan. The furthest western point is the island of Madagascar off the coast of Africa.

More specifically, Hawaiian is classified as a Polynesian language closely related to the language spoken in Tahiti, the Marquesas, and the surrounding island groups of the South Pacific. Early ancestors of the Hawaiian race originated from these groups, sailing their outrigger canoes from Southeast or Indo-Malay Asia around the north coast of New Guinea, through the islands of Melanesia and into Polynesia.

Variations in the core language evolved along the way, but certain words and verbal inflections continue to reveal the ancient ties between them. Instead of the Hawaiian term i'a for fish, people of Southeast Asia say ika or ikan. Instead of hale for house, they say fare, 'are, or vale. Instead of maka for eye, they say mata. Na Pali, the name for the towering cliffs in Kauai's North Shore, comes from the same root as the name of the Himalayan kingdom of Nepal.

By 1819, Calvinist Christian missionaries had succeeded in converting several adventurous Hawaiian seamen who had sailed on various trading ships to America's east coast.

The first missionaries to Hawaii knew that the Hawaiian language was a spoken language only, but they were eager to set it to writing to facilitate the translation of the Bible.

By 1823, three years after their arrival, the various missionaries established the Hawaiian alphabet, although not without disputes. Some argued that the k sound was closer to t, or that the flapped r sound was more of an l sound. When the final vote was taken, k was adopted over the t, and l was chosen over the flapped r. The consonants were established as h, k, l, m, n, p, and w, while the vowel sounds were recorded as the five distinctive *a, e, i, o*, and *u* sounds of Western romance languages. These 12 letters remain the official Hawaiian alphabet today.

For some time after Westerners began settling in the islands, Hawaiian continued to be spoken and written in government, business, and social circles of the Hawaiian kingdom. For years, it was used almost exclusively in newspapers. Then, as the outside culture came to predominate, with missionary schooling widespread and Hawaii emerging as the Pacific's key port, the use of Hawaiian fell into disfavor. It was forbidden in public schools by 1896, and by the start of the 20th century, it had been replaced by English in the territorial legislature.

Many Hawaiian households suppressed the use of the language in an attempt to conform to the standards of the day, and the art of chanting, which is the oral preservation of history and genealogy, diminished. The last Hawaiian language newspaper, *Ka Hoku O Hawaii (The Star of Hawaii)*, printed in Hilo on Hawaii Island, stopped its presses in 1948. In 1992, a monthly paper called *Na Maka O Kana*, aimed at Hawaiian-language students and published by the University of Hawaii, Hilo, began to offer news about sports, movies, and other activities in the Hawaiian language.

In the 1980s, it was estimated that only 2,000 native speakers of Hawaiian – about 300 of them residents of the privately owned island of Ni'ihau – remained in Hawaii. Today, the picture has brightened considerably. In 1979, the state legislature approved funding for the Office of Hawaiian Affairs (OHA), run for and by Hawaiians for the betterment of Hawaiians. The OHA assists the Department of Education in running language-immersion schools for children from kindergarten through 12th grade. Slowly, besides a few remaining *kupuna*, or elders, who are fluent enough to teach their native tongue, a younger generation of teachers is emerging.

Pronunciation guidelines

Every letter in Hawaiian is pronounced distinctly. Vowels have just one sound: *a* sounds like *ah*, *e* like *ay* (as in hay), *i* like *ee*, *o* like *oh*, and *u* like *oo*. Likelike Highway, for example, is correctly pronounced *lee-kay lee-kay*, not *like-like*. Keep these simple rules in mind when you see signs such as Kalaniana'ole Highway or Kapi'olani. And remember, glottal stops, called '*okina*, indicate that each vowel should be pronounced distinctly.

Words and phrases

In its development, the Hawaiian language has acquired several interesting grammatical complications, as well as a pronunciation system known for its complex vowel combinations and small number of consonants. The Hawaiian alphabet has eight consonants including the '*okina*. Each of the letters in this bunch is roughly similar in pronunciation to their equivalent letter symbols in English, with the exception of *w*.

h *hula* (Hawaiian dance)
k *kai* (sea)
l *lani* (heaven)
m *manu* (bird)
n *niho* (tooth)
p *pua* (flower)
w *wa'a* (canoe)

In Hawaiian, the letter *w* varies in pronunciation between a *w* and *v* sound. To English speakers, *w* often sounds like a *v* after a stressed vowel, as in the place name Hale'iwa. At the beginning of a word or after an unstressed vowel, *w* sounds like an English *w* as in the place names Waikiki and Wahiawa.

The five Hawaiian vowels come in both short and long duration forms. Pronunciation of vowels is similar to Spanish or Japanese: no sloppy or lazy sounds as found in English.

a as in father *nana* (look)
e as in hay *nene* (goose)
i as in beet *wiwi* (skinny)
o as in boat *lolo* (feeble mind)
u as in boot *pupu* (snack)

If you would like more *kokua* (help) with Hawaiian language, refer to three excellent books on the subject: *Spoken Hawaiian*, by Samuel Elbert; *Let's Speak Hawaiian*, by Dorothy Kahananui and A. Anthony; and *The Hawaiian Dictionary*, by Samuel Elbert and Mary Kawena Pukui.

Word list

ali'i **ancient Hawaiian royalty, nobility**
aloha **love, greeting, farewell**
'Ewa **toward 'Ewa**
hana hou **one more time, encore**
haole **technically all foreigners, now refers mainly to people of Caucasian ancestry**
hapa **half, part**
hapa-haole **part-Caucasian**
heiau **traditional Hawaiian place of worship, a temple**
ho'olaule'a **celebration, party**
imu **underground cooking oven**
kama'aina **island-born or longtime resident of Hawaii**
kanaka **man, person, especially a native Hawaiian**
kane **man**
keiki **child, children**
kokua **help, assistance**
lanai **porch, balcony, veranda**
lauhala **pandanus leaf, for weaving**
lu'au **traditional feast**
mahalo **thank you**
makai **toward the ocean**
malihini **newcomer or visitor to the islands**
mana **spiritual power**
mauka **toward the mountains**
mauna **mountain**
Mele Kalikimaka **Merry Christmas**
'ohana **family**
okole **rear end, buttocks**
'ono **delicious, tasty**
pakalolo **marijuana**
pali **cliff, precipice**
paniolo **cowboy**
pau **finished, completed**
pau hana **end of work**
poi **food paste made from taro roots**
puka **hole, opening**
pupu **hors d'oeuvre**
shaka **slang for an island hand greeting**
wahine **woman**

☉ The 'okina

Two symbols can be added to Hawaiian words to assist pronunciation: a glottal stop ('), called an '*okina*, and a macron, which is a horizontal line over a vowel, in which case it is drawn out. *Insight Guide: Hawaii* uses the '*okina*, but not the macron. The '*okina*, which gives a "hard edge" to a vowel or separates two adjoining vowels with distinct sounds, is necessary for basic pronunciation in normal conversation; the macron offers a more subtle pronunciation.

All place names in this guide that need them use a glottal stop, with three exceptions: Hawaii, Oahu and Kauai, also written as Hawai'i, O'ahu, Kaua'i. But the non-glottal spellings are so common and ubiquitous that most cartographers delete the glottal stop for these islands. Two islands requiring glottal stops for pronunciation are Ni'ihau *(nee ee how)* and Kaho'olawe *(kah ho o lah vay)*. We use these forms.

FURTHER READING

NON-FICTION

The Art of the Hula by Allan Seiden. Richly illustrated history of Hawaii's nature dance.

The Betrayal of Lili'uokalani by Helena G. Allen. All-important biography of Hawaii's last queen.

The Death of William Gooch by Greg Dening. Focusing on the murder of three British seamen on Oahu in 1792.

Diamond Head, Hawaii's Icon by Allan Seiden. A comprehensive look at Hawaii's renowned landmark.

Discovery by Bishop Museum Press. A superb collection of essays and photographs addressing ancient, contemporary, and future Hawaii.

Exalted Sits the Chief by Ross Cordy. An archeologist's view of Hawaiian history.

From Fishponds to Warships – An Illustrated History of Pearl Harbor by Allan Seiden. The full story, from geology and natural history to the war and the present day.

Haleakala: A History of the Maui Mountain by Jill Engledow. A look at the science of how Haleakala was formed, as well as the people who live there today.

Hawaii 1959–89 by Gavan Daws. A thorough history of Hawaii's first 30 years of statehood.

Hawaii: The Royal Legacy by Allan Seiden. The illustrated story of Hawaii's chiefs and Kings.

Hawaii's Birds by Hawaii Audubon Society. A local birdwatcher's bible.

Hawaii's Story by Hawaii's Queen by Queen Lili'uokalani. The memoirs of Hawaii's first and only reigning queen.

Hawaiian Dictionary by Mary Kawena Pukui and Samuel H. Elbert. The definitive reference on Hawaiian vocabulary.

Hawaiian Hiking Trails by Craig Chisholm. A must for backpackers and nature-seekers.

Hawaiian Legends by William Hyde Rice. Attractive reprint of a 1923 classic, with the addition of new photos by Boone Morrison.

Hawaiian Music and Musicians by George S. Kanahele. Hawaii's musical heritage.

Hawaiian Mythology by Martha Warren Beckwith. Definitive and comprehensive.

Hawaiian Son: The Life and Music of Eddie Kamae by James Houston with Eddie Kamae. The illuminating biography of the 'ukulele-playing co-founder of the Sons of Hawaii makes a great introduction to Hawaiian music.

Hawaiian Yesterdays by Ray Jerome Baker, with text by Ronn Ronck. A wonderful collection of historic photos by Hawaii's pioneer cameraman.

Honor Killing by David Stannard. The gripping real-life story of a crime that exposed Hawaii's underlying racial tensions in the 1930s.

History Makers of Hawaii by A. Grove Day. A biographical dictionary of the people who shaped Hawaii from ancient times to the present.

Kaho'olawe: Na Leo O Kanaloa by Wayne Levin, Rowland B. Reeve, Franco Salmoiraghi, and David Ulrich. Images of the Forbidden Island of Kaho'olawe.

Ka Poe'e Kahiko, the People of Old by Samuel Manaiakalani Kamakau. Important memoirs by a 19th-century Hawaiian historian.

Mark Twain's Letters from Hawaii by Mark Twain. Twain's look at Hawaii in the 1860s.

Na Leo I Ka Makani: Voices on the Wind by Palani Vaughan. A pictorial look at early Hawaii.

Oceanwatcher, An Above-Water Guide to Hawaii's Marine Animals by Susan Scott.

Pau Hana by Ronald Takaki. A history of plantation life.

Shoal of Time: A History of the Hawaiian Islands by Gavan Daws. A perfect introduction to the history of the Hawaiian Islands.

The Price of Paradise Volumes 1 and 2, edited by Randall W. Roth. A collection of essays highlighting important issues in contemporary Hawaii.

Volcanoes in the Sea by Gordon A. MacDonald. A historical and scientific look at Hawaii's spectacular volcanoes.

A Voyage to the Pacific Ocean, 1776–1780 by Captain James Cook and James King. Official account of Cook's discovery of Hawaii.

Waikiki Beachboy by Grady Timmons. A colorful history of Waikiki's famed beachboy era.

FICTION

The Descendants by Kaui Hart Hemmings. The novel that inspired the motion picture of the same name; about death, family bonding, and land ownership in Hawaii.

Fluke: Or I Know Why the Winged Whale Sings by Christopher Moore. This laugh-out-loud novel is based on humpback whale researchers who still conduct work off the coast of Maui every winter.

From Here to Eternity by James Jones. The novel that spawned a movie (and, in 2013, a musical); tells the story of military life on Oahu leading up to D-Day in 1941.

Hawaii by James A. Michener. An excellent saga revolving around Hawaii's history by the Pulitzer-winning author.

⊘ Send us your thoughts

We do our best to ensure the information in our books is as accurate and up-to-date as possible. The books are updated on a regular basis using destination experts, who painstakingly add, amend and correct as required. However, some details (such as opening times or travel pass costs) are particularly liable to change, and we are ultimately reliant on our readers to put us in the picture.

We welcome your feedback, especially your experience of using the book "on the road", and if you came across a great new attraction we missed.

We will acknowledge all contributions and offer an Insight Guide to the best messages received.

Please write to us at:
Insight Guides
PO Box 7910
London SE1 1WE

Or email us at:
hello@insightguides.com

CREDITS

INSIGHT GUIDE CREDITS

Distribution
UK, Ireland and Europe
Apa Publications (UK) Ltd;
sales@insightguides.com
United States and Canada
Ingram Publisher Services;
ips@ingramcontent.com
Australia and New Zealand
Booktopia;
retailer@booktopia.com.au
Worldwide
Apa Publications (UK) Ltd;
sales@insightguides.com
Special Sales, Content Licensing and CoPublishing
Insight Guides can be purchased in bulk quantities at discounted prices. We can create special editions, personalised jackets and corporate imprints tailored to your needs.
sales@insightguides.com
www.insightguides.biz

Printed in China

All Rights Reserved
© 2022 Apa Digital AG
License edition © Apa Publications Ltd UK

First Edition 1988
Fifteenth Edition 2022

Every effort has been made to provide accurate information in this publication, but changes are inevitable. The publisher cannot be responsible for any resulting loss, inconvenience or injury. We would appreciate it if readers would call our attention to any errors or outdated information. We also welcome your suggestions; please contact us at:
hello@insightguides.com

www.insightguides.com

Editor: Joanna Reeves
Updater: Maciej Zglinicki
Picture Editor: Tom Smyth
Cartography: original cartography Apa Publications, updated by Carte
Layout: Greg Madejak
Head of DTP and Pre-Press: Katie Bennett
Head of Publishing: Kate Drynan

Legend

City maps

	Freeway/Highway/Motorway
	Divided Highway
	Main Roads
	Minor Roads
	Pedestrian Roads
	Steps
	Footpath
	Railway
	Funicular Railway
	Cable Car
	Tunnel
	City Wall
	Important Building
	Built Up Area
	Other Land
	Transport Hub
	Park
	Pedestrian Area
	Bus Station
	Tourist Information
	Main Post Office
	Cathedral/Church
	Mosque
	Synagogue
	Statue/Monument
	Beach
	Airport

Regional maps

	Freeway/Highway/Motorway (with junction)
	Freeway/Highway/Motorway (under construction)
	Divided Highway
	Main Road
	Secondary Road
	Minor Road
	Track
	Footpath
	International Boundary
	State/Province Boundary
	National Park/Reserve
	Marine Park
	Ferry Route
	Marshland/Swamp
	Glacier / Salt Lake
	Airport/Airfield
	Ancient Site
	Border Control
	Cable Car
	Castle/Castle Ruins
	Cave
	Chateau/Stately Home
	Church/Church Ruins
	Crater
	Lighthouse
	Mountain Peak
	Place of Interest
	Viewpoint

CONTRIBUTORS

This edition was commissioned by **Sarah Clarke**, updated by **Maciej Zglinicki** and edited by **Joanna Reeves**. It builds on a previous edition by **Matt Villano,** who got married in Hawaii in 2004 and has visited many times since. He considers the islands to be his personal 'Happy Place,' especially during humpback whale season. Contributors to earlier editions include **Joyce Akamine, Kekuni Blaisdell, Cheryl Chee Tsutsumi, Joan Conrow, Betty Fullard-Leo, Jerry Hopkins, Alberta de Jetley, Larry Lindsey Kimura, Leonard Lueras, Ronn Ronck, Susan Scott, Lance Tominaga, Greg Ward, Marty Wentzel,** and **Paul Wood**. **Steven Greaves Photography** would like to thank Jacques, James, Nikole, Koa, George, Kika, and Jimmy.

ABOUT INSIGHT GUIDES

Insight Guides have more than 45 years' experience of publishing high-quality, visual travel guides. We produce 400 full-colour titles, in both print and digital form, covering more than 200 destinations across the globe, in a variety of formats to meet your different needs.
  Insight Guides are written by local authors, whose expertise is evident in the extensive historical and cultural background features. Each destination is carefully researched by regional experts to ensure our guides provide the very latest information. All the reviews in **Insight Guides** are independent; we strive to maintain an impartial view. Our reviews are carefully selected to guide you to the best places to eat, go out and shop, so you can be confident that when we say a place is special, we really mean it.

INDEX

MAIN REFERENCES ARE IN BOLD TYPE

A

accommodations 288. See
also camping
cabin rentals 272
resorts 158, 166, 57, 163, 173,
184, 233, 234
activities 10, 75. See also by name
admission charges 288
'Aiea 164
'Aikanaka 161
air travel 11, 284
Hawaii Island 284
history of 56
inter-island flights 285
Kauai 284
Maui 284
Molokai and Lanai 284
Oahu 284
'Akaka Falls 11, 241, 244
Alaka'i Swamp 263, 271
'Alau Island 199
'Alekoko Fishpond 279
Ali'i Kula Lavender Farm 191
Ali'iloa, Bill Lincoln 85
Aloha Friday 297
Aloha Stadium 163
Aloha Stadium Swap Meet 164
amusement and water parks
Wet'n'Wild Hawaii (Ko 'Olina)
167
'Anaeho'omalu 233
animals 288. See wildlife
Apaka, Alfred 84
aquaculture 93, 157, 212
aquariums and zoo
Honolulu Zoo (Waikiki) 134
Maui Ocean Center (Ma'alaea)
179
Sea Life Park (Makapu'u Point)
151
Waikiki Aquarium (Waikiki) 135
art and crafts 38, 280
courses 276
featherwork 38
jewelry 38
shopping for 294
textiles 38
art galleries. See museums and
galleries
astronomy 33, 35, 243
Keck Observatory (Hawaii
Island) 247
Onizuka Astronomy Complex
(Hawaii Island) 247
Au'au Channel 77
'Au'Au Channel 181, 182, 173
Aulani 166

B

Baldwin, Dwight 183
Barking Sands 271
baseball 163
beaches 9, 11, 23

access 58
Hawaii Island 235, 244, 256
Kauai 269, 263, 271, 268, 279
Lanai 221
Maui 173, 173, 184, 186, 187,
190, 197, 198, 199
Molokai 211, 214
Oahu 111, 150, 148, 156, 153,
167, 168
Waikiki 127
Beamer, Keola 85, 86
Beamer, Mahi 85
Bellows Air Force Station 151
Berger, Heinrich 81
bicycling 75, 192, 285
Biggers, Earl Derr 65, 131
The Adventures of Charlie Chan
65
Bingham, Hiram 46, 118
Bird, Isabella 242
bird life 25, 169, 177, 267, 272
albatrosses 168
goony birds 169
honeycreepers 263
moa (wild Hawaiian chickens)
272
mynahs 202
nene (Hawaiian Goose) 26, 248
Bishop, Charles Reed 139
Black Rock 184
boat trips and cruises 287
Hawaii Island 225, 232
Kane'ohe Bay 155
Kauai 270
Molokai 209
Oahu 133
bodyboarding 77, 150, 151, 168,
199, 279
Boiling Pots 244
Brennecke's Beach 279
Bronte, Emory 212
Brotman, Charles 87
Brower, Kenneth 33
Brown, William 125
Buck, Sir Peter 35
Vikings of the Pacific 35
business hours. See opening
hours
bus travel 11, 286
Hawaii Island 286
Kauai 286
Maui 286
Oahu 286

C

camping
Kauai 270, 271
Lanai 221
Maui 192, 197, 198, 199
Molokai 211, 214
canoeing, outrigger 79
Cape Kumukahi 249
Captain Cook (town). 232. See
also Cook, James

car rental 285, 286. See
also driving
restricted routes 200, 246
Carrere, Tia 87
Cartwright, Alexander Joy, Jr. 140
cathedrals
Our Lady of Peace (Honolulu)
121
St Andrew's (Honolulu) 121
caves 197, 198
Kaneana (Oahu) 168
Kazumura Cave (Hawaii Island)
253
Cazimero brothers 85
Central Oahu 163
Chain of Craters Road 254
Chang Apana 65
children 288
Choy, Sam 93
churches
Holy Ghost (Waiakoa) 191
Huialoha (Maui) 193
Ka'ahumanu Congregational
(Wailuku) 178
Kalua'aha 212
Kaulanapueo (Huelo) 196
Kawaiaha'o (Honolulu) 118
Moku'aikaua (Kailua) 225, 231
Our Lady of Sorrows (Kalua'aha)
212
Palapala Ho'omau (Kipahulu) 200
Siloama (Kalawao) 211
St Benedict's Painted Church
(Hawaii Island) 200
St Gabriel's (Wailua) 197
St Joseph's (Kaupo) 193
St Peter and Paul (Waimea Bay)
159
St Philomena's (Kalawao) 211
Cleveland, President Grover 51
cliff-diving 185
climate and weather 23, 289
Clinton, President Bill 58
clothing 297
cocoa 232
Coconut Coast 277
coffee 225, 231, 232, 296
Cook, James 34, 35, 38, 39, 189,
232, 263, 275, 281
coral reefs 23
cowboys 94, 191, 236
crafts. See art and crafts
crime and safety 167, 289
Crosby, Bing 85
Crouching Lion. See Kauhi
cruise ships 124, 242, 275, 285
culture and society 36, 64
customs regulations 289

D

Damien, Father 210, 211, 212
dance. See music and dance
de La Pérouse, Jean-François 187
Diamond Head 148, 151

Dillingham Airfield 160
disabled travelers 289
diving and snorkeling 10, 11, 23, 77, 79
    Kauai 269
    Lanai 218, 220, 221
    Maui 185, 187
    Ni'ihau 278
    Oahu 148, 149, 150, 155
Dole, James D. 219, 53, 165
Dole, Sanford 51, 53, 165
driving 149, 286, 287. See also car rental
    Hana Highway 195, 196
    in Honolulu 129

E

eating out.11 See also food and drink, restaurants
    food trucks 178
economy 19, 47, 57, 173
ecosystems 21, 23, 24, 255
Edgar, Thomas 42
Eisenhower, President Dwight D. 145
electricity 290
Ellison, Larry 59, 219, 99
embassies and consulates 290
emergencies 290
Emma, Queen 48, 49
environmental issues 26
    extinction of native species 27
    Great Pacific Garbage Patch 27
etiquette 290
'Ewa 111

F

Fagan, Paul 198
ferries 287
festivals and events
    Buffalo's Longboard Contest (Makaha) 167
    calendar of events 290
    Feast Day of Santa Cruz 69
    Fiesta Filipina 69
    Hale'iwa Arts Festival (Hale'iwa) 160
    Hawaiian International Billfish Tournament (Hawaii Island) 78, 231
    Hawaii International Film Festival 99
    Honolulu Marathon 134
    Ironman World Championship (Kailua) 231
    Ka Hula Piko Festival (Maunaloa) 87
    Makawao Rodeo (Makawao) 190, 191
    Maui Film Festival 99
    Merrie Monarch Festival (Hilo) 87, 243
    Molokai Ka Hula Piko festival (Molokai) 214
    Molokai-to-Oahu outrigger canoe race (Hale o Lono) 212
    Na Mele O Maui Song Contest and Hula Festival (Ka'anapali) 87

Prince Albert Hula Festival (Princeville) 87
Prince Lot Hula Festival (Moanalua Gardens) 87, 163
Queen Lili'uokalani Keiki Hula festival 87
rodeo (Makawao) 78
toronagashi festival (Hale'iwa) 160
Vans Triple Crown of Surfing (Oahu) 161
film and television 97
    50 First Dates 98
    Baraka 99
    Bird of Paradise 98
    Blue Crush 98, 166
    Blue Hawaii 98
    Fantasy Island 98
    Forgetting Sarah Marshall 98
    From Here to Eternity 98
    Girls! Girls! Girls! 98
    Hawaii 168
    Hawaii Five-O 98
    Jurassic Park 98, 268
    Just Go With It 99
    Lost 98, 153, 155
    Magnum P.I. 98
    North Shore 98
    Outbreak 97
    Pearl Harbor 98
    Pirates of the Caribbean 98
        At World's End 99
    Planet of the Apes 99
    Raiders of the Lost Ark 268
    Six Days, Seven Nights 98
    South Pacific 98, 267, 268, 269
    The Descendants 98
    The Devil at 4 O'Clock 99
    The Hunger Games, Catching Fire 98
    The Tempest 99
    Tora! Tora! Tora! 165
    Voodoo Island 98
    Waikiki Wedding 98
    Waterworld 99
fishing 179
    deep-sea fishing 78, 275
    game fishing 231
fishponds 154, 155, 212, 213, 234, 279
flora. See plant life
folklore. See mythology and legends
food and drink 91
    fish and shellfish 93
    Hawaii Regional Cuisine 92
    Koloa Rum Company (Koloa) 279
    local produce 93, 295
    malasadas 178
    Maui food scene 186
    plate lunch 94
    shave ice 94, 160
    shopping for 199
    Spam 94
    Tedeschi Winery 191
food trucks 178
forests 24, 153. See also rainforests
Fornander, Abraham 35
    An Account of the Polynesian

Race: Its Origins and Migrations 36
further reading 300

G

Garden of the Gods 11, 75, 219, 221
gardens. See parks and gardens
Gates, Bill 219
geography and geology 21, 207, 225, 270. See also volcanoes
Gilliom, Amy Hanaiali'i 85
golf 166
    Hawaii Island 233, 235
    Kauai 268, 277
    Maui 173, 184, 185, 186
government and politics 48, 50, 51, 54, 55, 68
Grant, President Ulysses S. 50
Gregg, John 281
Gregg, Robert 281

H

Ha'ena 269
Ha'iku 196
Halawa Bay 213
Halawa Valley 11, 211, 213
Haleakala 173, 189, 192
Haleakala National Park 192, 195, 199
Hale'iwa 11, 160
    Hale'iwa Jodo Mission 160
Halema'uma'u 259
Halona Blowhole 150
Hamakua Coast 225, 238, 244, 245
Hamoa Beach 199
Hana 197
    Hana Cultural Center & Museum 198
    Hana Ranch 198
    Ka'uiki Hill 198
    Travaasa Hana 198
Hana Airport 197, 284
Hana Coast 195
Hana Highway 195, 197
Hanakapi'ai 270
Hanakoa 270
Hanalei 268
Hanalei Bay 268
Hanama'ulu 275
Hanapepe 11
Hanapepe Town 275, 280
Hanauma Bay 77, 148
handicrafts. See art and crafts
Hansen's Disease exiles 207, 210, 211
Hapa 86
Hapuna Beach State Park 235
Hau'ula 156
Hawaiian Islands National Wildlife Refuge 169
Hawaiian Volcano Observatory 252
Hawaii Island 21, 42, 59, 107, 296. See also individual place names
Hawai'i Kai 149
Hawaii Ocean Science and Technology (HOST) Park 233
Hawaii Tropical Botanical Garden 244

Hawaii Volcanoes National Park 251, 225
Hawaii Water Sports Center 149
Hawi 11, 238
Healing Stones 164
health and medical care 292
Helm, Raiatea 85
heritage railways
Hawaiian Railway Society ('Ewa) 142
Lahaina Ka'anapali Railroad (Ka'anapali) 184
Hi'ilawe Falls 246
hiking 9, 75
Hawaii Island 238, 244, 246, 248, 251, 254, 255, 256
Honolulu 144
Kalalau Trail (Kauai) 75, 267, 270
Kauai 263, 270, 272
Kukui Trail (Kauai) 272
Lanai 219, 220, 221
Mahana Ridge Trail 76
Maui 185, 192, 196, 197, 198, 199, 200
Molokai 209, 211, 213
Munro Trail 79
Oahu 148, 150, 151, 156, 163
Pepe'opae Trail (Molokai) 209
Hilo 54, 225, 241
Banyan Drive 243
East Hawaii Cultural Center Gallery 243
Hawaii Tropical Botanical Garden 241
history 242
'Imiloa Astronomy Center 243
Kaiko'o 242
Lili'uokalani Gardens 243
Lyman Mission House and Museum 243
Mauna Loa Macadamia Nut Factory and Visitor Center 243
Pacific Tsunami Museum 243
Waianuenue Avenue 242
Hilo Bay 241
Hilo International Airport 284
Hindu Monastery 277
historic sites. See also temples
Kalaupapa National Historical Park (Molokai) 75, 210, 211
Kaloko-Honokohau National Historical Park (Hawaii Island) 233
Lapakahi State Historical Park (Hawaii Island) 72
Mauna Kea adze quarry (Hawaii Island) 246
Pu'uhonua 'O Honaunau National Historical Park (Hawaii Island) 37, 72, 232
Pu'ukohola Heiau National Historic Site (Hawaii Island) 235
history 10, 19
20th century century 53
monarchy 45
Polynesians, arrival of 33
statehood 55
US annexation 51
World War II 54, 146, 165, 187
hitchhiking 285

Ho, Don 84
Hokule'a, voyages of 35
Holualoa 230
Honaunau Bay 232
Honoka'a 241, 246
Honokohau 185
Honokowai 185
Honoli'i 244
Honolua/Mokule'ia Marine Preserve 185
Honolulu 57, 107, 111. See also Waikiki
Aina Moana State Recreation Area 125
Ala Moana Beach Park 125
Ala Moana Boulevard 124
Ala Moana Shopping Center 125
Ala Wai Canal 125
Ala Wai Yacht Harbor 125
Aloha Tower 124
Bernice Pauahi Bishop Museum 139
Bishop Square 122
Bishop Street 123
Boat Days 124
Cathedral of Our Lady of Peace 121
Chinatown 123, 290
East-West Center 145
Foster Botanical Gardens 124
Hawaii State Art Museum 122
Hawaii State Library 120
Hawaii Theatre 123
Honolulu Hale 119
Honpa Hongwanji Mission 143
Hotel Street 123
'Iolani Barracks 116
'Iolani Palace 115
Judiciary Building 117
Kawaiaha'o Church 118
Kewalo Basin 125
King Kamehameha the Great Statue 117
Kuan Yin Temple 124
Likeke Hale 119
Lyon Arboretum 145
Magic Island 125
Manoa Falls 146
Manoa Valley 144
Maunakea Marketplace 124
Mission Houses 119
National Memorial Cemetery of the Pacific 144
Neal S. Blaisdell Center 124
Nu'uanu 142
Nu'uanu Pali Lookout 143
Nu'uanu Stream 124
Oahu Cemetery 140
Oahu Market 124
Prince Kuhio Kalaniana'ole Federal Building 125
Punchbowl Crater 144
Pu'u 'Ualaka'a State Park 144
Queen Emma's Summer Palace 141
Royal Burial Ground and Tomb 116
Royal Mausoleum 141
sculpture of Father Damien 121
shopping 125
Soto Zen Mission of Hawaii 142

St Andrew's Cathedral 121
State Capitol Building 120
statue of Queen Lili'uokalan 120
Tantalus 144
University of Hawaii 145
Waipuhia Valley Falls 143
Ward Village Center 125
Washington Place 121
Honolulu International Airport 284
Honomanu 196
Honomu 244
Ho'okio Gulch 221
Ho-olehua Airport 208, 284
horseback riding 78
Hawaii Island 238, 246
Maui 191, 200
Oahu 155
hotels. See accommodations
hot springs 249
Hualalai 22, 229, 233
Huelo 196
Kaulanapueo church 196
Huialoha 200
Huialoha Church 193
Hui Ohana 85
Hulopo'e 218
Hulopo'e Bay 221

I

'Iao Needle 11, 179
'Iao Valley 178
Hawaii Nature Center 178
Kepaniwai Heritage Gardens 178
'Iao Valley State Park 179
'Ili 'ili 'opae Heiau 72
internet 292
irrigation 197

J

James Campbell National Wildlife Refuge 157
jet-skiing 155
Johnson, Jack 86
Josting, Edward 263

K

Ka'ahumanu 46
Ka'ahumanu, Queen 198
Ka'ala, Mount 168
Ka'anapali 184
Ka'anapali Beach 59
Ka'anapali Resort 184
Whaler's Village 184
Ka'apana, Ledward and Nedward 85
Ka'ena Point 160, 168, 169
Kahakuloa 185
Kahala 135, 149
Kahalu'u Beach Park 76
Kahana 185
Kahana Bay 156
Kahanamoku, Duke 128, 132
Kahanu Gardens 72, 170
Kahe Point 167
Kaho'olawe 107, 173, 187
Kahuku 157
Kahului 177, 178, 54
Kanaha Pond State Wildlife Sanctuary 177

Maui Arts and Cultural Center 177
Kahului Airport 284
Kahuna Falls 244
Kaiaka Bay 160
Kailua 225, 230. *See also* Kona
 Ahu'ena 230
 'Ahu'ena Heiau 225
 Hulihe'e Palace 225, 231
 Kailua Beach Park 153
 Kamakahonu 230
 Moku'aikaua Church 225, 231
Kailua 153, 229
Kailua Bay 153, 230
Kaiser, Henry J. 149
Kaiwio Pele 199
Ka Lae 225, **233**, 256
Kalahaku Overlook 192
Kalaheo 279
Kalakaua, King David 49, 83, 87
Kalalau Trail 75, 267, 270
Kalalau Valley 270
 Kalalau Valley Lookout 272
Kalalea Heiau 256
Kalama, Benny 84
Kalanikaula 213
Kalapaki 275
Kalapaki Beach 275
Kalapana 254
Kalaupapa National Historical Park 75, 210, 211
Kalaupapa Overlook 210
Kalaupapa Peninsula 210
Kalawao 211
 Siloama Church 211
 St Philomena's church 211
Kaleikini, Danny 84
Kaliuwa'a Falls 156
Kaloko-Honokohau National Historical Park 233
Kalua'aha 212
 Kalua'aha Church 212
 Our Lady of Sorrows Church 212
Kamae, Eddie 84
Kamahualele 35
Kamakau, Samuel M. 35, 42
Kamakawiwo'ole, Skippy and Israel 85
Kamakilo Village 277
Kamalo 212
Kamehameha II 46, 125
Kamehameha III 46, 125, 191
Kamehameha IV 48
Kamehameha, Lot 49
Kamehameha the Great 45, 125, 212, 230, 235
 birthplace of 237
 statue 238
Kamehameha V 49, 81, 208, 278
Kamokila Hawaiian Village 97
Kamuela. *See* Waimea
Kanaka'ole, Edith 85
Kane'aki 72
Kaneana 168
Kane'ohe 154
 Byodo-In Temple 154
 He'eia Fishpond 154
 Valley of the Temples Memorial Park 154
Kane'ohe Bay 154
Kanepu'u 221

Kanepu'u Preserve 79
Kapa'a 275, 277
Kapa'au 238
 Kamehameha the Great statue 238
 Kohala Tong Wo Society 237
Kapalua 180
 Kapalua Resort 185
Kapalua-West Maui Airport 284
Kapi'olani 47
Kapuaiwa Coconut Grove 208
Ka'u 251
Kauai 41, 57, 107. *See also* individual place names
 shopping 296
Ka'u Desert 255
Ka'u District 256
Kauhako 208
Kauikeaouli 46
Kaulakahi Channel 278
Ka Ule o Nanahoa 210
Kaumahina State Wayside 196
Kaumakaiwa 86
Kaumalapau Harbor 220
Kaunakakai 11, 208
Kaunolu 220
Kaunolu Bay 220
Kaupo
 St Joseph's Church 193
Kaupo 193, 200
Kaupo Gap 193, 200
Kaupo Ranch 200
Kawaihae 237
Kawela 212
Kawelo 161
kayaking 10, 79, 187
 Kauai 270
Kazumura Cave 253
Kealaikahiki 35
Kealakekua Bay 39, 42, 232
Keale, Moe 84
Kealohi Point, 154
Ke'anae 196
 Ke'anae Arboretum 197
Ke'anae Peninsula 196
Keauokalani, Kepelino 35
Keawa'ula Bay 168
Keawe, Auntie Genoa 85
Keck Observatory 247
Ke'e Beach 270
Keokea 191
Keomuku 221
Keopuolani, Queen 180
Keoua 45
Kepuhi Bay 214
Kihei 186
Kilauea 22, 22, 21, 107, 251, 249, 267
 Crater Rim Drive 252
 eruptions 249, 251
 Halema'uma'u Crater 252
 Kilauea Iki Crater 253
 Kilauea Visitor Center 251
Kilauea Point National Wildlife Refuge 268
Kina'u 47
Kipahulu 200
 Kipahulu Sugar Mill (Kipahulu) 200
 Palapala Ho'omau Church 200
Kipahulu Valley 200, 203

Kipuka 'Ainahou Nene Sanctuary 248
Kipuka Pua'ulu 255
Kohala 22, 225, 229
 Pu'u Kohala 45
Kohala Ditch 238
Kohala Mountains 237
Kohala Tong Wo Society 237
Kohumoku, George, Jr. 87
Koke'e 263, 272
 Iliau Nature Loop 272
 Koke'e Lodge 272
 Koke'e Museum 272
Koki Beach 199
Koko Head 75, 149
Kolekole Pass 165
Koloa 279
 Koloa Rum Company 279
Komohana 173
Kona 225, 229. *See also* Kailua
 Kona International Airport 229
 Kona Village Resort 233
Kona International Airport 284
Ko'olau Mountains 139, 153
Ko 'Olina 111, 163
 Wet'n'Wild Hawaii 167
Ko 'Olina Resort 166
Kualapu'u 210
 Molokai Museum and Cultural Center 210
 R.W. Meyer Sugar Mill 210
Kualoa Ranch 155
Kualoa Regional Park 155
Ku'ililoa Heiau 167
Kukuiho'olua 157
Kukui Trail 272
Kula 191
Kure Atoll 21, 23

L

Lahaina 76, 125, 173, 180
 Baldwin Home 183
 Banyan Tree 183
 Front Street 181
 Hale Pa'ahao 183
 Hale Pa'i 184
 Jodo Mission Buddhist Cultural Park 183
 Lahainaluna High School 183
 Malu'uluolele Park 183
 Pioneer Inn 181
 Wo Hing Society Temple 183
La'ie 156
 Mormon Temple 156
 Polynesian Cultural Center 156
La'ie Point 157
Lake Wai'au 246
Lanai 59, 63, 78, 173, 107, 173. *See also* individual place names
Lanai Airport 284
 Hotel Lanai 220
Lanai City 11, 219, 220
Lana'ihale 221
Lanaihale 79
land ownership 47, 57
language 19, 47
Lapakahi State Historical Park 72, 237
La Pérouse Bay 187, 191
Laulima Farm stand 199

Laupaho'eho'e 245
Laupaho'eho'e Train Museum 246
Laupaho'eho'e Natural Area Reserve 245
Lava Tree State Monument 249
lava tubes 253
Lawa'i Kai 280
Ledyard, John 43
Lee, Kui 84
Leeward Islands 169
legends. See mythology and legends
leis 88, 232, 294
leprosy colony. See Hansen's Disease exiles
LGBTQ travelers 293
Liholiho 46
Liholiho, Alexander 48
Lihu'e 263, 275
Grove Farm Homestead & Sugar Plantation Museum 276
Kauai Museum 276
Lihu'e Airport 284
Lili'uokalani, Queen 50, 83, 85. 121, 151
statue (Honolulu) 120
Limahuli 269
Lindbergh, Charles 200
Lingle, Linda 58
literature 35
mele 35
Lo'ihi 21, 254
London, Jack 211
The Cruise of the Snark 211
lu'aus 95
Lumaha'i 269
Lunalilo, King William 49, 118

M

Ma'alaea 179
Maui Ocean Center 179
macadamia nuts 243, 245
Machado, Lena 85
Makaha 167
Makaha Sons of Ni'ihau 85
Makaha Valley 168
Kane'aki Heiau 168
Makanalua Peninsula 210
Makapu'u Beach Park 151
Makapu'u Point 151
Sea Life Park 151
Makawao 78, 191
Pi'iholo Ranch 191
Makawao 11, 190
Makena 186
Makua Beach 168
Malo, David 35, 36
Manele Bay 218
Manele Boat Harbor 221
maps 293
Marcos, Ferdinand and Imelda 143
marijuana 234, 249
marine conservation districts 25
Hulopo'e Bay (Lanai) 221
Kealakekua Bay (Hawaii Island) 232
markets
Aloha Stadium Swap Meet 164

Hana 198
Hanalei 268
Kauai 268
Mars, Bruno 86
Maui 42, 57, 107. See also individual place names
shopping 296
Maunaiki 255
Mauna Kamakou 208
Mauna Kea 22, 241, 243, 246
Mauna Kea Beach Hotel 235
Mauna Lani Resort 234
Maunaloa 214
Mauna Loa (Hawaii Island) 22, 79, 231, 243, 248, 251
eruptions 244, 248
Mauna Loa (Molokai) 207
Mauna Ulu 253
Maunawili 151
Mavrothalassitis, George 93
McAllister, J. Gilbert 167
McKinley, President William 51
McNamara, Garrett 77
media 293
Melville, Herman 181
Menehune Ditch 279
Merriman, Peter 93
Michener, James 210
Hawaii 210
Midway Islands 169
Miloli'i 233
missionaries 46
Moanalua Gardens 163
Moanalua Valley 163
Mokoli'i 155
Mokualai 157
Moku'aweoweo 248
Moku Ho'oniki 213
Mokulau 200
Mokule'ia Polo Farm 160
Moli'j Fishpond 155
Molokai 23, 63, 107, 173. See also individual place names
Molokai Ranch 214
Molokini 187
Molokini Atoll 23, 77
money matters 293
budgeting for your trip 288
money-saving tips 11
tax 296
Mo'okini Heiau 237
Mo'oula Falls 213
movies. See film and television
Munro Trail 79, 221
Murdock, David 219
museums and galleries 9
Alexander & Baldwin Sugar Museum (Pu'unene) 179
Bailey House (Wailuku) 178
Baldwin Home (Lahaina) 183
Bernice Pauahi Bishop Museum (Honolulu) 139
East Hawaii Cultural Center Gallery (Hilo) 243
Grove Farm Homestead & Sugar Plantation Museum (Lihu'e) 276
Hana Cultural Center & Museum (Hana) 198
Hawaii Nature Center ('Iao Valley) 178

Hawaii State Art Museum (Honolulu) 122
Hulihe'e Palace (Kailua) 231
'Imiloa Astronomy Center (Hilo) 243
Kauai Museum (Lihu'e) 276
Koke'e Museum (Koke'e) 272
Laupaho'eho'e Train Museum (Laupaho'eho'e) 246
Lyman Mission House and Museum (Hilo) 243
Maui Arts and Cultural Center (Kahului) 177
Mission Houses (Honolulu) 119
Molokai Museum and Cultural Center (Kualapu'u) 210
Pacific Tsunami Museum (Hilo) 243
Parker Ranch Museum and Visitor Center (Waimea) 236
Tropic Lightning Museum (Schofield Barracks) 164
US Army Museum (Waikiki) 133
USS Bowfin Submarine Museum & Park (Pearl Harbor) 147
West Kauai Technology & Visitor Center (Waimea) 281
Wo Hing Society Temple (Lahaina) 183
music and dance 81
Aloha 'Oe 83, 151
hula 47, 83, 86, 214, 243
musical instruments 82, 294
slack key style 82
ukuleles 71
mythology and legends 19, 166, 198, 213, 254, 269
gnomes 35
Kamohoali'i 168
Kauhi 156
Maui 189, 244
menehune 279
Pehe and Makakehau 220
Pele 199, 229
Poli'ahu 246
sacred stones 128

N

Na'alehu 256
Nahiku 197
Na Leo Pilimehana 85
Na Palapalai 85
Na Pali 269
Na Pali Coast 75, 107, 267
Na Pali Coast State Wilderness Park 270
Napili 185
national and state parks 25
Haleakala National Park (Maui) 192, 195, 199
Hapuna Beach State Park (Hawaii Island) 235
Hawaii Volcanoes National Park (Hawaii Island) 251, 225
'Iao Valley State Park (Maui) 179
Na Pali Coast State Wilderness Park (Kauai) 270
Pala'au State Park (Molokai) 210

Polihale State Park (Kauai) 271
Pua'a Ka'a State Park (Maui) 197
Pu'u 'Ualaka'a State Park (Honolulu) 144
Russian Fort Elizabeth (Waimea) 281
Wai'anapanapa State Park (Maui) 197
Wailuku River State Park (Hawaii Island) 244
national historical parks and sites. See historic sites
National Tropical Botanical Garden 269, 280
nature reserves 25
Alaka'i Swamp (Kauai) 263, 271
Hawaiian Islands National Wildlife Refuge (Oahu) 169
Honolua/Mokule'ia Marine Preserve (Maui) 185
James Campbell National Wildlife Refuge (Oahu) 157
Ka'ena Point (Oahu) 168
Kamakou Preserve (Molokai) 209
Kanaha Pond State Wildlife Sanctuary (Kahului) 177
Kanepu'u Preserve (Lanai) 79
Kilauea Point National Wildlife Refuge (Kauai) 268
Kipahulu Valley (Maui) 200, 203
Kipuka 'Ainahou Nene Sanctuary (Hawaii Island) 248
Kipuka Pua'ulu (Hawaii Island) 255
Laupaho'eho'e Natural Area Reserve (Hawaii Island) 245
Waimea Valley (Oahu) 159
Nawiliwili 54
Nawiliwili Harbor 275
Neighbor Islands 57
newspapers 293
nightlife 230
Ni'ihau 41, 63, 107, 271, 277, 278
Niuli'i 238
North Kohala 225, 237
North Kona 233
North Shore (Oahu) 111
Northwestern Hawaiian Islands Marine National Monument 169
Nu'uanu Pali Lookout 11

O

Oahu 19, 41, 59, 54, 107. See also individual place names shopping 295
Obama, President Barack 59, 94, 153, 154
obsidian 230
off-roading 219, 78
Munro Trail 221
Ohe'o Gulch 195, 199
Olomana 151
Oneali'i Park (Royal Sands) 211
Onizuka Astronomy Complex 247
Onomea Bay 244
Opaeka'a Falls 277
opening hours 293
orientation 286

P

Pa'auhau 245
Pa'auilo 245
paddleboarding 77, 270
Pahinui, Gabby 84, 151
Pahoa 249
Pa'ia 190
Ho'okipa Beach 190
Mantokuji Mission 190
Pailolo Channel 213
Pakini Nui Wind Farm 256
Pala'au State Park 210
Palawai 220
Palawai Basin 220
Papa'aloa 245
Papa Ii, John 35
Papa'ikou 244
Papakolea Green Sand Beach 256
Papohaku Beach Camp 214
paragliding 79
parasailing 149
Parker, John Palmer 236
parks and gardens
Ala Moana Beach Park (Honolulu) 125
Foster Botanical Gardens (Honolulu) 124
Hawaii Tropical Botanical Garden (Hawaii Island) 244
Hawaii Tropical Botanical Garden (Hilo) 241
Kahanu Gardens 72
Kahanu Gardens (Maui) 197
Kapi'olani Park (Waikiki) 134
Kaumahina State Wayside (Maui) 196
Ke'anae Arboretum (Ke'anae) 197
Kepaniwai Heritage Gardens ('Iao Valley) 178
Kualoa Regional Park (Oahu) 155
Lili'uokalani Gardens (Hilo) 243
Lyon Arboretum (Honolulu) 145
Malu'uluolele Park (Lahaina) 183
Moanalua Gardens (Oahu) 163
National Tropical Botanical Garden (Kauai) 269
National Tropical Botanical Garden (Kauai) 280
Sacred Falls Park (Oahu) 156
Valley of the Temples Memorial Park (Kane'ohe) 154
Wahiawa Botanical Garden (Wahiawa) 164
Waimea Valley (Oahu) 159
Pauoa Bay 234
Pava'o, Dennis 85
Peahi 76
Pearl City 164
Pearl Harbor 50, 51, 107, 111, 146
Hickam Air Force Base 147
USS Arizona Memorial 145, 146
USS Bowfin Submarine Museum & Park 147
USS Missouri 147
World War II 54, 146
people 19, 279
Caucasians 70
Chinese 64, 237
ethnic diversity 48
Filipinos 67
indigenous Hawaiians 63, 208
Japanese 65, 242
Koreans 69
Marquesans 34
Mormon community 219, 156
Samoans 70
Tahitians 34
Pepe'ekeo 244
Pepe'opae Trail 209
petroglyphs 73, 163, 233
Puako petroglyph field 235
pets 288
Pi'ilanihale Heiau 72, 197
Pi'ilani Highway 198
pineapples 219, 163, 53, 165, 177
Dole Plantation 165
plant life 25, 21, 24, 267, 269
Cook Island pine 219
kukui trees 213
silverswords 25, 192
Pohakuloa 248
Po'ipu 275, 277
Poipu Beach 76
Polihale State Park 271
Polihua Beach 219
politics. See government and politics
polo 160
Pololu Valley Lookout 238
postal services 294
Preis, Alfred 145, 146
Presley, Elvis 124, 146, 150
Princeville 267, 268
Pua'a Ka'a State Park 197
Puako 73
Puako petroglyph field 235
public holidays 294
Pukalani 190
Puna 242, 249
Punalu'u Beach 256
Puohokamoa Falls 196
Pu'uhonua 'O Honaunau National Historical Park 37, 72, 232
Pu'u Keka'a. See Black Rock
Pu'ukohola Heiau National Historic Site 72, 235
Pu'u Kukui 179
Pu'unene 179
Alexander & Baldwin Sugar Museum 179
Pu'u O Hoku Ranch 213
Pu'u O Mahuka 72
Pu'uomahuka Heiau State Monument 159
Pu'u 'Ula'ula 192
Pu'u Wa'awa'a 230
Pu'uwai 278
Pyle, Ernest Taylor (Ernie) 144

Q

Queen's Medical Center 48

R

Radford, Arthur 145
radio 293
rail travel. See heritage railways

Rainbow Falls 244
rainforests 24, 111, 139, 195, 209, 251
Reichel, Keali'i 86
religion 37
 Christianity 47
 Polynesian deities 39
 sacred sites 165
 traditional beliefs 66, 160
restaurants 11. *See also* eating out, food and drink
Rhee, Dr Syngman 69
Rice, William Harrison 276
Rice, William Hyde 276
Robinson Keith and Bruce 278
Rowan, Chad 151
Royal Hawaiian Band 82, 83
royal stones 73

S

Sacred Falls Park 156
Saddle Road 246
salt ponds 280
Sandalwood Boat 209
Sandwich Islands 41
Sandy Beach 150
Schofield Barracks
 Tropic Lightning Museum 164
Schofield Barracks 164
Science City 192
sea travel 285, 287. *See also* cruise ships
Sheffer, Dr Anton 281
Shimabukuro, Jake 86
Shipwreck Beach 79, 221
shopping 294
 what to buy 294
Simeon, Sheldon 93
skydiving 160
Smith, Ernest 212
snorkeling. *See* diving and snorkeling
society. *See* culture and society
Sons of Hawaii 84
South Kohala 59, 234
South Kona 231
South Maui 185
South Point. *See* Ka Lae
sports venues. *See also* sports by name
 Aloha Stadium (Oahu) 163
 Mokule'ia Polo Farm 160
 The Ice Palace (Oahu) 164
Spouting Horn 279
Stadium Mall 164
state parks. *See* national and state parks
St Benedict's Painted Church 232
Steaming Bluff (Sulfur Banks) 252
Stevens, John B. 51
sugar 48, 50, 53, 177, 197, 244, 275, 276, 279
 Alexander & Baldwin Sugar Museum (Pu'unene) 179
 R.W. Meyer Sugar Mill (Kualapu'u) 210
sumo wrestling 71, 151
Sunday Manoa 85
Sun Yatsen 65, 237
surfing 8, 11, 76, 128, 161, 179

Hawaii Island 244
Kauai 267, 268
Maui 185, 200
Oahu 111, 158, 168
surfboards, shopping for 295
tuition 76, 161
Sweetheart Rock 220
swimming. *See also* beaches
 Hawaii Island 235
 Lanai 221
 Maui 196, 197, 199
 with dolphins 234

T

Tantalus, Mount 144
taro 196, 197
tattoos 38
tax 296
taxis 287
Tedeschi Winery 191
telephones 296
television 293. *See also* film and television
temples 27, 159, 232
 'Ahu'ena Heiau (Kailua) 225
 Ahu'ena (Kailua) 230
 Byodo-In (Kane'ohe) 154
 'Ili 'ili 'opae Heiau (Molokai) 72
 Kadavul (Kauai) 277
 Kalalea Heiau (Hawaii Island) 256
 Kaloko-Honokohau (Hawaii Island) 233
 Kane'aki Heiau (Makaha Valley) 168
 Kane'aki (Oahu) 72
 Ku'ilioloa Heiau (Oahu) 167
 Laka heiau (Molokai) 214
 Mantokuji Mission (Pa'ia) 190
 Mo'okini Heiau (Hawaii Island) 237
 Mormon Temple (La'ie) 156
 Pi'ilanihale Heiau (Maui) 72, 197
 Poli'ahu Heiau (Kauai) 277
 Pu'uhonua 'O Honaunau (Hawaii Island) 232
 Pu'ukohola Heiau (Hawaii Island) 235
 Pu'ukohola Heiau National Historic Site (Hawaii Island) 72
 Pu'u O Mahuka (Oahu) 72
 San Marga Iraivan (Kauai) 277
 Valley of the Temples Memorial Park (Kane'ohe) 154
 Wo Hing Society Temple (Lahaina) 183
theaters and concert venues
 Hawaii Theatre (Honolulu) 123
 Maui Arts and Cultural Center (Kahului) 177
 Neal S. Blaisdell Center (Honolulu) 124
 Polynesian Cultural Center (La'ie) 156
Thiebaut, Daniel 93
Thurston Lava Tube 253
tipping 297
tourism 57
tourist information 297

tour operators 297
tours
 helicopter tours 155, 209, 225, 270, 278
 Molokai rainforest 209
trains. *See* heritage railways
transportation 11, 284
tsunamis 233, 242, 246, 289
 Pacific Tsunami Museum (Hilo) 243
Tunnels Beach 267, 268
Turtle Bay Resort 158
Twain, Mark 181, 189, 210

U

'Ulupalakua Ranch 191
'Umi, King 247
Upcountry 190
'Upolu Point 237

V

Vancouver, George 35, 159
Vaughan, Palani 85
visas and passports 297
Volcano 254
 Volcano Art Center 255
 Volcano House 255
volcanoes 8, 19, 21
 eruptions 253
 Haleakala (Maui) 173, 189, 192
 Halema'uma'u (Hawaii Island) 259
 Hawaiian Volcano Observatory (Hawaii Island) 252
 Hualalai (Hawaii Island) 22, 229
 Kaiwio Pele (Maui) 199
 Kauhako (Molokai) 208
 Kilauea (Hawaii Island) 21, 22, 107, 249, 251
 Kohala (Hawaii Island) 22
 Komohana (Maui) 173
 Mauna Kamakou (Molokai) 208
 Mauna Kea (Hawaii Island) 22, 241, 243, 246
 Mauna Loa (Hawaii Island) 22, 79, 231, 243, 248, 251
 Mauna Loa (Molokai) 207
 Mauna Ulu (Hawaii Island) 253
 Palawai (Lanai) 220
 Pu'u Kukui (Maui) 179
 Pu'u Wa'awa'a (Hawaii Island) 230
von Kotzebue, Otto 35

W

Waha'ula 254
Wahiawa 164, 165
 birth stones of Kukaniloko 164
 Dole Plantation 165
 Wahiawa Botanical Garden 164
Waiakoa 191
 Church of the Holy Ghost 191
Wai'ale'ale 263
Waialua 212
Wai'anae 111
Wai'anae Coast 165
Wai'anapanapa State Park 197
Waihe'e, John 58

Waikiki 57, 59, 111, 125
accommodations 129
Atlantis Submarines 133
Halekulani hotel 131
Hilton Hawaiian Village 133
Honolulu Zoo 134
Kaimana Beach 134
Kapi'olani Park 134
Moana Surfrider Hotel 129
Queen's Surf Beach 134
Royal Hawaiian Hotel 130
Sans Souci 128
Statue of Duke Kahanamoku 128
Stones of Kapaemahu 128
Trump International Hotel
  Waikiki 131
US Army Museum 133
Waikiki Trolley 286
War Memorial Natatorium 134,
  135
Waikiki Beach 76, 107
Waikolu Lookout 209
Wailea 186, 59
Wailua 197, 277
Fern Grotto 277
St Gabriel's Church 197
Wailua Falls 199
Wailua River 277
Wailuku 175, 178, 185
Bailey House 178
Ka'ahumanu Congregational
  Church 178
Wailuku River 241
Wailuku River State Park 244
Waimanalo 148, 151
Waimanalo Beach 151
Waimanu Valley 246
Waimea 41, 225, 236, 281
Parker Ranch 236
Parker Ranch Museum and
  Visitor Center 236
Russian Fort Elizabeth State

Park 281
West Kauai Technology & Visitor
  Center 281
Waimea Bay 158
St Peter and Paul Church 159
Waimea Canyon 11, 107, 267, 271
Waimea-Kohala Airport 284
Waimea River 271
Waimea Town 275
Waimea Valley 159
Waimoku Falls 200
Waipahu 164, 166
Hawaii Plantation Village 166
Waipi'o Valley 79, 241, 245, 246
Waipouli 275, 277
walking 285. *See also* hiking
waterfalls 268
'Akaka Falls (Hawaii Island) 11,
  241, 244
Hi'ilawe Falls (Hawaii Island) 246
Kahuna Falls (Hawaii Island) 244
Kaliuwa'a Falls (Oahu) 156
Kauai 271
Manoa Falls (Honolulu) 146
Mo'oula Falls (Molokai) 213
Opaeka'a Falls (Kauai) 277
Puohokamoa Falls (Maui) 196
Rainbow Falls (Hawaii Island)
  244
Wailua Falls (Maui) 199
Waimea Valley (Oahu) 160
Waimoku Falls (Maui) 200
Waipuhia Valley Falls (Honolulu)
  143
water sports 149
weights and measures 297
West Maui 180
wetlands 24
whale-watching 10, 77, 173, 179,
  182, 186
whaling 47
what to bring 297

what to wear 297
Wheeler Army Air Field 165
Wilcox, George N. 276
Wilcox, Robert 50
wildlife 25. *See also* bird life,
  national and state parks, nature
  reserves, marine conservation
  districts
brown snakes 202
dolphins 25, 221
endangered species 77
feral donkeys 231
Hawaiian Monk Seals 25, 78,
  168, 169
hoary bats 25
mongooses 202
mountain goats 272
Polynesian rat 202
Portuguese man-o'-war
  jellyfish 213
sea turtles 25, 78, 169, 221, 256
whales 10, 25, 77, 173, 182
wild boar 245
wild horses 245
wildlife refuges. *See* nature
  reserves
wildlife-watching 77
Willie K 85
windsurfing 10, 153, 186, 190
Wong, Alan 92

Y

Yamaguchi, Roy 93
Yokohama Bay 168

Z

ziplining 79
zoo. *See* aquariums and zoo

INSIGHT ⊙ GUIDES

OFF THE SHELF

Since 1970, **INSIGHT GUIDES** has provided a unique perspective on the world's best travel destinations by using specially commissioned photography and illuminating text written by local authors.

Whether you're planning a city break, a walking tour or the journey of a lifetime, our superb range of guidebooks and phrasebooks will inspire you to discover more about your chosen destination.

INSIGHT GUIDES

offer a unique combination of stunning photos, absorbing narrative and detailed maps, providing all the inspiration and information you need.

PHRASEBOOKS & DICTIONARIES

help users to feel at home, when away. Pocket-sized with a free app to download, they go where you do.

CITY GUIDES

pack hundreds of great photos into a smaller format with detailed practical information, so you can navigate the world's top cities with confidence.

EXPLORE GUIDES

feature easy-to-follow walks and itineraries in the world's most exciting destinations, with our choice of the best places to eat and drink along the way.

POCKET GUIDES

combine concise information on where to go and what to do in a handy compact format, ideal on the ground. Includes a full-colour, fold-out map.

EXPERIENCE GUIDES

feature offbeat perspectives and secret gems for experienced travellers, with a collection of over 100 ideas for a memorable stay in a city.

www.insightguides.com